THE MAKING OF THE MAHATMA

[*Courtesy* : Publications Division, New De
Barrister Gandhi at the age of forty

Chandran D. S. Devanesen

The Making of the Mahatma

Orient Longmans

ORIENT LONGMANS LTD.   Regd. Office:

Hamilton House, ' A ' Block,
Connaught Place, New Delhi 1.

Regional Offices:

Nicol Road, Ballard Estate,
Bombay 1.

17 Chittaranjan Avenue,
Calcutta 13.

36A Mount Road, Madras 2.

3/5 Asaf Ali Road,
New Delhi 1.

Published by   C. M. Salis
Orient Longmans Ltd.,
36A, Mount Road, Madras 2.

Printed in India by   M. Swaminathan,
Amra Press
132, Lattice Bridge Road,
Madras 41.

Dedicated
to the memory
of
my uncles
J. C. Kumarappa
and
J. B. Kumarappa
faithful followers
of
Mahatma Gandhi

PREFACE

Bibliographies reveal that nearly three thousand books in several languages have been published dealing with the life and thought of Mahatma Gandhi. A reading of many of these books, however, indicates that certain approaches to the study of the Mahatma have been largely unexplored. In this book I have tried to attain certain fresh perspectives on the life of this great Indian.

Most biographies of Mahatma Gandhi seldom seem to rise above the level of uncritical admiration or sheer hagiography. They often ignore the forces which moulded Gandhi before he became a Mahatma—a force, himself, in history. Studies in cultural anthropology, psychology and sociology convinced me that the Mahatma has often been interpreted in too ethnocentric a fashion. It also became clear to me that while Gandhi was rooted in a rich Indian tradition he was subjected to very powerful forces of acculturation. I became interested in Gandhi, not just as a product of Indian history and culture, but as a person who had felt the intellectual and spiritual impact of more than one great civilization. My book investigates this aspect of Gandhi's character and personality.

I am convinced that the acculturative processes at work in Gandhi's life operated most decisively during his first forty years. A few days after his fortieth birthday Gandhi wrote a booklet entitled *Indian Home Rule*, later known as *Hind Swaraj*. As I read this booklet, I became certain that it marked the end of a mental and spiritual crisis in Gandhi's life. The booklet contains a statement of Gandhi's basic ideas and beliefs, and suggests the turning point at which he may be said to have become the Mahatma. This book then confines itself to these formative years which produced *Hind Swaraj*. Gandhi appears to have become a different and a more powerful personality with the composition of this booklet, which I have described as " The Manifesto of the Gandhian Revolution."

The first forty years of Gandhi's life falls into three periods: the Kathiawad Period (1869–1888), the London Period (1888–1891) and what may be termed his First South African Period (1893–1909). I have studied each period in order to understand the influences acting upon Gandhi and the changes taking place in his thought.

In describing the Kathiawad Period I have stressed the importance of regional culture in Gandhi's development. To treat Gandhi simply as an " Indian " seemed inadequate, for he came from a unique region of India which left an indelible mark on him. I have traced the role of the Gandhi family in Kathiawad history and politics, and have tried to evaluate the significance of Gandhi's early education and his belonging to the Vallabhacharya sampradaya. I have also described the various changes— religious, social and economic—that were taking place in Kathiawad during the nineteenth century. The British did not enter the peninsula until 1808, and did not establish effective control until 1862; Gandhi's boyhood, therefore, was passed in a region just beginning to feel the full impact of British rule. Although Gandhi's roots were deep in Kathiawadi culture, there is thus a certain freshness in his confrontation with western civilization which seems important.

The study of the London Period attempts to demonstrate how Gandhi responded to a society significantly different from anything he had known in Kathiawad. The fact that his Vaishnava heritage gave him an appreciation of middle class British Christianity is emphasized. Gandhi's use of Vegetarianism to steer himself through a period of strong acculturation is also studied, as is the role played by the London Vegetarian Society in discovering his potentialities as a leader. While Gandhi seems to have emerged from his London experiences with an appreciation for British culture, I have argued that his exposure to European civilization remained rather limited, partly because of his financial difficulties, which largely restricted him to London.

Gandhi's experiences in London obviously had not prepared him for the racial discrimination he met with in South Africa. I have traced his early optimism that racialism was a passing phenomenon easily remedied and his subsequent disillusionment. I have examined the steps by which Gandhi, rejected by Western civilization, concluded that the only alternative was to fall back on his own civilization. His transition from loyalty to the ideals of Empire to rebellion against them is outlined against the changing political background of South Africa. His experiences in South Africa led to a deep spiritual crisis and a desire to return to his mother-culture which culminated in the launching of Satyagraha and the writing of *Hind Swaraj*. It was South Africa that made the Mahatma.

In dealing with these phases of Gandhi's life I have attempted to recapture the historical atmosphere of each period. In order to achieve this sense of reality, especially in South Africa, I made use of many contemporary writings, memoirs and even guide books.

Throughout this book I have referred to the books read by Gandhi himself, in an effort to discover to what extent they influenced his thinking at different stages in his development. Neither his *Autobiography* nor the early volumes of his *Collected Works* note all the books he read, and more research is required to trace the full extent of all that he assimilated. I regret, for example, that I was not able to go to Ahmedabad to look into a collection of nearly twenty thousand books which Gandhi brought back with him from South Africa. Although I had the titles copied out for me, it would have been useful to determine how many of them he read himself.

I also draw attention to many minor and long-forgotten personalities who made even a small contribution to the life and thought of Gandhi.

To sum up, my book attempts to probe beneath some of the established stereotypes and legends that have grown up around the Mahatma in order more objectively to understand him as a great man produced by the historical forces of his times.

This book is based on the thesis I submitted to the Department of History of Harvard University in partial fulfilment of the requirements for the degree of Doctor of Philosophy in 1961. I express my thanks to Dr. K. I. Brown of the Danforth Foundation and Dr. Paul J. Braisted of the Edward W. Hazen Foundation for enabling me to be at Harvard from September 1956 to June 1958 as a post-graduate student. I was able to return to Harvard in 1961 for a period of six months to write the thesis through the generosity of the United Church Board for World Ministries and its secretary for India, the Rev. Telfer Mook. I must also thank my two supervisors, Dr. David Owen and Dr. J. H. H. Ingalls for their constant interest and encouragement. To Prof. David Owen, who is no more, I owe a special debt of gratitude for his great warmth and humanity. He enabled me to live in Winthrop House, of which he was then the Master, and he and Mrs. Louise Owen showed a personal interest in me which I can never forget. The list of people whose friendship and hospitality sustained me during the strenuous regime I imposed on myself to get the writing done is too lengthy but I must mention Dr. J. Edward Dirks who was then near at hand in Yale. I was also helped by several under-graduate and post-graduate friends of whom I must gratefully mention Dr. Thomas N. Tentler and Mrs. Pamela Belden Daniels.

I must also place on record my thanks to Dr. S. Gopal for helping me to prune a rather lengthy thesis, Mr. J. B. Appasamy for assisting with proof reading and Dr. M. Abel for working on the preparation of the index. I wish to thank the publishers for the speed with which they have worked to ensure the publication of the book during the Gandhi Centenary Celebrations.

The Bibliography will give the number of books I have consulted, and I wish to express my thanks to the Publishers whose material I have used.

Finally, I cannot but record my gratitude to my wife, who was with me in the States for a time helping and sustaining me, and to my three sons for their patience with and understanding of a father who was often absent from home both physically and mentally.

Tambaram,
September 1969.   CHANDRAN D. S. DEVANESEN

CONTENTS

Contents

LIST OF ILLUSTRATIONS

CHAPTER ONE

The Power of Tradition:
Gandhi's Kathiawadi Heritage

The analogy of a Chinese puzzle illustrates the historian's task in studying Gandhi as an historical figure. We must look at him as a product of a family which distinguished itself within the smallest box of the puzzle—that of Porbandar. This small Rajput state on the west coast of the peninsula was within a larger box labelled " Kathiawad." The history of Porbandar and the Gandhis cannot be understood without a knowledge of this unique region. Kathiawad, in turn, is within another box called " Gujarat " and cannot be understood without reference to it. All these boxes fit into the much larger box of India. Gandhi, as it were, first found his way out of these boxes into the wider world of England and South Africa. The Mahatma told Edward Thompson that he was at his profoundest in his childhood before his mind had been corrupted by education and society. Bemoaning the circumspection and the loss of uninhibited truthfulness in adulthood, Gandhi exclaimed, " Alas, alas, alas, a thousand times, alas."[1]

Gandhi as a Kathiawadi

This chapter presents a few aspects of this historical problem.

---

[1] R. Shahani, *Mr. Gandhi,* (New York, The Macmillan Co., 1961), p. 6.

Especially important is an examination of the implications of Gandhi's being a Kathiawadi; the significance of this fact has not yet been analyzed by any student of the Mahatma. Regionalism, an important factor in Indian history, played no small part in shaping the character and personality of the young Gandhi. He never lost some of his Kathiawadi characteristics, and his conception of nationalism was coloured by the area of India from which he came. The Mahatma superimposed certain idealized images, drawn from his early Kathiawadi experiences, on his vision of India. He wanted India to be like what he imagined Kathiawad to have been in the past. We shall, therefore, give an outline of Kathiawad's long past, even though it was not immediately responsible for producing Gandhi, for it served as a " construct," a mythological vision which influenced his thinking about the nature of Indian history and culture.

A major confusion in Indian history results from the failure to distinguish between the past which is truly dead and buried, and the contemporary reality which survived as a residue from vanished history. Gandhi was essentially a product of his own times. The study of Kathiawad in the nineteenth century is more important for understanding Gandhi than a knowledge of the ancient past. The historian may attempt, however, to throw light on the personality of Gandhi through proto-types and analogous situations in Kathiawadi history. In the present brief sketch of that extensive history there is a specific attempt to make Gandhi the central figure of such a " synoptic view " in order to understand how deep were his roots in " the breadth and diversity of the interests which surround the history of the province of Kathiawad."[2]

The residue of history survives largely in a cultural heritage

---

[2] *Ibid.,* p. 10.

2

as a living tradition. As we shall attempt to show later, the cultural tradition in Kathiawad was changing under the impact of the British when Gandhi was growing from childhood to young manhood. In this chapter some aspects of the caste and religious traditions which influenced the development of Gandhi are indicated. The nature of the changes induced by British rule will, therefore, be studied in some detail in the next chapter.

This emphasis on Kathiawad history is not merely an historian's submission to the academic passion. Gandhi was a Kathiawadi and thought of himself as one for nearly fifty years before he grew into the Father of the Indian Nation. When he was feted in Bombay on his return to India in 1915, the Mahatma was dressed as a Kathiawadi. With his usual good humour he tells us, " With my Kathiawadi cloak, turban, and *dhoti*, I looked somewhat more civilized than I do today... ."[3] It was at this gathering that Gandhi made his first Gujarati speech in India. He was still wearing Kathiawadi dress two years later when Rajendra Prasad met him in Bihar.[4]

Gandhi's first thoughts were about the need for an ashram where he could transplant his " Phoenix family " who had preceded him from South Africa. He told Gokhale that he would prefer the ashram to be " somewhere in Gujarat, as being a Gujarati, I was best fitted to serve the country through serving Gujarat."[5] Gandhi said the very same thing to Jamnalal Bajaj who pressed him to build the ashram near Wardha. Though he acquiesced many years later, at that time he replied, " I am a Gujarati. It is only by remaining in Gujarat that I can be able to serve better. I will serve

---

[3] M. K. Gandhi, *The Story of My Experiments with Truth*, (The references in this book are taken from an American edition entitled *Gandhi's Autobiography*, Washington, The Public Affairs Press, 1954), p. 456.

[4] Rajendra Prasad, *At the Feet of Mahatma Gandhi*, (Bombay, Hind Kitabs, 1955), p. 1.

[5] *Autobiography*, p. 478.

India by serving Gujarat."[6] It was only later that year, when the Kumbha Mela crowds hailed him at Hardwar, that he realized " what a deep impression my humble services in South Africa had made throughout the whole of India."[7] He felt the strong pull of destiny that would be national rather than provincial.

Gandhi would continue to have a deep and abiding interest in the province from which he came. Gujarat would see a literary renaissance stimulated by his contributions to the development of Gujarati. He would make an impact on Kathiawad by his fast at Rajkot in 1939 that would be more far-reaching in its consequences than the settlement made by Colonel Walker in 1807. Even in 1947, a few months before he was assassinated, he would remember the old family home in Porbandar with vividness and affection. " One can't forget that house," he said, " if you are on the third floor you have a lovely cool breeze. But if you are on the ground floor you cannot stay there even for a few minutes; it is so warm and stuffy."[8] The British were about to leave India. Gandhi had travelled a long way from that stuffy room on the ground floor where he was born.

The metal of which Gandhi was made came from the deep mine of Kathiawad's rich, historic past; he was the small but ancient peninsula's greatest gift to India and the world.

The Holy Land of Western India

Kathiawad, a small peninsula shaped like an elephant's ear, juts into the Arabian Sea nearly opposite the coast of Oman.[9]

---

[6] K. Kalelkar, (ed.), *To A Gandhian Capitalist*, (Bombay, Hind Kitabs, 1951), p. 17.

[7] *Autobiography*, p. 475.

[8] P. Gandhi, *My Childhood with Gandhi*, (Ahmedabad, Navajivan Publishing House, 1957), p. 4.

[9] The peninsula is bounded N. by the Rann of Cutch, E. by the Ahmedabad District and the Gulf of Cambay, and S. and W. by the Arabian Sea. Extreme length 220 miles, greatest breadth 165 miles, total area 23,400 sq.m.

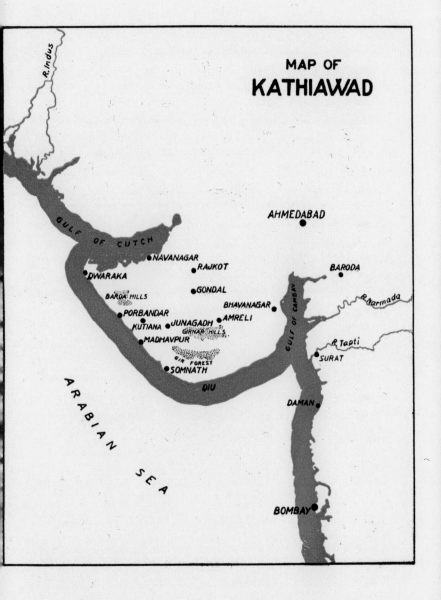

MAP OF
KATHIAWAD

It has produced characters as outstanding and diverse as Swami Dayanand Saraswati, the religious reformer, Ranjit-sinhji, the famous cricketer, Mohamed Ali Jinnah,[10] the creator of Pakistan, and Mahatma Gandhi, the Father of the Indian Nation. There must be some rational explanation for the emergence of such men from this region. Colonel James Tod, who played " the pilgrim in the wilds of Cat'hiawar,"[11] in 1822, thought it was the most interesting part of India. Few areas can compete with Kathiawad for the richness and variety of its history and culture. The waves of history in India found their way into this sea-girt pocket of land (it was probably once an island)[12] in swirls and eddies. Kathiawad is the story of India on a miniature scale.

Many observers have commented on the rich racial diversity of this peninsula which contains an amazing collection of peoples. Tod noted the shades of complexion ranging from the swarthy Bhils to the fair and occasionally blue-eyed Kathis.[13] Rapson considered it a region transitional between India and central Asia, because waves of invasions by Persians, Greeks, Scythians, and Huns have flowed into Kathiawad and spent their force there.[14] Muslim rule led to the infusion of some Turkish and Arab blood. The study of the origin and history of the various races in the peninsula is a fascinating subject in itself. Colonel J. W. Watson, for

---

[10] Hector Bolitho, *Jinnah: Creator of Pakistan*, (New York, The Macmillan Co., 1955), p. 3. Jinnah was born in 1876 in Karachi of Kathiawadi parents who had migrated from Rajkot.

[11] James Tod, *Travels in Western India*, (London, Wm. H. Allen & Co., 1839), p. 308.

[12] K. M. Munshi, *The Early Aryans in Gujarata*, (Bombay, University of Bombay, 1941), p. 2.

[13] *Travels in Western India*, p. 257.

[14] E. J. Rapson, *Ancient India*, (Cambridge, Cambridge University Press, 1912), p. 34.

example, thought the Kathis were descended from the ancient Hittites.[15] The recent paintings and sketches of a contemporary artist, Pradhumuna Tana, show that the people of Kathiawad retain something of an ancient aura. The young Gandhi grew up in an area where ethnic heterogeneity had led to a marked degree of social and religious tolerance.

From time immemorial, Kathiawad has been a land of temples and pilgrimages. Kinloch Forbes said, in the *Ras Mala*, that it has always been known to pious Hindus as " Dev desh "—the land of the gods.[16] In the *Tarik-i-Sorath*, Ranchodji Amarji called Kathiawad " the Holy Land of Western India."[17] The region is particularly sacred to the Vaishnavas because it contains Dwaraka, and many another spot, associated with the story of Sri Krishna. Sudamapuri, the ancient name of Porbandar, is derived from the story in the *Bhagavata Purana* of how a village was gifted to Sudama by Sri Krishna. To the Saivites there are few shrines more venerated than the ancient temple of Somnath. Kathiawad is also the cradle and the stronghold of Jainism. Its three sacred mountains—Girnar, Satrunjaya and Palitana—still attract thousands of Jain pilgrims. The old temples and shrines of Kathiawad are records of history in stone. Gandhi said of his father, " Of history and geography he was innocent."[18] Karamchand Gandhi may have been ignorant about the rest of India and the world, but this assertion could not have been applied to his knowledge of Kathiawad itself. No Kathiawadi could escape completely the determining influences of both history and geography with which the

---

[15] J. W. Watson, (ed.), *Gazetteer of the Bombay Presidency*, (Bombay, Govt. Central Press, 1884), Vol. VIII, Ch. III, p. 127.

[16] A. K. Forbes, *Ras Mala*, 2 Vols., (London, Oxford University Press, 1924), Vol. I, p. 9.

[17] R. Amarji, *Tarik-i-Sorath*, (trans.) James Burgess, (London, Trubner & Co., 1882), p. 1.

[18] *Autobiography*, p. 12.

peninsula was so abundantly endowed. Karamchand was a frequent visitor to the temples which dotted the land. His son, Mohandas, would learn much from him of the rich folklore and sacred geography of Kathiawad. The boy was surrounded on all sides by visible reminders of the past. To live in Kathiawad was a religious education in itself, for, as Tod put it, there was " no moving in this region without meeting at each step some objects interesting in themselves, or which have become so from association with the mingled history and mythology of past ages."[19]

Like Rajasthan, the peninsula is a land of Rajputs. The Charans and Bhats, the hereditary bards, kept alive the stories and legends of Rajput courage and chivalry through their ballads and *dohas*, the rhyming couplets well-known among the people. Karamchand must have spiced his conversation with many a familiar *doha*; and all the older Gandhis must have been raconteurs, not only with tales of the Jethvas of Porbandar, but also the other Rajput clans.[20] The boy Gandhi must have listened to many a story of the brave deeds of Rajput heroes and heroines. The songs and ballads would give him a tendency towards hero worship, and the rich tapestry of the legends would fill his mind with images and visions of a glowing past, a past which would inspire the Mahatma's conception of *Ramrajya*. The great Indian epics, the *Ramayana* and the *Mahabharata*, would appeal all the more to the grown man who had listened as a boy to the local epics of the Rajputs of Kathiawad. An idealized Rajput state was Gandhi's political ideal for India.

Gandhi confessed that as a boy he " used to be haunted by the fear of thieves, ghosts and serpents." The night held

---

19 *Travels in Western India*, p. 273.

20 See Thakur Shri Jessrajsinghji Seesodia, *The Rajputs: A Fighting Race*, (London, East and West Ltd., 1915), and Anil Chandra Bannerjee, *Rajput Studies*, (Calcutta, A. Mukherjee & Bros., 1944).

many terrors for him because he " would imagine ghosts coming from one direction, thieves from another and serpents from a third."[21]   The fear of snakes was natural enough in a country infested with them, and his fear of thieves and ghosts can also be explained rationally.   Not far from Porbandar were the Gir Forest and the Barda Hills—hiding places of dacoits and outlaws from time immemorial. Apart from the good hiding places afforded by a country of alternate jungle and high fields of wheat and *jowar* at harvest time, the vexed boundary question helped the dacoits; every Kathiawad dacoit knew exactly where the boundaries ended and thus took advantage of the inadequate laws of extradition.[22] C. A. Kincaid was fascinated by the ballads about their exploits and wrote about them in *The Outlaws of Kathiawar*.[23] The Mahatma remembered and admired the exploits of Mulu Manik, the most notorious of the Wagher dacoits.[24]   Some outlaws were fugitives from injustice; Gandhi resembles them in his attitude toward the British Empire. He deliberately " outlawed " himself from modern civilization in order to fight imperialism.

Ghosts were as real to the people of Kathiawad as their dacoits.   In 1849, Kavi Dalpatram Daya won the prize offered by the Gujarat Vernacular Society for original essays on Indian subjects with his paper on the *Bhoots* or ghosts of Kathiawad.   The essay was translated by Forbes in 1850 and incorporated into the last chapter of his *Ras Mala*.   The

---

[21] *Autobiography*, p. 33.

[22] Elizabeth Sharpe, *Thakore Sahib Sir Jaswant Singh of Limbdi*, (London, John Murray, 1931), pp. 57-58.

[23] C. A. Kincaid, *The Outlaws of Kathiawar*, (Bombay, Times of India Press, n.d.).

[24] M. K. Gandhi, *Speeches and Writings of M. K. Gandhi*,(Madras, G. A. Natesan .& Co., 1922), p. 351.   In his address to the Gujarat Educational Conference, October 20, 1917, Gandhi said, " the Barda Hills still bear witness to the valorous deeds of Mulu Manek and Jodha Manek."

powers possessed by the ghosts of Kathiawad are described as follows: " They take possession of a corpse and speak through its mouth; they exhibit themselves in the form which they possessed when living; they enter into a living man, and cause him to speak as they please; sometimes they afflict him with fever, or various other diseases; sometimes they assume the form of animals, and frighten people by suddenly vanishing in a flash of fire; sometimes remaining invisible, they speak in whispers. A *Bhoot* has been known to come to fisticuffs with a man, and to carry a man off and set him down in a distant place. It is even said that women are sometimes found with child by *Bhoots*."[25] With such formidable spirits said to haunt the land it is quite understandable that the boy Gandhi felt he was a coward since he dared not stir out of doors at night.[26]

In his youth Gandhi was much influenced by the folk culture and religion of Kathiawad. The simple faith of an old family servant woman, Rambha, left a deep impression on him in his childhood. The recollection of her faith comforted him in his loneliness in his early London days.[27] The young Gandhi's religion was the popular Hinduism of the annual festivals which he described so vividly for the English readers of *The Vegetarian*.[28] He would rediscover the literary and metaphysical traditions of Hinduism as he matured into the Mahatma.

An aspect of the influence of popular Kathiawadi thinking on Gandhi which needs to be explored is the general attitude of the people to natural calamities. Kathiawad suffered

---

[25] *Ras Mala*, Vol. II, pp. 375-376. See also C. A. Kincaid, *Lakshmibai, Rani of Jhansi and other Essays*, (Bombay, Times of India Press, n.d.), " Indian Ghosts."

[26] *Autobiography*, p. 33.

[27] *Autobiography*, pp. 47, 65.

[28] M. K. Gandhi, *Collected Works of Mahatma Gandhi*, 4 Vols., (New Delhi, Publications Division, Ministry of Information and Broadcasting, Govt. of India, 1958), I, pp. 37-44.

from earthquakes in the past. Tod surmised that the former Jethva capital, Ghumli, remained deserted because the earthquake which destroyed it had been viewed as an indication of divine displeasure.[29] Several earthquake shocks were recorded in the nineteenth century. In April, 1864, there was a shock, preceded by low rumbling noises and followed by vibrations, which caused considerable panic and excitement. Similar shocks were experienced in November, 1881, and September-October, 1898.[30] Kathiawad also suffered from terrible pests; the year 1814–1815 was called "the rat year." Captain Le Grand Jacob has left a graphic description of the dense masses of rats of a reddish shady colour that suddenly appeared at harvest time and devastated the crops.[31] The year of Gandhi's birth, 1869, was remembered as the year of the locusts. Robert B. Booth, the Agency Engineer, recollected the havoc the locusts wrought to the fields of *bajra* and *jowar* in the Rajkot area.[32]

The grim spectre of famine was never wholly absent from Kathiawad and the worst famines remained indelibly printed on the folk memory. The year 1559 A.D. was remembered by the peasants as "Jagdu Shah's famine" after a noble Bania of that name who succoured the hungry people with a never-forgotten liberality. The boy Gandhi would see almost daily the tower erected to Jagdu Shah's memory as it stood on the bank of the river Aji opposite to the town of Rajkot.[33] Repeated famines also explain the patterns of migration into Kathiawad (like the coming of the Kathis) as well as internal population movements within the peninsula. All these

---

[29] *Travels in Western India*, p. 417.

[30] W. W. Hunter, (ed.), *Imperial Gazetteer of India*, (London, Oxford University Press, 1908), p. 174.

[31] *Imperial Gazetteer of India*, p. 181.

[32] R. B. Booth, *Life and Work in India*, 1865–1899, (London, J. G. Hammond & Co., Ltd., 1912), p. 38.

[33] *Bombay Gazetteer*, VIII, pp. 190-191.

natural calamities gave a certain cast to the Kathiawadi mind which can be plainly seen in Ranchodji Amarji's description of a famine as " this heaven-sent calamity."[34] The Mahatma echoed the author of the *Tarik-i-Sorath* when he described the disastrous Bihar Earthquake as a punishment from God. Gandhi had not outgrown the ancient Kathiawadi explanation for natural calamities.[35]

K. M. Panikkar spoke of Kathiawad as having dominantly maritime traditions,[36] while K. M. Munshi said that the sea-faring activities of the Gujaratis were proverbial.[37] According to a Gujarati legend, Prince Vijaya sailed from Simhapura (Sihor) near modern Bhavanagar in Kathiawad and settled in Ceylon. There are evidences of trade with Persian and African ports and distant China. Hsuen-Tsang mentioned the foreign trade of Saurashtra, which he visited in 630 A.D. One Gujarati proverb runs, " He who goes to Java never returns; but if he does, he brings so much wealth that his grandchildren's grandchildren will not exhaust it." It originated from the existence of a Gujarati colony in Java in the seventh century A.D. Friar Oderic (1321 A.D.) crossed the Indian Ocean in a vessel manned by Gujaratis. Vasco da Gama and Albuquerque praised the nautical skill of Gujarati sailors. One of the titles of the Sultans of Gujarat was " Lord of the Sea," and during the Sultanate, the Sanger

---

[34] *Tarik-i-Sorath*, p. 188.

[35] See J. Prasad, "A Comparative Study of Rumours and Reports in Earth-quakes," *British Journal of Psychology*, XLI (December, 1950), 129-144, and D. Sinha, "Behaviour in a Catastrophic Situation: A Psychological Study of Reports and Rumours," *British Journal of Psychology*, XLIII (August, 1953), pp. 200-209.

[36] K. M. Panikkar, *Geographical Factors in Indian History*, (Bombay, Bharatiya Vidya Bhavan, 1951), p. 29.

[37] K. M. Munshi, *Glory that was Gujara Desa*, (Bombay, Bharatiya Vidya Bhavan, 1954), p. 355.

Rajputs of Navanagar in Kathiawad were noted for their skill in ship-building.[38]

Marco Polo complained bitterly that the Gujarati pirates were the worst in the world.[39] The Kathiawad coast was infested with them and they occupied even the temple of Somnath in 1880.[40] In 1808 the British obtained an agreement from the maritime states of Porbandar and Navanagar that they would renounce piracy.[41] In 1880, when Gandhi was eleven years old, Yashoda, the widow of the last of the Angrias, the pirate dynasty, was still alive.[42] "The suppression of piracy and slavery on the coasts of Arabia, the Persian Gulf, and Kathiawar," says James Douglas, "is a history by itself, and that history belongs to the Indian Navy."[43] Gandhi was born in the ancient port of Porbandar with the sound of the sea in his ears. The maritime past of Kathiawad was destined to shape his future. The Gujaratis continued their maritime enterprise into the nineteenth century and the Meman Muslim merchants of Porbandar were responsible for taking Gandhi to South Africa.

When the Mahatma presided over the Third Kathiawad Political Conference at Bhavanagar in January, 1935, he took delight in describing himself as "a native of Kathiawad."[44]

[38] Ibid., pp. 354-355; K. M. Munshi, Gujarat and Its Literature, (Bombay, Bharatiya Vidya Bhavan, 1954), pp. xxiv-xxvi; Asoke Kumar Majumdar, Chalukyas of Gujarat, (Bombay, Bharatiya Vidya Bhavan, 1956), p. 268.

[39] The Travels of Marco Polo, Aldo Ricci (trans.), Index and Introduction E. Denison Ross, (London, George Routledge & Sons, Ltd., 1931), p. 332.

[40] James Douglas, Bombay and Western India, 2 Vols., (London, Simpson Low & Co., 1893), Vol. I, p. 127.

[41] William Lee-Warner, The Native States of India, (London, Macmillan & Co., Ltd., 1910), p. 117.

[42] James Douglas, op. cit., I, p. 127.

[43] Ibid., I, p. 122; see also M. Malgonkar, Kanhoji Angrey: Maratha Admiral (Bombay, Asia Publishing House, 1959).

[44] M. K. Gandhi, The Indian States' Problem, (Ahmedabad, Navajivan Publishing House, 1941), p. 8.

All that was Kathiawadi for Gandhi was symbolised for him in that old stone house in Porbandar. He would create many meaningful images around his childhood home. Nehru became fond of quoting the following image that Gandhi had unconsciously based on that early childhood haven by the sea: " I want the culture of all lands to be blown about my house as freely as possible. But I refuse to be blown off my feet by any. I refuse to live in other people's houses as an interloper, a beggar, or a slave."[45] Gandhi's relation to Kathiawad can be seen most meaningfully in terms of that same old house. The Porbandar house of the Gandhis was built over a large tank, so that there was water under the verandah floor of the room in which Mohandas was born. The rain water drained into the tank through a pipe descending from the flat-topped roof. There was always a plentiful supply of water in the tank which was purer and tasted sweeter than the water in the wells in the vicinity. The tank served the daily needs not only of the Gandhis, but also of others living in the same street.[46] The fact that the Gandhis built their house over a tank to insure a constant water supply is a commentary on the turbulence of Kathiawadi history; it was a land where a man could be besieged in his own home. Gandhi, too, lived through some stirring times. Yet, wherever he went, his Kathiawadi heritage went with him. It was like the tank under the old house—a hidden source of refreshment in a life full of stress and strain.

An Outline of Kathiawad History

" They have a habit of writing history; they pretend to study the manners and customs of all peoples;" thus Gandhi

---

[45] *Nehru on Gandhi*, a selection arranged in the order of events, from the writings and speeches of J. Nehru, (New York, The John Day Co., 1948), p. 23.

[46] P. Gandhi, *op. cit.*, p. 5.

complained of the British in *Hind Swaraj*.[47]   This habit of the English was in evidence in Kathiawad, as it was everywhere else in India, throughout the nineteenth century.   When Gandhi was growing to manhood, the British had begun writing a good deal about the manners, customs and history of Gujarat with which the history of Kathiawad is intertwined. Colonel James Tod's researches for the writing of *Annals and Antiquities of Rajasthan*[48] led to an interest in Kathiawad with which so many Rajput houses in Central India were connected. His pilgrimage in the " Saura peninsula " resulted in *Travels in Western India*, one of the earliest British incursions into Kathiawad history, which appeared in 1839.   Tod's work bore fruit in the antiquarian researches of Sir A. Kinloch Forbes who established his claim to be the first modern historian of Gujarat with the publication of his *Ras Mala* in 1856.

Two decades after the appearance of the *Ras Mala*, the spade of the archaeologist was helping the historian in his study of legendary lore, inscriptions, and old manuscripts. The appointment of James Burgess in 1874 as Archaeological Surveyor and Reporter for Western India was a landmark in the exploration of the history of the region.   By the end of the nineteenth century, Tod's claim that Kathiawad is " a land containing subjects for many volumes and portfolios "[49] was amply justified.   Kathiawad owes much to scholarly British Civilians who rediscovered its ancient past.[50]   The

---

[47] M. K. Gandhi, *Hind Swaraj or Indian Home Rule*, (Ahmedabad, Navajivan Publishing House, 1946), p. 37.

[48] James Tod, *Annals and Antiquities of Rajasthan*, 2 Vols., (Calcutta, Unno Purna Printing Works, 1894).

[49] *Travels in Western India*, p. 258.

[50] Monographs on Kathiawad history found their way into the pages of the Gazetteers, the *Indian Antiquary* (edited by Burgess from 1874–1884), the *Journal of the Bombay Branch of the Royal Asiatic Society*, and the *Epigraphica Indica*. The foundations for future research were laid by men like John Wilson, Henry Cousens, Johann Georg Buhler, and George Buist.

Museum in Rajkot is named after J. W. Watson, with whom Gandhi's father served in the Rajasthanik Court.

The *Tarik-i-Sorath*, a history of Kathiawad written by Dewan Ranchodji Amarji about 1825, shows the influence of the Persian historians of Gujarat, just as Bhagvanlal Indraji, Bhau Daji, and R. G. Bhandarkar were products of a British era in the writing of Indian history. The work of these nineteenth century scholars, however, shows an admirable restraint and a healthy respect for the canons of historical writing compared to the propagandist historians of the nationalist era of the early twentieth century. Gandhi would be influenced by this later period of historical romanticism rather than by the more sober nineteenth century era, and for quite understandable reasons. When Gandhi reflected the contempt of the South African Whites for Indians, he wrote in *Hind Swaraj*: " It is a charge against India that her people are so uncivilized, ignorant, and stolid that it is not possible to induce them to adopt any changes."[51] The ignorant assumptions of the South African Whites cut him deeply. Gandhi himself was often referred to as " the coolie lawyer." He reacted strongly to this entire attitude by going to the other extreme, asserting that Indian civilization is superior spiritually to any other way of life the world has ever seen, just as some contemporary historians were doing. Some idea of the long history of Kathiawad in which Gandhi had his roots is necessary for understanding his vigorous defence of Hindu culture and his use of history in claiming a moral superiority for Indian civilization.

The Ancient and Medieval Period

It was the Marathas who called the peninsula " Kathiawad " after a small area occupied by the brave Kathis, whose

---

[51] *Hind Swaraj*, Ch. XII, pp. 43-44.

resistance they feared and admired.[52]   Its oldest name was
Kusvrata.   Since Indian Independence, the peninsula has
reverted to another ancient name—Saurashtra—which means
" the goodly land."   Kathiawad was known to Westerners
from early times; Ptolemy knew it as Syrastrene.[53]   There is
some evidence to show that Kathiawad formed part of the
Indus Valley Civilization in the prehistoric period.[54]   Though
Saurashtra is referred to in the Epics, the Puranas, and classical
Sanskrit literature, the early history of the peninsula is
blanketed in a mist of legend.   These legends, however,
exercised a powerful influence on the minds of the people, and
Saurashtra became one of the strongest centres of Vaishnavism
—the family faith of the Gandhis.   All the villages and
towns with which the Gandhis were associated were rich in
legendary lore concerning Sri Krishna.[55]   The Puranic
accounts are important for understanding the sacred geography
of Kathiawad and the religious and cultural ideas which
moulded the outlook of the people for centuries.

Inscriptions recording the repairs to the Sudarsana Lake,
an artificial reservoir which no longer exists, and the Girnar
Rock Edicts were discovered early in the nineteenth century,
throwing some light on the three well-marked epochs in

[52] In his early letters from London Gandhi spells it as " Kattywar," and in
his *Autobiography* as " Kathiawad."   Though it regained its old name of
" Saurashtra " after 1947, " Kathiawad " will be used for convenience in
this book.

[53] J. W. McCrindle, (ed.), *Ancient India as Described by Ptolemy*, (Calcutta,
Thacker, Spink & Co., 1885), p. 35.

[54] K. N. Dikshit, *Pre-historic Civilization of the Indus Valley*, (Madras, University
of Madras, 1939), p. 10.

[55] In 1869, James Burgess obtained an account of the Krishna legends from
Jatashankara Mujamdar, who had translated the *Tarik-i-Sorath* into Gujarati.
Mujamdar, in turn, had learned the legends from Ravi Maga, the
Vahiranchas (Keeper of the Genealogies) of the Chudasama rulers.   Burgess
incorporated the story of Revata into the introduction to his English transla-
tion of the *Tarik-i-Sorath*.

early Kathiawadi history.[56] It was during the first, the Mauryan period (c. 319-197 B.C.) that both Buddhism and Jainism probably found their way into the peninsula. It is only with the advent of the Mauryas that the real history of the peninsula begins. Asoka, the greatest ruler of this dynasty, inscribed fourteen Edicts containing his ethical teachings on the Rock of Girnar. Sudarsana Lake was built during this period.[57]

After the break up of the Mauryan Empire, in an intermediate period, Kathiawad was ruled by Greeks. The region formed part of the kingdom of Apollodotus, the Bactrian Greek, and later, of Menander, known in Buddhist literature as Milinda.[58] This intermediate period came to a close about 80 B.C.; the Bactrian Greeks were overthrown by the Partho-Scythians (Sakas) who entered India from Eastern Iran. The Saka tribe of the Ksaharatas, who controlled the area during this second epoch, invaded Kathiawad in the second century A.D. It was Rudradaman of this Saka dynasty who used the same rock of Girnar, on which Asoka had inscribed his edicts, to record his own achievements in Sanskrit. Rudradaman ruled Kathiawad through his Pahlava governor, Surisakha, who renovated the Sudarsana Lake.

The Kshatrapa-Saka rule in Kathiawad came to an end with the rise of the Gupta Empire (c. 380 A.D.). The Guptas formed the third epoch revealed by the Sudarsana Lake

---

[56] See K. B. Ardeshir Jamshedji, "The Sudarsana or Lake Beautiful of the Girnar Inscription," *Journal of the Bombay Branch of the Royal Asiatic Society*, XVIII, pp. 47-55.

[57] See *Epigraphica Indica*, VII, pp. 46-47.

[58] See H. G. Rawlinson, *Bactria: The History of a Forgotten Empire*, (London, Probsthain & Co., 1912); W. W. Tarn, *The Greeks in Bactria and India*; and A. K. Narain, *The Indo-Greeks*, (London, Oxford University Press, 1957). See also W. W. Tarn, "Notes on Hellenism in Bactria and India," *Journal of Hellenic Studies*, (1902); M. Foucher, *L'art du Gandhara*; and E. B. Havell, *Indian Sculpture and Painting*.

inscriptions. Kathiawad became an important province of the Gupta Empire because of its position as a trade emporium. During the reign of Skandagupta, one of the greatest of the Gupta rulers, Sudarsana Lake was repaired again; this fact, and a victory over the Huns (c. 456 A.D.) as well, was recorded on the Girnar Rock. The death of Skandagupta (c. 467 A.D.) heralded the disintegration of the Gupta Empire. Even before he died, the fierce Huns, under Toramana, had overrun the Punjab.

The collapse of the Gupta Empire led to the emergence of the Maitrakas as the rulers of the peninsula. These Maitrakas provide a solitary instance of a peninsular power strong enough to unite the region and extend their power to the mainland. At the height of their power they ruled over Malwa and Gujarat in addition to their native province of Kathiawad. Their capital was Valabhi, the modern Vala, which lies about eighteen miles to the north-west of Bhavanagar. The Maitrakas ruled for nearly three hundred years, from the fifth to the eighth century A.D. Though they were Saivites, the Maitraka rulers made Valabhi famous for its spirit of tolerance. Royal patronage was extended to Saivism, Vaishnavism, Sun-worship, Buddhism, and Jainism alike. Buddhism flourished under the Maitrakas, and Valabhi rivalled Nalanda as a seat of Buddhist learning.[59] Valabhi, however, was no less renowned as a *tirtha* (holy place) of Jainism. The famous Jain Council, encouraged by Queen Chandralekha, wife of Dhruvasena I, met at Valabhi in 526 A.D. and redacted the whole Jaina Canon, known thereafter as the Valabhi *Vachana*. After the fall of the Maitrakas, Buddhism disappeared, but Jainism continued as a living force in

---

[59] Valabhi was visited by Hsuen-Tsang early in the seventh century A.D. See S. Beal, *Buddhist Records of the Western World*, 2 Vols., (London, Kegan Paul, Trench, Trubner & Co., Ltd., 1906), Vol. II, p. 266.

Kathiawad.[60] The Jain religion was still taught in the *pathsalas* (schools) maintained by that community when Gandhi was a boy. It is to the achievements of Jainism under the Chalukyas, however, that we must look for the Jain cultural influences in Gandhi's outlook.

The immediate successors of the Maitrakas were the Pratiharas (c. 725-940 A.D.), who had also arisen as a result of the break up of the Gupta Empire. North India was convulsed at this time by the rivalries of Pulakesin, Harsha, and Dharmapala, giving the Pratiharas an opportunity to expand. The dissolution of Harsha's empire was followed by a brief ascendancy of Rajput kingdoms. This occurred during the interregnum between the end of the last great Hindu Empire and the conquest of Northern India by the Muslims. The Pratiharas were succeeded by their feudatories, the Paramaras, who had shrewdly allied themselves with their overlords' rivals, the Rashtrakutas. Like their former overlords, the Paramaras also came from the region of Mount Abu, a cradle-land of Rajputs. Kathiawad remained a distant outpost of the Paramara kingdom. The Paramaras, with their capital in Kanauj, could not subjugate the peninsula completely and their authority was challenged by the Chudasama rulers of Junagadh. The Paramara empire fell apart with the death of Bhoja in 1054 A.D.

The centre of power next shifted to Anahilavada Patan where a strong dynasty had emerged under Bhima Chalukya. His successors ruled Kathiawad until 1304 A.D., when they were followed by the Vaghelas. Great as is the record of the Chalukyas in Gujarat their doom was already writ. It was in their time that " the sun of the Rajpoots began to decline before the Moslem crescent, that a strange and furious invader

---

[60] See K. T. Virji, *Ancient History of Saurashtra*, (Bombay, Konkan Institute of Arts and Sciences, 1955).

burst upon the plains of India."[61]   The swarm of Muslim
invaders reached the gates of Anahilavada Patan in 1299 A.D.,
when it was besieged and captured by Ala-ud-din Khilji.
The last of the Chalukyan rulers disappeared, leaving behind
him nothing but the bitter-sweet memory of his daughter,
Dewul Rani, a fair prize carried off to Delhi, who there
inspired a long romantic poem in Persian.

The Muslim impact on Kathiawad took place in three
stages.   During the first phase the peninsula was exposed to
attack from two focal centres —Sind[62] and Ghazni.[63]   But
the threat to Gujarat became serious when the Khilji and
Tughluk dynasties had given Islam a firm footing in Northern
India.   Gujarat was ruled by the Viceroys of the Khiljis and
Tughluks for over a century.

The second phase began with the establishment of the independent Sultanate of Gujarat in 1403.   At this time Muz-
zafar Shah I threw off the authority of the last Tughluk ruler
after that dynasty had been enfeebled by the rapacity of
Timur.   One service rendered by the Gujarat Sultanate
before its collapse was the resistance it offered to the Portuguese.[64]   Unlike other Muslim kingdoms in India which
were established by foreign adventurers, the founder of the
Sultanate of Gujarat, Jafar Khan, traced his descent from a
family of Tonk Rajputs in what is now the Khaira district.
Their line, according to the author of the *Mirat-i-Ahmadi*,
extended " upwards to Rama Chandra whom the Hindus

---

[61] *Ras Mala*, I, p. 68.

[62] See H. M. Elliot, (ed.), *The Arabs in Sind*, (The Historians of India), (Cape
Town, Saul Solomon & Co., 1853).

[63] See Mohammed Habib, *Sultan Mahmud of Ghazni*, (Bombay, D. B. Tarapore-
vala & Co., 1927); Muhammad Nazim, *The Life and Times of Sultan Mahmud
of Ghazni*, (Cambridge, Cambridge University Press, 1931).

[64] E. Dosabhai, *A History of Gujarat*, (Ahmedabad, The United Printing &
General Agency Company's Press, 1894), p. 94.

worship as a god."[65] The Sultanate had an indigenous
flavour and the rulers frequently and easily took the daughters
of good Rajput families into their harems. As in other
Muslim kingdoms, foreign adventurers often rose to prominence ; but the vast majority of Muslims were Gujarati
by birth and outlook. As K. M. Munshi puts it, " The
Muslim rulers were accepted by the people as part of their
existence. Many Muslim communities consisted of Hindu
converts ; their proselytizing zeal had abated ; and their self-
interest linked them to a people who could replenish their
treasury when required."[66] These replenishers of their
treasury were usually *Bania* merchants. In spite of underlying tensions there was, on the whole, a comparative ease of
social relations between Hindus and Muslims in Gujarat and
Kathiawad. This is an important factor in studying Gandhi's
approach to the communal problem from the time of his
student days in London when he belonged to a Muslim organization, the *Anjuman Islamia*,[67] to the time of his assassination
in the hate-filled atmosphere of Delhi.

The third and final phase of the Muslim period was the
incorporation of the region into the Moghul Empire by Akbar
in 1573. Contemporary paintings of Shivaji show that in
dress and appearance he was indistinguishable from the Muslim nobility of the period. The impress of Muslim culture
spread over four hundred years is clearly seen in the author
of their downfall in Western India.

Reconstructing the atmosphere of this period K. M. Munshi
says, " In the sixteenth and seventeenth centuries, Gujarat
regained lost ground. It enjoyed a sort of settled existence

---

[65] E. C. Bayley, *Gujarat*, (The Local Muhammadan Dynasties), (London,
W. H. Allen & Co., 1886), p. 68.

[66] K. M. Munshi, *Gujarat and Its Literature*, (Bombay, Bharatiya Vidya Bhavan,
1954), p. 229.

[67] B. R. Nanda, *Mahatma Gandhi*, (London, George Allen & Unwin, 1959).

21

and grew prosperous again. The people succeeded in con-
fining political influences and stiffened social barriers so as to
secure contentment and happiness within narrow grooves.
Restricted life drove restive minds to harp upon the worth-
lessness of the world, while the prevailing contentment led
genial spirits of the age to create a new literary tradition."[68]
It is significant that Gandhi was fond of quoting poets like
Samal Bhatt and Akho, Mirabai and Narasimha Mehta, who
represented the other-worldly religious milieu of this period.

The Gandhi family originated in Kutiana,[69] a strategically
located frontier area close to Junagadh. The historic town of
Junagadh became the administrative centre of Muslim rule
over ' Sorath ' (the Prakritized name by which the peninsula
was known to Persian historians). The settlement of Sorath
by the Moghuls is described by Abul Fazl in the *Ain-i-Akbari*.[70]

" The year 1707 is a landmark in the history of Gujarat,
not so much because it marks the end of the long reign of
Aurangzeb, but for reasons that have a more important significance in history. From this date, or shortly after, we note
the decline of Moghul rule in Gujarat and the gradual emergence of a new political order," wrote Commissariat.[71] Captain Wilberforce-Bell maintained the same to be true for
Kathiawad. " The history of Saurashtra during the eighteenth century," he holds, " may be said to be that of the most
critical of the many transition stages in the eventful history of
the province."[72] The " new political order," however,
which eventually emerged in Western India in general, and
in Gujarat and Kathiawad, was not the work of the Marathas,

---

[68] *Gujarat and Its Literature*, p. 224.

[69] P. Gandhi, *op. cit.*, p. 6.

[70] F. Gladwin, (trans.), *Ayeen Akberry: or the Institutes of the Emperor Akbar*,
3 Vols., (Calcutta, 1834), Vol. I, Ch. VI, pp. 75-76.

[71] *Op. cit.*, p. 383.

[72] *Op. cit.*, p. 121.

who strove to supersede the Moghuls, but the achievement of the British.

The Maratha Period

The story of the rise of the Marathas begins with the career of Malhoji Bhonsle, a *sirdar* commanding a small body of Ahmednagar horse. His son, Shahji, furthered the family fortunes by shrewdly changing sides whenever it was to his advantage in the struggle between the Sultans of Ahmednagar and Bijapur, and the Moghul Emperor, Shah Jahan. In 1627, a son was born into the household of this military adventurer who laid the foundations of the Maratha power in India. When Shahji's son, Shivaji, plundered Surat for six days in 1664, the Maratha bid to oust the Moghuls had begun. Shivaji went on to become one of the great rulers of India.

The Maratha connection with Gujarat and Kathiawad became stronger in the time of Sahu, Shivaji's grandson. Sahu received a *firman* from the Emperor Bahadur Shah giving him rights of *chauth* and *sardeshmukhi* in that region in return for services rendered in putting down the uprising of the Sayyids, rebel Moghul nobles. Damaji Gaekwad was a Maratha officer who had distinguished himself in the wars against the Sayyids under the leadership of his commander and patron, Khanderao Dhabade. Sahu's recognition of Damaji's services led to the establishment of the Maratha principality of Baroda in Gujarat. The fortunes of Kathiawad were now linked to Baroda, and thus, to the activities of Damaji Gaekwad and his successors. Maratha incursions into the peninsula, in 1723, led to the formation of the Gohel Rajput kingdom of Bhavanagar in alliance with the Abyssinian Sidis of Janjira. In 1757 the Marathas began their annual incursions into the peninsula because the Gaekwad had agreed to pay the Poona Government half of the revenues of Gujarat proper and half of such tribute as he could collect in Kathiawad. It was this martial method of collecting the annual tribute known as *mulukgiri*, inherited from the Moghuls, which eventually brought Colonel Walker and the British into Kathiawad in 1807.

The seal was set upon the Maratha conquest of Gujarat in April, 1755, when Ahmedabad was finally occupied by the troops of the Peshwa and Damaji Gaekwad, after the capitulation of Jawan Mard Khan Babi, the Moghul governor. It was this joint occupation which accounts for the agreement between the Peshwa and the Gaekwad to share the revenues of Gujarat and the tribute from Kathiawad. Even while the Marathas were consolidating themselves in Gujarat, however, events elsewhere were preparing the way for their overthrow. The Peshwas were not able to fulfil Shivaji's vision of complete Maratha supremacy. The divisions among the Marathas had already seriously weakened them as can be seen in their defeat by the Afghans in the third battle of Panipat, in 1761.[73] This marked the further decline of the Maratha fortunes and paved the way for the success of the British in Western India, who wrote the next chapter in Kathiawad's long history.

The Muslim and the Maratha had come and gone, leaving Kathiawad in the hands of the British. Outwardly nothing was left but the empty shell of the past, like the shells left by the tide on the beaches of Sorath. Somnath was a desolate ruin,[74] and Valabhi, a mass of ruins in a forest of peloo trees.[75] The debris of the past was everywhere.[76] The British could

---

[73] See T. S. Shejwalkar, *Panipat*: 1761, (Poona, Deccan College Monograph Series, 1946).

[74] Edward Thornton, *A Gazetteer of the Territories Under the East India Co.*, (London, Wm. H. Allen & Co., 1858), p. 923.

[75] *Ras Mala*, I, pp. 18-19.

[76] See J. Burgess, *Report on the Antiquities of Kathiawad and Kachh*, (London, India Museum, 1876); H. D. Sankalia, *The Archaeology of Gujarat (including Kathiawar)*, (Bombay, Natwarlal & Co., 1941); Henry Cousens, *Somnath and other Mediaeval Temples in Kathiawad*, (Calcutta, Archaeological Survey of India, Vol. XLV, Imperial Series, 1931).

not be blamed for underestimating the task they had set themselves, because the power of tradition is not always visible like a ruined temple. It was there, however, and the British would themselves help to create a new pride in traditions that were reviving throughout the nineteenth century.

The study of history would lead to a heightened awareness of the heritage of Indian culture. Indians would relate themselves increasingly to the past as they learned to identify the threads of continuity on the loom of history, trying to tie them together again wherever they had snapped. Gandhi went to the Alfred High School which was also influenced by the British Public School tradition. As we have just seen, however, there were far older traditions which would shape the Mahatma as he began to realise his cultural heritage.

Gandhi's Bania Heritage

The Gandhis belonged to the Vaishya caste of the Modh Banias. Their ancestors were probably grocers before they entered the services of Porbandar State. The caste mores and traditions of the Banias need to be examined for an understanding of Gandhi. There has been too much of a tendency in the study of Gandhi, however, to look at the religious life of the Banias rather than their socio-economic role and their shrewd political capacities. The Banias were mentioned in Panini's *Grammar*, and their duties, along with those of other Vaishyas in general, were defined by the *Arthasastra*. The Bania caste has maintained certain consistent characteristics noted by the Europeans who first came into contact with them in Surat in the seventeenth century. Mandelslo, who travelled in Western India in 1638-1639, found them " a hardworking class, attached to trade and merchandise, with an extraordinary devotion towards religious matters."[77] The

---

[77] M. S. Commissariat, (ed.), *Mandelslo's Travels in Western India*, (London, Oxford University Press, 1931), p. 10.

Gandhis, however, were not distinguished as traders, but as professional servants of the Rajput rulers of Porbandar. Therefore, we must look for their prototypes in Banias who served the rulers of the past rather than in Banias exclusively confined to commerce. The best examples of Banias who distinguished themselves in politics and the service of the state are to be found in the Chalukyan and Vaghela periods of Gujarati history.

A. K. Forbes, Georg Buhler, Bhagvanlal Indraji, H. C. Roy and A. K. Majumdar have helped to reconstruct the political, administrative, economic, religious, social, and artistic achievements of the Chalukyas. The wealth of material is useful for the interesting light it throws on the Bania heritage aspect of Gandhi. The Banias and their mercantile and trade guilds played an important role in many activities of this period. They gained an important position for their community under the Chalukyas which they maintained right up to the time of the Vaghelas. The Banias produced some striking and versatile men and women during this era, now considered the Golden Age of Gujarat and Kathiawad. One of them was Udayana,[78] a prominent figure during the reign of King Kumarapala (c. 1143-1175 A.D.). He was a friend of the Jain Acharya, Hemachandra, and was probably the key figure behind a palace revolution which brought Kumarapala to power. His three sons were great temple-builders and enriched the Jain shrines at Satrunjaya and Broach.

Even better known are the two brothers, Vastupala and Tejahpala, great names in the Bania community in the thirteenth century when the Vaghelas were ruling in Dholka. These sons of a Jain merchant, Asaraja, became the chief officers of state under Viradhavala and Visaladeva. They were ably assisted by their wives, Lalitadevi and Anupadevi.

---

[78] *Ras Mala*, I, p. 189.

Enormously wealthy, they proved that they could also make efficient administrators and good military commanders. So great was their patronage of art and literature that contemporary writers were full of praise for them. The eulogies were not undeserved ; Vastupala established three libraries at a cost of eighteen crores of rupees. The white marble temples they built at Mount Abu at a cost of twelve crores and three lakhs of rupees (Rs. 120,300,000) are among the greatest monuments of Indian architecture.[79] Gandhi's career reflected many personality traits, long valued in his caste, such as industry, capacity, and astonishing versatility, which enabled Banias before him to achieve great success in varied fields.

The martial Rajput aristocracy and the pacific Bania oligarchy lived in a kind of dialectical tension with each other; they probably complemented each other's vices and virtues. Yet the Bania had proved that he was not lacking in courage, both moral and physical. In Balachandra's *Vasantavilasa*, the largest *mahakavya* (epic poem) on Vastupala, the warrior-merchant is advised to flee by a messenger from Sankha who argued that it will not be disgraceful for a Bania to retreat. Vastupala replies, " Messenger, it is a delusion to think that Kshatriyas alone can fight, and not a *Vanik*. Did not Ambada, a *Vanik*, kill Mallikarjuna in battle? I, a *Vanik*, am well-known in the shop of the battlefield. I buy commodities—the heads of enemies, weighing them in the scales of swords; I pay the price in the form of heaven."[80] Gandhi too had some experience of " the shop of the battlefield " as a stretcher-bearer in the Boer War and the Zulu Rebellion. Though a non-violent fighter, Gandhi's physical courage was never in doubt. The British writer, George Orwell,[81] and Lord

---

[79] *Gujarat and Its Literature*, p. 11.

[80] *Gujarat and Its Literature*, p. 117.

[81] George Orwell, " Reflections on Gandhi," *A Collection of Essays*, (Garden City, N.Y., Doubleday Anchor, 1954), p. 177.

Halifax,[82] a former Viceroy of India, are agreed that his natural physical courage was quite outstanding. He told an audience in Kathiawad in 1925, "Fleeing from the battle-field—*palayanam*—is cowardice and unworthy of a warrior."[83]

Gandhi's attitude to the Bania caste to which he belonged can be understood in terms of the " in-group " and the "out-group." Within the caste group, the Mahatma felt free to criticize the weaknesses and failings of his fellow Banias. He could also, however, defend them vigorously if the Banias were denigrated by an outsider. In February, 1927, the Bania and other Vaishya (trading communities) merchants of Dhulia in Maharashtra insisted on giving the Mahatma a separate reception at which they claimed him as one of themselves. Gandhi was frank to the point of rudeness and his speech contains a summary of his entire attitude to his fellow Banias. He attributed the British conquest of India to the cooperation extended to them by the Vaishyas. The British had usurped the functions of both the Kshatriya and the Brahman, while the Vaishyas served them in traitorous fashion. The Banias had forgotten the versatility they had been capable of in the past. " Our *Varnashrama Dharma* does not say that a Bania may not be a Kshatriya and fight for the honour of his mother and sister, nor does it say that a Bania may not acquire know-ledge like a Brahmana and serve like a Shudra."[84] It was a rather Kathiawadi point of view. The Mahatma also tried to rekindle in them a vision of their duties as they had been laid down in the *Arthasastra* and the Hindu scriptures. " I want us to be the Vaishyas of the *Bhagavadgita*, the Vaishyas whose natural calling is the protection of the cow, agriculture,

---

82 Lord Halifax, " Talks with Gandhi," *The Ladies' Home Journal*, (January 1957).

83 *The Indian States' Problem*, p. 601.

84 R. K. Prabhu, *This was Bapu*, (Ahmedabad, Navajivan Publishing House, 1945), p. 82.

and trade, for his own country."[85] There was one sentence in this exhortation, however, that must have been music in the ears of the listening Banias. "You can retrieve the situation today," said Gandhi, "by becoming true Banias again, by capturing again the whole of the national trade...."[86]

In 1931, when Gandhi was attending the Round Table Conference in London, an Englishman questioned him at a public meeting asking whether the rapacity of the Banias was not partly responsible for the poverty of India. The Mahatma's reply was sharp : "The Indian Bania is not a patch upon the British Bania and if we were acting violently, the Indian Bania would deserve to be shot. But then the British Bania would deserve to be shot a hundred times. The rate of interest charged by the Indian Bania is nothing compared to the loot carried on by the British Bania through the jugglery of currency and merciless exactions of Land Revenue."[87]

The Influence of Jainism

Nowhere else have the Jains preserved their traditions so strongly as in Kathiawad, the home and heartland of Jainism in India. Here Jainism wrote some of the most glorious chapters in its history, finding in King Kumarapala its Asoka. In Kathiawad, the historian looks back on a long vista of time to Hiravijaya Suri, spiritual leader of the Jains in Akbar's days ; to Hemachandra, literary genius and friend of King Kumarapala ; to Mahavira, the contemporary of Buddha— and beyond them to the legendary *thirthankaras*,[88] the twenty-

---

[85] *This was Bapu*, pp. 82-83.

[86] *Ibid.*, p. 82.

[87] *Ibid.*, pp. 96-97.

[88] See M. Bloomfield, *The Life and Stories of The Jaina Savior Parcvanatha,* (Baltimore, The Johns Hopkins Press, 1919).

four sages whom the Jains believe to have been born at suc-
cessive stages in the evolution of the world. The statues of
Neminatha, the Jain Krishna, show him to be black—black
as the darkness that obscures the dim past, leaving us only
shadowy legends.[89]

Gandhi could not escape the influence of Jainism since the
atmosphere of Kathiawad was impregnated with its teachings
and spirit. Gandhi's own conscious interest in Jain ethics
and philosophy dates from his days in South Africa. The
source from which he acquired a good deal of his knowledge
was a deeply religious Jain jeweller of Bombay, Raichand,
with whom he maintained a regular correspondence. Jainism
undoubtedly formed an important element in Gandhi's conception of Satyagraha.

Gandhi's faith in the efficacy of vows is traced to the influence of his mother, Putlibai. It is not unlikely, however,
that she herself was unconsciously influenced by old Jain
traditions. In 1185 A.D., twelve years after the death of
Kumarapala, Somaprabha wrote his *Kumarapala pratibodha*.
Kumarapala was already assuming heroic proportions as a
great benefactor of the Jains and there are many descriptions in this series of sermons of the vows he took at the insistence of his *guru*, Hemachandra.[90] Kumarapala is reputed
to have given up meat and wine, gambling, lechery and the
chase by assenting to the twelve vows of the Jain religion.[91]
It is not surprising that Kumarapala's successor resented this
attempt to turn the royal court into a monastery and reasserted the princely Kshatriya traits by inclining strongly to
the old Hindu *dharma*.

Perhaps, the influence of this story from Kathiawad's
medieval past is seen in the way Putlibai was reassured on

---

[89] *Tarik-i-Sorath*, pp. 47-48.
[90] *Gujarat and Its Literature*, p. 109.
[91] *Ras Mala*, I, p. 188.

the eve of her son's departure for distant England. In
Gandhi's own words: "Becharji Swami was originally a
Modh Bania, but had now become a Jain monk. He too was
a family adviser like Joshiji. He came to my help and said,
' I shall get the boy solemnly to take the three vows, and then
he can be allowed to go.' He administered the oath and I
vowed not to touch wine, women, and meat. This done, my
mother gave her permission."[92] The spirit of Hemachandra
may have triumphed over one destined to greater fame than
even Kumarapala, best known of the kings of Gujarat.

Jainism had achieved a remarkable degree of integration
between the clergy and the laity which explains their mutual
involvement in each other's affairs.[93] Hemachandra's influence over Kumarapala had an economic and political
edge useful to the Banias. A striking instance of a purely
economic measure was Kumarapala's renunciation of his
right to entail the property of those who had died without
leaving any male heirs.[94] Gandhi's Swadeshi programme
and his view of property as a trust were not totally unconnected with his appeal for certain types of big businessmen who
knew they could not develop their commercial enterprises on
a large scale until the British hold on India was broken.

The role of the Jain Acharyas in politics and the leaning of
the Banias towards Jainism need further examination for any
light they may throw on Gandhi. The Jain Acharya was
often a spiritual leader with a political usefulness. Part of
the attraction of Jainism for the Banias was the techniques
this religion had evolved for wringing economic, political and
religious concessions from their rulers. The Acharya, respected as the saintly symbol of the Jain community, sometimes

---

[92] *Autobiography*, p. 156.
[93] S.Stevenson, *The Heart of Jainism*, (London, Oxford University Press, 1915),
   p. 18; Sarma, *op. cit.*, p. 18.
[94] *Ras Mala*, I, p. 188.

played an important part in furthering their political interests. The Banias could not oppose the Kshatriya rulers as the middle-classes of Europe had done in their struggle with feudalism. Since the Banias were Vaishyas, they could not aspire after the political power of the Kshatriya as their respective positions were fixed in the caste hierarchy by the laws of *dharma*. Largely powerless to oppose the rulers physically, the Banias had to obtain their political goals by subtler methods. The non-violence of Jainism was sometimes exploited as the technique of a mercantile community unable to assert itself with either physical or political force against the rulers. This traditional element was not lacking in Satyagraha. Gandhi had no use for the weakling or the coward, but he admitted that Satyagraha was the weapon of the militarily weak against the strong. The Mahatma also tried to purge the technique of non-violence of the calculation and expediency associated with the efforts of a mercantile community to better its own interests.

Gandhi, consciously or unconsciously, imitated the combination of religious and secular interests seen in the Jain Acharyas and jewellers, while some of his political methods were also derived from them. For example, Gandhi's technique of the *pada yatra*, or walking tours, is strongly reminiscent of the Jain Acharyas. When Akbar invited Hiravijaya Suri to Fatehpur Sikhri in 1583, the Acharya refused the emperor's offer of a conveyance and escort. He walked the whole distance, bare-footed and surrounded by his white-clad monks.[95] Gandhi's Salt March to Dandi was as dramatic as Hiravijaya Suri's gesture.

Vijaya Dharma Suri, a Shrimali Bania, who became the Jain Acharya in 1893, was born a year before Gandhi at Mahuwa in Kathiawad. A biographer says of Vijaya Dharma

---

[95] *Ibid.*, p. 230.

Suri that "he proceeded from place to place bare-headed and bare-footed, with no conveyance but his bare feet, with no luggage but his begging bowl, with no girdle but his faith."[96] In 1903, Vijaya Dharma Suri walked from Kathiawad to Benares in order to establish a Jain college there. Gandhi could not have been ignorant of the activities of this Jain leader, so well-known in Kathiawad.

It had never been difficult for a Modh Bania to become a Jain, either in fact or spirit. Gandhi is a common enough name among the Jains of Kathiawad. There would be moments when the figure of the Mahatma would take on the visage and lineaments of a great Jain Acharya with that fusion of religion and politics which distinguished them in their role as leaders of their people.[97]

Gandhi and The Vallabhacharya Sampradaya

James Tod was so impressed by the richness and variety of religious life in Kathiawad that he wrote, "Besides this field for the enquirer into the natural history of men, there is one equally wide for investigating the history of all religions which have swayed the human mind in this sea-girt corner of Asia."[98] The Kathiawadi spectrum of religion ranges from Sun-worship to the strict monotheism of Islam. The Mahatma's religious roots were in a truly fertile spiritual soil. It is important to realize, however, that in the nineteenth century that spiritual soil was being ploughed both by local reformers like Sadhu Shantidas[99] and Sahajanand Swami[100]

---

[96] A. J. Sunavala, *Vijaya Dharma Suri: His Life and Work*, (Cambridge University Press, 1922), p. 34.

[97] See V. A. Sangave, *Jaina Community: A Social Survey*, (Bombay, Popular Book Depot, 1959).

[98] *Travels in Western India*, p. 257.

[99] N. A. Thoothi, *The Vaishnavas of Gujarat*, (Bombay, Longmans, Green and Co., 1935), pp. 99-100.

[100] K. G. Mashruwala, *Sahajanand Swami*, (Ahmedabad, Navajivan, 1923).

as well as the Protestant Christian missionaries from across the seas. Gandhi's religious outlook was largely a product of this religious ferment.

Dwaraka in Kathiawad is the most important centre of Vaishnavism. There is no evidence as to exactly when Vaishnavism became strong in Kathiawad ; it is probable, however, that it developed greatly when the peninsula was part of the Gupta Empire in the fourth and fifth centuries A.D. The Gandhis were Vaishnavas, worshippers of Vishnu in his incarnation as Sri Krishna. The more important fact though for the understanding of Gandhi is that the family had belonged, as far back as they could remember, to the Vallabhacharya sampradaya[101]—a sect founded by a Telugu Brahman, Sri Vallabha, in the fifteenth century. Vallabha was a contemporary of the Bengali mystic, Chaitanya ; the two Vaishnava saints are said to have met on more than one occasion. The religion of Sri Vallabha was based on *bhakti* (devotion) to Krishna in his *Ananda-swarupa*—in his form as a giver of bliss. At its best, the Vallabhacharya sampradaya was full of light and colour, a joyful expression of religion. The danger, however, in this kind of worship of Sri Krishna was that it sometimes results in eroticism attracting criticism.

The coming social changes of the nineteenth century, however, had been foreshadowed by the rise of a number of cults in Kathiawad in the eighteenth century. In 1724, Ranchod, a Bania, established a sect named after him as a protest against Brahmanism.[102] Nihal Daji, another Bania, introduced the Kabir sect into Gujarat about 1790.[103] Early in the nineteenth century Saela in Kathiawad was made famous by the presence in that town of a Bania saint, Lala Bhagat. The

---

[101] M. C. Parekh, *Sri Vallabhacharya*, (Rajkot, Harmony House, 1943), p. 371; Thoothi, *op. cit.*, p. 279.
[102] Thoothi, *op. cit.*, p. 120.
[103] *Ibid.*, p. 120.

34

beginnings of the new century also marked the rise of cults like that of Sadhu Shantidas directly opposed to the practices of the Vallabhacharis. In 1824, a Kunbi farmer called Madhavgar established a sect named after himself which was specifically opposed to the Maharajas. It is significant that Madhavgar was also in revolt against the practice of un-touchability.[104]

The most successful of these cults, however, was that of the Swaminarayan sampradaya, opposed strongly to " the gross Epicurianism of the Vallabh sect."[105] Sahajanand, the founder of the Swaminarayan sect, was born in Ayodhya in 1791, but he laboured in Kathiawad for nearly thirty years. The Swaminarayan sampradaya insisted on sexual purity and the *sadhus* of the sect took twenty-six vows relating to women ; seeing a woman or her portrait, or even pronouncing her name were among the prohibitions. Men and women were not allowed to worship at the same time in the Swaminarayan temples.[106] An order of female ascetics was established. Sahajanand was particularly successful among the peasants and tribal peoples of Kathiawad.

The young Gandhi was undoubtedly influenced by the charges of immorality aimed against his own sampradaya and his later attitude to sex certainly resembles that of the Swami-narayan sect. Later on he would come to value the *Bhaga-vata Purana* when it had been reinterpreted, like the *Song of Songs* in the Bible, in allegorical and spiritual terms. Despite his reaction to the earlier eroticism of the Vallabhacharya sampradaya, however, Gandhi owed much to his sect ; he was a true son of the *haveli* and would be inspired greatly by the teachings of Sri Krishna in the *Bhagavadgita*.

The Vallabhachari places of worship, called *havelis*, were

---

[104] *Ibid*., pp. 100-101.
[105] *Gujarat and Its Literature*, p. 267.
[106] *Ibid*., p. 267; Thoothi, *op. cit*., pp. 101-102.

different from Hindu temples in certain respects. The *havelis*, the private property of the Maharajas, were thrown open at certain times of the day. The daily ritual of worship of *Thakorji*, as the image of Sri Krishna is called, throws much light on certain aspects of Gandhi's outlook.[107] The congregational form of worship, for example, enabled Gandhi to appreciate the Christian services he attended as a student in London and partly explains his love of Christian hymns. Cardinal Newman's *Lead Kindly Light* was popular with the Vaishnavas of Gujarat before it became known as one of the Mahatma's favourite hymns.[108]

The interest Gandhi showed in dietetics can also be partly traced to the worship in the *haveli*; an incredible number of vegetarian dishes were cooked by the Vallabhacharis for the daily repasts of *Thakorji*. The Mahatma's noted cleanliness reflects the daily baths given to *Thakorji* as part of the ritual. The boy had learned the lesson of cleanliness from his Vallabhachari father who had risen several times a day from his death-bed in the interests of personal hygiene. Gandhi reacted, however, against the constant dressing up of *Thakorji* in fine clothes. He rejected the *ananda* or ecstatic aspects of *haveli* worship, assisted by music and flowers, and took what was in consonance with his asceticism. His own *bhakti* was directed towards Sri Krishna and Sri Rama in their heroic forms as warriors devoted to duty and truth.

The Vallabhachari practices in home and family life are also important for understanding the development of Gandhi. The joyful worship in the *haveli* was mirrored in the happiness of family life. Each family had a little shrine room where they gathered to sing devotional hymns. Just as there was no segregation of the sexes in the *haveli* so also the family religion was an experience shared by men and women. Sri Krishna

---

[107] Thoothi, *op. cit.*, pp. 337-350.
[108] *Ibid.*, p. 147.

was worshipped a great deal as Bala-Krishna, "the Holy Child," giving a dignity and respect to the children in the home. The great resemblances to Christian family life explains why Gandhi could appreciate the religion of the British middle-classes.

Speaking of religious life in Kathiawad, Manilal C. Parekh says, "The cultural and social predominance of the Brahmans has been for centuries no longer the rule as in other provinces, and the relations between different communities have been smoother than elsewhere."[109] Swami Dayanand Saraswati was a Brahman from Morvi in Kathiawad but his Arya Samaj met with success in areas of North India like the Punjab.[110]

The Bania had played a humanitarian and democratic role in the religious life of Kathiawad whether as a Jain or a Vaishnava. The Banias had produced a great Jain Acharya like Hemachandra and a Vaishnava saint like Lala Bhagat. During the first half of the nineteenth century, the leavening ideas of the Madhavgars, the Swaminarayans and the Christian missionaries had been at work among the Kathiawad Vaishnavas. There is hardly any need to look for the spiritual forerunners of the Mahatma outside the confines of the small peninsula where Gandhi was born.

---

[109] *Op. cit.*, p. 445.
[110] See Har Bilas Sarda, *Life of Dayanand Saraswati*, (Ajmer, Vedic Yantralaya, 1946).

CHAPTER TWO

Whirlwinds of Change:
Kathiawad in the Nineteenth Century

In 1898, Gandhi, then in South Africa, would write, "A reference to any map of the world would show that the Province of Kattywar is included in British India and is marked red."[1] He was defending the rights of Indians as British subjects. We shall now attempt to relate the story of how the coming of the British changed the environment of the peninsula where Gandhi spent his most formative years.

The "Reports of Proceedings in Kathiawar" of Major Alexander Walker are valuable sources of information for conditions in the peninsula at the dawn of the nineteenth century. Diwan Ranchodji Amarji, who knew him personally, said, "I have never seen a man so high and noble-minded as Alexander Walker, of little speech but great intelligence, acquainted with the affairs of government, versed in all political matters and capable of appreciating men of worth."[2] Jonathan Duncan sent Major Walker to Baroda to confer with Ananda Rao and his ministers while a military detachment was sent by sea to Cambay to deal with Malhar Rao and his insurgents. It was out of these events that

---

[1] *Collected Works*, III, p. 10.
[2] *Tarik-i-Sorath*, p. 204.

" affairs progressed rapidly towards that settlement which formed the groundwork of all future political relations in Gujarat."[3] The campaign against Malhar Rao reduced the Gaekwad to military dependence upon the British and led to the appointment of Major Walker as the Resident in Baroda in 1804.[4]

The financial stability of the Gaekwad's government depended to a large extent on the efficient and timely collection of the tribute from Kathiawad. Owing to the disturbed conditions in Gujarat, a *mulukgiri* force[5] had not been sent to Kathiawad to collect the tributary revenues which had fallen into arrears since 1798-1799. Babaji Appaji, the Gaekwad's able minister, accordingly went on circuit in the peninsula in 1802. He dealt severely with the recalcitrant chiefs and " finally liquidated the whole arrears of tribute due from that country, and established it in a state of subordination and order superior to any that had been witnessed for centuries."[6]

Babaji Appaji's success was in part due to the fact that the Kathiawadi chieftains knew he had the backing of the British ; thus the Gaekwad's government became keen to have their continued assistance in collecting the tribute. When Major Walker negotiated the Treaty of 1805 with Baroda, it was stipulated by the Gaekwad that one of the four battalions of Indian infantry stationed by the Bombay Government in Gujarat, should be available for service in Kathiawad, if necessary.

The need for the British to take some responsibility for the

---

[3] *Ras Mala*, II, p. 40; See Ch. II, " Anund Row Guikowar."
[4] See R. Wallace, *The Guicowar and His Relations with the British Government,* (Bombay, The Education Society, 1863).
[5] The term was derived from the Persian *mulk*, " country," and *giriftan,* "to take." See Surendranath Sen, *Administrative System of the Marathas*, (Calcutta, University of Calcutta, 1925).
[6] *Ras Mala*, II, p. 56.

mulukgiri tribute from Kathiawad had been the subject of correspondence between Bombay and Calcutta even earlier than 1805. On December 15, 1802, the Marquis of Wellesley and his Council expressed the view that " if an amicable arrangement could be made with the several chieftains of the peninsula for the regular payment of their tribute, without the necessity for the periodical advance of a military force, an acceptable service would thereby be rendered alike to the Guicowar state, and to the British interests in Goozerat." [7] But it was not until April 3, 1807, that the Bombay Government was able to act upon this agreed policy. Walker was now empowered to make a settlement of the *mulukgiri* tribute to Kathiawad. The choice naturally fell on him as an officer " uniting the essential qualifications of requisite information and local influences."[8] Thus the British entered Kathiawad half a century before the birth of Gandhi, and the changes they brought to the peninsula were destined to play a part in the shaping of his personality and ideas.

The *mulukgiri* expeditions of the Marathas were modelled on the tribute-collecting campaigns of the Moghuls. The last Moghul Viceroy to lead a *mulukgiri* force was Jawan Mard Khan Babi who levied the tribute in Kathiawad in 1751.[9] After him, the Marathas used troops of three or four thousand cavalry to exact the tribute but later their forces became rather irregular and ragged. Since the chieftains knew the Marathas were out to collect as much as possible, they did their best to resist these exactions. It was almost a point of honour with the Rajputs to object to paying the tribute.

The result was that the Marathas tended to concentrate on open towns and villages and usually chose the harvest season for their operations, both in order to gain a speedier com-

---

[7] *Ras Mala*, II, p. 57.
[8] *Ras Mala*, II, p. 58.
[9] *Bombay Gazetteer*, VIII, p. 304.

pliance with their demands and to be able to feed off the land. If a chieftain dared to resist the approaching Maratha forces " the Pindarees were thrown out on all sides, and the march of the army was thenceforth marked by every species of plunder and desolation ; the ripe crops were swept from the field, the villages were wantonly fired and destroyed, nothing was allowed to remain but the bare walls of the houses, and it frequently happened that every acre of his lands was left bare, and every hamlet in his territory reduced to a heap of smouldering ruins before the Rajput chieftain condescended to the payment of the tribute demanded."[10] The plight of the commercial classes like the Banias whose lives were constantly dislocated by these forays can be easily imagined. When one remembers how vehemently Gandhi protested against the British proposal to follow a " scorched earth policy," should the Japanese invade India, one is tempted to speculate as to whether there was not in his attitude something of the deep-seated aversion his Bania forbears must have felt for the perennial curse of the *mulukgiri* expeditions which so frequently devastated Kathiawad.[11]

Colonel Walker's joint expedition with Vithal Rao Devaji, in 1807, enabled the Gaekwad to obtain territories like the Amreli Mahals and Kodinar. But the important point is that Walker put an end to the ferocious system of *mulukgiri*, and had begun the pacification of the region which by the time of Gandhi's birth (1869), had led to the gradual emergence of settled conditions.

It must be conceded that the year 1807 was a kind of *annus mirabilis* in the peninsula. Apart from doing away with the pernicious system of *mulukgiri*, Walker captured Kandorna

---

[10] *Ras Mala*, II, p. 55.

[11] M. K. Gandhi, *Correspondence with the British Government* 1942–1944, (Ahmedabad, Navajivan Publishing House, 1945), p. 241.

from Jam Jasaji of Navanagar and restored it to its rightful owner, the Rana of Porbandar ; crushed the Waghers and Mianas ; and put down an abortive rebellion by Kunvar Prathiraj, one of the many Absaloms of Kathiawad history. Prathiraj's father, Haloji, was the same Rana of Porbandar whom Walker had protected from the avarice of the Jam. The Maratha administration of Kathiawad at this time was under Vithal Rao Devaji with his headquarters in Amreli. Between 1807 and 1820, the British role was one of assisting the Gaekwad to control the turbulent elements in Kathiawad ; they not only dealt with many internal feuds, but also repulsed an attempted invasion by Futteh Muhammad from Kachh in 1813.

The British also continued to help in the collection of the annual tribute. In 1817, Captain Ballantine, Political Agent of the Mahi Kanta, supervised the collection of the Peshwa's share of the revenues of Kathiawad. In 1818, the British acquired the Peshwa's rights in the peninsula by the Treaty of Poona negotiated by Elphinstone after the battle of Kirkee. A further step in the direction of British control was taken in 1820 when the Gaekwad agreed to the collection and remittal of his share of the tribute by them. The British did not assume paramountcy over Kathiawad till 1822 when the Nawab of Junagadh surrendered his rights. The early Political Agents, like Colonel Lang and Colonel Le Grand Jacob, did much to promote peaceful conditions. " This is no place to dilate on the campaigns in Kattywar, but they would form a volume of great interest, " says Edward Moor in another connection.[12] It is an interesting fact, however, that Kathiawad was in a partly disturbed condition to within a year of Gandhi's birth. (The Wagher Revolt in the 1850's was the last significant outburst of old violence as

---

[12] *Hindu Infanticide*, p. 299

Kathiawad began to cross the threshold from the feudal to the modern period.)[13]

Whatever the defects of Walker's settlement were, he tried to stabilize the whole nexus of economic and political relationships and created a reasonably secure social order which endured for half a century. He not only defined the relations between the Gaekwad and the chieftains, but also the feudal ties between these numerous overlords, both big and small, and their tenants called *bhayyats* and *girassias*. Walker froze these relationships as he found them and determined tenancy and occupancy rights throughout the peninsula. Kathiawad in the nineteenth century was a colourful mosaic of feudal patterns in which the constant proliferation of states had been ended by knitting them together with British law and authority. Its geographical compactness made it the most unique area in the whole of princely India.

The British impact was first felt by the *boomias*—the land-owning classes. Walker's settlement was based on the assumption " that a body of landlords, commanding respect from their hereditary title, may be a valuable bulwark to their land."[14] This policy worked so well that by the end of the century the hostility of the landlords had turned into a dependence upon the British for maintaining their *status quo*. Gandhi's fast at Rajkot in 1939 was directed against the very classes whom Walker had stabilized. The work of Walker and his successors was destroyed by two dynamic representatives of a new and radical middle-class, Vallabhbhai Patel and Gandhi, who tore open the quilted patchwork of feudalism forcibly stitched together by the British.

Walker's settlement, however, deserves to be remembered for generating the vital forces, including the right to the ownership of land and private property, which produced the

---

[13] *Ras Mala*, I, p. xiii; G. Smith, *op. cit.*, p. 201.
[14] *Ras Mala*, II, p. 300.

new social classes and their revolutionary representatives who would break it up when its historic usefulness had come to an end. A. K. Forbes, with remarkable insight, had anticipated that this would happen. Writing in the middle of the last century, he foresaw that " the victory which democratic tendencies had gained within the conquering nation itself, could not have failed sooner or later to influence the conquered ; the tempest which had broken upon the cliffs of England was sure before long to make itself felt in the higher rising of the surges which rolled upon the beach of Soreth. . ."[15] Gandhi was born in a house on " the beach of Soreth."[16]

Looking back at Walker's settlement after a century had elapsed, Wilberforce-Bell could claim its immediate result was " that Kathiawad became blessed with peace such as the peninsula had not enjoyed for very many years."[17] Violence and disorder had been endemic for so long that " *Pax Britannica* " was certainly no meaningless euphemism as far as Kathiawad was concerned. For centuries the Jains had tried to rid the country of violence and disorder by preaching *ahimsa*. It is not surprising, therefore, that this blood-drenched soil should have finally produced a prophet of non-violence of the stature of Mahatma Gandhi. There ought to be a symbolic painting of the child Gandhi, based upon the legendary past, balancing himself on one foot upon the top of a many-headed serpent with its tail held in his hand. The snake would then represent the spirit of violence tamed by a British middle-class ; for " the Waghela of Sanund and the Gohil of Peerum could not hope to escape the arm which had reft their hereditary power from McKenzie and McShimei."[18] The child born in 1869 could grow up in safety to preach his gospel of *ahimsa* to the world.

---

[15] *Ras Mala*, II, p. 295.
[16] *Ibid.*, II, p. 295.
[17] Wilberforce-Bell, *op. cit.*, pp. 164-165.
[18] *Ras Mala*, II, p. 295.

Kathiawad, like the rest of India, began to change rapidly after the Mutiny. Gandhi's childhood and boyhood were passed against this vigorous background of increasing social momentum which made Kathiawad a different place from the peninsula the British first entered. The three forces that operated together in Kathiawad, for example, to eradicate infanticide—the British administration, the Christian missionary movement, and an educated Indian public opinion radiating from Bombay—continued to exert an influence on Kathiawad. But by the end of the eighties when Gandhi sailed for England there were many significant differences in the situation.

In 1844, Bhau Daji could write appreciatively of the British Government that " through them some of the most abominable and horrible practices in India have been abolished. Human sacrifices, Suttee, Infanticide of various kinds, Thuggism, Slavery, Tragga, Dhurna, etc., are no longer allowed to inflict shame and disgrace on India."[19] By 1855, however, John Wilson was pointing out that " Thyaga and Dharana are already terms which we have to explain to India's people as well as to foreigners."[20] How dim the recollection of what India was like in the eighteenth and early nineteenth centuries had become can be seen in Gandhi's *Hind Swaraj* where he debunks the *Pax Britannica* as any justification for British rule.[21] By that time, Indians were no longer seeing India through the eyes of Ram Mohun Roy or Bhau Daji, but with the romantic vision of Max Muller. Yet Max Muller is rightly honoured by Indians for he helped to restore their sense of self-respect, and encouraged them to believe that the greatness of their past justified their demand for freedom at a time when the official British policy was

---

[19] *Essay* cited, p. 23.
[20] *Op. cit.*, p. 440.
[21] *Op. cit.*, Ch. VIII, p. 31.

justifying their subjection in terms of their contemporary wretchedness.

Christian Influences in Kathiawad

The attempt to probe into the nature of the Christian influences at work in Kathiawad and the kinds of responses they evoked, particularly in the nineteenth century, is important from two points of view. First, there is general agreement that the Western impact on India was mediated through the British administration, English education, and the Christian missionary movement.[22] These channels by which Western culture and civilization were communicated were inevitably and unavoidably inter-connected. Therefore, the story of the establishment of British authority over Kathiawad needs to be complemented by the history of missionary activities in the peninsula in order to get a clear picture of the kinds of forces that were at work while Gandhi was growing up.

In the second place, we know that Christian activities were creating a negative response in the youthful Gandhi; but biographers of Gandhi have not examined what was actually happening at the time. After telling us that toleration for all faiths was inculcated in him the Mahatma adds, " Only Christianity at the time was an exception. I developed a sort of dislike for it! "[23] The conflict of religions plays an important role in the meeting of two civilizations and is reflected by individual personalities. Gandhi's attitude to Christianity changed in many ways and he was destined to be described as the most Christ-like man of the twentieth century. But he never truly rose above some aspects of his early

---

[22] See, for example, A. R. Desai, *Social Background of Indian Nationalism*, (London, Oxford University Press, 1948); and S. Natarajan, *A Century of Social Reform in India*, (Bombay, Asia Publishing House, 1959).

[23] *Autobiography*, p. 49.

emotional reaction to missionary activities in Rajkot; it continued to colour his attitudes to Christians and Christianity for the rest of his life. The history of the missionary movement in Kathiawad ought, therefore, to throw some interesting light on the sociological origins of Gandhi's highly determinative reactions to Christianity as a boy.

The Christian Church had been in India for a longer time than is generally realized.[24] A few miles outside Madras there is Parangimalai—the Hill of the Ferenghis (or foreigners) —commemorating the legend that St. Thomas, the Apostle, came to India. The hill, which overlooks the growing airport of Madras, is said to be the spot where he lived before his martyrdom. *The Acts of St. Thomas*, ascribed to Abdias of Babylon, say he was invited to northern India by a shadowy king called Gondophernes, whose coins have been found. St. Thomas is said to have been in India from about 52 A.D. to his martyrdom in 67 A.D. The Church historian, Eusebius, claims that St. Pantaenus of Alexandria was in India at the close of the second century A.D. One of the bishops at the Council of Nice held in 325 A.D. was John of Persia and Great India. The Nestorians came to India about 496 A.D. and established Christian communities on the West Coast. These Malabar or Syrian Christians acknowledged the Patriarch of Antioch; a section of the Syrian Christians continue to do so to this day. Alfred of England, the absentminded king who burned the cakes, sent gifts to the church of San Thome, a suburb of Madras, where the Apostle, according to legend, is buried.[25]

In the popular mind, however, the coming of Christianity is usually associated with the advent of the Europeans at the

---

[24] See P. Thomas, *Christians and Christianity in India and Pakistan*, (London, George Allen and Unwin, 1954).

[25] Capuchin Mission Unit, *India and Its Missions*, (London, Macmillan & Co., Ltd., 1923), pp. 81-82, 87-88.

end of the fifteenth century and within a few years of the discovery of the New World by Christopher Columbus. In 1487, the emissary of the Portuguese king, Dom Joao II, Pedro da Covilham, reached Calicut by the land route. Eleven years later, on May 16, 1498, Vasco da Gama's ship, piloted by a Gujarati, Malemo Cana, dropped anchor off this small port on the West coast of India. The Spaniards and the Portuguese had opened up a whole world which the Pope obligingly divided between them. An entirely new era in history had begun with far-reaching consequences for India. Many were the invaders who had been absorbed into India; but the Portuguese set in motion a train of events that would tend to absorb India into the world.

Kathiawad's connection with the Europeans began peacefully with the establishment of a Dominican mission on the island of Diu. But, by 1507, the Portuguese, who had attacked Mahim and Bombay, were embroiled with Sultan Mahmud Begada of Gujarat. His deputy in Sorath, Malek Aiaz, defeated a Portuguese fleet with the help of a squadron sent by the Sultan of Turkey. The struggle was continued by Sultan Bahadur (1526–1537). He was killed by the Portuguese in a fracas at Diu and they could not be dislodged from the strong fort they had contrived to build on the island.

The Reformation and the Counter-Reformation in Europe began to make themselves felt along the coasts of India. It was soon apparent that the aggressiveness of the Portuguese was both economic and religious. They brought their brand of fanaticism to an India, weary of the intolerance of the Muslims, and glad for the respite afforded by Akbar's eclecticism. Goa, captured by the Portuguese in 1510, became the seat of their authority, both civil and ecclesiastical. The Inquisition was introduced in 1560, and the Grand Inquisitor was more feared and respected than either the Archbishop or the Viceroy of Goa. The Inquisition was temporarily suspended in 1774, but was resumed three years later; it was still functioning when Dr. Claudius Buchanan visited Goa in 1808 and was not finally abolished till 1812.[26]

In the latter half of the nineteenth century Catholic missionary activity was largely confined to Diu, where there were the Cathedral of St. Paul and a few monasteries. There were only a few Portuguese and Eurasian Catholics in Rajkot.[27] Gandhi reacted against the activities of Protestant missionaries, though he was probably unaware of the denominational differences among Christians in that period of his life. This fact, however, makes it possible to narrow down the field of enquiry, since there was only one Protestant mission at work in Kathiawad in the nineteenth century. This was the Indian Mission of the Irish Presbyterians. The story of how they happened to go to Kathiawad is an interesting example of the kinds of circumstances that often conspired to make Christianity indistinguishable from British Imperialism in the eyes of the Indian people.

Since Bombay was a centre of Marathi and Gujarati, missionary ideas were being mediated through both languages and had an influence in the two regions where these tongues were spoken. But the earliest mission fields in Gujarat itself were Surat and Ahmedabad; the London Missionary Society established itself in Surat in 1815, while the Society for the Propagation of the Gospel worked in Ahmedabad for a short time. The London Missionary Society set up a printing press in Surat in 1821 which published and distributed thousands of tracts and booklets in Gujarati; some of them found their way into Kathiawad through John Wilson. The London Society later handed over its work in Surat to the Irish Presbyterians. The press continued to flourish under the new management and the New Testament in Gujarati appeared in 1857; the Gujarati Old Testament followed in

---

[26] J. M. Mitchell, *In Western India*, (Edinburgh, David Douglas, 1899), p. 42.
[27] *Bombay Gazetteer*, VIII, p. 434.

4

1861. The first Report of the Gujarat Tract and Book Society founded in 1852 shows that fifteen tracts were printed, six of them translations of foreign writers and nine of them written in India.[28]

The first and only Protestant mission to Kathiawad in the nineteenth century was an offshoot of the work of the Church of Scotland Mission. In 1839, Dr. Alexander Duff, the great Scottish missionary educator of Calcutta and a friend of Ram Mohun Roy, visited Ireland and spoke with such eloquence that the three hundred Presbyteries of the Synod of Ulster decided to establish a mission in India. The Irish response to the missionary appeal was rather belated and the Irish Presbyterian Mission was about the very last of such societies that had been at work for more than half a century. Therefore, they were really in a quandary as to where to locate their Mission in India. Reverend George Bellis, the Secretary of the new Society, wrote to Calcutta, Bombay, and Madras asking for suggestions which could be submitted to the Synod of 1840.

It is not surprising that no helpful replies were received from either Calcutta or Madras—both now old mission fields where there were hardly any " unoccupied " areas left. But Dr. John Wilson, who had visited Kathiawad in 1835, sent off an exhaustive report, later described as " an apostolic epistle," on the needs and advantages of this region. The Synod acted promptly and the first Irish Presbyterian missionaries, the Reverend Alexander Kerr and the Reverend James Glasgow, reached the hospitable home of Wilson on Malabar Hill in Bombay, accompanied by their wives, at the end of February, 1841.

The two missionaries had obtained the Company's permission to come to India, but their arrival in Bombay immediately raised some delicate political issues. The Company's

---

[28] M. A. Sherring, *History of Protestant Missions in India* 1706–1835, (London, The Religious Tract Society, 1884) Ch. VIII.

policy towards missionaries had softened considerably in the territories directly administered by it. Yet, hitherto no missionary had been allowed to enter a native state. Would Kerr and Glasgow be permitted to enter Baroda and the native states of Kathiawad? That they eventually did was due to the tact and influence of John Wilson who succeeded in bringing round the Governor of Bombay, Sir James R. Carnac, an " Old Indian " of the Madras Army who had previously been Resident at Baroda and Chairman of the Court of Directors. Wilson was helped to win over the Governor by Sir J. P. Willoughby, then the Chief Secretary.

Three months had passed in negotiations with the Government during which time the two Irish missionaries learned Gujarati, while their wives nursed the babies born soon after their arrival. They then set off for Kathiawad accompanied by none other than John Wilson himself. Their journey gives us a graphic picture of the inaccessibility of Kathiawad only a quarter of a century before Gandhi was born. The first lap was a gruelling sea voyage of three hundred miles from Bombay to Gogha in an open " Bunder " boat, without decks or cabins, manned by Indian sailors. The missionaries with their wives and children huddled together on straw mats spread on the floor of the boat while the sun beat down making them faint with thirst. At Gogha, they transferred to springless bullock carts which jolted along a parched, roadless countryside teeming with game. The indomitable Wilson divided his time between shooting to replenish the food supplies and preaching in some of the villages through which they passed. Their bullock carts arrived at Rajkot after eight weary days.

The acting Political Agent in Rajkot, Captain Le Grand Jacob, had not been very enthusiastic about the coming of the missionaries. Policy gave way to a natural sympathy, however, when the worn-out little party arrived, and the small British colony rallied to their support. They arrived at

Rajkot on June 3, 1841; only eight days later the Glasgows lost their infant daughter for whom the journey had proved too much. Worse was to follow; both Wilson and Kerr came down with the dreaded "Gujarat fever" which we know today as malaria. On August 16, a second burial service was held—for Kerr. Wilson went back to Bombay leaving the two bereaved families to found the first Protestant mission in Kathiawad.

The mission in Rajkot was strengthened early in 1842 by the arrival of the Reverend Robert Montgomery and the Reverend A. D. Glasgow. A small trickle of missionaries had begun and the first meeting of the newly constituted "Presbytery of Kathiawar in Rajkot" was held on January 30, 1843. One of the decisions made was to send Montgomery and Reverend J. H. Speers to Porbandar. It was John Wilson who had suggested the establishing of a mission station in Porbandar; he had visited it in March, 1835, and found the response to his preaching in the bazaar so friendly that he had been able to distribute many Gujarati tracts. It was recognized as an important commercial centre because of its brisk trade with the Konkan and Malabar coasts and with the ports of Sind, Baluchistan, the Persian Gulf, Arabia, and East Africa.

Montgomery and his family, accompanied by Glasgow, reached Porbandar in February, 1843 after a journey of nine days by bullock cart; Speers followed them later. Montgomery's diary, which told the story of the unsuccessful attempt to found a mission station in the capital of the Jethvas, has been preserved.[29] Rani Rupaliba, the Regent during the Rana's minority who had caused much unpleasantness to Gandhi's grandfather, had died two years previously. The young Rana Vikmatji's reception of the missionaries was

---

[29] The Foreign Mission Office of the Irish Presbyterian Church, Belfast, kindly permitted the making of a microfilm copy of the diary.

cordial at first. On February 24, he sent them his salaams and " a quantity of almonds and candy sugar " which was " according to the custom of the country a mark of respect." Three days later, Glasgow and Montgomery were invited to meet the Rana at the palace. When the missionaries presented Vikmatji with a Gujarati New Testament, he looked at the title page and asked, " Who is Jesus? " Glasgow launched into a lengthy explanation which convinced the Rana that Jesus was an incarnation worshipped by the English. After this friendly interview, a school was started and Montgomery and Speers settled down to the study of Gujarati. They also preached regularly in the neighbouring villages. If their activities were disapproved, there were no open signs of it during the first eight months the missionaries lived in Porbandar.

But in October a real storm blew up, because the first Christian convert in Kathiawad was baptized in Porbandar that month. Montgomery's Gujarati *munshi* (teacher) was Abdul Sulam, the son of a much respected Muslim *mullah* of Porbandar, Mir Mohammed. He had a brother, Abdul Rahman, who was attracted by the religion of the missionaries and asked for baptism. When he was baptized, unfortunately in the presence of two friendly British lieutenants, strong passions were aroused in the town and violence was feared. The Rana quite understandably sided with his Muslim subjects, who controlled a good deal of the trade of Porbandar, and refused to intervene to protect the missionaries and their solitary convert. In the end the mob had to be dispersed by the Captain of the British troops stationed in the town. The little mission in Porbandar had lost the goodwill of the Rana and become hopelessly dependent on the British military authorities for protection.

It is interesting, however, that the disturbance over the first Christian convert in Porbandar became linked with the disturbance in Bombay over the conversion of two young

Parsis in 1839. One of them was Dhanjibhai Nauroji who served the Church in Surat after receiving an education at the New College, Edinburgh. There he met Abdul Rahman, also now a minister, and married his daughter. The whole Porbandar family, including the eighty-four-year old father, Mir Mohammed, had become Christians and were living in Surat which was safer for them than any place in Kathiawad.

The conversion of Abdul Rahman made the position of the mission in Porbandar so difficult that Montgomery's letters were full of statements concerning the uncooperative attitude of the Rana. The missionaries were boycotted in the shops and bazaars and it became impossible to rent a house or buy a plot of land. Vikmatji was reported to have told a prospective seller, " So you are selling land to the English ? They'll want to buy the palace next." Montgomery's diary tells how the position of the mission became so hopeless that it was closed down in 1845.[30]

Forty years later there were some signs of change. In 1886 the British Administrator of Porbandar, Mr. Frederick Lely, was able to appoint a Christian, Joseph Chhaganlal, to head the Police force of the State.[31] His home was both the church and the social centre of the tiny Christian community for nearly fifty years. A century after the arrival of the Irish Presbyterians a handsome church was dedicated in Porbandar through the efforts of the Reverend George Wilson, a frequent visitor to Gandhi's Ashram in Ahmedabad between 1925–1937. The state of Porbandar made ample amends for the past; the land on which the church stands and a sum of Rs. 3,000 were donated to the Presbytery of Kathiawad. The Heir Apparent laid the foundation stone and the Rana

---

[30] For a character sketch of Montgomery, see B. M. Malabari, *op. cit.*, pp. 14-15.

[31] Gandhi's brother, Karsandas, was also employed in the Porbandar State Police.

himself opened the building on November 7, 1942. The Rana could afford to be generous; it was not Christianity but a militant Indian nationalism directed by the son of his own grandfather's dewan which now seriously threatened the *gadi* that the Jethva Rajputs had occupied for a thousand years.

The importance of these little-known facts concerning the visit of John Wilson to Kathiawad in 1835, and the activities of the Irish Presbyterians in the town and the neighbouring villages, consists in the impressions they must have left on the Gandhi family and the attitudes they are likely to have formed towards Christianity. Gandhi's own impressions, apart from what he might have unconsciously imbibed from his family, were based largely on what he saw and heard in Rajkot. The missionaries in Rajkot opened a school within a month of their arrival; it was the first school where English was taught in the peninsula. Gandhi related that he went to a primary school and claimed that he could clearly recollect his experiences there and even the names of the teachers. He went from there to a " suburban school " and then to the Alfred High School at the age of twelve.[32]

The primary school Gandhi went to could have been a school run by the Irish Presbyterians. Bishop F. B. Fisher, who was a close friend of Gandhi, tells us that Mohandas began learning English quite early and that his first teacher was Irish. The teacher sounds like a missionary because he made the boy copy out sentences from the Sermon on the Mount on his slate.[33] Bishop Fisher is not always accurate in his information and he may be mistaken, though he says he was told about it by Gandhi himself. But if Gandhi did

---

[32] *Autobiography*, p. 15.

[33] F. B. Fisher, *That Strange Little Brown Man Gandhi*, (New York, Ray Long & Richard R. Smith Inc., 1932).

go to a mission school, why does he not say so when he had such a clear recollection of it? A very likely explanation is that he quite rightly feared that too much might be made out of the fact at the time he was writing his autobiography.

The two immediate reasons for Gandhi's aversion to Christianity were street-preaching and various rumours he had heard about conversions in Rajkot. On one occasion he says he stood at a corner near the Alfred High School listening to a missionary. He concluded that the missionary must be attacking the Hindu religion and its gods because he had been told that was what missionaries did. Preaching in towns and villages was certainly carried on by the few missionaries in Kathiawad as did others throughout India. The missionary preaching in a bazaar or under a village banyan tree was a familiar sight in India in the nineteenth century. This faith in the efficacy of the spoken word had its roots in the Reformation and the Methodist revival of the eighteenth century. A Wesley or a Whitfield preaching in the open fields to grimy-faced miners was a very different thing from preaching in India. The East India Company banned it on more than one occasion and usually with good reason. Even John Wilson was disturbed by the excesses of some missionaries; he warned them that they were "too frequently inclined to speak on the folly of idolatry" and they presented the Gospel to Indians "in any manner which was destitute of solemnity."

It is interesting, however, that the missionary Gandhi had listened to denied the Mahatma's charges in a letter written to him forty years after the incident.[34] The missionary in question was the Reverend H. R. Scott; he had been the sole representative of the Irish Presbyterians in Rajkot from 1883 to 1887. In his memoirs of Kathiawad, Booth, the Agency

---

[34] H. R. Scott, *Christian Missions: Their place in India*, (Ahmedabad, Navajivan Press, 1941), pp. 11-12.

Engineer, referred appreciatively to Scott and his wife. "They were long resident at Rajkot," he remembered, "and very popular with natives as well as Europeans. They both possessed a marvellous power of attracting the natives, who held them in high esteem and their mission schools were well attended."[35] It is worth comparing Gandhi's account of the "vague" rumours he had heard about the conversions in Rajkot and the preaching incident as he told it to his first biographer, Joseph Doke, with his later narration of the same events in his autobiography. With regard to Scott himself, Gandhi told Doke, "Later, I got to know him and to admire him."[36] When Gandhi replied to Scott in 1926, the Indian atmosphere of the time had led him to stiffen his attitude to missionaries and missions.

In 1881 there were six hundred and five Indian Christians in Kathiawad and only twenty-nine in Rajkot—fifteen men, eight women, and six children. Some of them were Bhils and some were servants of the British residents. They worshipped in Gujarati every Sunday in the Mission Bungalow and attracted very little notice.[37] But when the Reverend H. R. Scott arrived in Rajkot in 1883, he attracted a number of high caste men into the church like Pitambar Shamji, Kunvarji Mansingh, and Kahanji Madhavji. It was the conversion of men from good families including some Brahmans and a Jain *sannyasi* that caused the commotion in Rajkot which had an effect on the young Gandhi's mind.

The biographies of many of these converts in Rajkot are now available. A study of them makes one feel that at this impressionable age, Gandhi, rather unthinkingly, accepted the loose allegations about them which were current at

---

[35] *Op. cit.*, pp. 294-295.

[36] *Op. cit.*, p. 20.

[37] *Bombay Gazetteer*, VIII, p. 169.

Rajkot.[38] He believed that the converts were expected to eat beef and drink liquor, change into European clothes, wear a hat, and abuse the religion of their forefathers. The boy Gandhi can hardly be blamed for accepting this stereotype of what a Christian convert was supposed to be like because of the identification, inevitable at that time, of Christianity with Western civilization. The converts were often forced to become dependent on the missionaries because of the persecution and ostracism. It is worth comparing this mental picture Gandhi formed of them with a description of these Christians of Rajkot as they really were in the 1880's. " In respect of food, dress and clothes," says the Kathiawad section of the *Bombay Gazetteer* of 1884, " these native Christians scarcely differ from natives of similar position. Animal food is allowed, though from its cost, few are able to procure it; the use of opium and of intoxicating drinks is forbidden."[39]

Gandhi never did give up his early attitudes which were further strengthened by seeing the westernized, Colonial-born Indian Christians of Natal. When he visited the Reverend Kali Charan Bannerji in Calcutta in 1901, he could barely conceal his surprise at finding that he lived simply and wore Indian clothes. As late as 1925 his correspondence with Reverend Scott over the preaching incident shows him still firmly holding on to his stereotyped image of the Indian Christian.[40] Gandhi was only reflecting the popular view—a view which had been established long ago while the Moghuls still ruled in Delhi. It was the Roman Catholic mission to the Moghul Court which established the stereotype. The Chaplains to Sir Thomas Roe's embassy were told, " Christian

---

[38] R. H. Boyd, *Trophies for the King*. A series of five pamphlets published from 1950 onwards in Belfast.

[39] *Op. cit.*, p. 169.

[40] *Christian Missions: Their Place in India*, pp. 11-12.

religion, devil religion. Christian much drink, much do wrong, much beat, much abuse others."[41]

The Englishmen were told this at a time when the Emperor Jehangir could drink any of their number under the table. The boy Gandhi was not worried by the fact that many of the Parsis in Kathiawad were liquor merchants though he would criticize them as the Mahatma. The point really is that, in the emerging cultural conflict, to become a Christian seemed to be the most extreme form of selling out to the dominant civilization. The solution for many sensitive Hindus like Gandhi was to accept Christ while rejecting organized Christianity and its packaging of Western culture. Another solution was to try to assimilate Christ to Indian culture.[42] The absorbent capacity of Hinduism was frustrated by the fact that Christianity, like Islam, was too monotheistic and dogmatic. The solution, therefore, could only be largely political—namely, to prevent further conversions and to contain the Christian community as a socially useful but politically powerless entity within the body politic.

The facts that missionary work in Kathiawad began as late as 1841 and that the Irish Presbyterians were the first to enter a native state must be borne in mind. Kathiawad was reacting to Christianity when Gandhi was a boy, in the way that Madras, Calcutta, and Bombay had reacted earlier.[43] The feelings of dislike and opposition were still sharp and raw and they are reflected in Gandhi's own feelings. Even though Gandhi had a few intellectual objections to Christianity —such as his rejection of the assumption of the uniqueness of

---

[41] Mayhew, *op. cit.*, p. 47.

[42] See P. C. Mazoomdar, *The Oriental Christ*, (Boston, George H. Ellis & Co. 1910); and Swami Akhilananda, *A Hindu View of Christ*, (New York, The Philosophical Library, 1949).

[43] See *The First Hindoo Convert: A Memoir of Krishna Pal*, (Philadelphia, American Baptist Publishing Society, 1852).

Christ—his objections, on the whole, were those most popular. He reflected the mass mind rather than the outlook of Hindu intellectuals like Sri Arabindo and Radhakrishnan. The latter had just graduated from the Madras Christian College, while Gandhi was writing *Hind Swaraj*. Christian intellectuals, including missionaries like Nicol Macnicol, A. G. Hogg, and Albert Schweitzer, would have to come to grips with Hindu philosophy. But the missionaries would find the greatest obstacle to their work in Gandhi—and for four interesting reasons.

Firstly, the missionaries with their evangelicalism and puritanism met in Gandhi their opposite type within Hinduism —the Hindu evangelical and puritan who was a product of the curious blending of Hinduism with Victorian morality produced by the impact of Christianity. Romain Rolland speaks of " Gandhi's evangelical heart beating under his Hinduism."[44] These Hindu evangelicals could combine a sacred thread with an Oxford accent or clinch an argument about birth control with a quotation from the Hindu scriptures. The missionary and his opposite Hindu number could and often did meet happily on some common ground like Prohibition by unconsciously bringing together John Wesley and Hemachandra. The new middle classes of Victorian India bore some resemblances to the great middle class of Victorian England.

Secondly, by the time Gandhi returned to India in 1915, it was no longer the conversion of individuals from the upper castes which Hinduism feared, but the secession of masses of " untouchables " in a developing situation in which leaders of the depressed classes like Dr. B. R. Ambedkar were prepared to use the threat of mass conversion for political bargaining. Gandhi was quick to realize that the problem of " Untouchability " constituted a real danger to the Hindu community

---

[44] R. Rolland, *Mahatma Gandhi*, (New York, The Century Co., 1924), p. 49.

and fought hard to prevent mass secessions from the Hindu fold. Untouchability, like infanticide, became largely a political rather than a religious issue; and Gandhi used every possible argument—racial and cultural, rational and irrational —to prevent conversion from one religion to another. What Ram Mohun Roy's Brahmo Samaj did to prevent the conversion of young Hindu intellectuals, Gandhi's Harijan Sevak Sangh did to prevent the conversion of the depressed classes, but in a much more economic and political rather than religious and intellectual fashion than had been the case a century before. Then Ram Mohun Roy had written a witty polemic, *Conversation between a Missionary and Three Chinese*, in the style of Voltaire, to disprove the doctrine of the Trinity. This difference in orientation explains why some missionaries felt Gandhi was a shrewd politician even while recognizing the nobility and sincerity of his work for the " untouchables."

Thirdly, by becoming the most Christ-like man of the twentieth century Gandhi produced Gandhism which expropriated the role of the missionary movement in India. J. C. Browne described his book on *Indian Infanticide* as " nothing more than a sketch of the course pursued by a Christian people for the suppression of a most inhuman practice among their heathen dependents."[45] The " heathen dependents " had done a considerable amount of thinking for themselves by the time Gandhi grew up, and they were beginning to follow " the course pursued by a Christian people " as inspired by their own ancient scriptures. The liberal idealism of Ram Mohun Roy and Bhau Daji continued to find expression in M. G. Ranade and G. K. Gokhale till their moderate outlook, which accepted many Western and Christian values, was swept aside by the militant Hindu

---

[45] *Op. cit.*, p. 56.

revivalism of B. G. Tilak. Hinduism in the twentieth century with its programmes of educational, medical, and social uplift, with its militancy and its cultural messianism, would look rather like the Christian missionary movement of the nineteenth century. Yet it was precisely this movement which modern Hinduism so vehemently repudiated in the process of winning recognition for itself as one of the great religions of the world.

Fourthly, the charge that the British Government and the missionary movement were undermining the cultural and religious life of India was accompanied by a developing national consciousness which asserted the moral, ethical, and spiritual self-sufficiency of Hinduism and the superiority of Indian culture over Western civilization. It would soon be forgotten that both these attitudes were largely fostered by a distinguished line of Western scholars from Sir William Jones to Max Muller, and by Western movements like Unitarianism and Theosophy. A school of thinkers was developing in the West, with interesting affiliations to Hindu philosophy, which was trying to rescue Christ from a Christianity that had got enmeshed in materialism and violence; Paul Tillich would express the rather anarchistic gropings of this school in a more sophisticated theological fashion.[46] As Appendix I of *Hind Swaraj* shows, Gandhi would come to read with avidity many of these critics of Western civilization, ranging from New England to Russia.

The wheel set in motion in Kathiawad by Jonathan Duncan and Alexander Walker over infanticide had turned full cycle. If John Wilson could return to the Bombay he loved so dearly he would be astonished to discover that, in Gandhi, India had produced a prophet who sought, in the great missionary's own language, the " moral renovation " of the West. *Ex*

---

[46] P. Tillich, *The Protestant Era*, (translated with a concluding essay by James Luther Adams), (Chicago, University of Chicago Press, 1948)

oriente lux—though the filament inside the bulb was partly of Western manufacture. If Wilson, on the other hand, could have the opportunity also to look at the West with its scientific rationalism, its secular materialism, its piled-up armaments and its race prejudice he would probably be on Gandhi's side— like C. F. Andrews. He, most likely, would sympathise with those aspects of Gandhi's critique of the West based on the assumption that it was a Christian culture that had apostasied—it had developed a degenerate materialistic civilization.[47]

Like Ram Mohun Roy before him, Gandhi rejected Christianity, but not Christian ethics. Gandhi's social and religious outlook was infused with many Christian values. The ethical source of his conception of Sarvodaya, which he derived from Ruskin's *Unto this Last*, is rooted ultimately in the Christian view of the worth and dignity of man. It is not surprising that on more than one occasion Gandhi was accused of sedulously fostering Christianity. The assassination of the Mahatma on a Friday brought forth many comparisons between the closing events in the life of Christ and the life of Gandhi. The prophet of non-violence had tried to rescue Christ from a West which he felt was denying Christian ethics while worshipping the Galilean in their churches. Perhaps a

---

[47] Sources for Christian activities in Kathiawad: R. Jeffry, *The Indian Mission of the Irish Presbyterian Church*, (London, Nisbet & Co., 1890); R. H. Boyd, *Courier of the Dawn*, (Belfast, 1940), which describes the work of the pioneer missionaries; R. H. Boyd, *The Prevailing Word*, (Belfast, 1951), which describes the work of the Mission from 1840–1950. The Annual Reports of the Irish Presbyterian Mission are available from 1870 onward. The *Oriental Christian Spectator* published in Bombay is also a valuable source as is G. Smith's *Life of John Wilson*. Books dealing with Gandhi's attitude to Christian Missions: *Christian Missions: Their Place in India*, (Ahmedabad, Navajivan Press, 1941), and Clifford Manshardt, (ed.), *The Mahatma and the Missionary*, (Chicago, Henry Regenery Co., 1949), contain selected writings of Gandhi on the subject. S. K. George, *Gandhi's Challenge to Christianity*, (Ahmedabad, Navajivan Publishing House, 1947), and the writings of J. C. Kumarappa and J. B. Kumarappa are interesting for the light they throw on Gandhi's influence on some Indian Christians.

similar fate is overtaking Gandhi in India. Homage and lip-service are being paid to the Mahatma by men who have no intention of following his teachings.

India After the Mutiny

Gandhi was born a decade after the Mutiny, when events both in India and abroad were accelerating the tempo of life. The primary lesson the British learned from the Mutiny, which did not find a place in the liberal statement of policy contained in the Queen's Proclamation of 1858, was the need for greater political and military control over the vast sub-continent through the development of better communications. The Mutiny, therefore, led to the growth of railways and telegraphs which, in their turn, set in motion trends towards a greater economic unification of the country. The building of railways and roads received further impetus from the American Civil War, 1861–1865. The demand for Indian cotton, created by the blockade of the Southern States, helped to lay the foundations of the textile industry; thus, it studded Western India with cotton mills and brought prosperity to Bombay and turned Ahmedabad, the old capital of the Sultans of Gujarat, into a great industrial city.[48] It was in the 1860's that many industrial developments began and it was in that decade that the man was born who would attack machinery as evil. Gandhi and the Indian industrial revolution arrived together.

" Yellow, leonine, imperious, there is in her something of the caprice, of the almost treachery, of beautiful women who have swayed the wills of the world " was how Sister Nivedita (Margaret Noble) described the Ganges.[49] But by 1870 the

---

[48] Frenise A. Logan, " The American Civil War: A Major Factor in the Improvement of the Transportation System of Western India," *The Journal of Indian History*, (April, 1955).

[49] M. Noble, *The Web of Indian Life*, (London, Heinemann, 1904), p. 5.

currents of the Thames were mingling swiftly with the currents of the Ganges; steamboats churned those ancient waters and the steel arches of railway bridges were reflected in them. The Marchioness of Dufferin visited one of these bridges being built over the Ganges and described the " very alarming walk on thin planks at an enormous height over the river."[50] The Railway Age had dawned in India and Gandhi, like many others on both sides of the Atlantic, disliked the steam engines that were destroying more than the peace of the countryside. There were only about a thousand miles of railways when Gandhi was born; by 1887 they had increased to 15,245 miles. He would state his objections to railways in *Hind Swaraj*.

Gandhi was also born at a time when India was being brought into closer contact with the Western world. In 1870, a year after his birth, the Suez Canal, " M. de Lessep's magnificent ditch," as Edwin Arnold called it,[51] was opened with incalculable results for the traffic between East and West. It was the culmination of the improvements in communications which had begun earlier in the century. In 1825, the Hooghly River was entered by the first steamship, the *Enterprise*, which, two years later, manoeuvred off the seashore of Madras for the edification of Sir Thomas Munro and a vast crowd of spectators. In 1838, a monthly service (with an overland trip between Suez and Alexandria) reduced the journey to London to forty-five days. By 1843 the Peninsular and Orient Line had reduced the journey to London to a month. Two little steamships flying the

---

[50] The Marchioness of Dufferin and Ava, *Our Viceregal Life in India. Selections from My Journal*, 1884-1888, 2 Vols., (London, John Murray, 1889), Vol. II, p. 14.

[51] Edwin Arnold, *India Revisited*, (London, Trubner & Co., 1886), p. 25. Eighteen years later Gandhi noted that the Canal was as wide as the Aji at Ramnath, the river which flowed past Rajkot. *Collected Works*, I, " London Diary,", p. 15.

5

Peninsular and Oriental flag, the *Vectis* and the *Valetta*, plied to and fro between Alexandria and Marseilles "plunging with rolling paddles and diving prows."[52] The Overland Route was celebrated in a play of the same name of which there was a performance in Simla as late as September, 1888, the month in which Gandhi arrived in England.[53]

The completion of the overland telegraph line in 1865 brought London closer to Calcutta. New nerve centres of a sophisticated Indian way of life were springing up as cities and towns were bound together by a network of railways. Moncure Conway, who visited Calcutta in 1884, has left us a vivid picture of the new middle class society of the period. Describing a typical gathering of the Indian intelligentsia he wrote, "All present were Hindu gentlemen, mainly professional men, so fluent in English and talking with so much wit that I could fancy myself dining with my fellow Omarites of our Omar Khyam Club (*sic*) in London.... They were all friends, men of the world in a high sense; and if, with their culture, their refined faces and manners, they could all be transferred to Boston, there would be a glad cry that its literary era had returned."[54] In 1903 an American traveller, E. R. Scidmore, could speak of "the watering-place atmosphere of Calcutta" where "the life is the life of London, a London with the chill taken off and the sun shining gloriously" except for the presence of numerous turbanned and bare-footed servants, the creaking of *punkahs* and the use of Hindusthani words. It was a Calcutta where everyone eagerly awaited *The Times*.[55]

The Mutiny had reduced the influence of the old feudal aristocracy and increased the importance of the English-

---

[52] *India Revisited*, (London, Trubner, 1886), p. 4.

[53] *Our Viceregal Life in India*, p. 297.

[54] Moncure Conway, *My Pilgrimage to the Wisemen of the East*, (Boston Houghton Mifflin, 1906), p. 245.

[55] E. R. Scidmore, *Winter India*, (New York, The Century Co.,) p. 94.

educated middle class of lawyers, doctors, and teachers. Gandhi himself played with the idea of becoming a doctor before deciding to be a lawyer; hundreds of other young men were facing a similar professional choice at that time. This dynamic new class emerging from the universities of Calcutta, Bombay, and Madras (all established in 1857), along with a sprinkling of those educated in England, clamoured for greater representation in the Government services; demanded a larger measure of local self-government; established the Indian National Congress in 1885 with the help of a British Civilian, Allan Octavian Hume, the son of the Benthamite Radical, Joseph Hume; and laid the foundations of the liberal nationalism of the latter half of the nineteenth century while Gandhi was still in his 'teens.[56] Gandhi would turn against this Anglicised middle class with its Western outlook and reserve some of his sharpest criticism for the doctors and lawyers in *Hind Swaraj*.

The abolition of slavery in the Empire in 1833 resulted in waves of emigration to areas where cheap labour was needed. Throughout the nineteenth century the forefathers of the Indians overseas were finding their way as indentured labourers or shopkeepers and itinerant traders along the far-flung arteries of the British Empire stretching between Fiji in the Pacific and Guiana in South America.[57] In November, 1860, nine years before Gandhi was born, the first batch of Indian labourers landed at Durban, in South Africa. Indian students were becoming a familiar sight in the streets of London and the quads of Oxford and Cambridge. Surendranath Bannerjea, Romesh Chandra Dutt, and Behari Lal Gupta returned from England in 1871. In the last decade

---

[56] Surendranath Bannerjea's *A Nation in Making*, contains much useful material relating to this period.
[57] C. Kondapi, *Indians Overseas* 1835–1949, (London, Oxford University Press, 1951).

of the century Ranjitsinhji, an Indian Prince and a Cambridge
Blue, whom Gandhi knew in London, was delighting the
cricket-loving English crowds with his wizardry.

Indian seamen, of course, had found their way to Europe
long before the educated Indians could pluck up courage to
cross the Black Water. Their numbers increased with the
opening of the Suez Canal. When the first Peninsular and
Orient steamer passed through the Canal in 1870 she was
towed by her Indian lascars and tied up at night. A passenger
was even heard to remark that it must be a pleasant change
for the lascars to go out into the sunlight and have some good
exercise.[58] Kathiawad supplied many of these men.

Indian women, too, were exploring the world. Some of
them were the wives of the humble indentured labourers while
others were the intrepid *ayahs* who accompanied British
children to and from England. Edwin Arnold on board the
Paramatta in 1885 described how " the quiet, patient *ayahs*
glide about like cats, purring Hindusthani songs, and ceaselessly
watching and fondling the blue-eyed English children."[59]
At the turn of the century another traveller on board the
Victoria noted that several children were " tended by nose-
ringed Indian nurses."[60] Other women were pioneers of
educational and social reform like Dr. Anandabai Joshi, the
first Indian woman to go abroad for medical studies,[61] and
Pandita Ramabai who went to England in 1883 and visited
America in 1886. The Ramabai Association of Boston for
assisting her work in India was formed in 1887.[62]

---

[58] Denis Kincaid, *British Social Life in India* 1608–1937, (London, George
Routledge & Sons, 1938).

[59] *India Revisited.*

[60] James Wells, *Across India*, (Glasgow, Kennedy, Robertson & Co., Ltd.,
1901), p. 20.

[61] *London, Trubner's Record*, (1888), p. 42.

[62] Clementina Butler, *Pandita Ramabai Saraswati*, (New York, F. H. Revell Co.,
1922), and Mrs. E. F. Chapman, *Some Distinguished Indian Women*, (London,
W. H. Allen & Co., 1891).

Better communications had shifted the real seat of power from Calcutta to London. Viceroys, either willingly or reluctantly, had to keep their ears attuned to the India Office and the debates in Westminster. What Ram Mohun Roy had realized at the beginning of the century was now more widely known, and Indians were looking more and more to the House of Commons to redress their grievances as the seat of Imperial authority; they were studying the shifts in British party politics and trying to influence British public opinion. In 1866, Dadhabai Naoroji founded the East Indian Association and the sending of deputations to London became a feature of Indian political agitation. A kind of Indian lobby developed with the help of many interested Englishmen including some Members of Parliament and former British officials. Dadhabai Naoroji decided to enter the House of Commons to be a spokesman for India there. He was busy nursing his London constituency while Gandhi was a student in England; and Naoroji became the first Indian to be elected to the British Parliament in 1892. British Members of Parliament, like Alfred Webb and Charles Bradlaugh, visited India and presided over Congress sessions. British and Indian politics were partly intertwined in a phase that lasted into the first decade of the twentieth century.

While the distance between India and the West was decreasing, the social gulf between educated Indians and the British was widening. With the arrival of British women in increasing numbers and the establishment of a separate and exclusive way of life after the Mutiny, mutual suspicion and distrust were poisoning the relations between the two peoples.[63] Wilfred Scawen Blunt, who attended the

---

[63] P. J. Griffiths, *The British Impact on India*, (London, Macdonald, 1952), Ch. XXXIII; H. J. S. Cotton, *New India*, (London, Kegan Paul, Trench & Co., 1885), pp. 30-45; C. E. Carrington, *The British Overseas*, (Cambridge University Press, 1950); Denis Kincaid, *British Social Life in India*.

Conference of the Indian Association in December, 1883, noted the growing ill-feeling between the Indians and the British.[64] It was in that same year that passions had been aroused by the Ilbert Bill. Sir Henry Cotton complained that it was common to hear British Civilians say that they loved the country and the common people but disliked the educated Indians.[65]

The British Government was becoming a vast, impersonal bureaucracy. H. Caldwell Lipsett felt that the British Civilian was being stripped of individual personality as he became a mere cog in a machine. And, unlike many officials before the Mutiny, he no longer thought of India as his home as it was now so easy to get away to England for a holiday.[66] Guy Wint points out that the British Government became suspicious and distrustful of the very middle classes which it had brought into being as a result of the Mutiny. When the Government became distant and aloof with no further desire to promote social change, the educated Indians had to develop their own leadership.[67] But when they succeeded in doing so through the Indian National Congress they found the Government unsympathetic to their aspirations. The British could afford to ignore the educated classes—a " microscopic minority," in the words of Lord Dufferin. The Mahatma would shatter this complacency of the British by turning the Congress into a mass organization.

All these developments underlay the turmoil of the last three decades of the nineteenth century which presents a fascinating panorama of movement filled with interesting men

---

[64] W. S. Blunt, *India Under Ripon*: *A Private Diary*, (London, T. Fisher Unwin, 1909).

[65] *New India*, p. 44.

[66] H. C. Lipsett, *Lord Curzon in India*, (London, Everett, 1903), p. 94.

[67] Guy Wint, *The British in Asia*, (New York, Institute for Pacific Relations, 1954), p. 68.

and women who were responding or reacting, co-operative or rebellious, but all quickened and stimulated by this meeting of two civilizations within the context of Victorian imperialism. It was a meeting filled with elements of good and bad, attraction and hate, optimistic and pessimistic forebodings. The keynote of it all was the resurgence of Indian society and culture. The seed sown by the Brahmo Samaj in Bengal, the Prarthana Samaj in Bombay, and the Arya Samaj in the Punjab was now bearing fruit in an Indian nationalism of many flavours. The reformers, attacked now by both the orthodox and the ultra-nationalists, stood their ground with courage. Politics had not assumed the priority that it would in the twentieth century, and these men and women were as noted for their interest in religious or social reform as they were for their political opinions. They were much more versatile, much more truly educated, and much more interesting than many of the political types who would dominate India in the twentieth century.

Kathiawad, which had remained remote and inaccessible right up to the Mutiny, was steadily integrated into the rest of India by threads of cotton and rails of iron, as cotton presses and ginning factories, roads and railways developed in the peninsula. New and stimulating currents of thought travelled along the railway lines into Kathiawad. The boy Gandhi sitting at his desk in the Alfred High School felt the stirrings of this new India. But as fresh horizons opened out to his wondering view, the pull of London would prove even more compelling than the pull of Bombay. Since Kathiawad was a part of princely India, the British continued to play an important role in the affairs of the peninsula; their reforming impulses had not weakened here to the same extent as they had in British India. We must, therefore, turn to the changes inaugurated in Kathiawad by the British after the Mutiny to understand more fully the background of both the rapid change against which the childhood and boyhood of Gandhi were passed as well as the urge to go to England which he says completely possessed him.[68]

The history of Kathiawad in the nineteenth century must be set within the wider framework of British policies towards the princes in order to follow the sequence of developments in the peninsula after the Mutiny. It is difficult to understand this " veritable museum of sovereignties "[69] known as Kathiawad without a knowledge of the larger background.

Jonathan Duncan, as Governor of Bombay, and Alexander Walker, as Resident at Baroda, had to implement the policies of four Governors-General in the short space of three years. The Treaty of 1805 with Baroda, negotiated by Walker, followed the pattern of subsidiary alliances vigorously promoted by the Marquis of Wellesley; this brother of the Iron Duke was ruthless in his attitude to the Indian States at a time when England was engaged in a grim struggle with Napoleon. The Company feared that Wellesley's zeal had imperilled rather than ensured the security of India, however, and he was recalled. Cornwallis, an old man in his seventies, was sent out for a second term to exercise a conciliatory influence, but died shortly after his arrival. Barlow was deputised to act for Lord Minto, who reached India in 1807. It was Minto, also pledged to a policy of moderation, who was responsible for the nature of Walker's settlement of Kathiawad. There were no separate treaties with each chieftain, but rather a general acceptance of the feudatory system in the area.[70]

---

[68] *Autobiography*, p. 54.

[69] K. M. Panikkar, *Indian States and the Government of India*, (London, Martin Hopkinson Ltd., 1932), p. 181.

[70] *Indian States and the Government of India*, see Appendix 1; see also Anil Chandra Bannerjee, " Lord Minto and the Rajput States," *Journal of Indian History*, Vol. XXII, (April, 1943).

When Lord Moira (later the Marquis of Hastings) succeeded Lord Minto in 1813, the fear of France had receded. The Company began to act like a paramount power and not as one among many competitors for supremacy. It was during this phase that the British acquired the tributary or *jamabandi* rights of the Peshwa, the Gaekwad, and the Nawab of Junagadh over the peninsula. Though they continued to share the tribute with the Gaekwad and the Nawab, they emerged as the dominant political power. Though the British were the *de facto* rulers they did not claim a *de jure* sovereignty as well, because of the policy of non-interference followed by Lord William Bentinck. In 1830, the Court of Directors unequivocally stated that the rulers of Kathiawad were entitled to the exercise of their powers within their kingdoms and that British rights were limited to the collection and distribution of the tribute.[71] The reasons for this policy of neutrality were outlined by Sir John Malcolm in 1825. He held that the security of the Company's " vast oriental possessions is involved in the preservation of native principalities which are dependent on us for protection " and argued that " their coexistence with our rule is of itself a source of political strength, the value of which will never be known till it is lost."[72] A similar point of view was expressed by Sir John Shore writing in 1834;[73] and the same point of view was put forward with vehemence and sincerity by James Tod.[74]

The policy of annexation followed by Auckland, Ellenborough and Dalhousie was partly responsible for the uprising of 1857. The Mutiny, however, proved a great turning

---

[71] *Indian States and the Government of India*, p. 19.

[72] *Ibid.*, p. 16.

[73] John Shore, *Notes on Indian Affairs*, 2 Vols., (London, John W. Parker, 1837), Vol. II, pp. 70-105.

[74] *Annals and Antiquities of Rajasthan*, I, pp. 115-118, 177.

point in the relations between the British Government and the Indian States. Canning recognized that the loyalty of several Princes had acted as a breakwater against the crashing waves of revolt and the Queen's Proclamation took special note of the fact. "We shall respect the rights, the dignity, and honour of Native Princes as our own," the Proclamation said, "and we desire that they, as well as our own subjects, should enjoy that prosperity and that social advancement which can only be secured by internal peace and good government."[75]

The problem of good government in the Indian States, however, was one that had agitated many minds even before the Mutiny. Sir Thomas Munro firmly believed that the system of subsidiary alliances was to blame for the growing corruption and poverty of the Indian States. In 1853, *The Times* complained editorially that the Indian Princes had been given power without responsibility; and the iron hand of the British preserved their thrones for them despite "their imbecility, their vice and their crimes." The result was a chronic anarchy in most States with no checks on the folly, extravagance or incompetence of the Indian rulers.[76] Looking back at this period when no interest in the internal administration of the Indian States was taken by the Supreme Government, K. M. Panikkar says that the courts of many Indian Princes became "the theatre of the most degraded debauchery and the most horrible mis-government."[77]

The Kathiawad States were no exception to this general rule. Describing them in 1856, Kinloch Forbes wrote, "A sleepy indulgent, *dolce far niente* kind of spirit pervades these

---

[75] Directorate of the Chamber of Princes, *The British Crown and the Indian States*, (London, P. S. King & Son Ltd., 1929); see the General Foreword by L. F. Rushbrook Williams.

[76] *Indian States and the Government of India*, p. 24.

[77] *Ibid.*, p. 22.

states and it is probably not unacceptable to the inhabitants, who have as little love of innovation and comprehend improvement as little as their masters."[78] But a close scrutiny of many of the Kathiawad States would have revealed that intrigue, debauchery, and violence were endemic beneath the placid-looking surface. The marks of the cannon balls that thudded against the walls of the Gandhi home in Porbandar sometime during the 1830's are visible reminders of those days when subjects could find their lives suddenly jeopardised by the uncontrollable wrath of the ruler. The furious Rani who besieged Gandhi's grandfather, Uttamchand, in his own home was typical of these petty rulers who often needed the restraining hand of the Political Agent in Rajkot to keep their arbitrary powers within bounds.

As late as 1869, the year of Gandhi's birth, an unfortunate political incident took place in Porbandar. When Rana Vikmatji went to Broach to visit an exhibition, the State was administered by his son Madhavsinhji. The Prince was led into drunkenness and dissolute habits by evil associates and excessive indulgence so ruined his health that he died. Rana Vikmatji was so grieved and angered by what had happened when he returned that he ordered the nose and ears of the ringleader of this vicious group to be cut off. When this was done, this man, called Lakshman, threw himself down from the terrace of the palace and died. The British Government degraded Porbandar to a Third Class State, since mutilation, which was a common form of punishment meted out by rulers like Meraman Khavas in the eighteenth century, was now considered a crime.[79]

The short-sightedness of the policy of abdicating responsibility for the internal government of the Indian States between 1813–1855 was thrown into sharp relief by the blazing light

---

[78] *The Bombay Quarterly Review*, VII, (1856), p. 195.
[79] Wilberforce-Bell, *op. cit.*, pp. 222-223.

of the Mutiny; yet the British were too preoccupied with restoring order and balancing the budget to pay it much attention. British civil and military officials tended to think of Kathiawad as a pleasant holiday resort or a sportsman's paradise. The famous Kathi horses made pig-sticking and cross-country riding a delight.[80] The jungles were full of panther, while antelopes and *nilgai* (blue buck) fed in hundreds over the plains. The *bhids* (meadows) abounded in partridge, quail, snipe, wild duck, rock grouse, bustards, and florican. The streams were full of murrel and pike.[81] The most famous shooting resort was the Nal Bauli, a fresh-water lake at the head of the Gulf of Cambay.[82] The British love of shooting gave offence to the Jains and created a stereotype of a race indifferent to the taking of life. Gandhi, while sharing the Jain feeling, would appeal to the sportsmanship of the British, especially in South Africa, another area famous for its game.

Keatinge's Reforms, 1863-1867

Kathiawad had relapsed into a colourful but stagnant feudal backwater. It was rescued from this somnolent condition after the Mutiny by A. Kinloch Forbes, Political Agent (1859-1860) who proposed, and Colonel R. H. Keatinge, who initiated, an era of reforms lasting from 1863-1882. Keatinge, who was Political Agent from 1863-1867, ranks with Walker as one of the ablest men who administered Kathiawad. A good soldier who had won his VC in the Mutiny, he was a tall fine-looking man with a manner that

---

[80] John Bowle, the author of *Western Political Thought*, was very much impressed by Gandhi, when he visited Westminster School in London in 1930, and told me that " he had the jaw of a pike."

[81] James Douglas, *op. cit.*, II, p. 70.

[82] Robert B. Booth, *Life and Work in India*, (London, J. G. Hammond & Co., 1912), pp. 36-37. The author was Engineer to the Kathiawad Political Agency from 1865-1899.

was bluff and terse but kind.[83]   He was a man of tremendous drive and energy; there was no aspect of life in Kathiawad that did not feel the impact of his personality.   Whether he was distributing better ploughs and steam pumps to the agriculturists, or planning the education of the princes, his consuming passion was the improvement of the peninsula. Though his methods were paternalistic he was truly sensitive to the need for change.

Keatinge's great achievement was to introduce measures to rectify the defects which had revealed themselves in Walker's settlement.   This settlement or *Fael Zamin* was made for ten years in the first instance, but became permanent after 1820. Mountstuart Elphinstone, the last and the greatest of the Residents in Poona, who had effected the settlement of the Deccan, analysed the results of Walker's *Fael Zamin* in a Minute dated April 6, 1821.   He concluded that the settlement had been beneficial to two classes—the chiefs and the *ryots*.   The chiefs had been confirmed in their authority over their subjects and the British were there to uphold their rights.   The *ryots* were vested with what they had never possessed before—a proprietary right to the land they occupied which they could sell without the consent of their landlords, and from which they could not be evicted so long as they paid their taxes.[84]

Elphinstone also pointed out that several classes were left discontented by the *Fael Zamin*.   Many of the *girassias* and *mulgirassias*, who were the tenants of the chiefs, and some sections of the commercial classes (including Banias) felt

---

[83] *Life and Work in India*, p. 20.
[84] *Ras Mala*, II, p. 305; *Bombay Gazetteer*, VIII, p. 303. Elphinstone's views as Governor of Bombay are important in the study of Kathiawad. Kenneth Ballhatchet's study of him from 1817–1830 entitled *Social Policy and Social Change in Western India*, (London, Oxford University Press, 1957), is a useful work.

77

disgruntled right up to the 1860's. Lawlessness also continued into the 1860's because numerous types of fighting men had lost their employ, and the predatory tribes like the Mianas and the Waghers could no longer live off plunder by land and piracy by sea. Keatinge extended the land settlement to the *girassia* class and stabilized their relations with the chiefs. This was in keeping with what was happening all over India; a major result of British rule was a widespread agrarian settlement. Keatinge also stimulated the commercial classes by his programme of road making and the steps he took to introduce railways. This aspect of Keatinge's reforms was necessitated by the impact of the American Civil War on Kathiawad. Keatinge took to the field himself in 1865–1866 in the campaign against the Waghers in order to prevent them from becoming a rallying force for all the turbulent elements in the peninsula. He instituted a system of passes called *parvanas* to restrict the carrying of arms.[85] Though Keatinge left Kathiawad in 1867, the policies of his successors as Political Agents followed the lines laid down by him.

When Walker entered Kathiawad in 1807, he found that all the landowners, big or small, exercised an unrestrained power over the people living on their *khalsa* lands. Whether it was the punishment of a criminal or the increasing of the rents, the landlords followed traditional methods and ancient usage without supervision by anybody. Walker had to decide rather arbitrarily as to who would continue to exercise such powers, and who would no longer do so and become subordinate to another. This created a class of discontented *girassias* who felt their rights had been ignored; they could also point to instances where Walker had given rights to upstart *girassias* who had taken advantage of disturbed conditions to declare themselves independent.

---

85 *Bombay Gazetteer*, VIII, p. 264.

Kathiawad had not experienced a centralized administration for so long that the *girassias* resented any loss of independence which the *Fael Zamin* involved for them. The chiefs took every advantage of the settlement to extend their powers over the *girassias*. Since there was no higher authority to whom he could appeal, the *girassia* who had a grievance, usually resorted to the only method open to him from time immemorial —he went *baharwativa* by choosing to become an outlaw. It was recognized as the traditional method of gaining redress and was governed by laws of sanctuary known as *sirna*. The Gir Forest was the analogue of Sherwood Forest which sheltered many a Kathiawadi Robin Hood and his merrie men; but they were not pleasant altruistic characters, since a boundless desire for revenge made them barbarous and cruel.[86]

Girassia discontent and the serious proportions which *baharwativa* had assumed showed the British that all was not well between the chiefs and their vassals. The British Raj was reluctant, however, to extend its jurisdiction over the states by introducing judicial institutions. Kinloch Forbes was not facetious when he described the traditional style of justice in Kathiawad as resembling the judicial system of England under Alfred. A wronged man could try *dharna* for redress—that is, the sitting on the doorstep of the evil-doer till he relented. He could ask the Charan or Bhat, who had gone *bahandari* or surety for him, to fulfil his obligations by committing *traga* in the presence of the offending party. The bold Charan would then inflict wounds on himself or commit suicide to make the opponent yield. The one hundred and fifty-seven chiefs who executed the *Fael Zamin* with Walker gave the honour of their Charans and Bhats as surety for keeping these agreements.[87] An aggrieved person could

---

[86] Wilberforce-Bell, *op. cit.*, p. 203; *Bombay Gazetteer*, VIII, Ch. IX.
[87] *Bombay Gazetteer*, VIII, p. 136.

also resort to *jhansa*, the sending of a written ultimatum threatening to burn the offender's house over his head if he did not make amends by a stated date. Trials by ordeal were common; there were both hot and wet ordeals. An accused was often asked to take an oath at the grave of a holy man or at a sacred shrine.

If justice was rough and ready, punishment was quick and tolerably humane. The village or caste *panchayat* might demand a meal for the caste group in the village, or the chief might board one or more of his armed men called *mohsals* who had to be fed by the offender. If this failed his goods were seized and auctioned. The British also used this system of boarding *mohsals* to punish recalcitrant chiefs; but the proud Rajput would accumulate an army of them before yielding. Fining was very common. The British utilized the practice by creating the Infanticide and Messenger (Mohsal) Funds into which were paid the fines inflicted on the chiefs. The death penalty was hardly ever resorted to. The first instance of it recorded by the British was during the famine of 1812–1813 when some men were executed in Bhavanagar State for killing and eating a cow in their hunger.[88]

In 1821, Elphinstone had discussed, in the light of what had been experienced elsewhere in India, the evils that might result from the attempt to introduce a western type of judicial system into a feudal and agrarian society like Kathiawad. The security of property rights was offset by the protection given to the money-lender. In 1825, Bishop Heber criticised the introduction of "Adawlut Courts" which helped to recover debts and tried to control rates of interest, but really only resulted in a system which "strips the weaver of his loom, the husbandman of his plough, and pulls the roof from the castle of the feudal chieftains" and leads to the abandon-

---

[88] *Bombay Gazetteer*, VIII, p. 324; Wilberforce-Bell, *op. cit.*, p. 194.

ment of once prosperous villages.[89] The situation in Kathiawad was becoming so serious that the British established a Chiefs' Court in 1831, presided over by the Political Agent assisted by three or four chiefs, which enabled the weaker states to punish capital offences and restrained the rulers from committing crimes against each other. The Political Agent, however, had difficulty in getting the chiefs assisting him to pass truly deterrent sentences.[90]

The instituting of the Chiefs' Court turned the Political Agent's Camp (he toured frequently accompanied by an Arab bodyguard) into an astonishing spectacle. Wherever the Political Agent went, his Camp swarmed with thousands of complainants all hoping to lay before him their grievances against the chiefs. Trying to get the Political Agent to use his influence with the chiefs became an alternative to *baharwativa*. Something had to be done, and the 1860's saw much discussion of the constitutional and legal position of the British in the peninsula.[91]

In 1863, the Bombay Government failed to convince the Secretary of State for India that the ruling of the Court of Directors in 1830 no longer held good; India had since come under the Crown. It is interesting that Sir Henry Maine, with whose works Gandhi would become familiar, argued that the Kathiawad chiefs were supreme within their own territories. In his celebrated Minute of 1864, he rejected the Austinian view on the grounds that the example of Kathiawad proved that sovereignty is divisible.[92] But Sir Bartle Frere, Governor of Bombay from 1862–1867, eventually succeeded in establishing the claim of paramountcy over the peninsula and enabled Keatinge to press on with his reforms. Thus,

---

[89] Heber, *op. cit.*, II, p. 145.
[90] *Bombay Gazetteer*, VIII, p. 329.
[91] *Ibid.*, p. 331.
[92] K. R. R. Sastry, *op. cit.*, p. 17.

6

Gandhi's boyhood coincided with a period when the British were assuming greater control over Kathiawad.

Another area in which the British sought to clarify the extent of their legal powers was in the question of the right to interfere in the relations between a chief and his vassals. In 1860, the Bombay Government referred the question to Calcutta and the matter was finally decided by Lord Cranborne's Despatch of January 31, 1867, dealing with the case of *Palitans* vs *Dajibhai of Sejalia*. It stated that the *girassias* were entitled to look to the paramount power of the British for the enforcement of the obligations of the rulers under the *Fael Zamin*.[93]

In the meantime, in 1863, Keatinge had classified all the *taluqdars*, or landed-proprietors, into seven categories; and he had defined the nature of their respective jurisdictions in terms of their position as chiefs and the extent of their possessions. The authority of the chiefs of the one hundred and eighty-eight states of Kathiawad now varied from powers of life and death and unlimited civil jurisdiction to the right to imprison for fifteen days or inflict a fine of fifteen rupees. The more important chiefs were encouraged to develop civil and criminal courts and to build proper jails instead of the dungeons in their palaces. The law administered by the smaller *darbari* courts was the customary law modified by local or tribal usage, but new codes based on the Civil and Criminal Procedure Codes of British India were introduced in the larger states. A new class of pleaders and vakils grew up. In 1873, rules were framed governing the practice and remuneration of legal practitioners and the scale of registration fees for legal documents was fixed in the following year by the Kathiawad Agency.[94] Police forces were also organized.

---

93 *Bombay Gazetteer*, VIII, Ch. IX.
94 *British Enactments in Force in Native States*, Vol. IV, pp. 182, 190-191.

In brief, there was a great improvement in law and order paving the way for the rapid progress of the peninsula.[95]

An important result of Keatinge's classification of the Kathiawad States was to bring more than 2000 square miles directly under British administration by depriving smaller proprietors of some of their jurisdiction and taking over the residuary powers of the smaller states. This area amounted to nearly a quarter of the peninsula; it was divided up into one hundred and forty-six *talukas* and each was placed under an official with limited powers called a *thanedar* who looked after the cluster of villages in his circle. These *thanas* increased the sources of revenue available to the British Government and provided them with the agencies needed to introduce changes. What British India was to the Princely States these *thana* circles became to Kathiawad.

Keatinge also divided the whole province into four districts, or *prants*, presided over by an Assistant Political Agent. He created a Civil Station in each *prant* to serve as district headquarters, with courts and offices for the judicial and executive administration of the area. The Assistant Political Agents toured the *prants* " hearing complaints, advising the chiefs, punishing crime and generally entering into all the wants of the people and the country."[96] Each of these British Officers was provided with an Indian assistant. The work of the *thanedars* in each *prant* was supervised by these officials. The four *prants* were Jhalawad, Hallar, Sorath, and Gohelwad; as a native of Porbandar, Gandhi belonged to the Sorath *prant*. He recorded that he won scholarships in the fifth and sixth standards reserved for boys from Sorath, but modestly ascribed his achievement to the fact that there were not many students from his *prant* in his class.[97]

---

[95] W. W. Hunter, (ed.), *The Imperial Gazetteer of India,* 9 Vols., (London, Trubner & Co., 1881), Vol. V, pp. 308-311.

[96] Booth, *op. cit.*, p. 25; *Bombay Gazetteer*, VIII, pp. 330-331.

[97] *Autobiography*, p. 26.

The object of Keatinge's classification of the *taluqdars* was to continue the policy of creating a stable class of landowners loyal to the British. He also wanted the princes to take the lead in harnessing the energies of the entire landowning class for constructive developments. He saw clearly that the *Fael Zamin* had led to the demoralization of the once war-like chiefs. If Walker stabilized the landed aristocracy, it was Keatinge who reactivised them and encouraged them to become a socially responsible class. He tried to give them a sense of pride by reviving their martial Rajput traditions. Keatinge deliberately fostered a new sort of pageantry by giving the princes gun salutes and investing the more enlightened of them with the new Order of the Star of India for good administration. He also encouraged them to travel in India and Europe, and it was Keatinge who conceived the idea of building a college in Rajkot for the education of the princes.

Keatinge, who left Kathiawad in 1867, faithfully reflected the changed attitude to the Indian States after the Mutiny. Lord Mayo, who became Viceroy early in 1869, evinced a keen interest in the princes while stressing the theory of paramountcy. He summed up the new attitude at a great Durbar held in Rajputana. " If we support you in your power," he declared to the princes, " we expect in return good government."[98] In 1870, the opening of the Rajkumar College in Rajkot by Sir Seymour Fitzgerald was symbolic of the new era in Kathiawad. He was the first Governor of Bombay to visit the province and provided an opportunity for an impressive display of pageantry. A long procession of princes mounted on their elephants and accompanied by their colourful retinues met the Governor three miles outside Rajkot.[99] Even if it were only a lavish display typical of an

---

[98] *The British Crown and the Indian States*, p. 64.
[99] Booth, *op. cit.*, pp. 63-64.

imperialistic era, it did at least have the merit of enabling the chiefs to cross the boundaries of their states on a peaceful mission. The sluggish states of Kathiawad had begun to stir with new life as Gandhi was born.

The Rajasthanik Court

It was the reforming zeal of the British which brought the Gandhi family from Porbandar to Rajkot about 1875. In 1873, a method of settling disputes between the chiefs and their vassals was evolved which proved highly successful. This was the Rajasthanik Court, in existence till 1899, in which Gandhi's father served as an assessor for a time. It was a sensible compromise between British administrative efficiency and the old feudal method of settling disputes between the chiefs and their *bhayyats* and *mulgirassias*. The Court, whose decision was final, was presided over by a British Officer assisted by two assessors from a list of six names drawn up by the chiefs. The *girassias* were encouraged to appeal first to their own chiefs for a clarification of their rights. If they were not satisfied by the chief's interpretation of the position they could appeal to the Rajasthanik Court. The chief or the complainant could object to an assessor with whom he was dissatisfied. The decisions of the Court were recorded after discussion of each case with both the chief and his tenant.

The Court, which had been objected to at first by some of the chiefs, succeeded in winning their confidence. The *girassias*, too, learned to trust the court and many a doubtful and obscure case was finally settled. Though the court's decisions were legal and binding, its procedure was informal and friendly. Its method of arbitration and conciliation had the avowed object of settling and not prolonging disputes. Recalling it to mind many years later, Gandhi would describe it as a very influential body. It is a curious way of describing a court of law, but that is what it was—not a place of litigation but a body using its good offices to produce harmony and

85

agreement. The Rajasthanik Court proved so satisfactory that the *baharwativa* was eliminated before the end of the century.[100]

Colonel J. W. Watson was President of the Rajasthanik Court from 1873–1886; it was during his tenure of office that Gandhi's father worked with him as an assessor. The choice of Karamchand Gandhi from the list of six names submitted by the chiefs shows that the Gandhis' of Porbandar had a good reputation as conciliators and men of independent judgment. The young Gandhi must have imbibed the spirit of reconciliation as he listened to his father talking to parties engaged in disputes when they called at his home in Rajkot. Though Gandhi makes only two passing references to the Rajasthanik Court in his *Autobiography*,[101] it probably had a greater effect on the development of his thinking than is generally realized. It is likely that his dislike for the British-style courts of Kathiawad and Bombay, his rejection of lawyers in *Hind Swaraj*, and his conception of the function of law were rooted in his memories of his father's work as an arbitrator in the Rajasthanik Court and his unconscious idealization of its methods and aims.

Kathiawad and The American Civil War

Another important factor in the backdrop of Gandhi's youth is the economic change which was sweeping over the peninsula. The effects of the American Civil War began to be felt in Kathiawad by 1863, and resulted in a period of rapid economic improvement which lasted till the famine of 1878–1879. This famine was so bad that there was a falling off in imports and a stoppage of house building.[102] The

---

[100] *Bombay Gazetteer*, VIII, pp. 32-33, 316-317, 331; Wilberforce-Bell, *op. cit.*, pp. 230-231, 235, 254.
[101] *Autobiography*, pp. 11, 15.
[102] *Bombay Gazetteer*, VIII, p. 247.

economic boom in Kathiawad is part of the story of cotton in Western India. The secession of South Carolina provided Bombay with an opportunity which both the British and Indian merchants of that city were not slow to grasp, and for five years the world's cotton trade was transferred from the Southern States of the Union to Western India. Bombay became the New Orleans of the eastern hemisphere.

The price of Indian raw cotton rose from three pence to nineteen pence per pound and the quantity exported gradually doubled. In 1860–1861, Bombay exported cotton worth seven million sterling; in the last year of the "American War," as it was called, while the amount exported still remained little more than three hundred and fifty-five and a half million pounds, Bombay received more than thirty million sterling for it. The high degree of prosperity which it brought for a time to Western India can be gauged from the trade passing through the port of Bombay. The normal export and import trade of about 40 million sterling rose in 1865–1866 to over 75 millions. If the trade of Sind were added to this figure it would give an amount which was double the ordinary sea-board trade of Bengal, Madras, and Burma in the same period.[103]

In the eighteenth century, cotton was a cottage industry in Kathiawad in a self-sufficient rural economy. The village women used spindles called *rentias* to spin the yarn which was woven into coarse fabrics on handlooms by Dheds and the Muslim Bohras and Tarias.[104] In the 1780's Kalavad was famous for a very fine *dangari* or cotton cloth called *pankoru* which was worn even by the chiefs.[105] But the story of Fair Dholera, as the cotton from Kathiawad was known in the markets of Bombay and Europe, belongs to the nineteenth

---

[103] G. Smith, *op. cit.*, p. 573.
[104] *Bombay Gazetteer*, VIII, pp. 248-249.
[105] *Ibid.*, p. 503.

century. Bhavanagar was the chief port for the export of Kathiawad cotton till the British opened Dholera in 1802. Though much of the trade had returned to Bhavanagar by 1846 the name of Dholera clung to the Kathiawad cotton.

When the effects of the "American War" began to be felt the price of Fair Dholera in the Bombay market rose from an average of 8 s. (Rs. 4) a *man* to £3.10 s. in 1864–1865. Large tracts in Kathiawad were turned over to cotton cultivation and prosperity was in the air. Copper and brass were imported in large quantities and the use of metal pots instead of earthenware became general. The use of gold and silver ornaments, like the armlet worn by Gandhi's brother,[106] also became widespread. The abundance of money led to reckless gambling and speculation on the part of the trading classes.[107] Though the Panic of 1867 affected Kathiawad adversely like the rest of Western India, cotton had established itself as the chief export; and by the 1880's the peninsula was supplying one-sixth of the cotton exported from Bombay.[108]

The cotton trade inevitably led to the development of the textile industry in Kathiawad and the establishment of steam presses and gins and spinning and weaving mills. Several Indian merchants and British firms from Bombay had established agencies in Kathiawad for buying cotton. J. M. Drennan, a British businessman, was the pioneer who introduced textile machinery and opened up a new outlet for Indian capital in the peninsula. Before 1864, the cotton went to Bombay from the Kathiawad ports as loose bales, called *dhokdas* and *kothlis*, in small sailing vessels called *pattimas*. Then a number of Indian screw presses, with screws made of local *babul* wood and frames imported from Malabar, were set up for binding the cotton into half-pressed bales. But

---

[106] *Autobiography*, p. 40.
[107] *Ibid.*, pp. 205, 248.
[108] *Imperial Gazetteer of India*, V, p. 311.

steam presses worked faster and turned out full-pressed bales. By the 1880's there were seven steam cotton presses in Kathiawad.

The first press in Bhavanagar started in 1871 was the Volkart-United Press owned by the Volkart United Press Company. Four more presses followed—the Bhavanagar Cotton Press (1872), West's Patent Press Company Ltd., (1877), the Fort Press Company Ltd., (1877), and the New Indian Press Company Ltd., (1882). The Bhavanagar State exempted these enterprises from taxation and gave them easy terms for the leasing of land and the use of water. A cotton press was also opened in Mahuva in 1877 by the Bhavanagar Cotton Manufacturing Company Ltd., and another at Wadhwan by Gaddum and Company.

The introduction of cotton ginning proved a more hazardous undertaking. Drennan started The Wadhwan Cotton Gin and Press Company in 1866 with factories in Wadhwan and Dhanduka. The buildings of the Wadhwan factory which housed sixty gins were washed away by floods in 1867. The Dhanduka factory was taken over by the Dholera Press and Ginning Company Ltd., but was not a thriving concern. The factory started at Limbdi by Messrs. W. & A. Graham of Bombay was a failure while the small factory with ten gins established in Vala proved too expensive. In 1870, the British Government loaned two lakhs of rupees to Drennan to open a cotton press and a ginning factory with fifty Platt's Macarthy gins at Dhoraji in Gondal State. Everything seemed to go wrong with the enterprise—the manufacturers failed, there were quarrels with the patentees, and the boats bringing the machinery foundered. The factory was saved only by the extension of the railway to Dhoraji.

In 1873, when Bhavanagar was jointly administered by E. H. Percival and Gourishankar Udayashankar, steam spinning and weaving mills were started by Messrs. Forbes and Company of Bombay with every encouragement from the

State. When the Bombay firm went bankrupt in 1879 the mills were mortgaged to a local banker, Venishankar Lakshmishankar, under whose efficient management the Company, which had been reorganized as the Bhavanagar Cotton Manufacturing Company Ltd., started showing a profit. The mills used cotton grown in Kathiawad and, apart from a small export trade with China, produced cloth for local consumption.[109] When Gandhi went to Bhavanagar in 1887 to join the Samaldas College, he was in the most industrialized town in the peninsula.[110]

The development of the cotton trade and the textile industry led in turn to improvements in transport and communications. In 1807, Colonel Walker had made the protection of the rough highways one of the objects of the *Fael Zamin*; the chiefs specifically undertook to guarantee the safety of travellers.[111] Though the British were entitled to spend one per cent of the tribute for making roads it amounted to only Rs. 7000 per annum. Therefore, prior to 1866, Kathiawad did not have a single road. In 1839, a trunk road of 1400 miles was built connecting Calcutta with Delhi and Peshawar, and in the following year another road linking the capital with Bombay via Agra and Ahmednagar was completed. But it was only when the railway line from Bombay reached Ahmedabad that transport began to improve in Kathiawad.

Colonel Keatinge was responsible for the opening of a new Civil Station at Wadhwan and he realized the advantages of connecting it with the *Bombay, Baroda and Central India Railway* on the mainland. He succeeded in getting the Bombay

---

109 *Bombay Gazetteer*, VIII, pp. 251-252.
110 *Autobiography*, p. 52. Since Gandhi came to dislike the machine age it is worth recording that the machinery in the factory, so efficiently managed by a Bania banker, was supplied by Curtis, Parr & Modeley and Hetherington of *Manchester* and Lord Brothers of Todmorden. The engines came from W. & J. Yates of Blackburn; *Bombay Gazetteer*, VIII, p. 265.
111 Lee-Warner, *op. cit.*, p. 250.

Government to survey the terrain between Wadhwan and Ahmedabad, but not to build the railway. A sum of Rs. 20,000 had now accumulated in the Road Fund and Keatinge was keen to utilize it. He persuaded the chiefs whose territories would benefit by the building of the railway to give subsidies for the making of a good carriage road from Rajkot to the Kathiawad boundary and personally supervised the construction of the first thirty miles of it as far as Choteels. With further help from the chiefs he developed a scheme for a network of roads from Rajkot to Jamnagar, Bhavanagar, and Jetpur.[112]

The maintenance of the roads, however, constituted a serious problem and they were so utterly neglected by the contractors who were in charge of them that they were in danger of disappearing altogether. In 1874, a severe monsoon caused havoc to the roads, stopping all traffic for days together. The Rajkot-Wadhwan Road was reduced to mire and slush. The story of how Gandhi's father tried to cover the one hundred and twenty miles from Rajkot to Porbandar in 1883 forms part of the history of road transport in Kathiawad. He covered the distance in three days in stage coaches ordered for him by the Thakore Saheb, but arrived all bandaged up because his carriage had overturned. It is not surprising that the mishap took place on the third day and the last lap of the journey. The further westward one travelled the worse the roads became.[113] They were a sad commentary on the fact that prosperity had deserted the western ports for centres nearer the mainland from where the best cotton came.[114]

The railway age began in Kathiawad with the completion

---

[112] Booth, *op. cit.*, p. 45.

[113] Years later, in 1904, Gandhi would tell the story about a cartman and the ruts of the roads of Kathiawad to illustrate a point, *Collected Works,* IV, p. 121.

[114] *Autobiography*, p. 20.

of the line between Wadhwan and Ahmedabad in 1872. It immediately increased the importance of Wadhwan which became the chief centre of the cotton trade. It also spelled out the ruin of Dholera. A drawback of this port was the delay caused by the early monsoon which meant storing bales of cotton till the country craft and small freighters could sail again. The cotton, however, could now be shipped by rail from Wadhwan in all weathers. The other centres of the cotton trade like Bhavanagar and Dhoraji were quick to realize the need for lines linking them with Wadhwan. The Bhavanagar and Gondal States co-operated to build the Bhavanagar-Gondal Line in 1880 which fulfilled this object. All these changes called for an improvement in the revenue system of the peninsula. In 1808, Colonel Walker had estimated the total revenues of Kathiawad at about Rs. 51,95,550 of which Rs. 9,79,880 was paid as tribute. By the 1860's the revenues of Kathiawad were increasing while the tribute remained stationary. The tribute had been augmented by the various fines inflicted on the chiefs which were credited to funds for socially useful purposes. The Infanticide and Messenger Funds, for example, were used to create an educational system in the 1840's. With the improvement in law and order the system of fining was no longer a source of income. The Political Agents had to persuade the chiefs to contribute to the various development funds which they were not always willing to support. There was no way of checking the accounts maintained by the chiefs, and most of them made no distinction between the states' revenues and their private incomes.

The Kathiawad Agency took two steps to improve this situation. The first was to clarify the sources of the income of the chiefs through the Rajasthanik Court which had called for a proper land survey. The Court abolished *veth*, or forced labour, but gave the chiefs the right to levy an improvement cess or *sudhara* at the rate of two annas for each acre of cultivable land. Another collection permitted by the Rajasthanik Court was the *deshdan*, or levy, on cotton which had to be paid by subordinate *girassias* and owners of rent-free lands. Thus, the states could benefit by the prosperity brought by the cotton trade. These revenues were to be utilized for improved general welfare through schools, hospitals, public works, and the creation of police forces. By 1879, the Agency had created a general local fund to which every chief and landed proprietor had to contribute a fixed amount for general welfare. By the 1880's the total revenues of Kathiawad were triple the figure given by Walker in 1808. It was in this way that the British created a revenue system though the amount of the tribute remained unchanged into the twentieth century.[115]

At the time Gandhi was a boy, the Kathiawad described by K. M. Munshi, in which the towns were camps of ruling chiefs and the villages were the homes of a hard-working and oppressed peasantry, was rapidly passing away.[116] The changes unleashed by the British were breaking up the once almost impregnable economy of self-sufficient villages. The coming of modern forms of transport enabled the mercantile and new industrial classes to draw a formerly unyielding countryside into the orbit of their operations. The American Civil War and the cotton boom of the 1860's had placed the Kathiawad peasant at the mercy of a fluctuating world market. A process of industrialization and urbanisation was at work altering and transforming the life and outlook of the people. By the 1880's Kathiawad was a very different place from the war-like little peninsula Walker rode into in 1807.

In 1939 Dharmendrasinhji, the Thakore Saheb of Rajkot, faced with a Congress agitation in his State led by Gandhi, issued a notification which read: " We appeal to our loyal

---

[115] *Bombay Gazetteer*, VIII, Ch. X.
[116] *Gujarat and Its Literature*, p. 27.

and devoted subjects not to be driven away by outside whirlwind (*sic*) guiding the destinies of the subjects of all states of Kathiawar."[117] The beleaguered ruler's ungrammatical appeal was strangely belated because the whirlwinds of change had been blowing through the peninsula for over a century. C. F. Andrews unconsciously perpetuated a half-truth when he claimed that the boy Gandhi " was brought up in a Hindu environment which had little connection with the outside world."[118] On the contrary, winds from the outside were blowing strongly in the decades in which Gandhi was growing up. In the next chapter we shall attempt to trace the influence of this period of reforms and economic changes on the man who looked to Dharmendrasinhji like a whirlwind from the outside.

---

[117] *The Indian States' Problem*, (Notification No. 72 of 1938–1939), p. 451.
[118] C. F. Andrews, *Mahatma Gandhi's Ideas*, (New York, Macmillan, 1930), p. 31.

CHAPTER THREE

The Gandhis of Porbandar

Having looked at the way in which Kathiawad was being transformed by the British impact, we must now turn to a study of the Gandhi family. The importance of the family is universally recognized; but the joint family system of India, with its determinative caste and religious affiliations, makes it even more necessary to study familial relations for the understanding of historic personalities. The influence of the family on Gandhi is especially clear in his early days.[1] The problems connected with his desire to go to England were more than financial; he had not yet reached a stage where he could act independently. The number of people who had to be consulted reflects the network of relationships involved when any important family decision had to be made, aggravated, in this instance, by the fact that his mother was a widow. The defiance of caste mores and prejudices involved in going to England demanded courage, not only from Gandhi, but from his whole family.

Even after Gandhi emerged as a striking individual, family ties were still meaningful to him. During most of his life he

---

[1] See *Collected Works*, I, " Why He Went to England," pp. 55-56, for the young Gandhi's account of the Bania family system.

was never without the company of relatives, male and female, old and young, the only exception being the years he spent in England. This explains the utter sense of loneliness he felt till he found his feet in London. He took a number of relatives to South Africa, like Chhaganlal and Maganlal, who became his trusted helpers. After returning to India, Gandhi was frequently consulted about family matters. A few months before his death, two young relatives came all the way to Delhi from Kathiawad to consult him about the old family house in Porbandar.[2]

Gandhi listed a love for their " clan " among his father's virtues.[3] The Gandhis possessed a sense of family cohesion and social mobility long before Mohandas appeared on the scene. The feeling of pride in their achievements became marked when his grandfather, Uttamchand, became Dewan of Porbandar under Rana Khimaji (1813–1831). We must, therefore, try to trace the origins of the Gandhi family, the role they played in the history of Kathiawad, and the impact on them of changing conditions in the peninsula, to understand how this particular family produced such a great national leader.

The Gandhis called themselves Modh Banias because they belonged to a section of this trading caste which claimed to have come to Kathiawad from Modhera in Gujarat.[4] Modhera is a town in the Vadarli *taluqa* of Baroda which was once populous and wealthy. There are many ruins in the vicinity, such as an old temple called Sita's Chavadi which was once dedicated to Sun-worship. (According to James Burgess it was probably built in the eleventh century.) Modhera was a frontier town of the Chalukyan Kingdom of

---

2 P. Gandhi, *op. cit.*, p. 4.
3 *Autobiography*, p. 12.
4 G. S. Ghurye, *Caste and Race in India*, (New York, Alfred A. Knopf, 1932), pp. 31-32.

Anahilavada Patan when Siddharaja ruled over it. The town is known in Jain legends as Modherpura or Modhbank Patan. There is no record of when and why the Modh Banias migrated to Kathiawad. Modhera, however, was captured by Ala-ud-din Khilji, and some Modh Banias may have moved westwards to Kutiana during the chaos following upon the collapse of the Chalukyas.[5]

The Gandhis were living in Kutiana in the eighteenth century but again there is no way of knowing when they settled there. The *Tarik-i-Sorath* seems to supply what is only a faint clue. Ranchodji Amarji says that the cultivating classes of Junagadh were immigrants from Gujarat.[6] There was a great deal of cultivation all along the banks of the Bhadar which flows past Kutiana. The Gandhis, as money-lenders, may have accompanied a wave of peasant migration to Kutiana from the mainland. It is interesting that Modhera was a frontier town of the Chalukyas while Kutiana was a frontier fortress of the Chudasama Rajputs. It suggests that the forbears of the Gandhi family were adventurous Banias prepared to brave the hazards of a frontier existence.

Though the Gandhis moved to Porbandar in the eighteenth century, they still remained in contact with Kutiana. Gandhi's father retired to Kutiana having incurred the wrath of Rana Vikmatji's mother when she was Regent. It was from there that his father returned to succeed Uttamchand as Dewan. The Gandhis owned houses in Kutiana till quite recently, and they still own land in the district. This plot of about two acres belongs to the joint family and is dedicated to the maintenance of the temple of the family deity.[7]

If Kathiawad is a miniature of India, the Kutiana district

---

[5] *The Imperial Gazetteer of India*, (London, Oxford University Press, 1908) see *Modhera*.

[6] *Tarik-i-Sorath*, p. 27.

[7] P. Gandhi, *op. cit.*, p. 8.

is a miniature of Kathiawad. It reflects both the geography and history of the peninsula. Kathiawad is a well-watered land; and Kutiana is watered by the Bhadar, the peninsula's largest river, which rises in the Mandav Hills and flows for one hundred and fifteen miles into the Arabian Sea. It is a saying in the areas through which the Bhadar passes that it is fed by ninety-nine tributaries. Kutiana is rich and fertile because of its *gher* lands, subdivided into *vel* and *chel*, which are twice as productive as ordinary soils. Immediately after the rains, small boats can sail the twenty-five miles from Kutiana to Navibandar at the mouth of the river. Timber, lashed together to form rafts, used to be taken up stream. Part of the area was once a desert, and nearby are hills which " have reverberated with the sounds of gallant cavalry hoofs for centuries."[8]

Ranchodji Amarji, who knew Kutiana well, tells the legend about the origin of the town in his *Tarik-i-Sorath*.[9] The name is said to be derived from a Charan woman, called Kunti, who used to graze her flocks at this spot and founded a *nes* or hamlet which grew into a village. It bore her name which became corrupted into its present form. So much did Kathiawadi history lap the walls of this town that it is not surprising to find Kutiana the home of famous bards and poets like Bhat Rao Lakhan, Sorathia Saraswat Vaikunth, Kshatri Haridas Bhagat, Bhat Thakurdas and Bhat Bhupat Singh.[10] The town was guarded by two strong forts, one of them built by a Bania governor called Kalidas. A look at a map of Kathiawad will explain the strategic location of Kutiana. Situated on the north bank of the Bhadar, it commanded the fords across the river and occupied a pivotal position in relation to three important regions. Kutiana

---

8 *Ibid.*, p. 6.
9 *Op. cit.*, pp. 49-50.
10 *Bombay Gazetteer*, VIII, Ch. XII, see " Kutiana ", pp. 525-526.

constantly changed hands, but never so frequently as in the eighteenth century after the collapse of Moghul power in the peninsula. The old stones of the fortresses of Kutiana could tell many interesting tales of sieges and battles, echoing the noise and din of many a confusing epoch in Kathiawadi history.

Since Kutiana was the gateway into three important regions, we must look at each of them in turn to understand the balance of forces still operating when the Gandhis began their rise to prominence in the eighteenth century. The first region, the most important and most coveted area called the Nagher, lies to the south of Kutiana with the Bhadar forming a natural northern boundary. The Nagher is the fertile coastal strip which extends south-eastwards in a curve from Madhavpur to Jafarabad. This is the oldest region of Kathiawad and the ports which dot the coastline were known to the Alexandrine Greeks in the second century A.D. It was thickly populated when the hinterland was still covered by dense jungles and immensely wealthy because its ports made it a trade emporium. Also, since the Nagher was (and still is) the Holy Land of Vaishnavism, its temples attracted a considerable pilgrim traffic. Up to the British period, when the development of Bombay and the introduction of railways ruined the coastal ports, the Nagher exerted a powerful pull which explains a great number of the internal rivalries within the peninsula and the frequent invasions from distant parts of the mainland.

Kutiana also guarded the old routes leading into the second region, the heart of the peninsula where the Chudasama Rajputs from Sind had established themselves as feudatories of the Chavadas of Anahilavada Patan. Their first capital was at Wanthali. Later they moved closer to the protective barrier of the Girnar Hills after the building of the Uparkot, the strong fortress of Junagadh. Jainism flourished in this region during the eight centuries of their rule, from the eighth through the fifteenth centuries A.D. Gandhi's mother was born in the village of Datrana which belonged to the Vadal revenue sub-division of Junagadh State.[11] This village, twelve miles north of Junagadh, has an interesting connection with Ra Mandalika, the last of the Chudasama rulers. It is known as the birthplace of the Charan woman, Nagbai. According to the legend repeated in the *Tarik-i-Sorath* and familiar to every Kathiawadi bard, Nagbai cursed Ra Mandalika for trying to violate the chastity of her beautiful daughter-in-law, Minbai, and foretold his defeat by the Muslims. There is a shrine and a memorial stone which commemorate Nagbai; her descendants, called Goviala Charans, were still living in the village in the 1880's.[12]

The third region which Kutiana serves as a gateway is to the northwest: the Barda Hills, the coast of Okhamandal, and the ancient island of Beyt. It was through this area that many tribes and races from Sind and Kachh came treading on each other's heels, driven southwards by the pressure of the Huns and the Muslims. By about the ninth century A.D. this region was occupied by the Jethvas, whose rulers still sit on the oldest surviving *gadi* in Kathiawad. The ruins of Ghumli testify to the prosperity the Jethvas had achieved by the thirteenth century. They were overthrown, however, by Jadeja Rajputs from Kachh at the beginning of the fourteenth century; and they never recovered again till the chaos following the decline of the Moghul Empire revived their long-cherished ambition of penetrating southwards into the Nagher.

It was the fatal lure of the Nagher which converted Kutiana into a Muslim *kasbah*. During the Chalukyan Era the rulers of Anahilavada Patan fought the Chudasamas for the control of the rich trade and pilgrim traffic of the western coast. Hemachandra's *Dvyasrayakavya* describes the conflict between

---

[11] P. Gandhi, *op. cit.*, p. 18.
[12] *Bombay Gazetteer*, VIII, p. 408.

Ra Graharipu and Siddharaj for the mastery of this region. Kumarapala also extended his sway over Kathiawad. But by now the Muslims had become conscious of the wealth of the Nagher. The maritime raids from Sind were followed by the terrible incursion of Mahmud of Ghazni, and the Nagher was gradually engulfed by the Muslim tide. The Sultans of Gujarat completed the work of the Ghoris and the Tughluks when Ra Mandalika surrendered to Mahmud Begada in 1472–1473. Like the Gujarati Sultans, the Moghuls stationed a *fauzdar* in Junagadh and a governor in Mangrol. Kutiana was occupied by a garrison of Muslim *Kasbatis*.

The Muslim conquest of Sorath did not diminish the trade of the ports of the Nagher; on the contrary, a flourishing commerce developed with Muslim lands. Kutiana, too, became populous and prosperous. It was during Muslim rule that the rich and powerful Bania, Kalidas, built one of the two forts. The other was built by Prince Halim, who later became Sultan Muzafar, when he was Fauzdar of Sorath. Kutiana was renamed Muzafarbad after this popular prince who did much to develop the town. It is by this name that Kutiana is known in old Persian deeds. A Persian inscription in the Juma Mosque, built in 1539 A.D. during the reign of Sultan Mahmud III of Gujarat by Ibrahim Nizam Jharmi, uses Muzafarbad as the town's name. During the Moslem occupation, Kutiana became famous as a dress-making town; its *kachas*, *lunghis*, *dhotars*, *mirkhanis*, *gajianis* and *alavachas* were in great demand. Dyers also enjoyed a flourishing trade. Both Hindu and Muslim fairs were held in Kutiana. One annual fair was held on the seventh and eighth day of the dark half of the month of Shravan at the temple of the Nagnath Mahdev. Another fair, lasting for several days, was held at the shrine of Pir Miskin Shah during the Muslim festival of Shabibarat.[13]

---

[13] *Bombay Gazetteer*, VIII, see " States and Places."

The decline of Moghul authority began in Kathiawad towards the end of the long rule of Aurangzeb. It produced an unsettled state of affairs in Sorath which had an adverse effect on Kutiana. The loosening hold of the Moghuls led to a revival of the powers of the peninsula, and the old habit of internecine strife reasserted itself. The Muslim garrisons of the towns, following the example of the Fauzdar of Sorath and the Rajput States, threw off the Moghul yoke in the general confusion of the eighteenth century. The *Kasbatis* of Kutiana, caught between several rival states, plunged into a career of reckless adventurism that brought nothing but disaster to the town. During this troubled period, the Gandhis emerged as minor officials of the Rana of the Jethva Rajputs.

As the Moghul Empire decayed under the onslaught of the Marathas, the Jethvas became strong enough to contend for the control of the Nagher with the Muslim Babis of Junagadh, who had become independent of Delhi. The period also saw the growth of Navanagar under Meraman Khavas, the slave from Dhrangadra who dominated the feeble Jam, and the rise of the Gohel Rajput state of Bhavanagar. The Jethvas were taking advantage of the disorders following upon the death of Aurangzeb, as were others in Kathiawad and all over India. The British arrived in the peninsula exactly a hundred years after the last great Moghul died; they ended the chronic state of incessant warfare which had disrupted life in Kathiawad throughout the eighteenth century.

It is significant that the Gandhis emerge as a prominent family in the midst of the chaos and confusion of the decay of the Moghul Empire. India in the eighteenth century was no place for the weak. It produced a crop of adventurers, some of them brilliant and able, some of them despicable and cruel like vultures gathered to feast on a dying carcass. But all of them needed money, and their economic needs gave a fillip to the class of money-lenders and revenue farmers. The Gandhis were Banias, a class that certainly financed the resurgent states of Kathiawad in the eighteenth century. By the middle of the century they had become associated with the Jethva Rana in his bid for power.

The Jethva successes up to the annexation of Kutiana in 1749 were due not only to the collapse of the Moghul government of the peninsula, but also to the disturbed conditions in the neighbouring states of Navanagar and Junagadh. Sultanji's ambitions were thwarted though, by the rise of two remarkable men—Meraman Khavas of Navanagar and Dewan Amarji of Junagadh. Meraman Khavas was a household slave who accompanied Ba Depabai of Halwad to Navanagar on her marriage to Jam Lakhaji. He reduced the Jam to a puppet by 1756, and dominated north-western Kathiawad till his death in 1800. Dewan Amarji, a Nagar Brahman, was born in Mangrol about 1742. This extraordinary man, his brothers, and their sons comprised the most influential family in Kathiawad till the turn of the century. One of his sons was Ranchodji, the author of the *Tarik-i-Sorath*, one of the main sources for the history of the period. Amarji served the Muslim Babis so well that when Walker entered the peninsula, Junagadh was still the leading state of Kathiawad.

In 1759, the fickle *Kasbatis* of Kutiana handed over the town to Hashim Khan, a member of the Babi family. By the 1770's it was clear that the Jethvas had already reached their high water mark with the occupation of Kutiana in 1749. But Sultanji was bent on a career of expansion despite one disaster after another. In 1774, he called on his kinsman, Jadeja Khumboji of Gondal, to help him drive away the Sheikh of Mangrol who had taken Navibundar in a night attack. In 1778, he incurred the wrath of Meraman Khavas by building a fort at Bethali on the Navanagar border. Sultanji vigorously defended the fort against the powerful army of the Khavas; but in the end he had to ask Dewan Amarji to intervene on his behalf. The Khavas withdrew his forces but Sultanji had to agree to the dismantling of the fort.

Dewan Amarji, at the age of eighteen, had arrived at Junagadh in time to rescue Nawab Mahabat Khan from his discontented Arabs. By the 1780's he had made Junagadh so powerful that he incurred the enmity of the rulers of the three neighbouring states of Navanagar, Porbandar and Gondal. In 1782, Sultanji and Jadeja Khumboji laid siege to Kutiana. They were driven off by the invincible Amarji before the forces of Navanagar could join them. Meraman Khavas changed sides and joined Amarji in laying waste the territory of Sultanji. The enemies of Dewan Amarji now accomplished their purpose by treachery. They played upon the jealous fears of Nawab Hamid Khan and, in 1784, bribed him into murdering this great Dewan who had served him and his father so faithfully.

Sultanji made a last bid to revive his waning fortunes by removing his capital to Porbandar in 1785. This act marked a century which had elapsed since the Jethvas surreptitiously built a fort there. In 1787, he occupied the fort of Chorvad when its chieftain, Sanghji, a kinsman, was killed by Alia Hathi of Malia. A more spectacular success was his capture of Verawal which he took in a night attack. But these successes were short-lived. In 1789, the Nawab of Junagadh descended on the Nagher and took both Chorvad and Verawal after some bitter fighting. Sultanji also lost the fort of Kandorna which was captured for the Nawab by Govindji, who was Amarji's brother and governor of Kutiana. At the end of the century, while the rebel Bania, Kalian Sheth, was ravaging his lands, Sultanji was embroiled with the Sheikh of Mangrol. The defeat of Kalian Sheth by Ranchodji at Kutiana was no real compensation for the unhappy state of affairs to which the kingdom of the Jethvas had been reduced during Sultanji's long rule.

Despite all the defeats he sustained, Sultanji was never lacking in a reckless sort of courage. His defence of Verawal

against the Nawab of Junagadh has an epic quality to it.
Sultanji tried to succour his loyal Arab garrison by provisioning
them by sea from Porbandar and cannonading the Nawab's
camp with guns mounted on boats. What this kind of warfare
entailed for the civil population can be seen from the devasta-
tion of Chorvad, when cows and donkeys fed on its famous
pan leaves, while the people had no other shelter left but the
shade of the plantain trees.[14] Things had reached such a
pass that Sultanji was deposed by his son, Haloji, in 1804.
Three generations of Gandhis served this remarkable man as
daftaris in Porbandar. Since Gandhi's grandfather was
Sultanji's grandson's dewan, he must have known Sultanji
who lived till 1813.

Though the information available is rather scanty we can
now try to trace when and why the Gandhis became associated
with the Jethvas.[15] The first known Gandhi is Lalji, who
lived six generations before Mohandas (born in 1869).
Allowing an average of twenty-five years for each generation,
or a total of one hundred and fifty years, that would take us
back to 1719. This was the year after Rana Khimoji had
claimed Porbandar as his own. The Jethvas held Kutiana
from 1749 to 1759. The fact that Lalji's son Ramji, and his
grandson, Rahidas, were both *daftaris* or assistants to the
Kamdar (dewan) of the Rana of Porbandar shows the
importance of this decade in the history of the Gandhis.

Rahidas Gandhi was given a gift of land by the Nawab of
Junagadh which the Gandhis still use for the maintenance of
the family shrine in Kutiana; this land was a *dharmada* or
religious tenure. It is probable that this Nawab was Mahabat
Khan who was saved by Dewan Amarji in 1758. Amarji
went to Porbandar to secure the services of an Arab Jamadar,
named Salmin, whose men stormed the Wagheswari Gate of

---

[14] *Tarik-i-Sorath*, p. 184.
[15] P. Gandhi, *op. cit.*, p. 8.

the fort of Junagadh. The Arab mercenaries of Porbandar would certainly have dealings with the *daftari*, since they were directly paid by the Dewan of the State. This is only conjecture but it is not impossible that Rahidas Gandhi, in his capacity as *daftari*, enlisted the aid of the Porbandar Arabs. A grateful Nawab would be likely to reward Rahidas since the family came from Kutiana which was in his territory. Also, it would be wise to take the land on a *dharmada* or religious tenure, since the *Kasbatis* of Kutiana would respect this even in those uncertain days.

If the Gandhis left Kutiana for Porbandar between 1749–1759, it was a wisely timed move. Sher Khan Babi made himself independent of the Moghuls in 1730. This defection of the Fauzdar of Sorath encouraged the *Kasbatis* of Kutiana to do the same, and they invited Niamat Khan Lodi of Somnath Patan to become their governor. When Mahabat Khan became Nawab in 1758, confusion still reigned in Junagadh. His aunt set up her grandson as a rival; hardly had this problem been resolved through the intervention of Jadeja Khumboji, when the Arab mercenaries, to whom the State was in arrears, seized the Uparkot. As we have seen, the timely arrival of the youthful Amarji saved Mahabat Khan, but it took some years for even this clever dewan to restore order. In 1759, the *Kasbatis* of Kutiana defected from Rana Sultanji II and made Hashim Khan Babi their governor. The oppressive rule of Hashim Khan came to an end in 1770, when Amarji restored Kutiana to Junagadh. The town continued to change hands with bewildering rapidity and fell on such evil days that it was mortgaged to Raghunathji, another son of Amarji, in 1805.

Apart from the disorder in Kutiana after it fell into the hands of the Muslim *Kasbatis*, there were many economic motives that could have influenced the Gandhis to move to Porbandar. Kutiana was no longer the good trading centre it had been under the Moghuls. Conditions probably became

difficult for the Bania merchants with the seizure of both
political and economic power by the *Kasbatis*. The brief
period during which Kutiana was ruled by the Jethva Ranas
would have given the Hindu merchants an opportunity for
expanding their trade. The Jethvas were keen to make
Porbandar into a flourishing port and would naturally
encourage Banias to settle there. The textile industry in
Chhaya would benefit by the confusion in Kutiana. The
Nawab's mint in Junagadh closed down at the beginning of
the eighteenth century, and was reopened only in 1780 by
Dewan Amarji; but Rana Sultanji's mint functioned throughout the century. Sultanji founded Aditiana in 1748, and a
trade in Porbandar stone had sprung up. Porbandar also
became noted for its fairs; half the number of fairs in Kathiawad
in the nineteenth century were still being held in this area.
The Gandhis would have seen a rising Hindu power in
Porbandar and opportunities for making their fortunes (which
no longer existed in Kutiana) in the vigorous attempts of
Sultanji to control the trade of the ports of the Nagher. The
rise of the Gandhis must be seen against the background of the
attempt of a Hindu kingdom to reassert itself after the collapse
of the Moghul Empire, and the opportunities it provided for
a commercial class like the Banias for economic enterprise and
employment in the state services.

By the 1770's the Gandhis were prosperous enough to buy
a house in Porbandar; this was eight years before Sultanji
moved his capital there from Chhaya. This house, which
is a quarter of a mile from the sea, was purchased by Harjivan
Gandhi in 1777 A.D. The sale deed in the name of Gandhi's
great grandfather is still preserved. The hand-made paper is
slightly damaged by insects but the old writing in the
Devanagari script is clear and legible.[16] Perhaps the old

[16] P. Gandhi, *op. cit.*, p. 4.

document had more sentimental value for Gandhi than we realize. Both hand-made paper and the Devanagari script were dear to the heart of the Mahatma. The old Gujarati words of the document spelled out more than a common transaction; they announced that the Gandhis, a family as sturdy as the Porbandar stone of which the house was built, had arrived. They would achieve even greater prominence in the nineteenth century.

The great achievement of Gandhi's grandfather was his salvaging of the State of Porbandar from the ruinous condition into which it had sunk as a result of the fifty years of warfare waged by Sultanji II. We must, therefore, trace the events leading up to the reign of Rana Khimaji under whom Uttam-chand " brought honour and fame to the Gandhi name."[17] Haloji had deposed his father, Sultanji, in 1804, but the change of rulers brought no respite to Porbandar. The Makrani and Arab mercenaries had helped Haloji in the hope that he would settle their arrears of pay. The state was practically bankrupt, however, and the mercenaries were becoming desperate. A quarrel broke out between the Makranis and the Arabs. As a result, eight hundred Makranis suddenly left the Rana's capital and seized the fort of Kandorna some sixteen miles away. As they had no faith in Haloji's offer to settle their arrears, the destitute Makranis declared they would sell the fort to the highest bidder.

The death of Meraman Khavas in 1800 released Jam Jasaji from the clutches of his powerful slave, but he proved no less ambitious. The Nawab of Junagadh refused the offer of the Makranis, but the Jam closed with it and occupied Kandorna. He failed to reckon with the presence of Walker and the Marathas who were in the peninsula. Haloji appealed to Walker who advanced on Kandorna and took it after a

---

[17] P. Gandhi, *op. cit.*, p. 8.

brief assault in November, 1807. Haloji had to pay for the restoration of Kandorna though. He gave a *nazarana* (tribute) of twenty thousand rupees to the Gaekwad's Government and agreed to the farming out of the revenues to Sundarji.[18]

Kunvar Prathiraj, Haloji's son, resented these impositions and rebelled against his father; he seized the fort of Chhaya. The Rana had become so feeble that he could not dislodge the Kunvar. Once again he appealed to Walker who sent a force to assist him. Prathiraj, with his wife, surrendered after he had been wounded in the fighting. It was on this occasion that his grandmother, Sultanji's wife, had her feet cut off by the *sipahis*, greedy for her gold anklets.[19] Haloji had to make more concessions to the British. A detachment of one hundred men was stationed in the fort and the British lent him fifty thousand rupees to clear his debts to the Gaekwad. It was this Prathiraj who succeeded Haloji as Rana Khimaji in 1813, and made Uttamchand Gandhi his Kamdhar.

Rana Khimaji needed a good administrator who could help him put his finances in order and solve some of the difficult boundary problems that had greatly reduced the size of his state. He found the man he needed in Uttamchand Gandhi. The Rana obviously became very attached to his able Kamdhar. The Gandhi family still hands down the story of how Rana Khimaji himself participated in the marriage ceremonies of Uttamchand's two eldest sons. Khimaji employed all the six sons of Uttamchand. Before the Rana died he gave this Gandhi a written assurance, as was the custom in those days, that the office of dewan would be hereditary in the Gandhi family. The promise was kept by Khimaji's successors; Tulsidas, Mohandas Gandhi's uncle, succeeded his father, Karamchand, as Dewan in the 1870's.

---

[18] *Tarik-i-Sorath*, p. 92.
[19] *Ibid.*, p. 92.

Two of Gandhi's brothers, Lakshmidas and Karsandas, were employed by the State of Porbandar.

Prabhudas Gandhi points out that it was almost a tradition for the Gandhis to be more influenced by their uncles than by their fathers.[20] Uttamchand owed the beginnings of his career to his uncle, Daman Gandhi, who was a *daftari* in Porbandar when Khimaji was the Rana. It was still the usual practice in the early nineteenth century for the Ranas to farm out the revenues to contractors. Daman Gandhi found Uttamchand a position as a customs contractor at Mithi Mandvi where the port dues, including the pilgrim tax, were collected. The young man also found time to help his uncle in his office. On one occasion Daman Gandhi happened to be away when the Rana sent for him. Uttamchand took it upon himself to meet Khimaji, who was so favourably impressed that he entrusted the *daftari's* young nephew with a difficult mission the day after their first meeting. The Collector of Customs at Madhavpur was proving intractable, because he was receiving encouragement from the officials of Junagadh. Khimaji asked Uttamchand to go to Madhavpur to deal with this difficult situation. Uttamchand exceeded the expectations of the Rana by negotiating a treaty with the State of Junagadh which settled all the outstanding boundary questions and increased the size of Porbandar. It was due to Uttamchand's efforts that the British eventually recognized Porbandar as a First Class State.

Uttamchand's other creditable achievement was to improve the finances of Porbandar. As we have seen, the revenues of Porbandar were farmed out to Sundarji in 1809. This Sundarji (known also as Sundarji Shivaji and Sundarji Khatri) was none other than the man who gave information to Jonathan Duncan regarding the female infanticide practised by the Jadeja Rajputs. Beginning as a horse trader supplying

---

[20] P. Gandhi, *op. cit.*, p. 33.

the British Army, he used his influence with the British officials
to become a revenue farmer on a large scale and wielded
quite an influence in Kathiawad politics.[21] The debt to this
Kachhi merchant's firm had grown to such proportions that
Porbandar hardly had any revenues of its own. Uttamchand
found a loophole in the mortgage deeds which enabled him
to turn the income from sources other than land revenues and
the ports into the Rana's treasury. So great was Uttamchand's concern for the finances of Porbandar that, when his
sons were married, he turned over the presents he received
to the Rana, who was touched and surprised, because such
scrupulous behaviour was rather unusual in those days.
Mohandas inherited his careful handling of public funds from
his grandfather.

When Khimaji died in 1831 his son, Vikmatji, was only
eleven years old. Khimaji had married two wives; one was
a Vala from Dhank and the other a Jhala from Ranpur.[22]
One of them was Rupaliba, the mother of the boy ruler, who
became Regent in 1831. Like most female Regents she was
susceptible to the influence of the women of the *zenana* and
priests. She probably had very little notion of state finance
with the result that Uttamchand's careful husbanding of the
resources of Porbandar must have looked like parsimony to
her. Uttamchand's protection of Khima Kothari, the State
Treasurer, who had fallen foul of her, enraged Rupaliba to
such an extent that she besieged Uttamchand's house and
ordered a cannon to bombard it. The Political Agent in
Rajkot had to intervene and Uttamchand retired to Kutiana.
Rupaliba was obviously a spirited woman. Her conduct
suggests that she was the wife who was with Khimaji when,
as Kunvar Prathiraj, he was captured by Walker's *sipahis* at

---

[21] *Tarik-i-Sorath*, pp. 218-219.
[22] Tod, *Travels in Western India*, p. 420.

Chhaya. Her Regency was by no means a failure. She built the temple at Kedareshwar in Porbandar and the water tank called Mitha Talav near the city.[23] She was probably inspired by the example of Ahalya Bai of Indore who had repaired the temples in Somnath Patan in 1783.[24]

Uttamchand Gandhi achieved prominence when a turbulent era in Kathiawad was coming to an end. Old Sultanji, who saw the collapse of the Moghuls, the rise of the Marathas, and the triumph of the British in Western India, died in 1812. Jam Jasaji of Navanagar and Sheikh Mian of Mangrol died in 1814, and Wakhatsinhji of Bhavanagar, in 1816. Nawab Hamid Khan, who took Chorvad and Verawal from Sultanji, died in 1811. Though the best part of his career lies in the nineteenth century, Uttamchand Gandhi bears a resemblance to eighteenth century figures like Dewan Amarji. This astonishing Nagar Brahman and his family were well-known in Porbandar; Mangalji and Ranchodji, his nephew and son respectively, had served Rana Sultanji. The Gandhis, though only humble *daftaris* of Porbandar at the time, would see in this amazing family that dominated the politics of Kathiawad for half a century, all that they themselves aspired to be.

Uttamchand Gandhi was a manly Hindu whose daily exercise, even after he had retired to Kutiana, was horse-riding. Like Dewan Amarji and Premaji Lohana (Sultanji's Kamdhar who recruited a Muslim army for him),[25] Uttamchand could command the loyalty and respect of his rough Arab bodyguard; they did not desert him when Rani Rupaliba attacked his house. When Uttamchand valiantly saluted Nawab Hamid Khan II with his left hand, because his right

---

23 *Bombay Gazetteer*, VIII, Ch. XIII, " Porbandar."
24 *Tarik-i-Sorath*, pp. 66-67.
25 *Tarik-i-Sorath*, pp. 165-166.

was still pledged to Porbandar, it was a thoroughly eighteenth century gesture.[26]

The Gandhis from this time forward had a nostalgia for these affluent days when they could invite the whole of Porbandar to a family wedding by pasting rice on the city gates in the traditional manner. The high position of Uttamchand Gandhi as Kamdhar brought them power and social prestige. Tod describes the status of this important official in Rajput courts who was traditionally drawn from one of the Vaishya castes. The whole of the territorial and financial arrangements were vested in the kamdhar or dewan. He appointed the civil governors of the districts and farmed out the revenues of the state. All the departments concerned with expenditure were under him. " He becomes," says Tod, " a most important person as the dispenser of the favours of the sovereign. Through him chiefly all requests are preferred, this being the surest channel to success. His influence necessarily gives him unbounded authority over the military classes with unlimited power over the inferior officers of the state."[27] He had a personal bodyguard to enforce his commands. The office was usually hereditary.

Uttamchand was the last Kamdhar of Porbandar in the old style; the times had changed by the time Karamchand succeeded him. Ranchodji Amarji describes Premaji Lohana as a bold man who had " become haughty and fat like a tumour in the exuberance of his power."[28] If Gandhi's grandfather did not care to imitate Sultanji's Kamdhar it was not simply because Porbandar was passing through some lean years, but because he was of a different calibre. By the

---

[26] In 1751, the Peshwa treacherously attacked Damaji Gaekwad's camp and made him a prisoner. After that incident, Damaji Gaekwad never saluted the Peshwa with his right hand but only with the left. Dosabhai, *op. cit.*, p. 189, fn.

[27] *Annals and Antiquities of Rajasthan*, I, p. 448.

[28] *Tarik-i-Sorath*, p. 88.

8

time of Gandhi's birth, his grandfather had assumed some of the proportions of a legend. The boy Gandhi carried with him an inspiring image of this great ancestor who belonged to a virile and colourful age; he would regret the passing of that era when he became a man. Only a decade before he was born, the spirit of that age tried to reassert itself through the Mutiny. When Gandhi was born in 1869 and old Sultanji's great grandson was the Rana of Porbandar, the last of the Moghuls had died only seven years previously. Gandhi was linked to that age through Ota Baba, as his grandfather was popularly known. It was not, as Prabhudas Gandhi asserts, Karamchand who inherited Uttamchand's " brilliance, brains, love of truth and courage."[29] Karamchand had some of his father's fire but not all of it. It was Mohandas Karamchand Gandhi who came from the same mould as Ota Baba, who had made the Gandhis into a distinguished Kathiawadi family.

Gandhi's father, Karamchand, began his career in the service of the Porbandar State as personal accountant and letter-writer to Rana Khimaji. Upon the death of Khimaji, his son Vikmatji (born April 1, 1819), succeeded to the *gadi* on June 20, 1831; Rupaliba, his mother, became his Regent. It was during her Regency that John Wilson visited Porbandar. Rani Rupaliba had no use for the Gandhis, but their temporary misfortune came to an end when she died in 1841. Vikmatji was a young and inexperienced ruler when the Irish Presbyterian missionaries opened a Mission Station in his capital in 1843. According to the agreement with the British made by his grandfather, Haloji, a regiment under British officers was still stationed in Porbandar. Once a year the young Rana was pestered by the Political Agent for trouble-some returns relating to female infanticide among the Jethva

---

[29] P. Gandhi, *op. cit.*, p. 15.

Rajputs. He needed wise counsel and he turned to his father's dewan, Uttamchand, for help. Ota Baba's suggestion that his fifth son, Karamchand, be appointed Dewan was accepted and Karamchand returned to Porbandar about 1847. He was then about the same age as the Rana.

Rana Vikmatji[30] was born in 1819, a year before the British established their headquarters at Rajkot. He died in 1900 at the age of eighty-one, and his long life was lived against the background of all the changes in Kathiawad in the nineteenth century. Vikmatji continued throughout this period to be a feudal figure; he lived in rather miserly fashion and was obviously out of tune with the times.[31] As a result of Keatinge's reforms, Porbandar was recognized as a First Class State and a salute of eleven guns was conferred upon Vikmatji in 1865. In 1869, the British induced him to go to Broach to visit an exhibition being held there so that he might have some idea of the world beyond the confines of slow-moving Porbandar. The Rana benefited very little from the excursion. The first thing he did on his return was to mutilate the man who had corrupted his son, Madhavsinhji. Porbandar was degraded to a Third Class State. Six years later Karamchand Gandhi left for Rajkot to serve as an assessor in the Rajasthanik Court. Mohandas Gandhi, who knew Rana Vikmatji personally, described his character to Joseph Doke in the following words: " Firm-minded, singularly chaste in morals, keen-sighted, often cruel, so independent that he quarrelled with the political agent, so stubborn that he raised a Civil War, so niggardly that his dependents were almost starved, and yet with compensating characteristics which won their affection."[32]

---

[30] His title was " His Highness Rana Shri Vikramatji Khimaji of Porbandar."
[31] E. Sharpe, *op. cit.*, p. 86.
[32] Joseph Doke, *An Indian Patriot in South Africa*, (London, The London Indian Chronicle, 1909), p. 13.

The three decades during which Karamchand was Dewan of Porbandar were, on the whole, quiet and uneventful years. Porbandar began to catch up with the other states of Kathiawad only after Vikmatji was deposed in 1886. It was placed under a British Administrator and the Rana's grandson, Bhavsinhji, was sent to the Rajkumar College at Rajkot. Progress had been so slow in Porbandar that even the lighthouse was not built till 1876. Karamchand's twenty-eight years in Porbandar were happy though. He liked his work because the Rana trusted him, and his simple ways endeared him to the people. He would receive his visitors every morning at Raghunathji's temple, chatting with them in informal and friendly fashion while peeling and cutting vegetables. Uxorious by temperament, Karamchand was also happy in his married life. He was deeply attached to his fourth wife, Putlibai, whom he married in 1857.[33] Though the mother of Mohandas was twenty years younger than Karamchand, she shared his hospitable ways and enjoyed looking after the numerous relatives and friends who daily filled the house. Mohandas, the last child, and son of Karamchand's old age, grew up in a warm and friendly home that was almost like an ashram. When Gandhi became known as Bapu, and was hailed as the Father of the Nation, it was a tribute to Karamchand and the domestic felicity of the Gandhi home.

In the 1860's, the State came into closer touch with the British Administration in Rajkot, not only through Keatinge's reforms, but also because of the activities of the Waghers, a fierce tribe in Okhamandal whose traditional occupation had been piracy. Having been deprived of the means of their

---

[33] There seems to be some confusion as to whether Gandhi's statement that Putlibai was his father's fourth wife (*Autobiography*, p. 11) was correct. P. Gandhi claims that Karamchand married only thrice, (P. Gandhi, *op. cit.* p. 187).

[*Courtesy* :   Publications Division, New Delhi.

The house at Porbandar where Gandhiji was born.

livelihood by the British and the Marathas, they became highwaymen and dacoits. In the 1860's, they entered the western Kathiawad states and created a considerable disturbance. In October, 1860, they seized Kodinar from the Gaekwad's soldiers and plundered it. By 1865, their activities had become such a threat to law and order that Colonel Keatinge himself led a force which dislodged them from the Gir Forest. In the same year a fund was started to support a special punitive force; the states most affected, Junagadh, Gondal, Navanagar and Porbandar, contributed to it. This force of five hundred men was stationed at fifteen outposts and the whole area was divided into an Eastern and Western division. In 1867, Lieutenant Gordon was put in charge of the Navanagar, Gondal and Porbandar levies in the Western Division. In the same year, Captains Henry Hebbert and Charles La Touche were killed by the Waghers in an encounter at Tobar Hill. In May, 1868, the dacoits were surrounded at Wanchurda in Porbandar territory by a force, assisted by the Rana's troops, led by Jamadars Lakha and Mubarik. Their famous leader, Mulu Manik, was killed and the Wagher revolt ended.[34]

The part played by Porbandar brought Karamchand to the notice of British officials in Rajkot; thus, in 1875, Colonel J. W. Watson chose him to serve on the Rajasthanik Court. We have already discussed the significance of Karamchand's association with this interesting institution. When his term of office in the Rajasthanik Court came to an end, Karamchand was in his fifties. The Gandhis had moved to Rajkot in time to escape the famine of 1876–1877 which was particularly bad in Porbandar. The poor died in such large numbers that their bodies were thrown into shallow pits near the beach where they were eaten by hyenas, jackals, and dogs.[35]

---

[34] Wilberforce-Bell, *op. cit.*, pp. 210-211, 214-220.
[35] R. B. Booth, *op. cit.*, p. 212.

Karamchand's financial worries were beginning and, knowing how irregular some rulers could be in paying even the salaries of their dewans, he laid down some stringent conditions before he agreed to serve the small State of Wankaner. The young ruler of this Jhala Rajput principality, twenty-four miles to the north-east of Rajkot, was Banesinhji (born, 1842) who succeeded to the *gadi* in 1861. Karamchand must have served him as Dewan in the late 1870's as Banesinhji died in 1881 at the age of thirty-nine. The relations between the young ruler and his elderly Dewan were stormy, and on one occasion, Karamchand protested against the Raja Saheb's interference by fasting publicly.

In the 1880's, Karamchand served as Dewan of Rajkot. This small Jadeja Rajput State was founded in the second half of the sixteenth century by Vibhoji, the third son of Jam Sataji of Navanagar. The ruler, Bawajiraj, was a minor; therefore, his grandmother, Naniba, administered the State till 1867 when Keatinge entrusted its management to Captain J. H. Lloyd. Keatinge then sent Bawajiraj to the Rajkumar College in 1870. The young ruler, now a college graduate, was given full power as Thakore Saheb in 1876. It was Bawajiraj who arranged for stage coaches to rush Karamchand to Porbandar in 1883 for the wedding of his sons, Karsandas and Mohandas. Karamchand was on good terms with Bawajiraj. Although he resigned, owing to a disagreement with the Thakore Saheb, he received a pension for nearly three years till his death in 1886.

Karamchand was not as happy in Rajkot as he had been in Porbandar. Apart from financial worries, his health, which had never been very good, caused much anxiety to the family. Asthma, a fistula, and the after-effects of his bad accident on the way to Porbandar were taking their toll; death hovered constantly over the saddened home in Kaba Gandhi Lane. After his sunny childhood in Porbandar, a shadow fell across the boyhood of Mohandas in Rajkot. Torn by anxiety for his father, distracted by a jealous passion for his attractive young wife from the time he was thirteen, struggling with text books in an unfamiliar language (since few people he knew actually spoke English), he became morbid and introspective. He felt a sense of guilt about all sorts of matters because the sounds from the sick room of his dying father prevented him from any natural enjoyment of life. In 1901, he would write to his son Manilal, "When I was younger than you are today I used to find real enjoyment in looking after my father. I have known no fun or pleasure since I was twelve."[36] His boyhood was a training period in the art of self-denial, though he did not begin to feel he had achieved mastery over himself till he was thirty-six.

Karamchand's decision to go to Rajkot ultimately proved to be an even more momentous decision than that of Lalji Gandhi's son when he decided to go to Porbandar. When Ramji Gandhi became a *daftari* in the service of the Rana, he paved the way for Uttamchand who became the first dewan in the family. When Karamchand became associated with the British Government through the Rajasthanik Court, the family moved closer into the orbit of a power far greater than that of Rana Sultanji. It put his youngest son on the road that would eventually make the Gandhis the most famous family in the whole of India. Though Karamchand once said of Mohandas, "Manu will bring honour to the family name," he could not know that the boy was destined to make that name known throughout the world.[37]

Rajkot was a different place from the sleepy little port of Porbandar. Even Kasturba, the merchant Nakanji's daughter, was a little different because she had grown up in Rajkot; Mohandas resented the independent manner in which his wife would set off for the temple or to visit her

---

[36] P. Gandhi, *op. cit.*, p. 31.
[37] P. Gandhi, *op. cit.*, p. 24.

friends. Two worlds met in Rajkot—the old historic world of the Jadeja Rajputs and the new world of the British Cantonment and Civil Station. The old city and the new Civil and Military Station confronted each other across an unsavoury *nullah*, feeling each other out, and then either responding with mutual appreciation or reacting with mutual dislike. The rapidly changing face of Rajkot was the changing face of Kathiawad. It was the administrative hub of the peninsula; the newly built roads and railway lines, and the influences and ideas that were transforming the life of the land formed its spokes.

The old city, with its fort of white stone built by Lakhaji Jadeja,[38] stood on the bank of the Aji, which Burgess considered the prettiest river in Kathiawad.[39] The Aji flows northwards past Rajkot and empties itself into the Gulf of Kachh. It was noted for its good water, and before the building of a reservoir in the 1890's, the whole city (including its cattle) drank, washed, and bathed in it. In London, the young Gandhi would vividly remember his baths in the Aji and the long lines of cattle going out of the town to pasture.[40] Like all old Kathiawadi towns it was enclosed by fortified walls. The narrow, crooked streets were deliberately made tortuous and irregular to afford shelter and protection to the defenders in case an enemy gained access to the town. The four main gates were also strategically located; the outer gate opened into a court from which a second gate led into the city. The gates were placed between walls of solid masonry six to ten feet thick, and their doors were made of strong teak wood ten to twelve feet wide and twenty to thirty feet high. The huge doors were studded with large iron spikes in case elephants were used to ram them. The walls and bastions were full of

---

[38] *Tarik-i-Sorath*, p. 94.
[39] *Tarik-i-Sorath*, p. 5.
[40] *Collected Works*, I, pp. 34-35.

loopholes for shooting and platforms for sallying forth against attackers. It was a strong reminder of a feudal era that was passing away.

In 1820, the British Government acquired about two square miles on a perpetual lease from the Thakore Saheb of Rajkot. A Military Cantonment and a Civil Station grew up side by side, flanking a road a mile long. Like similar cantonments anywhere in India the military section was neatly laid out with bungalows for the British officers, the regimental mess, orderly rooms and parade grounds. Adjoining this area were the sepoy barracks for the Indian infantry, cavalry, and artillery troops with simple quarters for married and unmarried men. The roads and compounds were fenced with prickly pear or cactus. The civil section was dominated by a rambling building known as the Kothie— the residence of the Political Agent. Nearby were the public offices and courts for the transaction of Agency business. Further down the road were the bungalows of the Assistant Political Agents and the Civil Surgeon. The bungalow of the Irish Presbyterian Mission, and Anglican Church, a Roman Catholic Chapel, a schoolhouse, a civil hospital, and a jail completed this typical sample of British life in India. [41]

Gandhi was obviously familiar with this life of the Cantonment. This is proved by the fact that he frequently compared what he saw on his voyage to England in 1888 with the locality he knew. The bungalows in Aden reminded him of the bungalows in the Rajkot Cantonment. In Malta, Gandhi thought the park in Valetta was not as good as the public gardens of Rajkot. Gandhi, who had watched the sahibs playing tennis in the Cantonment, made the understandable mistake of landing at Tilbury clad in white flannels in late autumn. He discovered, to his dismay, that the tennis

---

[41] R. B. Booth, *op. cit.*, pp. 24-33, *passim*.

flannels suitable for recreation in Rajkot, were not the standard clothes of Englishmen.[42]

An ailing father, the tender love of his mother, the half-mocking, half-serious affection of his wife, all kept Gandhi close to home where he tended his little garden or busied himself in the sickroom. But he would encounter the British officials riding their horses like centaurs on his solitary walks, or watch them strolling with their memsahibs while the band played in the public park. Sometimes he would go down to the banks of the Aji with his bold Muslim friend, Sheikh Mehtab, and other boys, and they would talk about the Sahibs and imitate them by smoking cigarettes. Or they would ask why the British ruled the country, and Sheikh Mehtab, conscious perhaps that his meat-eating forbears had once held sway too, would solemnly assure the boys that it was because they were not vegetarians. Talk led to experiment; Gandhi with his daring Muslim companion would go to a Rest House, furnished in British style, to break his Vaishnava tradition by eating curried mutton. At other times he would overhear gossip about the arrogant behaviour of the British or about the Missionary Sahib's corruption of young men by giving them beef to eat and brandy to drink. For what other reason could those young men possibly visit the Padre Sahib and his wife in their bungalow in the Civil Station? So the two worlds eyed each other, and each acquired a superficial knowledge of the other. At one vital point, however, the meeting was more penetrating. Gandhi went to the Alfred High School, which was part of the system of education established by the British.

Mountstuart Elphinstone had written his Minute on Education in 1824; Alexander Duff had started the first English School in Calcutta in 1830; and Macaulay had sent his famous Despatch of March 7, 1835; yet, the Political Agent

---

[42] *Collected Works*, I, pp. 14, 19; *Autobiography*, p. 61.

reported in 1842 that Kathiawad was still very backward educationally. Hardly a chief could read or write; books were rare and the funds for education pitifully inadequate. There were *dhooli-shalas* (so called because the children learned to write on sand) like the one Mohandas Gandhi attended in Porbandar,[43] and *pathshalas* like the one where B. M. Malabari, the Parsi author and reformer, got his early education.[44] English schools were first introduced into Kathiawad by the Irish Presbyterian missionaries soon after their arrival in 1841. In 1846, the Political Agent, Mr. A. Malet, laid the foundations of an educational system by recommending that an English and vernacular school should be opened in Rajkot under the direction of the Agency.

A lakh of rupees (Rs. 100,000) from the accumulated amount in the Infanticide Fund had been invested and the interest set apart for education. In 1847, Malet suggested that donations from the rulers and private subscriptions should be added to the Education Fund, but progress was slow because of the tardiness of the Princes. In 1852, the Bombay Board of Education rather reluctantly accepted some responsibility for education in Kathiawad. Colonel Lang pressed the need for a central school in Rajkot and in 1853, the Local Committee of the Agency was reorganized to form a Board of Education which included the dewans of the leading States. In June, 1853, the Board selected an able headmaster, Mr. Bhogilal Pranvalabhdas, to be the first head of the Central School at Rajkot and superintendent of the other schools in the peninsula. In 1857, the Board of Education was converted into a Department, and the Kathiawad Schools were supervised by the Inspector of Education of the Northern Division of the Bombay Presidency. An Englishman, E. Giles, was the Inspector when Mohandas Gandhi was a schoolboy in Rajkot.[45]

---

[43] P. Gandhi, *op. cit.*, p. 27.
[44] J. Singh, *B. M. Malabari*, (London, G. Bell & Sons, Ltd., 1914), pp. 8-12.
[45] *Autobiography*, p. 15; Dosabhai, *op. cit.*, p. 11, fn.

As we have seen, Kathiawad progressed rapidly in the 1860's; education also expanded greatly. In 1864, the educational budget amounted to Rs. 11,100. In June, 1865, Mr. Gopalji Surbhai was appointed Deputy Educational Inspector for Kathiawad; District Committees were set up in each of the four *prants* which had come into being through Keatinge's reforms. It is interesting that the representatives of the States wanted education to be free though it was finally decided that the schools would be fee-levying. In 1865, there were seventy-one schools (including thirteen for girls), 4189 pupils and a budget of Rs. 20,000. By 1882, there were six hundred and thirty schools (including fifty-three for girls), 36,848 pupils and the budget had risen to Rs. 219,400. The cesses and levies sanctioned by the Rajasthanik Court had made it possible for the States to contribute most of the budget.[46]

The foundations for the education Gandhi received at Rajkot were laid in 1853 when a central school was established. In 1867, the Rajkot English School, as it was known, was raised to the rank of a high school of the second grade. It became known as the Kathiawar High School, since it was the only one in the peninsula, and the Headmaster was Mr. Uttamram. In 1870, the Nawab Saheb of Junagadh went to Bombay to be presented to H. R. H. the Duke of Edinburgh. On his return he expressed a desire to commemorate the occasion in some suitable form. Upon the advice of the Political Agent, he agreed to donate a lakh of rupees for giving new buildings to the Kathiawar High School, which was outgrowing its cramped quarters in the Civil Station. The spacious new buildings of the Alfred High School, as it was now called after the Duke of Edinburgh, were designed in the Norman-Gothic style by Booth, the Agency Engineer.

---

[46] *Bombay Gazetteer*, VIII, Ch. XI, see "Education", and Booth, *op. cit.*, Ch. VI, *passim*.

The chief official at the opening on January 4, 1875, was Sir Philip Wodehouse, Governor of Bombay.

The Alfred High School lived in the shadow of the Rajkumar College founded in 1870 and was inevitably influenced by its British public school traditions. The Parsi Headmaster of the Alfred High School, Dorabji Edulji Gimi, obviously took his cue in educational matters from Chester Macnaghten, the Principal of Rajkumar College. The Parsis were the best Indian cricketers at that time and Gimi, like Chester Macnaghten, who was a Cambridge Blue, believed strongly in the values of the game. Gandhi tells us that he made gymnastics and cricket compulsory. Mohandas admired the popular Headmaster, who was a good teacher and disciplinarian, but came into conflict with him over the rule of compulsory games at four every evening. He could not get Gimi to exempt him in order that he might nurse his father and was fined on one occasion for being late for games. Gandhi admits that he had a false notion that " gymnastics had nothing to do with education." [47] But Mohandas ended his schooldays happily enough. He was given a farewell by the staff and students on the eve of his departure for England and he made a brief little speech reported in the *Kattyawar Times*. [48]

Karamchand wanted his son to have a good education. He probably sensed the importance of Rajkot as an educational centre in 1870, when the Rana of Porbandar attended the opening of the Rajkumar College. The Alfred High School was functioning in its new buildings when Karamchand came to serve at the Rajasthanik Court. When he went to Wankaner, he left the family in Rajkot so that the education of his sons would not be interrupted. In spite of his ill health he stayed on in Rajkot only for the sake of Mohandas's education, since Karsandas had discontinued his studies after his

---

[47] *Autobiography*, p. 27.
[48] *Collected Works of Mahatma Gandhi*, I, (*Kattyawar Times*, July 7, 1888), p. 2.

marriage. The privations endured by Lakshmidas, the eldest brother, in order to support Mohandas in London was the fulfilment of their father's wishes.[49]

The important position occupied by Rajkot in the life of the peninsula was not lost on Gandhi, the boy, though he became more aware of its significance as a man. When he led the agitation for constitutional reforms in that familiar town in 1939, he said, " Rajkot is the hub of Kathiawad, and if Rajkot is given a popular government, other States of Kathiawad will of their own accord and without any further civil resistance fall in line. There is no such thing as perfect coincidences on this earth. Its beauty lies in its multitudinous variety. There will be, therefore, a variety of constitutions in Kathiawad States. But let the trunk be true."[50] It was an unconscious tribute to the British who had made Rajkot the trunk through which flowed the sap bringing fresh vitality to the many-branched tree of Kathiawad. He also paid a graceful tribute to the city that had contributed so much to his early development. " Rajkot is no doubt an insignificant place on the map of India," he said, " but it is not insignificant for me and my wife. As a child she was brought up in Rajkot though born in Porbandar."[51] He was right to mention his wife. Neither of them could ever forget the formative influences of Rajkot.

The Wave of Reform

Gandhi referred to " a Wave of Reform "[52] in Rajkot and yet confessed that he never read a paper till he got to London. His knowledge of Indian religious and social reform movements was the fruit of later reading during his first period in

---

[49] The account of the progress of education in Kathiawad is based on the *Bombay Gazetteer*, Ch. II and R. B. Booth, *op. cit.*, Ch. VI; See H. H. Sir Bhavsinghji, *Forty Years of the Rajkumar College* 1870-1910, (London, 1911).

[50] *The Indian States' Problem*, p. 228.

[51] *Ibid.*, p. 153.

[52] *Autobiography*, p. 32.

South Africa. The problems confronted there drove him to acquire a better perspective of contemporary Indian culture. His activities during his visit to India in 1901 were those of an exile hungry for a better understanding of his country and eager to become acquainted with the leaders of Indian religious, social, and political thought. Gandhi's vague allusions to the wave of reform passing over Rajkot, however, indicate that British rule, missionary activities and western education were having an impact on the traditional way of life of various communities in Kathiawad. The experiences he described show a conflict between his Vaishnava upbringing and the disturbing desires for social freedom.

The Parsis, who came from Persia in the eighth century A.D. to preserve their Zoroastrian faith, were the first to respond powerfully to the British impact on the western coast of India. The British wisely extended religious tolerance to the Parsis and the Banias, the two most enterprising commercial communities of Western India who contributed greatly to the consequent development of Bombay.

By the time Gandhi was a boy studying in a school presided over by an able Parsi headmaster, the social and educational progress of this ethnic group had exerted a great influence on Gujarat. The Parsi reformer, Mulla Firoz (1758—1830), helped to revive the Gujarati language. Naoroji Furdunji (1817–1885) founded the Young Bombay Party whose watchword was "Reform." He exerted a great influence over future leaders like Dadhabhai Naoroji, V. N. Mandlik, Sorabji Shapurji and Bhau Daji. The organ of the Young Bombay group was a Gujarati newspaper, *Rast Goftar*. Furdunji and his disciples established the first girls' school, the first library, the first literary society, the first debating club, the first political association, the first organization for improving the condition of women, the first institution for social and religious reform, the first law association and the first educational periodicals maintained by Indians in Western

India. Furdunji visited England thrice where he spoke on behalf of the Bombay Association and the Poona Sarvajanik Sabha. He even enlisted the support of John Bright for the cause of Indian Reform.[53]

One of Furdunji's proteges, Sorabji Shapurji (1831–1893), contributed a great deal to the development of Gujarati journalism. He started a Gujarati monthly called the *Jagat Mitra* and edited the *Bombay Samachar*, the oldest Gujarati paper. This too was founded by a Parsi, Furdunji Marzben in 1812. In 1851, Shapurji started another Gujarati journal called the *Jagat Premi*. He was also one of the founders of the *Rast Goftar* in 1858. A series of articles for *Rast Goftar* flowed from his pen describing the cotton factories, iron foundries, shipbuilding yards, and coal pits he saw in England on his visit in 1863. He was keenly interested in the education of women and contributed many articles to a feminine journal, *Stribodh*, begun in 1857 by Karsandas Mulji.[54]

In 1909, Gandhi wrote an article at the request of the Gujarat Literary Association in which he acknowledged that the Parsis "were a Godsend to Gujarati." In the same article, he pointed out that Gujarati could gain a great deal from Parsi enterprise. "Several Gujarati newspapers are in the hands of Parsis," he said, "and it is up to them to protect the future of the language."[55] Gandhi owed more than just a little literary inspiration to the influence of the Parsis, however. The only outstanding national leader Gandhi was familiar with during his student days in London was Dadhabhai Naoroji. Significantly he turned to this Parsi and, later, to another leader, Sir Muncherjee Bhownagree, for support after he had founded the Natal Indian

---

[53] G. P. Pillai, *Representative Indians*, (London, George Routledge & Sons, Ltd., 1897), pp. 237-245.

[54] *Ibid.*, pp. 247-255.

[55] P. Gandhi, *op. cit.*, p. 65.

Congress. When Gandhi took his family to South Africa he dressed them in the Parsi style.[56] The small Zoroastrian community in South Africa headed by his close friend, Parsi Rustomji, gave him their support. When Gandhi returned to South Africa from London in November, 1909, the Parsi industrialist, Ratanji Jamshedji Tata, donated Rs. 25,000 to his Satyagraha Fund. Before he adopted Gokhale as his Guru, Gandhi looked to Parsi leaders like D. E. Wacha and Sir Pherozeshah Mehta for support and guidance. This influence of the Parsis on the young Gandhi is today a largely forgotten fact.

The progress of the Parsis did combine with social reform among the Bania and Bhatia Vaishnavas of Western India in the person of a very courageous leader, Karsandas Mulji (1832–1874). When Mulji was a student in the Elphinstone Institution, he began writing a paper on " Remarriage of Hindu Widows " for an essay contest sponsored by an association called Guzarati Dayan Prasarak Mandli. He was ostracised for this action by his family. After becoming headmaster of the Gokuldas Tejpal Seminary, he became connected with *Rast Goftar* as a regular contributor. In order to reach the members of his own community more effectively, Mulji started a weekly Gujarati paper called *Satya Prakash* in which he ventilated his ideas on religious and social reform. His articles were stirring up the Banias and Bhatias when he created a great sensation, the repercussions of which lasted for several decades—he exposed the immoral activities of the Maharajas of the Vallabhacharis, a Vaishnava sect.

There were about twenty of these Maharajas in western India who claimed descent, as we have seen, from the Telugu Brahman, Sri Vallabhacharya (c. 1478–1521). The Maharajas visited Kathiawad periodically, being received

---

[56] *Autobiography*, p. 229.

with great ceremony. They maintained four *thanaks* or centres at Junagadh, Amreli, Porbandar, and Navanagar.[57] The controversy in 1862 over the Maharaj Libel Case involving Karsandas Mulji and a Gosainji Maharaj from Surat was still echoing in Porbandar, a centre of the Vallabhachari sect, when Gandhi was a boy. He tells us that he gained nothing from the Vaishnava *haveli* in Porbandar because he heard rumours that immorality was practised there and lost all interest in it. It is impossible that this celebrated case should not have been known to members of the Gandhi family who were Vallabhacharis. Varjivandas Madhavdas, a witness for the prosecution, was questioned on the claim that " the Raja of Porbandar was disgusted with the worship of a Maharaj on account of his immoralities."[58] The case lasted for forty days beginning on January 26, 1862, and created a great stir. Karsandas was exonerated by the Judges, Sir M. Sausse and Sir Joseph Arnold, but he was severely assaulted outside the court.

The sufferings of the early reformers are illustrated by another aspect of the career of Karsandas. He and his family were persecuted because he had the temerity to visit England which was a breach of caste rules. Karsandas died shortly thereafter (1874) in Kathiawad.[59] Gandhi was the first Modh Bania to follow in the footsteps of Karsandas Mulji by going to London; and, like him, he was excommunicated from his caste. When one remembers the tragic fate of Karsandas in his last unhappy days when he was shunned and humiliated, we must admire the pioneer courage of the young

---

[57] Bombay Gazetteer, VIII, p. 155, fn.

[58] *Report of the Maharaj Libel Case*, (Bombay, 1862), Appendix, p. 10; *History of the Sect of the Maharajas or Wallabacharyas in Western India*, (London, Trubner & Co., 1865), was published anonymously. Manilal C. Parekh thinks it was the work of Karsandas Mulji, assisted by John Wilson, *op. cit.*, p. 369.

[59] G. Parameswaran Pillai, *op. cit.*, pp. 279-284.

Gandhi when he defied the rules of his caste. The times had changed, but only fourteen years had elapsed since the death of Karsandas; it was still a courageous act for a boy in his teens. Just before he sailed from Bombay he was surrounded[60] by a mob of Modh Banias near the Town Hall. Gandhi left India with the jeers of his own people ringing in his ears.

The experience through which ideas of Indian social reform reached the mind of the young Gandhi in Rajkot was his early marriage. It is a curious coincidence that B. M. Malabari, the Parsi reformer, published an article in the *Hitechhu* in 1883, the year of Gandhi's marriage at the age of thirteen, entitled "The Horrors of Infant Marriage." Half a century of discussion of the subject had made no impression on the conservatism of the Gandhis. Kasturba was the third little girl betrothed to Moniya, as Gandhi was known as an infant in Porbandar; the other two had died previously. When Gandhi left for England in 1888, he and Kasturba had been married for five years; the young couple had lost their first baby when both were only sixteen; she had already borne him two children. Gandhi had to struggle with the problems of marriage, sex and parenthood even before he had reached manhood. Had the reform movement, which was battling with these problems, succeeded earlier, Gandhi might have been spared these onerous responsibilities at so tender an age.

Gandhi's account of his early married life, which he describes as "Playing the Husband," indicates some contact with the thoughts and ideas of the social reformers of the period. "About the time of my marriage," he says, "little pamphlets costing a pice, or a pie (I now forget how much) used to be issued in which conjugal love, thrift, child marriage, and other such subjects were discussed."[61] It was this search for

---

[60] *Collected Works*, I, p. 58.
[61] *Autobiography*, pp. 22-25.

meaning in his relations with Kasturba that led Gandhi to
think about social problems in Rajkot. His struggle with the
problem of vegetarianism assumed significance and importance
after he went to London. Other problems like smoking,
lying, and stealing were never really serious issues. It was
the shock of his early marriage that proved to be the foundation
stone of Gandhi's later career as a social reformer.

The Sin of Machinery

" Machinery is the chief symbol of modern civilization; it
represents a great sin," wrote Gandhi in *Hind Swaraj*.[62] Some
of Gandhi's dislike of industrial civilization can be traced to
the difficult decades of the 1880's when he keeps referring to
" the poverty of my family."[63] The famine of 1878-1879
had added to the general distress though it temporarily
arrested the population growth. The population of
Kathiawad was estimated at 1,475,700 in 1842. By 1872,
it had risen to 2,343,899, showing an increase of about 59%.
Owing to the famine, the rise during the next eight years was
only 1·08%. But price levels rose and many people migrated
to the mainland and Bombay. There were 45,000 Kathia-
wadis in the city of Bombay by 1908.[64]

" An economic change is at work among the native population, the result of which it is difficult to forsee," said the
" Kathiawar " section of the *Bombay Gazetteer* in 1884. The
Kathiawad Agency was aware of the dislocation and discontent caused by the introduction of machinery; for there
had been agrarian riots in the Bombay Presidency in 1875.
They hoped that industrialization would ultimately benefit
the peasant classes of Kathiawad by drawing the non-

---

[62] *Op. cit.*, p. 69.
[63] *Autobiography*, p. 52.
[64] *Bombay Gazetteer*, VIII, " Population "; *Imperial Gazetteer*, 1908, " Kathiawar."

agricultural castes like the Kolis and Ahirs into the towns to form a fixed labouring community. As the *Gazetteer* put it, " The pressure of population on land will thus be reduced and the tillage of the soil will be left to those classes who will do it justice. If this expectation is realized, landowners, cultivators and labourers will benefit by the introduction of steam and machinery into the province." The Agency also made some efforts to improve agriculture. Cattle fairs and vegetable shows were held at Wadhwan in 1874 and 1880 and at Kundla in 1875.[65]

The growth of towns in Kathiawad, however, drained off not only landless workers but also the village *intelligentsia*, leaving the rural areas stagnant and unprogressive. The new towns like Rajkot, Wadhwan, and Bhavanagar contributed to the growth of a faster-moving kind of urban life—one full of vigour and vitality; but they also became overcrowded and insanitary. The Agency and the more enlightened Princes made strenuous efforts to improve sanitation and other civic amenities. The rate of change was bewildering, however, and the spread of plague to Kathiawad brought a new form of terror to the narrow streets and lanes of the towns.

The introduction of steam power and machinery into the cotton industry provoked various forms of economic conflict. The Indian screw-presses were forced out of Bhavanagar. They managed to survive for a time by moving inland to centres close to the railway lines, since freight charges were more favourable to half-pressed bales; they found no dearth of work during the cotton season.[66] But the competition of the steam gins was bitterly resented by the owners of the hand-ginning yards. The steam ginning factories built by Drennan at Wadhwan and Dhandhuka were strongly opposed

---

[65] *Op. cit.*, pp. 243, 252.
[66] *Ibid.*, p. 251.

by the local Mahajans, or associations of the employers of hand-ginning labour. The Government-subsidized factory opened by Drennan met with violent opposition from the Mahajan at Dhoraji. The *ads* or yards crowded with workers sitting in lines and using the hand gin (called a *charkha* in Kathiawad) employed a larger number of labourers who were paid at a piece rate; but the steam gins worked faster with fewer hands. The *ads* managed to compete successfully with the factories for a long time.[67]

The handloom textile industry collapsed and practically disappeared because of the competition from Manchester which caused hardship to Hindu and Muslim weavers. A few Arabs continued to weave fine gold brocades, scarves, and cloth at Junagadh with State patronage, but the handloom weaving at Verawal was destroyed by competition from piece-goods imported from Bombay and Europe. The same story was repeated at Amreli where there were about a thousand handlooms providing employment for Banias, Tarias, Bohras, and Khojas. Before the coming of machine-made textiles, Amreli was noted for its *pachedi* shawls, *dhotis*, coverlets, and *pagris* (turbans). The export trade had moved away to Dhoraji, Wadhwan, Rajkot, and Bhavanagar and the maritime states in the west compensated for the loss of their commerce by taking to imports. Navanagar, for instance, developed a large import trade of cotton piecegoods when its handloom industry was destroyed. Machine-made goods from Bombay, Manchester, and Birmingham flowed into Kathiawad through the western ports. The value of imports of cloth in 1876-1877 amounted to Rs. 117,708; in 1879-1880 it had risen to Rs. 185,284.[68]

---

[67] *Bombay Gazetteer*, VIII, pp. 251-252.
[68] *Ibid.*, pp. 246, 257, 261, 367.

Other Kathiawad cottage industries and handicrafts also suffered from foreign competition, such as the perfumed *pudi*, or powders, of Navanagar and the soaps from Wadhwan. Many continued to buy locally-made hair oils like *phulel* and *sugandhray tel* and scents like *attar* of roses. Typically Indian products like *agarbatti* (scented sticks) and *soneri*, the gold and silver thread of Navanagar, managed to survive. The wood and ivory workers of Mangrol and the copper and brass artisans of Sihor led a struggling existence. The village smiths suffered from the import of cheap farm implements, knives, and axes from Bombay.[69]

Prior to 1866, the only form of travel in Kathiawad was on horses, camels, and elephants or in gaily coloured and decorated but uncomfortable bullock carts. Kathiawad horses were famous; and the deeds of sires and dams were woven into tales and ballads in days when a man frequently owed his life to the speed and endurance of his faithful steed. The horses were bred on the shores of the Rann mainly by the Kathis. The Persian histories always refer to them as the Kachhi horses. The Moghuls imported Arab stallions which were landed at many of the Kathiawad ports and helped to improve the local breed. Horses were so common that in 1801 Jam Jasaji levied an *asp vera* or horse tax. Famous cavalry regiments of the Company (like the Seventeenth Dragoons) were horsed in Kathiawad. With the coming of modern transport even the Rajputs forgot how to ride; a bit of romance faded away with the disappearance of the equine age.

With the horse went also the livelihood of many different groups of people from grass-cutters to saddle-makers. The best saddles came from Kundla and Muli. When Gandhi's wedding procession made its way through the narrow, winding

---

[69] *Bombay Gazetteer*, VIII, Ch. VI, "Kathiawar Crafts."

lanes of Porbandar, he probably rode seated on one of these beautiful saddles made of broadcloth stuffed with wool and embroidered with coloured silks and gold and silver thread.[70]

Camels were as useful as horses and also figure in old romances and tales of war. In 1839, camels from Kachh and Kathiawad were used in the First Afghan War. As late as 1881, the Navanagar Durbar owned a herd of six hundred camels. The mangoes from Kodinar passed through the Gir Forest on the backs of camels on their way to the markets of the peninsula.[71] In 1888, Gandhi rode a camel from Dhoraji to Porbandar in his eagerness to talk to his uncle about going to London; he had changed his mode of transport because the journey from Rajkot to Dhoraji by bullock cart had been too slow.[72] His camel must have passed the men laying down the railway from Dhoraji to Porbandar; Lord Reay, the energetic Governor of Bombay, had turned the first sod in 1887 for the line which was completed in 1889.

Rail and road transport brought improved postal facilities to Kathiawad. The first British Post office was opened at Amreli in 1863. The mailbags were carried by sturdy runners in laps of seven to eight miles. One relay of runners carried the post from Ahmedabad to Veeramgum and from there to Wadhwan. The other postal route left the railway at Surat. The mail was taken across the Gulf of Cambay by ferry boat, and then relays of runners covered the one hundred and twenty miles to Rajkot in two days if the weather was fair. During the monsoon the mails were expected when they arrived. When the rivers were flooded the mails were carried across the torrent by hardy swimmers with the bags strapped to their shoulders. The railways destroyed the livelihood of these brave *dak* runners and the building of bridges made the

---

[70] *Bombay Gazetteer*, VIII, p. 98; Wilberforce-Bell, *op. cit.*, p. 113.

[71] *Ibid.*, pp. 359, 563; E. Dosabhai, *op. cit.*, p. 273.

[72] *Autobiography*, p. 54.

swimmers unnecessary.[73]   The Bhadar was bridged at Jetpur in 1877, the Keatinge Bridge was built at Wadhwan in 1878, the Peile Bridge over the Bhadar and the Kaiser-i-Hind Bridge at Rajkot in 1879.   The footfalls of the *dak* runners died away as the number of post offices increased.   There were thirty-nine Imperial Post Offices in 1872–1873; they had increased to seventy-eight by 1879–1880.

There were no banks in Kathiawad even in 1884.   There had been a branch of the old Bank of Bombay at Bhavanagar from 1864 till it crashed in the Share Mania in the wake of the failure of Overend, Gurney & Company.   The merchants were able to transfer large sums of money from one town to another because of a class of men known as Angarias who travelled throughout the peninsula and to the mainland making cash transactions possible.   An Angaria party consisted of about fifteen trustworthy armed men, mainly Rajputs, Kolis, and Bhils, under a headman called a *mukadam*.[74]   The railways destroyed the Angaria parties and another colourful body of men were consigned to the limbo of the past.   The function of the Angarias was taken over by the railway police; a small force of seventy-three men was organized early in 1880, the successors of the Arab *sibandis* and Gaekwadi *sowars* of a bygone age.

There were many other groups of men to whom the coming of the railways was no blessing at all.   The Dhoraji-Porbandar line destroyed the occupation of the lumbermen who poled the timber rafts up the Bhadar and its tributaries to Jetpur, Uplets, and Vanthali during the rainy season.   The extension of the railways to Jhalawad stopped the pack-bullocks that came from Mewad, Marwar, and Malwa bringing dyes and going back laden with stone, salt, and grain.   It was easier

---

[73] R. B. Booth, *op. cit.*, p. 43.
[74] *Bombay Gazetteer*, VIII, p. 203.

for the Bania and Bohra merchants to import *sorangi* dyes by rail; the dyers who once bought the *sorangi* from the itinerant traders with their pack-bullocks had to pay a higher price for it. Also badly hit were the cart-men, who came from Gujarat with mangoes and other fruits, and the peddlers carrying groceries, cloth, and vegetables on their backs or on a bullock.[75]

In 1875, Sir Philip Wodehouse, Governor of Bombay, came to Rajkot to open the Alfred High School. This was about the time that Karamchand Gandhi came to Rajkot with his family to serve as a member of the Rajasthanik Court. A Durbar was held at which the young Thakore Saheb of Bhavanagar summed up the changes overtaking Kathiawad in his address of welcome. "Your Excellency," he stated, " the country, as you will yourself see, is in a state of peace; justice is improved, commerce is increasing, factories are rising, roads and bridges are being built, schools are multiplying." There was, however, one significant omission and the Governor made pointed reference to it in his reply: " It is not surprising that you should hesitate to undertake the construction of railways without strong reasons for believing that you will ultimately receive an adequate return for the outlay."[76] The hesitation of the Princes was partly justified because they were discovering a new form of their ancient rivalries in the building of railways. The rulers of the western states like Navanagar rightly feared that the building of railways in the east of the peninsula would ruin the trade of their ports. The fears of the Jam were real. By the 1880's, the fine railway buildings of Sihor stone from the Ranio Hill reflected the prosperity brought to Bhavanagar and Gondal by the steam locomotives, while the rapidly dwindling trade of the western ports proved how right the Jam had been.

---

[75] *Bombay Gazetteer*, VIII, pp. 244, 247, 579.
[76] R. B. Booth, *op. cit.*, pp. 76-78.

The Gandhis of Porbandar

The maritime States like Navanagar and Porbandar could not stay out of the race; they were soon involved in the fierce competition of the Railway Age in Kathiawad.

Gandhi's boyhood fell during this gloomy decade that followed the prosperity of the cotton boom when money was so plentiful that a farmer is said to have plated the spokes of his bullock cart with silver.[77] The tide of sudden prosperity receded with the termination of the American Civil War in 1865, leaving behind the wreckage of British, Parsi, and Hindu business firms and the scandalous collapse of the Bank of Bombay. The pawnbrokers and the money-lenders reaped a harvest of gold and silver jewelry. The stimulus of the cotton trade, however, continued to promote the capitalist enterprise of the commercial classes of Kathiawad; but not on the scale required to solve its economic problems aggravated by rising prices, the pressure of the population on the land, and the dread spectre of famine.

In 1925, Gandhi paid a happy visit to Kathiawad. The gloomy events of the Rajkot Fast, when Kasturba was imprisoned in this town where she had spent so many years of her life, were still in the future. Mahadev Desai told readers of *Young India* briefly about how the now famous son of Kathiawad was feted and honoured.[78] But Gandhi's speeches, interesting for the fragments of reminiscence they contain, are full of awareness of what he called " the ever-deepening poverty of Kathiawad." As he analysed the causes for that poverty, Gandhi voiced the inarticulate feelings of the grooms and syces, camel-drivers and pack-bullock owners, weavers and peasants, village smiths and saddle-makers, lumbermen and boatmen, *mukadams* and *dak* runners, who had all been swept aside ruthlessly by the coming of modern civilization.

---

[77] B. M. Malabari, *op. cit.*, pp. 99-100.
[78] *Young India*, (Feb. 26, 1925), " I Cry to Conquer."

" In my view," he said, " the starting of mills and ginning factories in Kathiawad will not make for the people's prosperity, but will be in the nature of a disaster."[79]

The Birth of a Conservative Radical

The association of the Gandhis with the Ranas of Porbandar must be interpreted in terms of the economic and political consequences. These explain why Gandhi came to demonstrate Lord Acton's dictum that there are few things more powerful than a revolutionary mind in a conservative mould. The Gandhis aimed at both economic and political power when they entered the service of the Jethva ruler. They gained their objective when Gandhi's grandfather became Dewan of Porbandar, but their success was belated; the British were already in the peninsula effecting changes that would strip them of both economic and political status. What they were left with was a tradition of religion and culture which they could put to use by overlaying it with an English education in order to join one or another of the new professions. They clung to the past, disliked the present, and hoped for a better future.

The British discovered, through their trade with Surat from the beginning of the seventeenth century, that, in the words of Linschoten, " The Gujaratis and Banyas are the most subtile merchants in the whole of India."[80]   In 1616, Henry Lord, Preacher to the Honourable Company of Merchants at Surat, newly arrived, was intrigued by the Banias and Parsis. Of the Banias he wrote, " According to the busie observance of travailers, inquiring what novelty the place might produce, a people presented themselves to mine eyes, cloathed in linnen garments, somewhat low descending, of a gesture and garbe,

---

[79] *Ibid.*, (Jan. 8, 1925), " Kathiawad Political Conference ", *passim.*
[80] J. Douglas, *op. cit.*, I, p. 35.

as I may say, maydenly and well nigh effiminate; of a counteanance shy and somewhat estranged, yet smiling out a glosed and bashful familiarity, whose use in the compainies affaires occasioned their presence there. Truth to say, mine eyes, unacquainted with such objects, took up their wonder and gazed, and this admiration, the badge of a fresh travailer, bred in mee the importunity of a question. I asked what manner of people those were, so strangely notable, and notably strange? Reply was made, They were Banians."[81] Many other travellers like Mandelslo and Grose were impressed by their combination of industry and piety. Only Dr. Fryer strikes a discordant note: he calls the Banias the vermin of India, a mass of sordidness, blood suckers, horse leeches, cheats, liars, and dissemblers.[82] The legends relating how both the Chalukyas and the Chudasamas were betrayed to the Muslims by a Bania suggest that the vulgar opinion of the learned doctor was close to that of the common people.

Phillip Anderson described how Gerald Aungier induced the Banias to settle in Bombay through a pact with Neema Parekh, a leading merchant of Diu, promising them liberal treatment and religious toleration. The policy of the British was in such sharp contrast to that of the Portuguese that Parsis and Banias flocked to Bombay and turned a fishing village into a prosperous city.[83] While Gandhi's grandfather was serving Rana Khimaji, many of his Parsi and Bania contemporaries were becoming merchant princes through their commercial enterprise in Bombay and other cities of Western India. The best known among them was Sir Jamsetji Jijibhai (1783–1859) who began with Rs. 120 and ended as

---

[81] P. Anderson, *The English in Western India*, (London, Smith, Elder & Co., 1856), p. 52. The quotation is from Henry Lord's *A Discovery of Two Forreigne Sects in the East Indies*.

[82] J. Douglas, *op. cit.*, I, p. 150.

[83] *Op. cit.*, p. 127.

a millionaire. Two well-known Bombay magnates, Sir Manguldas Nathubhai (1832–1890), a Kapol Bania from Kathiawad, and Gokuldas Tejpal (1832–1868), a Bhatia from Kachh, were contemporaries of Gandhi's father.

The answer to whether or not British rule and modern civilization enriched or impoverished the commercial classes like the Banias depends on certain explicable vagaries. The Gandhis belonged to a part of Kathiawad which was ruined by the cotton trade and the coming of the railways. With the exception of the Laburkua crop grown in a tiny area near Mangrol, the cotton grown in Sorath was of an inferior quality; and even this poor variety was exported mainly from the Junagadh harbours of Verawal and Mangrol rather than the ports of Porbandar. Further, the railways absorbed the greater portion of the export trade of the small western ports and concentrated it at Wadhwan in the north-east and Bhavanagar in the south-east. The growth of a compensatory import trade did not benefit the ports of Porbandar to the same extent as the ports of the more vigorous States of Navanagar and Junagadh. In 1881–1882, the exports of Navibundar amounted to Rs. 39,206 and the imports to Rs. 41,261; in 1882–1883, they had fallen to Rs. 17,409 and Rs. 32,580 respectively. The decline of the Porbandar trade was attributed to the crushing port dues, the great competition from Verawal and Bhavanagar, the absence of good road and rail communications, and the ineptness of the Rana.[84]

The economic backwardness of Porbandar is reflected in the steady impoverishment of the Gandhis, who took to the professions or migrated. Gandhi had two step-sisters, Pankunwarbehn and Mulibehn. Karamchand found employment for Pankunwarbehn's husband, Damji Mehta, and his

---

[84] *Bombay Gazetteer*, VIII, pp. 248-249, 545, 579-580, 618-619; *Imperial Gazetteer*, (1908) " Kathiawar ", p. 180.

two sons, Lakshmidas and Karasandas, as officials in the Porbandar State Service. Mulibehn's descendants migrated to Bombay; her grandson, Maturadas Trikamji, was once Mayor of the City. Lakshmidas's eldest son, Samaldas Gandhi, also migrated to Bombay and became editor of *Vande Mataram*, a Gujarati newspaper.[85] It was the decline of the Porbandar ports which also led the Memon Muslim merchants to migrate to Zanzibar and South Africa making it possible for Gandhi and an impressive number of his close relatives to go to Natal. The Gandhi fortunes were at a low ebb, but they were still not lacking in a spirit of adventure. Like many families in a difficult period of transition their family pride would increase in inverse proportion to their poverty.[86] Respected but poor, friendly with the rich and powerful, but alienated from them, they would naturally develop a contempt for the *nouveau riche* and lean towards radicalism in politics.

For most of the nineteenth century the political loyalty of the Gandhis was directed towards the Princes. A disenchantment with princely rule began in the 1870's when the Gandhis were not averse to working with the British; Karamchand's effectiveness as an assessor of the Rajasthanik Court was followed by his unhappy spell as Dewan of Wankaner. But once again the Gandhis were rather belated; Karamchand's best years were over and he was too much of a dewan in the old style to compete with the new men like Sir T. Madhava Rao or Satyendranath Tagore who became the first Indian Civil Servant in 1863. Another blow to the Gandhis was the forced abdication of Rana Vikmatji in 1886 and the appointment of a British administrator when Gandhi's uncle, Tulasidas, was the Dewan. The confidence that Colonel J. W. Watson

---

[85] P. Gandhi, *op. cit.*, p. 19.
[86] *Collected Works*, I, p. 10. Gandhi regretted the flattery he employed when he approached the Thakore Saheb of Rajkot for financial help in 1888.

showed in Karamchand Gandhi was not extended by the
British to his sons. Frederick Lely, the Administrator of
Porbandar, had no time for the nephew of the man he had
supplanted; Tulasidas described him as a good man but was
too nervous to see him personally on behalf of Mohandas.
E. C. K. Ollivant, Political Agent from 1890–1895, who was
rude to Gandhi, dismissed his plea on behalf of his elder
brother, Lakshmidas, alleging that he was an intriguer.

The poverty of his family drove Gandhi to seek help from
British officials for his education in England when paternalism
was in decline.[87] The young Gandhi's faith in British
benevolence met with disappointment in his brief encounter
with Lely, a tough, efficient and busy Civilian who was
putting Porbandar back on its feet after the long maladminis-
tration of the Rana. Neither Lely nor Charles Ollivant bore
any resemblance to " Huzur Alexander Walker Saheb "
whom Ranchodji Amarji described as " Amir-like." Walker
could find time to exchange courtesies or to relax at a nautch
given by a local notable. The new Civilians had lost the
common touch possessed by an old Company official like
Keatinge who travelled about lying full length in a bullock
cart with his coat off, his shirt sleeves rolled up and a single
sowar for an escort.[88]

This new attitude was reflected in the code of behaviour for
British officials laid down by Sir Richard Temple. " While
cautious not to allow interested persons to make separate or
personal representations to him regarding matters under
investigation," he wrote, " he cannot be too accessible to all

---

[87] E. Thompson and G. T. Garratt, *Rise and Fulfilment of British Rule in India*,
(Macmillan & Co., Ltd., 1934), Book VI, (1859-1885), See " Decline of
Paternalism " and Book VII, See " Bureaucracy in Operation."

[88] R. B. Booth, *op. cit.*, p. 62.

sorts and conditions of Natives "[89]—a curious echo of the Book of Common Prayer. Sir Richard practised what he preached. His tour of Kathiawad in 1876 included a visit to Jetpur and an audience there with eighteen Kathi chiefs. After a good breakfast and a smoke, His Excellency fell sound asleep. The Kathi chiefs arrived, and the Governor slept on as no one dared wake him; the best part of the morning wore away and the descendants of a fearless breed departed tamely after a fruitless wait.[90]

The utter helplessness of the boy at this period was the making of the man. His father, whose companionship had meant so much to him, had died in 1886. Rana Vikmatji had been deposed, his uncle had lost much of his influence, and the whole family was in financial straits. His mother was torn between her ambition for him and her fear of an unknown land and ostracism by their caste. Only Lakshmidas agreed loyally with the wise old Brahman, Mavji Dave, that the times had changed so greatly that the way to retrieve the family fortunes was to send Mohandas to England. The appeal to the British Administration had failed and no help could be expected from his caste. Gandhi had reached the point when there were only two alternatives open to him—to sink to the bottom or win his way to the top, not wholly as a member of a collective, but as an individual in the making, impelling himself upwards through a determination born of his own inner resources.

Gandhi was hardly aware of what his inner resources were

---

[89] *India in* 1880, (London, John Murray, 1881), 2nd ed., p. 47. In some ways the British Officials in the Indian States were more powerful than those in British India. Joseph Chailley in his *Problems of British India*, (London, Macmillan & Co., Ltd., 1910), said, " the attitude of the political officer while ordinarily deferential in form (although even this is sometimes lacking) is the attitude of a servant who directs his nominal master, haughty, polite, impertinent and ironical ", p. 259.

[90] R. B. Booth, *op. cit.*, p. 120.

as he struggled with the problem of his passage to England. How he came to discover that he possessed sources of strength in his religious and cultural heritage is the story of his English and South African years. When Gandhi went to Porbandar to meet his uncle, the old man was setting off on a pilgrimage to Benares; he had no inkling of the very different kind of pilgrimage his young nephew was about to embark on.

The Young Bengal of the 1840's was matched by the Young Bombay of the 1860's. Young Bombay drank less deeply of the heady wine of Western literature, was more sober, more cautious, but was not lacking in courage in its devotion to Social Reform. Gandhi's desire to go to England showed that Young Kathiawad had arrived. It was different in many respects from both Young Bengal and Young Bombay; it was much less cosmopolitan and much more provincial, much less uprooted and much more related to the past. The Western impact did not have the same force; the conservative barrier of numerous semi-independent feudal states made it more diffusive and less corrosive. Nor had the British been in the peninsula for very long compared to other parts of India. Kathiawad was " new ground " in Toynbee's phrase;[91] the very freshness of the British impact contributed to the development of a personality who was strikingly different from the types of leaders who had emerged elsewhere in India. It is probable that no other region could have produced such a forceful blend of conservatism and radicalism.

---

[91] Toynbee points out that Galilee had been conquered for Jewry by the Maccabees rather less than a century before the birth of Jesus. The British had hardly been in Kathiawad for half a century when Gandhi was born. See D. C. Somervell, *The Study of History*, 2 Vols., (New York and London, Oxford University Press, 1956), I, p. 99.

CHAPTER FOUR

Portrait of a Young Indian
as a Late-Victorian

A Young Man at Sea

In June, 1891, *The Vegetarian* published an interesting interview with Gandhi, who had sailed back to India earlier that month, in which he explained why he had gone to England as a student. He stated frankly that it was due to ambition, the desire for status, and the hope of improving his economic position by joining a lucrative profession.[1] He had thought highly of the legal profession, though his uncle had ranted against the "big lawyers" and their Anglicised ways. Though he does not say so, there was also an element of *mimesis* in the desire he expressed "to see England, the land of philosophers and poets, the very centre of civilization."[2]

While, as Gandhi himself has indicated, there were economic and sociological reasons compelling him to go to England, his overmastering desire to do so can also be studied as due to what Erik H. Erikson has called an "identity crisis."[3] His decision to go abroad was the result of an inner turmoil which

---

[1] "Why He Went to England?" *Collected Works*, I, pp. 53-63.
[2] *Ibid.*, p. 54.
[3] E. H. Erikson, *Young Man Luther*: *A Study in Psychoanalysis and History*, (New York, W. W. Norton & Co., Inc., 1958), pp. 14-15.

he described as a fire burning within him.[4] Precocity in Indian children is not unusual since there is no nursery, actual or symbolical, in a joint family; from birth the child belongs to the little society of the family and has varying degrees of intimacy with a number of persons, both young and old. The child soon becomes a little man or woman but no real adulthood is conferred; the sense of responsibility is left undeveloped by withholding the right of making decisions. Gandhi was hardly aware of the plans for his marriage.

The result of such an upbringing is usually some form of a " delayed identity crisis." Suicide is sometimes the only way out for young Indians who feel they are adult but are not allowed to exercise freedom of choice because of conflicts with the traditional pattern of life. The stealing-in-order-to-smoke episode in Gandhi's boyhood was a form of protest. " Our want of independence began to smart. It was unbearable that we should be unable to do anything without the elders' permission. At last, in sheer disgust, we decided to commit suicide! "[5] An older Gandhi was a bit amused by the boy Gandhi who had toyed with the idea of suicide in the Kedarji Mandir, and had rejected it by the time he and his friend reached the Ramji Mandir; but it reveals that an inner conflict was latent in him from his early teens. The boy who played with the idea of self-destruction would show an interest in the high incidence of suicide among the indentured Indians in Natal.

From where did Gandhi get his unusually sensitive conscience? How is it that he was the only one in a class of boys who refused to cheat when encouraged by the teacher to correct a misspelled word during an annual inspection? It could have been due to the fact that there was a difference of forty years between him and his father. As B. R. Nanda

---

[4] *Collected Works*, I, p. 54.

[5] *Autobiography*, p. 39.

148

points out, Gandhi's father was in some ways more an object of reverence than a companion to the boy who did nightly obeisance to him.[6] The care bestowed on the ailing father closely parallels the daily attention Vallabhacharis give to the image of *Thakorji* in their *havelis*; the sickroom had become rather like a shrine.[7] If to displease such a parent seemed like displeasing God, it would explain how the boy's precocity took the form of an early concern with ethical problems. Further, the overly obedient and undefiant child would find compensation by leading campaigns of civil disobedience and defying a mighty Empire through a relationship to God stressing obedience to the inner voice and truthfulness.[8] The sickroom had also served as a confessional. However, Gandhi usually also told his mother his sins before he went to his father to ease his guilty conscience. The grown man never hesitated to confess his failures to his Mother-country because he could find consolation and forgiveness from his Father-god. A man's deepest religious understanding is often rooted in his deepest human relationships.

After his father's death Gandhi began " incessantly brooding over these things "—things like the difficulty of getting a good job, the lack of influence, the lack of money. The inner conflict was so acute that it expressed itself in physical symptoms; he suffered from constant headaches and nose-bleeding.[9] These ailments were not unconnected with his growing desire to find a way out, even a kind of escape, by going to England; he described it as " a secret design " in his mind. One way of breaching the barriers of orthodoxy was to say that it was necessary to go abroad for the sake of one's health; it is not

---

[6] *Op. cit.*, p. 20.

[7] Thoothi, *op. cit.*, see pp. 342-350, for an account of the daily washing, dressing and feeding of *Thakorji* by the Vallabhacharya priests.

[8] He was not always in agreement with his father though he usually obeyed, *The Indian States' Problem*, p. 21.

[9] *Collected Works*, I, p. 54.

surprising that Gandhi's physical disorders were attributed to a hot climate. Once Gandhi had decided in April 1888, that he must go to England, his persistence and determination were astonishing. His mother's fears, his father-in-law's nightly arguments, his wife's tears, his brother's vacillating moods, the indifference or malice of jealous relatives, the opposition of his caste—nothing could stop him. So great was his eagerness to depart that he says, " Sleeping, waking, drinking, eating, walking, running, reading, I was dreaming and thinking of England and what I would do on that momentous day."[10]

On September 4, 1888, the young Gandhi stood at the rails of the steamer *Clyde* watching the shoreline of Bombay fade as evening turned to night. He was haunted by the tearful face of his mother, the sobbing of his wife. Looking back on it all soon after he reached London he confided to his diary " . . . I must write that had it been some other man in the same position which I was in, I dare say he would not have been able to see England. The difficulties which I had to withstand have made England dearer to me."[11]

It is a pity that the diary Gandhi kept in England was lost and that only the twenty pages copied out by Chhaganlal have survived; it shows that the youth was as frank and as subjective as the man. This fragment also shows that the young Gandhi was by no means an uninteresting person; the older Gandhi tended to exaggerate the shyness and timidity of the youthful Mohandas. At nineteen, Gandhi was a popular young man with that capacity for making friends which characterized him all his life. He lists the names of eighteen out of a crowd of fifty relatives and friends who assembled in the Gandhi home in Rajkot on the eve of his

---

[10] *Collected Works*, I, p. 57.
[11] *Ibid.*, p. 12.

departure. He was met by other friends at Gondal, Jetpur, Wadhwan, and Dhola; his brother, Lakshmidas, and his bosom friend, Sheikh Mehtab, accompanied him to Bombay. More than a dozen others boarded the *Clyde* to bid him farewell. He was already something of a leader and his shyness on the ship and in England were largely due to the difficulty of adjusting to another culture and society.

The seven weeks Gandhi spent on board the *Clyde* before he landed at Tilbury, on October 28th, were a kind of unplanned and haphazard " orientation course " which gave him a foretaste of life in England. Like any normal youngster of that age, Gandhi was curious and interested by all he saw and heard as the *Clyde* called at Aden, Port Said, Brindisi, Valetta,[12] and Gibraltar.

A prophet usually seems sombre and unappreciative of nature in his old age; if he is of the ascetic type he will seem to have renounced the appreciation of natural beauty. But in his youth even Jeremiah could see beauty in an almond tree, and the young Gandhi was responsive to the changing glories of sea and sky. " On one moonlight night I was watching the sea. I could see the moon reflected in the water. On account of the waves, the moon appeared as if she were moving here and there. One dark night when the sky was clear the stars were reflected in the water. The scene around us was very beautiful at that time."[13] The stars reminded him of diamonds, of fireworks that had thrilled him in Rajkot, as he watched them dance on the sea for several nights. What happened to that lad breathing in the salt air and communing with the mystery of the starry heavens? It was this question which underlay the controversy between Tagore and Gandhi; the poet was appalled by the

---

[12] Indian troops were stationed in Malta in 1878 as a result of the Treaty of San Stephano.
[13] *Collected Works*, I, p. 13.

elemental crudity of the prophet. Romain Rolland, in a stimulating discussion of the correspondence which passed between Gandhi and Tagore, awarded the palm to the prophet; a poet was too much of a luxury in poverty-stricken India.

The young student stirring his cup of cocoa in his cheap London room had no time to look out of the window at the moon. In South Africa the moon looked cold and chill like the staring, hostile white faces in the street. In India it was always a dark night of sighing, groaning poverty. But the twinkle of the stars could break out of his eyes sometimes; and there could be a look on his face like the upturned, delighted look on the face of the boy watching fireworks in Rajkot.[14]

The *Clyde* reached Plymouth late at night. Gandhi was eager to get a first glimpse of England but could see no lights because of a dense fog. " Really I was very anxious to see it but could not."[15] The England Gandhi reached in 1888 was really not very easy to see or understand. C. F. Andrews probably overstated the case when he claimed that " those years in England were among the most eventful in his whole life."[16] South Africa was still in the offing. But Late-Victorian England did leave its mark on Gandhi; the process began from the moment he set foot in the Victoria Hotel. " I was quite dazzled by the splendour of the hotel. I had never in my life seen such a pomp."[17]

Gandhi would see many forms of Victorian pomp in a London that had just celebrated the first Jubilee of the Queen. Despite contemporary pessimism, England was both rich and powerful; Gandhi may have passed the new buildings of the

---

14 Fireworks were frequently mentioned in his article entitled " Some Indian Festivals " in *The Vegetarian*. *Collected Works*, I, pp. 37, 40, 41.
15 *Collected Works*, I, p. 20.
16 *Mahatma Gandhi's Ideas*, p. 17.
17 *Collected Works*, I, p. 21.

Midland Bank and the London offices of Lloyds. It was an age of high finance portending the rise of the famous Big Five Banks. The name of the ship which brought Gandhi to England was the *Clyde*; it commemorated a shipyard that was helping Britain to maintain her position as the proud mistress of the seas. By the turn of the century England owned five-eighths of the world's shipping.

London seemed a blaze of lights to the youth accustomed to the dimly-lit lanes of Rajkot. After Gandhi's eyes had got used to the lights in Regent Street and Oxford Street,[18] where Hutton and Bagehot had wandered together, he discovered that others beside himself were noting the squalor and misery hidden behind the dazzling facade of pomp and circumstance. The poverty of London's poor was ghastly; panaceas for the removal of their misery poured out in books and two-penny pamphlets.

" *The Condition of England* " so Gandhi entitled Chapter V of *Hind Swaraj*. " The Condition of England " had been ventilated by Carlyle, appalled by the ugliness of the new industrial civilization, in *Past and Present*; Gandhi, influenced by Ruskin and Tolstoy, superimposed the borrowed phrase on his own impressions and images of England in the eighties. If the *joshi*, the family astrologer,[19] could have properly forecast the child's future in twenty years, he would have been struck by the fact that Mohandas was destined to go to an England eminently suitable for creating a ferment in one whom history would mould into a revolutionary figure. The eighteen-eighties have been described as the epilogue of one era and the prelude to another, a phantasmagoric period

---

[18] *Collected Works*, I, p. 40.
[19] Gandhi told his first biographer, Joseph J. Doke, that the family astrologer cast his horoscope and helped to choose his name, *M. K. Gandhi: An Indian Patriot in South Africa*, (London, The London Indian Chronicle, 1909), p. 18.

in the waning light of late afternoon.[20]   The dark shadow of
the eighties never lifted in the mind of Gandhi: *Hind Swaraj*
shows that it coloured his attitude to modern civilization.

The England to which Gandhi came had been dominated
by the alternating leadership of Gladstone and Disraeli from
1868 to 1885.   Though a realignment of parties was taking
place, the echoes of that " personal duel on a grand scale "[21]
had not yet died away.   In 1886, Gladstone's Irish Home
Rule Bill had split the country and alienated a section of the
Liberals led by the Birmingham Radical, Joseph Chamberlain.
Lord Salisbury's Ministry was in power throughout Gandhi's
stay in London; his domestic policies seemed like concessions
to Lord Randolph Churchill's Tory Democracy on the one
hand, and Joseph Chamberlain's Municipal Socialism on the
other.   In foreign affairs his suave diplomacy paid golden
dividends in Africa; the town of Salisbury in Southern
Rhodesia was deservedly named after him.

Gandhi came to a London where the spirit of Chartism
seemed to have revived; Trafalgar Square had become the
rallying point of organized discontent.   London was suffering
from a " local Malthusian tension; "[22] the experience of
Midland and Northern towns was repeated through the
influx of large numbers of rural labourers due to a depression
in agriculture.   The situation helped to focus attention on
the condition of both rural labour and the London poor.
Improvement set in after 1885 when, thanks partly to the
agitation led by Joseph Arch, a section of rural labour had
been enfranchised; the example of Birmingham and the
activities of Socialists and Trade Unionists led to the establish-

---

20 G. M. Young, *Victorian England*: *Portrait of An Age*, (London, Oxford
   University Press, 1953), pp. 112, 148.
21 Winston S. Churchill, *The Great Democracies*, (Vol. IV of A History of the
   English Speaking Peoples), (New York, Dodd Mead & Co., 1958), p. 283.
22 Young, *op. cit.*, p. 159.

ment of the new London County Council. The revived spirit of London was symbolised by the popularity of John Burns of Battersea, the labour leader.

The distress and the agitation rather than the signs of change would naturally be more visible to the young Gandhi who saw the terrible winters of 1889 and 1890 and the London Dock Strike. As Gandhi tramped " the miles of suburban villa and wastes of urban slum "[23] (partly for exercise and partly to save cab fares), as he passed " the drink-steeped liquor shops, the foul and degraded lodgings "[24] in search of a cheaper place to live, he would become aware of the East End described by Engels in 1885 as " an ever spreading pool of stagnant misery and desolation."[25] Gandhi admired a student he knew who lived even more cheaply than he did by taking rooms in the heart of the East End. Before leaving England in 1891, Gandhi, thinking of class differences in London, wrote, " Death would soon be knocking at the door of a delicately nurtured lord trying to imitate an East End labourer."[26]

The boy, Mohandas, had vaguely sensed injustice in the attitude of others to his outcaste playmate. The young Gandhi's perception of the inequality of man would be heightened by years spent in London, where concern for the poor was passing from sentimentality into an age of statistics and scientific study accompanied by political agitation. Engels' *Condition of the Working Class* appeared in 1845. Henry Mayhew had launched a campaign against the evils of sweatshop labour rampant among the East End tailors; he published

---

[23] *Ibid.*, p. 145.
[24] William Morris, quoted in J. W. MacKail, *The Life of William Morris*, 2 Vols., (1899), Vol. II, p. 21, (Cited by Crane Brinton, *English Political Thought in the Nineteenth Century*, London, Ernest Benn Ltd., 1954, p. 261.)
[25] G. M. Trevelyan, *British History in the Nineteenth Century and After*, (London, Longmans, Green & Co., 1956), p. 399.
[26] *Collected Works*, I, p. 36.

his *London Labour and London Poor* in 1851. Henry Fawcett's optimism in 1865 in his *Economic Position of the British Labourer* was offset by Karl Marx's first volume of *Das Kapital* in 1867. In the eighties the problem of pauperism found a keen student in Charles Booth; his social concern was shared by his cousin, Beatrice Potter, who married Sidney Webb in 1893. Both began an inquiry in 1887 that would continue for sixteen years; a part of his great work appeared in his *Life and Labour of the People of London* in 1889.

It is significant that Gandhi was in Britain at a time when Socialism and the "new Trade Unionism," two forces that led to the formation of the Labour Party, were taking effective root in that country. So little of Robert Owen's doctrines had survived that Morley could say, in 1881, that in no other country had there been such a lack of interest in Socialism as in England.[27] Not long afterwards a British politician would startle the House of Commons by saying, "We are all socialists now." British Socialism of the eighteen-eighties was inspired by mid-century continental socialists, Henry George and Karl Marx. William Morris was an admirer of Fourier and Proudhon, while H. M. Hyndman popularised Marx, much to the annoyance of Marx himself who could not bear the reincarnation of his ideas in his top-hatted, frock-coated disciple. Henry George, who had seen misery in the streets of Calcutta, published his *Progress and Poverty* in 1879; his best-seller enjoyed a vogue in an England interested in "three acres and a cow" as a possible solution to the problem of the landless labourer.[28]

Among those attracted by the Democratic Federation formed by Hyndman in 1881 was the writer, Edward

---

27 D. C. Somervell, *English Thought in the Nineteenth Century*, (London, Methuen & Co., Ltd., 1957), p. 197.
28 Robert L. Heilbroner, *The Worldly Philosophers*, (New York, Simon and Schuster, 1953), pp. 175-182.

Carpenter, whom Gandhi would read in South Africa. In 1884, the newly-named Social Democratic Federation was split by a schism; William Morris and about half the membership broke away to form the Socialist League. The splinter group was itself splintered in 1889 by an anarchist faction and disappeared into oblivion. The S. D. F. continued to be influential till 1893 when it was overshadowed by the Independent Labour Party led by Keir Hardie. A significant parallel development, which also began in 1884, was the Fabian Society. The germinal *Fabian Essays* appeared in 1888; Gandhi met one of its contributors, Annie Besant, in London in 1889, and another, George Bernard Shaw, in 1931.

In his *Autobiography* Gandhi reveals an interest in the " new Trade Unionism " rather than in the formal socialistic ideas of the period. " The dock labourers' strike," he writes, " had come to an early termination owing to the efforts of John Burns and Cardinal Manning."[29] An older Gandhi was more interested in the " early termination " of the settlement rather than the promotion of industrial disputes.[30] But is this really what the young Gandhi felt when the dock workers walked out in the summer heat of August, 1889? What did he really feel as the strike spread from Tilbury to London, as John Burns maintained the morale of the ragged strikers by his fiery speeches to them on Tower Hill before their daily procession through the City and West End? Did the doughty leader's reference to India strike any sort of a chord within him? " This, lads," said John Burns, " is the Lucknow of Labour, and I myself, looking to the horizon can see a silver gleam—not of bayonets to be imbrued in a brother's blood, but the gleam of the full round orb of the

---

[29] *Autobiography*, p. 99.
[30] See, for example, his article entitled " Strikes " in *Young India*, February 16, 1921.

dockers' tanner."[31] To try to find the young Gandhi it is
necessary to dig below the surface of the older Mahatma's
accumulated years and experience.

The fact that it was Gandhi who interested Narayan
Hemachandra in Cardinal Manning's role in the Dock
Strike is in keeping with the bent of his mind at this time.
The image of the humanitarian religious leader appealed to
him more than that of John Burns, the rough Trade Unionist,
capable of using violent and profane language. It was Miss
Manning of the National Indian Association who introduced
a Gandhi, tongue-tied from shyness, to the older man, Hemachandra, scarcely tongue-tied in spite of his lack of English.
The name of this good lady may have prompted the conversation that led to Hemachandra's suggestion that they should
call on the Cardinal whose " name was then on every lip."
Cardinal Manning was living in great simplicity in a roomy
but barrack-like mansion in Carlisle Place, Vauxhall Bridge
Road. " As soon as we were seated, a thin, tall old gentleman made his appearance and shook hands with us." The
thinness was due to the Cardinal's vigorous asceticism. A
great deal of history looked out of his penetrating grey eyes
set in a face with a high and expansive forehead.

Manning was born in 1808, a year after Walker entered
Kathiawad. He had studied at Oxford with Pusey, Gladstone, and Newman. In 1850, he had protested against the
Privy Council's decision in favour of George Cornelius Gorham.
Among his varied social interests was the problem of child
marriage in India in which B. M. Malabari had interested
him. For a few fleeting moments of history the lives of
two great religious leaders touched and parted. The young
Indian would have to pass through many a fiery ordeal before
he emerged with a saintliness wedded to social service akin

---

[31] Churchill, *op. cit.*, p. 365.

A Young Indian as a Late-Victorian

In *Hind Swaraj*, Gandhi reflected the pessimism of the decade when he wrote, " Several English writers refuse to call that ' civilization ' which passes under that name. Many books have been written upon that subject. Societies have been formed to cure the nation of the evils of civilization."[36] He was forty when he wrote those sentences, but he had lived in London when George Bernard Shaw said, " That our own civilization is already in an advanced stage of rottenness may be taken as statistically proved."[37] It was a time when William Morris could say, " the leading passion of my life has been its hatred of modern civilization."[38] Morris, whose works Gandhi would read in Pretoria, was among the writers who would lead the Mahatma to change his earlier attitude; for those were not the views of the young Gandhi who described London in 1891 as " the very centre of civilization." It was the brutal experience of South Africa that drove him to a reassessment of his student days; it was the cruel episode of colour prejudice that made him one with other nineteenth-century figures in Europe, Russia, and America who abominated modern civilization, symbolised by what they considered an all-consuming monster—the machine—which destroyed the souls of men, making them cruel and predatory.

Recessional

When Gandhi was trying to describe the *Diwali* festival for readers of *The Vegetarian*, he was reminded of the illuminations in that landmark of Victorian London—the Crystal Palace.[39] It was here that Disraeli made his famous speech in 1872, when Gandhi was a child of three. It marked the new

---

[36] *Op. cit.*, p. 24.
[37] John Bowle, *Politics and Opinion in the 19th Century*, (New York, Oxford University Press, 1954), p. 418.
[38] *Ibid.*, p. 427.
[39] " Some Indian Festivals," *Collected Works*, I, p. 40.

11

feeling of Imperial pride in a generation enfranchised by the Reform Act of 1867. Gandhi came to an England full of proud, Imperial enthusiasm which continued unabated till after the First World War. Gladstone was still admired but no longer followed; what the young Indian student was impressed by were his powers of oratory and the felicity of his domestic life.[40] Gandhi wrote a great deal more about Salisbury, whose directness and candour appealed to him.[41] But in later years Gandhi, in his approach to the British, would appeal to the moral tradition of Gladstone in politics.

Queen Victoria became Empress of India when Gandhi was eight; he would remember her first Jubilee more clearly since he was then a schoolboy in the Alfred High School. Something of the fascination the Queen had for the British people was felt in India. In 1875, Sir Mancherjee Bhownagree published his Gujarati translation of the Queen's *Leaves from the Journal of Our Life in the Highlands*. She was extolled in Sanskrit when Vidya-Bhaskar Pandit Lalchandra published a collection of poems entitled *Jubilee Paramodika* in 1889.[42] Gandhi was in Rajkot in 1896 when preparations for Victoria's Diamond Jubilee had begun. He served on the Celebrations Committee;[43] was indignant when he found a lot of insincerity in some of the members; carefully tended the tree he planted to celebrate the forthcoming event; and taught his children the British National Anthem. Today a younger generation of Indians have very little idea of how regretfully Gandhi withdrew his loyalty to the Crown and how long he took to come to the conclusion that he must

---

40 " Some Indian Festivals," *Collected Works*, I, p. 67; *Autobiography*, p. 252.

41 " Lord Salisbury," *Collected Works*, III, pp. 427-429, Gandhi's obituary on him in *Indian Opinion*.

42 V. P. Lalchandra, *Jubilee Paramodika*, (Ajmere, Friend of Rajputana Press, 1889).

43 *Autobiography*, p. 212.

become a rebel. " Hardly ever have I known anybody to cherish such loyalty as I did to the British Constitution,"[44] are his own words. The first four volumes of his *Collected Works* fully bear out this claim.

By the 1880's, *The Microcosm of London*,[45] depicted by T. Rowlandson and A. C. Pugin, had turned into the macrocosm of Empire. A motley crowd of nationalists and revolutionaries attracted by the steadily growing freedom of British society and what Gandhi later called " the free atmosphere of the great metropolis "[46] were making London the Mecca of political refugees.

It was the Irish discontent that could be most loudly and clearly heard when Gandhi was a law student. During the three years Gandhi was in London, Parnell occupied the forefront of the stage of British politics; when he arrived in September, 1888, the allegations made earlier by *The Times* in a series of articles entitled " Parnellism and Crime " were being examined by a special commission of three judges. Despite Parnell's recent defection to the Conservatives, the hopes of his Liberal supporters revived when he was exonerated in February, 1889; the popularity of the Irish leader would be an asset to Gladstone in the forthcoming General Election. These Liberal expectations were doomed in November, 1890, however, when the suit of O'Shea and Parnell opened in the Divorce Court.[47] The young Gandhi missed the drama of the event; he was busy dabbling in Theosophy at the time. When he returned to London in

---

[44] For Gandhi's deep appreciation of Queen Victoria, see *Collected Works*, IV, pp. 449-450.

[45] T. Rowlandson and A. C. Pugin, *The Microcosm of London*, (London and New York, The King Penguin Books, 1947).

[46] *Collected Works*, III, p. 375.

[47] R. Barry O'Brien, *The Life of Charles Stewart Parnell*, 2 Vols., (New York, Harper & Brothers, 1898). Robert Rhodes James, " Charles Stewart Parnell," *History Today*, January, 1957.

1909, he would be reminded of Parnell and Irish affairs as he discovered that Indian nationalism was passing through an Irish phase; other Indians, who had not missed the significance of the Irish struggle, were busy applying its lessons to India.

One of the four letters of introduction Gandhi carried with him to London was addressed to Dadhabhai Naoroji. Though he attended several meetings addressed by the veteran Indian leader, he found courage to hand over the letter only towards the end of his stay as he was worried about his prospects in India. Dadhabhai, with his white beard, was an impressive figure. Gandhi felt he was obtaining *darshan* when he was in his presence; he missed much of the political significance of what this magnificent old Parsi was doing in England at the time—but not completely. He was the first Indian leader to whom Gandhi appealed as he launched the struggle over the Indian Franchise in Natal; he knew that Dadhabhai was the spokesman of Indian aspirations in Britain.

The foundations of the Indian agitation in Britain were laid by sympathetic Members of Parliament among whom are listed the illustrious names of Edmund Burke and John Bright. The approaching debates on the renewal of the Charter of the East India Company inspired John Dickinson to form the India Reform Society in 1853. Dickinson supplied John Bright with material for his great speeches on India which had a decisive effect on Canning's policies after the Mutiny. These speeches influenced the nature of the Queen's Proclamation of 1858, which Gandhi would constantly refer to in South Africa. In 1883, John Bright gave his approval to the formation of an informal Parliamentary committee for co-ordinating action on Indian affairs; he acted as chairman of its small executive. Backed by this Indian Committee, John Slagg, the Senior Member for Manchester, moved for a full inquiry into the Indian administration. Lord Randolph Churchill, then at the India Office, agreed to the proposal. Slagg's motion was swept aside by the general election which brought Salisbury to power in 1886. While Gandhi was in London, Salisbury's Ministry was acting as a damper where Parliamentary endeavours on India's behalf were concerned. The idea of an Indian Parliamentary Committee was revived during the short-lived Liberal Ministry of 1892; it finally came into existence on July 27, 1893, through the efforts of Sir William Wedderburn. The Working Committee included the first Indian Member of Parliament—Dadhabhai Naoroji.

When Gandhi reached London in 1888, the Congress Agency's office, located at 25 Craven Street in the Strand, was churning out printed speeches and pamphlets by the thousands. The expenditure for the first seven months amounted to £1700 and the pressing need was for more funds. Both Hume and Dadhabhai were incredibly energetic for men of their age; the former shuttled back and forth between India and England while the latter held the Congress fort in the Strand.

All these activities found a focus in the effort to elect Dadhabhai to the House of Commons in the General Election of 1892. The idea of electing an Indian to Parliament was suggested to Hume by R. T. Reid in 1885, but the lesson of Irish tactics in the House was there to inspire Indians with the idea. The campaign to elect Dadhabhai from Finsbury gathered momentum in 1890, the year in which Gandhi began attending his meetings. In February, 1890, the British Committee launched a journal called *India*; it appeared at irregular intervals till it became a monthly in 1892; it was a weekly from 1898 till its demise in 1921. Bradlaugh returned from India in February, 1890, to spark further interest in Indian problems after having attended the Congress Session in Bombay the previous December. February saw an article by Bradlaugh on the Indian Congress in the *New Review* and an interview with him in the *Scottish Leader*; it also saw an article in the *Fortnightly Review* by an irate Kipling who vented his spleen on British and Indians alike. In March,

1890, Sir Charles Dilke's *Problems of Greater Britain* was commended by *India* for its fair and impartial treatment of British India.

The Indian appeal to Finsbury intensified in April. On Monday, April 14, a great meeting was held in Forester's Hall in Clerkenwell Road, addressed by Surendranath Bannerjee and Dadhabhai; Sir William Wedderburn was in the chair. Unfortunately, W. S. B. McLaren, John Bright's nephew, could not be present, but the Anti-Corn Law League atmosphere must have pleased old Hume when he read the account of the meeting in the pages of *India*; he was back in England, but in mourning for his wife. Four days later another meeting was held at Kensington in Horn's Assembly Rooms. *India* reported that though " the night was stormy, a cold north-easter blowing and rain falling," those who attended it were not disappointed because of " Mr. Surendranath Bannerjee's exciting and enthralling oratory."[48] Two years later the friends and supporters of India felt gratified when the voters of Finsbury, despite Salisbury's appeal that they should not vote for " a black man," sent Dadhabhai to the House of Commons. In 1895, the Conservatives made amends for Salisbury's rudeness by putting up Sir Mancherji Bhownagree as their candidate for North East Bethnal Green; he retained his seat for ten years and proved very useful to the Indians in South Africa.

The 1880's had their politically conscious students also, like the one who wrote a letter to the Editor of *India* in April, 1890, assuring him that Indian students in Britain while " busy with their professional studies " are " in their hearts not forgetful of their native land."[49] At Surendranath Bannerjee's meeting on April 22, 1890, in Plymouth, the

---

[48] *India*, April 25, 1890.
[49] *India*, April 11, 1890.

other speaker was a young Muslim student, Syed Ali Imam. Gandhi was obviously on the fringe of these political activities; he was busy till June, 1890, studying for the London Matriculation which he had failed the previous December, and had found an outlet for his energies in vegetarian activities. In the year that Syed Ali Imam went to Plymouth to address a political meeting, Gandhi went to Portsmouth to attend the International Vegetarian Conference.

Gandhi was not forgetful of his native land though, and gathered much that was useful when he got to South Africa. In 1894, he organized the Natal Indian Congress and in 1898 he was the "Johannesburg Correspondent" of *India*,[50] the journal that had mirrored so much of the Indian effort to enlist the sympathy of the British public during his student days. In 1921, he defended the decision of the Congress to abolish both the British Committee and *India*; he preferred that the £ 45,000 sent annually to London since Hume's day should be spent on spinning wheels or primary schools.[51]

It is an interesting coincidence that the Kimberley diamond field was discovered about the time Gandhi was born; the curtain had begun to lift on the drama of the conflict between Briton and Boer which in turn would lead to the partition of Africa among the European powers.

During Lord Salisbury's second Ministry from 1886 to 1892 Africa was successfully divided up by the European powers through a series of diplomatic manoeuvres which prevented any resort to arms. In 1891, Salisbury talked about what was happening in his usual sardonic fashion. A month before Gandhi returned to India, Salisbury told a Glasgow audience, " When I left the Foreign Office in 1880 nobody thought about Africa. When I returned to it in

---

[50] *Collected Works*, III, p. 17, fn. 1.
[51] " India and The British Committee," *Young India*, January 19, 1921. See also " Foreign Propaganda," *Young India*, March 9, 1922.

1885, the nations of Europe were almost quarrelling with each other as to the various portions of Africa they could obtain. I do not exactly know the cause of this sudden revolution."[52] If he really did not, it was a highly profitable species of ignorance for all concerned; Britain, France, Germany, Belgium, and Portugal sliced up most of Africa between them.

When Rhodes died in 1902, Gandhi was moved by the passing of a man who was considered a colossus in Africa; the young Indian lawyer had not yet lost his faith in the British Empire and its builders.[53] But Gandhi was singularly uninterested in international affairs as a student; something of the long isolation of Kathiawad clung to him all his life. In his later years he was usually content to leave the steering of the Congress Party in foreign affairs to Nehru; he was humble enough to allow others to fill in the gaps in his knowledge and experience. He was, therefore, probably unaware of the smell of gun powder that hung threateningly in the air during the last two decades of the nineteenth century until the shock of the Boer War. Even while Britain was acquiring an area more than fifty times as large as herself, punctuated by moments of national rejoicing presided over by the dauntless spirit of an adored Queen, some men there were capable of seeing ominous signs and portents of impending struggles on a massive scale. As the fate of the Boers of the Transvaal hung in the balance, some consciences, including that of J. A. Hobson, were stirred.

The young Gandhi could not know that he was destined to play a prominent part in bringing about a recession of imperial power. But in curious fashion some would find his image mirrored in the imagery of Kipling, the imperialist poet. Despite his English education in India and England,

---

[52] Keith Hutchison, *op. cit.*, p. 28.
[53] *Collected Works*, III, pp. 236-237.

A Young Indian as a Late-Victorian

Gandhi retained that essential seriousness and integrity which Kipling missed in "muddied oafs and flanneled fools;" he had hardly anything in common with the cricket enthusiasts of Rajkot. On the other hand, he was no other-worldly dreamer like the gentle but ineffective Lama in *Kim*, though Joseph Doke compared him to another of Kipling's characters, "Purun Dass."[54]   Richard B. Gregg and S. K. George saw in Gandhi the type of personality Kipling depicted in *If*; there are elements of truth in this perception of Gandhi's character in that well-known poem.[55]   The gentle Mahatma looked like one of Kipling's "two strong men," standing face to face with the West, and challenging it to shed its imperialism and racial superiority in order to merge itself in a wider humanity.

Playing the English Gentleman

Every Indian who goes to the West shares to some extent in the experiences of the young Gandhi. Though conditions have changed greatly, the problems of Indian students overseas are not completely different from those he encountered during his three years in London.[56]   Each Indian who goes abroad involves himself in an inter-cultural experiment; the development of the social sciences and various branches of psychology now give us many insights into the nature of this experience.[57]

---

[54] *Speeches*, Appendix I, p. 3.

[55] *Op. cit.*, p. 14.

[56] When Gandhi was in England in 1931 an Indian student asked him, "Why are you so uncharitable to those who drink?" R. K. Prabhu, *This Was Bapu*, (Ahmedabad, Navajivan Publishing House, 1945), p. 5. For studies of students abroad see Richard D. Lambert and Marvin Bessler, *Indian Students On An American Campus*, (Minneapolis, University of Minnesota Press, 1956), and Cora DuBois, *Foreign Students and Higher Education In The United States*, (Washington, American Council On Education, 1956).

[57] See Report No. 41, *Working Abroad: A Discussion of Psychological Attitudes and Adaptations in New Situations*, (New York, Group for the Advancement of Psychiatry, 1958).

The word " shock " was frequently used by Gandhi during his first forty years, and, quite often, he used it in an unconscious psychiatric sense. The Mahatma had become largely immune to shocks; he delighted in shocking others, sometimes with dead earnestness, at other times with an impish chuckle and a twinkle in his eye. It could be argued that Gandhi was shocked into becoming the Mahatma. The shocks of his boyhood, like his early marriage and his father's death, were cushioned by the traditional pattern of Kathiawadi culture which was still strong though showing signs of disintegration. The young Gandhi who went aboard the *Clyde* began to receive what is called a " culture shock,"[58] it was as if he had been thrown into the Arabian Sea before he had learned to swim. Gandhi, like the little boys he watched at Aden, would prove a good swimmer in the cross-cultural currents of his age. Bishop Fisher described the Mahatma as " what the Scotch call canny—wise in the psychology of peoples."[59]

Gandhi's frequent references to his early shyness needs some analysis. Why was the Mahatma, who lived so much in the public eye, the shy creature he was in London? A psychiatrist may trace his boyhood shyness to persistent constipation and other childhood experiences inducing a feeling of inner insecurity.[60] But his shyness on board the *Clyde* was partly the diffidence of any traveller beginning an exploration of another culture. Like Gandhi, thousands would remember the first impact of the strange atmosphere of a ship's dining saloon and the supercilious-looking waiters

[58] See " Symposium No. 7," *Application of Psychiatric Insights to Cross-cultural Communication*, (New York, Group for the Advancement of Psychiatry, 1961).
[59] *Op. cit.*, p. 2. Incidentally, Gandhi could swim and enjoyed showing that he was still quite good at it in his fifties. See *Reminiscences of Gandhiji*, pp. 99-100.
[60] For Gandhi's admission that he suffered from constipation as a man, see *Collected Works*, III, p. 259, and *Autobiography*, p. 329.

170

of whom one hesitated to ask about the food till one learned
the art of judicious tipping—even if they did not react by
spending two days in the cabin eating sweetmeats and fruits
brought from home. The early rising in order to get to the
bathroom also has a familiar ring about it; Gandhi expressed
his surprise over " the arrangement of the English water
closets " and noted the strange Western habit of using toilet
paper.[61] The youth whose previous experiences of European
society was limited to asking a favour of two British officials,
Lely and Watson, kept away from his fellow passengers for a
few days. But there are few things more interesting than
one's first long sea voyage and Gandhi was soon enjoying
himself. The sense of shock, however, returned with redoubled
force when he left the small and tolerably friendly, though
strange, world of the ship for the bewildering impersonal
world of London. " Everything was strange—the people,
their ways, and even their dwellings."[62]

When Gandhi moved from the Victoria Hotel into lodgings,
loneliness closed on him in that terrifying way which it can
in big cities. He was uneasy and unhappy with no one to
share his misery. With nothing in particular to do all day,
he was sleepless at nights. Ringworm, a legacy from his
crowded quarters in Bombay, added physical discomfort to
his mental distress. He had bravely held back his tears at
Rajkot lest it should be felt he was too weak to go to England.
Now that he was there he gave full rein to his unhappiness
and the tears streamed down his cheeks. The kindly
Dr. Mehta[63] quickly realized the mental strain his young

---

[61] *Collected Works*, I, p. 13.

[62] *Autobiography*, p. 63.

[63] Pran Jivan Mehta, a distinguished student of the Grant Medical College and
a Barrister-at-Law of the Middle Temple, became Chief Medical Officer of
Idar State. He continued to help Gandhi in South Africa and visited him
in Durban in 1898. *Collected Works*, III, p. 109.

compatriot was feeling and moved him into rooms with another Indian with a much longer experience of English life. Richmond, however, was too far from the Inns of Court, and Gandhi moved into lodgings kept by an Anglo-Indian family in West Kensington. Here he began to find his feet in both a metaphorical and literal sense; he gradually gained confidence as he wandered about through the miles of streets with the set purpose of finding a vegetarian restaurant.

The number of Indian students in England were so few that no one was particularly concerned about them and the problems they encountered on their arrival. The student had to depend on letters of introduction, mainly to other Indians in London. Except for Dr. P. J. Mehta and the rather impatient fellow-Indian student in Richmond, Gandhi had no one to advise and help him. During the first four months he carried on a lonely struggle with problems which fall into the five areas of clothes, food, money, sex, and religion. The fact that Gandhi was not enrolled in any educational institution, but was a private student, threw him entirely on his own resources. On November 6, 1888, he joined the Inner Temple[64] and decided to take the Matriculation of the University of London as a private candidate in December, 1889. During the early part of 1889, Gandhi tried his hand at what he called " playing the English gentleman." The approach of the Matriculation Examination sobered him and made him realize that, since his time was entirely his, his paramount need was a disciplined life. Gandhi began to

---

[64] " The Inns of Court, on the road between the city and Westminster, were the seat of a learned trade-union that linked up the general public with the political and governmental world. The lawyers were still what the clergy had once been, the organization through which a clever son of the people had the best chance of rising to worldly greatness in an age of privileged aristocracy." G. M. Trevelyan's comment is interesting in the light of the subsequent careers of both Mahatma Gandhi and M. A. Jinnah, a student of Lincoln's Inn; *op. cit.*, p. 29.

learn the balance between freedom and discipline. His religious sense told him that the enormous freedom he enjoyed would destroy his integrity if he did not take himself in hand. Gandhi's financial circumstances were such that what seemed morally right had also become economically imperative.

As the inner man changed in Gandhi so did the clothes worn by the outer man; his changing dress provides a clue to his changing images of himself and the roles he desired to play until, in 1921, he finally adopted the famous loin cloth of the Tamil peasants when they told him they were too poor to buy *khadi*.[65] The young boy at the Alfred High School wore a *dhoti*, a long frock coat reaching below the knees, and a skull cap, later replaced by a Kathiawadi turban. Going to England involved a visit to a Bombay tailor to acquire the rudiments of an English wardrobe—" Some of the clothes I liked and some I did not like at all."[66] Tying a necktie was a nuisance at first and the short jacket made him feel naked.

Within four months the raw youngster from Kathiawad had acquired expensive sartorial tastes which included Bond Street clothes and a double watch chain of gold sent at his request by a patient elder brother. A contemporary has left us a vivid description of Gandhi as he appeared in Piccadilly Circus in February, 1890: " He was wearing a high silk top hat burnished bright, a Gladstonian collar, stiff and starched; a rather flashy tie displaying almost all the colours of the rainbow under which there was a fine striped silk shirt. He wore as his outer clothes a morning coat, a double-breasted vest, and dark striped trousers to match and not only patent leather boots, but spats over them. He carried leather gloves and a silver-mounted stick, but wore no spectacles. He was, to use the contemporary slang, a nut, a masher, a

---

[65] *This Was Bapu*, p. 67.
[66] *Autobiography*, p. 59.

blood—a student more interested in fashion and frivolities than in his studies." [67]

Gandhi's reversion from Bond Street to the Army and Navy Stores was dictated by economy rather than nationalist feeling. He continued to be punctilious about dress as a student and a young lawyer. It is not till the writing of *Hind Swaraj* that we find him critical of clothes as a symbol of Western civilization. But the young Gandhi was at an impressionable age when many humble people were still contributing to his thinking without his being aware of it. One of them was Narayan Hemachandra, the Indian who stuck to his Indian clothes in London and was later arrested in America for being " indecently " clad. The young conformist secretly envied the bolder compatriot and never forgot him. When Gandhi was in London in 1931, he wore even less than Narayan Hemachandra who had twitted him saying, " You civilized fellows are all cowards. Great men never look at a person's exterior. They think of his heart." [68] As Gandhi strode briskly through the East End on his morning walks, clad in a loin cloth and a shawl, he may have remembered—with affection—the taunting laughter of one of the many men in the past who had left their impress on him.

Not only his interest in clothes, but also Gandhi's brief lessons in dancing, French, elocution, and music, mirror the image of what it took to make a gentleman in an England where the social structure had long been showing signs of change. It was not only young Indian students who were trying to make themselves into English gentlemen but a whole generation whose fathers were enfranchised by Reform Bills, freed from irksome religious disabilities, and enriched by growing trade and industry. In the eighteen-thirties and

---

[67] Sachchidanand Sinha, *Amrita Bazaar Patrika*, Republic Day Souvenir, January 26, 1950. (Quoted by B. R. Nanda, *op. cit.*, p. 28.)

[68] *Autobiography*, p. 99.

forties, Alexander Bell had made a reputation for himself as a professor of elocution. The *Standard Elocutionist* used by Gandhi was almost certainly the work of Alexander Melville Bell. Bell's *Standard Elocutionist*, a book of four hundred and six pages, contained " the principles of elocution and relative exercises; followed by an extensive collection of classified extracts in prose and poetry adapted for reading and recitation." The first edition was published by D. R. Collie and Sons of Edinburgh in 1860; Gandhi very probably used the edition printed in 1873. He began his lessons with a speech by Pitt and was overcome by a feeling of futility. " But Mr. Bell rang the bell in my ear and I awoke."[69]

Gandhi's dancing lessons, so different from the Kathiawadi folk dances he had watched as a boy,[70] remained in his memory for a long time; he talked about Western dancing to the Kathiawad Political Conference in 1925, pointing out that what is a normal form of recreation for young Englishmen is often a disturbing experience for young Indians.[71] His French lessons induced him to visit the Paris Exhibition in 1890. His violin lessons appear to be part of his attempt to become an English gentleman, but there is more to it than appears on the surface. It is significant that the boy Gandhi came to appreciate the power of song and music through the drama; he used to play on a concertina for his father the tunes he liked in the stories he saw enacted. The " itinerant showmen " and " a certain dramatic company " mentioned by Gandhi conceal some interesting developments in the Gujarati stage.[72] The modern Gujarati stage owes its beginnings to the pioneer efforts of the Parsis of Bombay. By the time Gandhi was a boy, the Gujaratis themselves had

---

[69] *Autobiography*, p. 71.
[70] *Collected Works*, I, p. 38.
[71] *The Indian States' Problem*, p. 12.
[72] *Autobiography*, p. 16.

begun to take an interest in the drama and itinerant companies were organized. *Harischandra*, the play which moved the boy so greatly, was written by Dewan Bahadur Ranchodbhai Udayaram who contributed much to the revival of the Gujarati drama.[73] On board the *Clyde* the young Gandhi overcame his shyness and played the piano in the ship's saloon. He had an ear for music before he decided to try his hand at the violin.

When Gandhi visited Romain Rolland in 1931 he requested the French author to play some Beethoven for him on the piano.[74] The Mahatma, who listened to Rolland's rendering of the Andante of Beethoven's *Fifth Symphony* and the *Les Champs Elysees* of Gluck, had already articulated what the small boy playing on a concertina had come to feel about music. His views were expressed in an article entitled, " Democracy *vs* Mobocracy " in the *Young India* of September 8, 1920. " Our great stumbling block," he wrote, " is that we have neglected music. Music means rhythm, order. Its effect is electrical. It immediately soothes. I have seen in European countries, a resourceful superintendent of police by starting a popular song, controlling the mischievous tendencies of mobs. Unfortunately, like our Shastras, music has been the prerogative of the few, or the banter of prostitutes, or high class religious devotees. It has never become nationalized in the modern sense." He went on to say that the singing of national songs should be made " compulsory " and that the people should be taught " mass music."

The paths by which the Mahatma reached these conclusions are astonishing in their diversity. The revival of the Gujarati stage, the traditional culture of the Indian courtesan reflected feebly by the prostitutes of Rajkot, the singing of religious

---

[73] Thoothi, *op. cit.*, p. 292.
[74] *This Was Bapu*, pp. 150-151.

mendicants, Vaishnava devotional music and Kathiawad
garbis, all have blended with a boy's experience with Western
instruments like the concertina, the piano, and the violin,
with the Indian student's experience of mass singing in a
growing British democracy, with the young lawyer's experience
in South Africa when Alexander, the Police Superintendent
of Durban, saved him from a mob by getting them to sing
popular songs. Gandhi expressed his views before the world
became aware of Adolf Hitler's abuse of Wagner's music;
Gandhi's intention though was not to rouse the mob but to
mould the massive Indian crowds, whose pushing and shoving
he disliked, into an orderly and disciplined people. The
" West End Riots " were still green in the memories of
Londoners when Gandhi arrived in 1888, but such scenes
were never repeated and he had come away with an admiration for the well-behaved crowds in the capital of the world's
most disciplined democracy.[75]

In recounting the obstacles he had to surmount in order
to go to England, Gandhi put money at the head of the list.
The sensitive youth felt humiliated by what he had to go
through in the months prior to his departure. Lavish promises
(accompanied by traditional oaths) were made which were
not fulfilled. In one case Gandhi's bold friend, Sheikh
Mehtab, forged a letter in order to remind a man of his
promise. He also hated the fulsome flattery he had to resort
to when he appealed to the Thakore Saheb and the Political
Agent for help.[76] When he finally sailed it was with money
borrowed from friends. His account of the voyage has many
references to the expenses he reluctantly incurred. It is
summed up in the picture of the young Gandhi watching

---

[75] The admiration increased when he was in England in 1914. " London in
these days was a sight worth seeing. There was no panic but all were busy
helping to the best of their ability." *Autobiography*, p. 426.

[76] *Collected Works*, I, p. 10.

with delight the antics of the boys diving for coins thrown by passengers when the ship was at Aden. " Ourselves did not throw a single pie," says Gandhi in his quaint, still developing English.[77] He could play the Bania when he had to. After his initial spending spree in London had ended, the Bania tradition of frugality and parsimony stood him in good stead. " I kept account of every farthing I spent and my expenses were carefully calculated. Every little item, such as omnibus fares or postage or a couple of coppers spent on newspapers, would be entered, and the balance struck every evening before going to bed."[78] If £ 666 is all he had, it was certainly an achievement to have survived on it for three years.[79]

Looking back on the experience the Mahatma read a sermon to young men: " Let every youth take a leaf out of my book and make it a point to account for everything that comes into and goes out of his pocket, and like me he is sure to be a gainer in the end."[80] But the young Gandhi had moments when he felt irked by his financial limitations. He talked with friends about the possibility of going to Oxford or Cambridge, but was deterred by the expense involved. One of these friends was probably Ranjitsinhji to whom he had a letter of introduction. Gandhi's autobiography is as significant for what it omits as for what it includes.[81] He does not mention that he knew and sympathised with Ranjit-sinhji whose succession to the *gadi* of Navanagar had become uncertain. But in 1925, Gandhi claimed that he and Ranjit-sinhji " were friends in our youth " and that they used to

---

[77] *Collected Works*, I, p. 14.

[78] *Autobiography*, p. 72.

[79] " Letter to Mr. Lely," *Collected Works*, I, p. 22.

[80] *Autobiography*, p. 72.

[81] *Autobiography*, pp. 341-342. " I know that I do not set down in this story all that I remember. Who can say how much I must give and how much omit in the interests of truth?"

meet "very often" in London.[82]   The need for economy
also limited Gandhi's desire to travel both in England and on
the Continent.   The only trips he made out of London were
to Portsmouth, Brighton, and Ventnor in the Isle of Wight,
as well as Paris.   In Paris, the young Gandhi bemoans the
expensive lunch he had at the top of the Eiffel Tower.

The Mahatma was right in claiming that his economic
hardship in London ultimately benefited him.   But poverty
also disfigures and limits a man's experience of life and Gandhi
did not have much scope for exploring the full range of Western
culture.   He was more limited than even the average middle-
class Indian student in England at the same time.   Gandhi
seemed to move either in the world of landladies, cheap
lodgings, and restaurants or the posh world of hotel lobbies
and ship saloons.   He was a paying guest once in an English
vegetarian home and the only English children he mentions
are those who ran shouting after Narayan Hemachandra in
his shirt and *dhoti*.   He met the members of the British middle-
class at worship in their churches or at work in their societies—
only occasionally when they were at play (the young Gandhi
could enjoy a rubber of bridge),[83] or in the intimacy of their
homes.   Gandhi, however, bears a familial resemblance to
other young men destined to become well-known who were
also struggling along in London about the same time—
among them George Bernard Shaw, just emerging from
obscurity, and H. G. Wells, then a penurious school master.

The Perfect Way in Diet

When we turn from externals to inner needs, the most
immediate area which concerned the young Gandhi was the
hollow feeling in his stomach—he felt he was starving in the
midst of plenty because of his vegetarian vow.   " I was a

---

[82] *The Indian States' Problem*, p. 32.
[83] *Autobiography*, p. 95.

179

good eater and had a capacious stomach. . . "[84] He was
hungry and miserable till he discovered that London had
vegetarian restaurants. Many a street in London had some
romance attached to it; in the light of the past it was a romantic
moment when a young Indian turned into Farringdon Street,
and his eyes filled with happiness as he saw the Central
Restaurant advertising vegetarian food. Biographers of
Gandhi like Vincent Sheean and B. R. Nanda see in that
moment the beginnings of a life of ascetic holiness and a
return to the religious and moral ideas enshrined in the
Vaishnava practice of vegetarianism. But the Vegetarian
Society did two other things for Gandhi. It gave him a
sense of mission and launched him on his career as an organizer,
speaker and propagandist. It also brought him into contact
with a group of vegetarians, thinkers and writers, some of
whom lived in " Queer Street," but nearly all of them
influenced by Ruskin and involved in some form of radical
reaction to the industrial civilization of the West. They had
sympathy for the working class and lived on the fringes of
proletarianism though none of them were proletarians. It
was in the Memorial Hall also on Farringdon Street, not far
from the Central Restaurant, that the Labour Party was
conceived on February 27, 1900.

The word " vegetarianism " came into use about 1847,[85]
and had some of its roots in the earlier interest in diet reform
and model menus for working poor. Vegetarianism had an
attraction for artists and writers who had experienced some
measure of poverty themselves. Charles Kingsley once
described Shelley as a " lewd vegetarian "[86] and George
Bernard Shaw's vegetarianism was well-known. It is
significant that the oldest Vegetarian Society in England was

---

[84] *Autobiography*, p. 65.
[85] " Vegetarianism," *The Encyclopedia Britannica,* 11th ed., XXVII, p. 967.
[86] G. M. Young, *op. cit.,* p. 5, fn.

started in the Radical stronghold of Manchester which was also the home of its journal, *The Vegetarian Messenger*. In 1889, Gandhi, fortified by reading Salt's *Plea for Vegetarianism*, had solved the problem of where and what to eat and could get on with his studies. It was in the following year that he began to take a serious interest in vegetarian activities, though he knew of the Manchester Vegetarian Society and occasionally read *The Vegetarian Messenger*. But it was his friendship with Dr. Josiah Oldfield, the editor of *The Vegetarian*, the journal of the London Vegetarian Society, which turned Gandhi into a useful and active member.

Gandhi joined the London Vegetarian Society on September 19, 1890, and later accompanied Dr. Oldfield to the International Vegetarian Conference at Portsmouth where the young student read a paper which appeared in *The Vegetarian Messenger*. It was the Indian enthusiast who organized a Vegetarian Society in Bayswater and persuaded Edwin Arnold, with whose works he had become acquainted the previous year, to be its President. In 1891, Gandhi, a member of the Executive Committee of the London Vegetarian Society, was speaking and writing on behalf of Vegetarianism. In May he read his paper on " The Foods of India " to a meeting in Bloomsbury and in June he addressed the Band of Mercy in Upper Norwood. Between February and June of 1891 a series of articles appeared in *The Vegetarian* from the pen of the young Indian who had represented London at the meeting of the Federal Union of Vegetarian Societies.[87]

On February 20, 1891, Gandhi attended an important meeting of the Executive of the Vegetarian Society at which a decision had to be taken as to whether Dr. Thomas Richard Allinson, who had been advocating birth-control, should be allowed to continue as a member. Dr. Allinson was a well-

---

[87] *Collected Works*, I, pp. 354-355.

known contributor of articles on health and dietetic problems
to *The Weekly Times and Echo*. In 1887, his articles were
published in two volumes entitled *Medical Essays*. Two years
later he published his *Leaflets for Young Men* and had already
upset some by boldly printing a pamphlet entitled *Gonorrhoea
or Clap*, in 1890, when the more puritanical members of the
London Vegetarian Society moved to expel him. Gandhi
was too shy to read his speech which defended Allinson,
though he did not like his views on birth-control; and the
President had to get someone else to read it for him.
Allinson was expelled but a young Indian had learned to
stand by his convictions in a difficult situation.[88]

Turning from Gandhi's activities to his reading, one is
impressed by his desire to understand all the implications of
the Vegetarian creed. His dietetic experiments and his
reading were intimately connected to both his need of money
and poor health. The first writer on Vegetarianism
Gandhi became familiar with was Henry Stephens Salt
(1851–1939). This old Etonian began a long literary career
with the book which Gandhi bought for a shilling and read
from cover to cover. The slim volume of one hundred and
fifteen pages was published by the Vegetarian Society of
Manchester in 1886 and was entitled *A Plea For Vegetarianism
and Other Essays*. The first and fourth essays were published
in *Time* in February, 1883 and January 1886 respectively.
The rest appeared at different times in *The Food Reform
Magazine*, *The Dietetic Reformer*, and the Vegetarian Society's
Annual. The book makes interesting reading in the light of
Gandhi's subsequent development. Salt hoped that meat-
eating would disappear like cannibalism though " . . . a
Vegetarian is still regarded, in ordinary society as little better
than a mad man, and may consider himself lucky if he has

---

[88] " Shyness My Shield," *Autobiography*, pp. 81-84.

no worse epithets applied to him than humanitarian, senti-
mentalist, crotchet-monger, fanatic, and the like."[89] These
words must have soothed the youth, smarting under the
taunts of his Indian room-mate in Richmond. In 1906,
Salt published a book of verse called *Consolations of a Faddist*.
In later life the Mahatma gaily called himself a faddist
also.

In the opening essay, " A Plea For Vegetarianism," Salt
pointed out that " the first and most obvious advantage of a
vegetarian diet is its economy "[90] which greatly appealed to
Gandhi. In " Morality in Diet," Salt claimed that
Vegetarianism is " a system which claims to be at once most
moral, most wholesome, and most economical ... the three
great advantages, the three chief aspects! "[91] " Good Taste
in Diet " is largely a tribute to Ruskin and his Society of
St. George. Gandhi read Salt's commendation of " the
works of Mr. Ruskin, a teacher whom we Food Reformers,
in common with all who strive after a purer life, must revere
above all living writers,"[92] but he did not have the fore-
knowledge of the influence that writer was destined to exert
on him. Another essay which must have helped the young
man who had taken a vow not to touch alcohol is " Some
Results of Food Reform " in which Salt claimed that " in
ninety-nine cases out of one hundred the Vegetarian will be
a total abstainer " and that " if Food Reform be once established, Drink Reform will automatically follow."[93] Salt
also asserted that a fleshless diet makes smoking impossible.
" Medical Men and Food Reform " contains the germ of
Gandhi's arguments against doctors in *Hind Swaraj*. " The

---

[89] *Op. cit.*, p. 7.
[90] *Ibid.*, p. 8.
[91] *Ibid.*, p. 22.
[92] *Op. cit.*, p. 37.
[93] Salt, *op. cit.*, p. 42.

truth," said Salt, " is that medical men are very far from being infallible either in their individual opinion or collective judgements."[94] Salt also provided Gandhi with the assurance that Vegetarianism was not impossible in cold climates in his essay entitled " On Certain Fallacies." The essay on " Vegetarianism and Social Reform " is important for the light it throws on the later ideas of Gandhi who also believed in " the indirect influence of Vegetarian principles in carrying out any plan of social reform."[95]

When Gandhi arrived in London, Salt had edited *A Shelley Primer* and was writing for the *Westminster Review*. He was particularly prolific in 1890; he edited Godwin's *Political Justice*, Thoreau's *Anti-Slavery and Reform Papers*, and also published *The Life of H. D. Thoreau*. Gandhi never met him, but Salt's now forgotten book made an impact on his mind which was deep and lasting in its influence on many of the Mahatma's attitudes.[96]

A prominent writer on Vegetarianism whom Gandhi met at Ventnor was Howard Williams. He had read *The Ethics of Diet*: *A Catena of Authorities Deprecatory of the Practice of Flesh-eating*[97] published by Williams in 1883 and correctly described it in his autobiography as an attempt " to make out that all philosophers and prophets from Pythagoras and Jesus down to those of the present age were vegetarians."[98] Another book that Gandhi found attractive was *The Perfect Way in Diet* by Anna Kingsford, 1846–1888. The book was a translation of her thesis in French for the degree of M.D. she received from the University of Paris and was published

---

[94] *Ibid.*, p. 54.

[95] *Ibid.*, p. 114.

[96] See *Salt and his Circle* (with a Preface by Bernard Shaw), (London, Hutchinson, 1951).

[97] Manchester, F. Pitman, 1883.

[98] *Autobiography*, p. 68.

in London in 1881.[99] When Gandhi was in South Africa he corresponded with her collaborator, Edward Maitland. Gandhi's own dietetic experiments in London were inspired to a considerable extent by the writings of Dr. Allinson whom he met in 1890.[100]

Vegetarianism, however, not only helped Gandhi to solve his dietetic problem, but broadened his interests; it even led him to do some research in Indian history. He read the Histories of India by James Mill and Sir W. W. Hunter in search of material for his paper on " The Foods of India."[101] Vegetarianism had led him into a field which he would find invaluable in South Africa when confronted by the assumption that Indians were a barbarous and uncivilized people. It was Vegetarianism which gave him the habit of meeting prominent people; the young Gandhi spent a lot of time meeting well-known people until, as the Mahatma, he became one of the most visited and interviewed men of his times. If the germ of the Indian National Congress lay in the recollections of the young Allan Octavian Hume of the Anti-Corn Law League's agitation, the germ of the Indian agitation in South Africa lay in the young Gandhi's experience of Vegetarian activities in England.

Cleansing the Heart of Passions*

Several students of Gandhi suggest that he is a fit subject for analysis " from the standpoint of Freudian psychology."[102]

---

[99] (London, Kegan Paul, Trench & Co.). See Edward Maitland, *Anna Kingsford: Her Life, Letters, Diary and Work*, 2 Vols., (London, George Redway, 1896).

[100] *Autobiography*, pp. 68, 438.

[101] *Collected Works*, I, pp. 44, 47.

*Lines from the chapter on Gandhi's experience in a boarding house in Portsmouth. See *Autobiography*, p. 96.

[102] J. K. Mathews, *The Techniques of M. K. Gandhi as Religious*, unpublished Ph.D. thesis, Columbia University, 1957, p. 16.

The young Kathiawadi who arrived in London was, on his own admission, a sexually virile male whose mind was often "hovering about the bedroom." Bound by the oath to his mother to keep away from women, the young man's struggle for self-control was probably much sharper and more painful than the autobiography written by the Mahatma in his fifties seems to reveal. It was in England that Gandhi began a long process of self-discipline which would so alter his relations with women that Millie Graham Polak would find an appealing "womanliness" in him,[103] and a young female relative, Manubehn Gandhi, would write a book of reminiscences about the Mahatma entitled *Bapu My Mother*.[104]

The three women closest to Gandhi before he went to England were his mother, his wife, and his sister-in-law. He could tease his mother, making her laugh or cry, but with his wife he had to maintain a certain reserve in public, however friendly or passionate they were in private. His relations with his sister-in-law would be the pattern which obtained with most of his female relatives—a mixture of affection and the traditional forms of behaviour prescribed by custom. With other women of his own class he would establish agnatic relationships calling them "sister" or "mother" in terms of their age and status. For instance, his landlady in Bhavanagar, where he resided as a student for a brief time in 1888, treated him like her own son and wept when he left.[105] The system of *purdah* was there to regulate relationships; the silken veils were strong barriers to any forms of behaviour suggestive of sex. The symbol of sex was a woman outside this circle of relationships—the prostitute. It was through

---

[103] " Mahatma Gandhi has been given the love of many women for his womanliness," *This Was Bapu*, p. 30.

[104] Manubehn Gandhi, *Bapu My Mother*, (Ahmedabad, Navajivan Publishing House, 1949).

[105] *Collected Works*, I, p. 6.

his friend, Sheikh Mehtab, that Gandhi came to know something of the lure of these women in the lanes of Rajkot, though he escaped the temptations of the local brothels.

In a society where the sexes were so rigidly compartmentalised it was natural that friendships between young men were often akin to that between David and Jonathan, with a love surpassing the love of women. It explains the enigma of Gandhi's strong attachment to his friend Sheikh Mehtab which broke finally only in Durban. The usual explanation given is that Gandhi wanted to reform the young reprobate. But obviously Sheikh Mehtab, who stopped the bigger boys from bullying smaller lads,[106] and was gay, bold, and daring, satisfied a need in the shy and timid Gandhi. The young Muslim was the embodiment of all the temptations that Gandhi spent a life-time in overcoming. His fondness for Sheikh Mehtab obsessed him completely at times. " Once I was to go with Zaverchand but an hour before the time of my departure a serious accident took place. I was always quarrelling with my friend, Sheikh Mehtab. On the day of departure I was quite engrossed in thinking about the quarrel...On our way I was buried in the madcap thoughts of London on one side and the thoughts of Sheikh Mehtab on the other. Amidst thoughts I came unconsciously in contact with a carriage. I received some injury. Yet I did not take the help of anybody in walking. I think I was quite dizzy. Then we entered the house of Meghjibhai. There I again came in contact with a stone unknowingly and received injury. I was quite senseless."[107] The fainting fit was probably due to constipation, but this punished Sheikh Mehtab to such a degree that a reconciliation was effected. Later on he accompanied Gandhi to Bombay. In London he could not forget the friend against whom his family had

---

[106] P. Gandhi, *op. cit.*, p. 30.
[107] *Collected Works*, I, p. 6.

once warned him; in spite of his own financial difficulties he sent Sheikh Mehtab gifts of money.[108]

Gandhi took Sheikh Mehtab to South Africa and broke with him there when he caught him inviting prostitutes to the house they shared. Looking back on that long association he said, "Infatuation had completely blinded me."[109] But Gandhi was haunted by Sheikh Mehtab in the person of his own son. The Mahatma failed with his eldest son as he failed with the friend of his youth.[110] The friend and the son, so like each other, are pathetic in their failures but they underline the fact that Mahatmas are not easy to live with; the greater the demand for puritanism and asceticism, the greater the rebellion against it. Gandhi broke with Sheikh Mehtab, not simply because his association with him after becoming a public figure would harm him, but also because he had outgrown the need for his friend. Gandhi had become the stronger of the two men; it was his own manliness that would now attract strong men like Motilal Nehru and Vallabhbhai Patel to his side.

When Gandhi went to England he was plunged into a society where the relations between men and women were not only traditionally freer but also in a state of flux. Ibsen took the title of his play, *The Doll's House*, performed in London in 1889, from Dickens, which is an unconscious commentary on the way in which the doctrine of the Two Spheres was changing throughout the nineteenth century. The two worlds of men and women had begun to inter-penetrate both economically and intellectually in rapid fashion by the eighteen-eighties. Before Gandhi had to take his stand on a question relating to Dr. Allinson's birth-control propaganda,

---

[108] P. Gandhi, *op. cit.*, p. 30.
[109] *Autobiography*, p. 203.
[110] For a revealing account of Gandhi's relation with *Harilal*, his eldest son, see "Satyagraha in South Africa" by Pragji Desai in *Reminiscences of Gandhiji*, Chandrashanker Shukla, (Ed.), (Bombay, Vora & Co., 1951), pp. 82-84.

A Young Indian as a Late-Victorian

Annie Besant and Bradlaugh had been tried and convicted for publishing Knowlton's pamphlet, *The Fruits of Love*, which contained some crude information about contraceptive methods.[111]   Annie Besant was present at the great demonstration in Trafalgar Square organized by Hyndman in 1886, and, two years later, she initiated the " New Unionism " by leading a successful strike of London girls employed in making lucifer matches.   Gandhi met her soon after her conversion to Theosophy.

Gandhi was most at ease with older people in England because he could relate himself to them by means of the mother or father image.   He obviously liked motherly women such as Miss Manning and the unnamed lady he met at Brighton whose London house he visited regularly for a time on Sundays.   He warmed towards older men like Dr. P. J. Mehta, Narayan Hemachandra and Frederick Pincott.   It also explains why Gandhi enjoyed working with a much older group like the Executive of the London Vegetarian Society.   The women who made him uneasy were the young ones with whom he could flirt; highly emancipated types with whom he was expected to engage in intellectual conversation, and women who smoked or drank.   They were outside the range of his earlier relationships in Kathiawad.

Like most other young Indians in London at that time, Gandhi took out the daughters of his landladies and indulged in some mild flirtation, but was saved from going any further by his shyness and reticence.   He was inhibited by his oath and by his lack of money as taking a young woman out involved expenditure on cab fares, theatre tickets and food.   But his feeling of guilt, due to the concealment of the fact that he was married, came to a head when he felt he was getting too

---

[111] The still strong prudery of the 1880's is seen in *How to be Happy Though Married*, (New York, Charles Scribner's Sons, 1886), in which the anonymous author avoided any reference to the physical aspect of marriage.

involved with a young woman. He relieved his mind of " the canker of untruth " by a cathartic process characteristic of him—confession leading to a healthier relationship.

One is surprised to find that Gandhi read so much into his mild experiences. Why was he so sure that the landlady in Portsmouth or the rather healthy, out-door girl, the landlady's daughter in Ventnor, was wanting to seduce him? It was partly due to the tension within himself as he struggled to remain loyal to his vow; the desire to seduce became confused with the fear of being seduced. " Remembering the vow I had taken before my mother, I fled from the scene. To my room I went quaking, trembling, with beating heart, like a quarry escaped from its pursuer."[112]

But there was a deeper and more unconscious cause for his nervousness. The social freedom exhibited by these young women would unknowingly raise in his mind the feared image of the sex-symbol—the prostitute—like the prostitute on whose bed he had sat in Rajkot without daring to consummate what he had gone there to do. Flirtation made him afraid that he was getting too dangerously involved in " the banter of prostitutes." Gandhi's fears were rooted in the Indian image of the prostitute; but others beside him were appalled by the knowledge that, in a disintegrating Western culture, sexual morals were drifting dangerously close to unprofessional prostitution. Adultery no longer required the daring of a Tristan; thanks to contraceptives, Iseult was accessible and available.[113]

Gandhi's response, however, to the pattern of sex-relations in England was not all negative. It gave him a new conception of conjugal ties and strengthened his conviction that early marriage is a mistake. The young Indian admired Mrs. Gladstone's devotion to her husband and saw in that

---

[112] *Autobiography*, p. 95.

[113] See Denis de Rougement, " The Myth *v*. Marriage," *Love in the Western World*, (Garden City, New York, Doubleday, 1957).

distinguished couple the supreme example of conjugal love.[114] He also sensed that greater freedom between the sexes could lead to comradeships, free of sexual promiscuity. He had to see the activities of the Suffragettists in London, however, before he consented to the mass participation of women in the political struggles in South Africa. When the scared Indian student had turned into the Mahatma he could inspire the warmest feelings of friendship in both Eastern and Western women.[115] Eleanor Morton's *The Women in Gandhi's Life*[116] studies the richness and variety of those friendships. Perhaps the most moving of them all was the friendship between the Mahatma and Madeleine Slade, the daughter of a British admiral.

The theme of the holy man and the prostitute runs through the history of religion. Opposites in so many respects, yet they are linked together in the spiritual agony of the flesh striving towards a higher humanity. The prostitute is the troubled blood in the holy man; the holy man is the aspiration towards purity in the prostitute. Though he did not succumb, the seductive image of the prostitute remained a temptation in the life of the young Gandhi. He fled from the prostitutes of Rajkot. In fleeing from the landlady in Portsmouth he felt he was fleeing from all the pursuing shapes from the brothels of that seaport.[117] As his mind dwelt on the temptations of Portsmouth[118] he might have remembered how he was asked if he wanted a girl in Brindisi.[119] On his way to South Africa in 1893 he fled from a Negro prostitute in Zanzibar.

---

[114] *Autobiography*, p. 252.

[115] Moulana Shaukat Ali told the Executive Club of Chicago on March 6, 1933, " Mahatma Gandhi is not much to look at but has a wonderful winning way with the ladies, a charm that is very loveable." *Gandhi as Others See Him*, p. 93.

[116] Eleanor Morton, *The Women in Gandhi's Life*, (New York, Dodd, Mead, 1953).

[117] *Autobiography*, pp. 94-96.

[118] In 1904 he noted that sixty per cent of those arrested for drunkenness in British seaport towns were women. *Collected Works*, IV, p. 235.

[119] *Collected Works*, I, p. 17.

The figure of the prostitute continued to haunt him in South Africa; the males among the indentured labourers so outnumbered the females that Gandhi found " the very distinction between a married woman and a concubine ceased to exist among these unfortunate people."[120] The Gandhi who showed such righteous indignation when he found his friend with a prostitute in his " nice little house in a prominent locality" of Durban, was both angry and afraid. Although he felt it proper to break with his friend, the Mahatma, sadly remembering more than one broken friendship strewn along the path of a holy man, wrote, " Howsoever you may repair it, a rift is a rift."[121] The rift was more than a rift with a friend. It was a rift with an old temptation, a besetting sin. "I saw a prostitute inside. I asked her to leave the house, never to return." He banished her not only from his house but also from his own mind and soul.[122] But like Buddha and Jesus the Mahatma stepped over her fallen body only to turn and raise her up. In 1921, the Mahatma met more than two hundred prostitutes in Barisal who volunteered to join the Congress. He wrote, " for me the two hours I passed with these sisters is a treasured memory."[123] The Mahatma could now stretch out his hand to these women without the fear of temptation or calumny that had unnerved the young Indian lawyer in Durban.

The Religion of the British Middle-Class

The lines separating the classes were still clearly visible when Gandhi went to England and, as an Indian student, he came into closest touch with the British middle-class.[124] The

---

[120] *Satyagraha in South Africa*, (Ahmedabad, Navajivan Publishing House, 1950), p. 22.
[121] *Autobiography*, p. 204.
[122] *Autobiography*, pp. 201-204.
[123] " Our Fallen Sisters," *Young India*, September 15, 1921.
[124] Halevy, *op. cit.*, p. 336.

moral and religious ideas of this middle-class made an indelible impact on the thoughts and feelings of the young Hindu. Gandhi was exposed to a curious mixture of surviving Evangelical piety and esoteric cults like Theosophy trying to fill a growing spiritual vacuum in the middle-class. The explanation for it, of course, is that he was never a proper university student immersed in the intellectual climate of a British institution of higher learning. Gandhi, like Lord Acton and unlike Nehru, " was excluded from the direct influence of the English public school and university."[125]

The Inns of Court, where Gandhi was enrolled, lay between the City and Westminster; the scattered group of picturesque, old buildings set around pleasant grass courts near the Thames, was connected with the busier thoroughfares by winding lanes, archways, and gates.[126] Prior to the nineteenth century students lived in these rambling inns and had the advantage of being in close touch with experienced lawyers and judges. Gandhi studied in his room or a public library and attended a dinner in the Inner Temple six times a term; his presence was always welcome to some of his fellow-students as he gave away his wine. But the law dinners were not the most fruitful kind of contact to have with his peers. Gandhi studied law seriously, but his impersonal and isolated role as a student filled him with anxiety towards the end of his stay; he sought out Frederick Pincott for advice as to how to become a successful lawyer. Gandhi sensed what he had missed when he saw Cambridge in 1931; there is an underlying note of wistfulness in the account of his visit to the University where Ranjitsinhji and Nehru had studied—it might also have been his *alma mater*—had he the money.[127]

---

[125] Crane Brinton, *op. cit.*, p. 199.

[126] Jeanette Eaton, *Gandhi: Fighter Without a Sword*, (New York, William Morrow & Co., 1950), p. 33.

[127] C. Rajagopalachari and J. C. Kumarappa, (Ed.), *The Nation's Voice*, (Ahmedabad, Navajivan Publishing House, 1947), p. 197.

13

When Gandhi took the Matriculation Examination of the University of London, he was involved in a curriculum which reflected certain social and economic trends in the period following Forster's Education Act of 1870. He took Chemistry for his first attempt because it had been a compulsory subject in India, but switched to Heat and Light when he failed. What might have been the complexion of Gandhi's mind had he continued with Chemistry and Physics after the London Matriculation? It would have brought him into real contact with the continuing debate between religion and science. "It was, perhaps, unfortunate," wrote R. B. MacCallum, "that in this utilitarian age the most obvious and popular form of science to be advocated in schools and the easiest to provide and demanded by parents was Chemistry, cultivated at the expense of physics and biology. To this day the radical complexion in politics of many of our scientists is not unconnected with the fact that they or their fathers, heard their studies dismissed as ' stinks ' by boys and masters who were wont also to arrogate to themselves other assumptions of superiority."[128] Gandhi never got involved in the social overtones of " stinks " because there were no laboratories in which private candidates could work. The Indian medievalist in Gandhi was strengthened by his fondness for Latin. What he did take away, however, from Late-Victorian England was its faith in evolution; the Mahatma was a believer in the perfectability of Man. What Marx believed was possible through a reordering of society, Gandhi believed was possible through a reordering of the inner man; they resemble each other in their utopianism and perfectionism, two dangerous fallacies critically analysed by Reinhold Niebuhr.

It is interesting that the Englishman who introduced Gandhi to the Christian Scriptures was a vegetarian and a

---

[128] *Victorian Years*, p. 437.

seller of Bibles from Manchester.[129]   But it was the beginning of a life-long study of the Bible which Gandhi's later love for the Gita did not destroy.   Commenting, in 1916, on the words of Jesus, " Children, how hard it is for them that trust in riches to enter the kingdom of God.   It is easier for a camel to go through the eye of a needle than for a rich man to enter into the kingdom of God," (St. Mark 10 : 25) Gandhi said, " Here you have an eternal rule of life stated in the noblest words the English language is capable of producing."[130] What Gandhi assimilated from the Bible was supplemented by his knowledge of the Victorian sermon and the popular hymns of the period.   Charles Haddon Spurgeon, at the Metropolitan Tabernacle, Joseph Parker at the City Temple, and Dean Farrar at the Abbey were still famous preachers when Gandhi was in London; he heard them all and he regularly attended Parker's mid-week service for young men. " The form of preachers," says G. M. Young, " was canvassed like the form of public entertainers, and the circulation of some Victorian sermons is a thing to fill a modern writer with despair."[131]   Gandhi's lecture to the Muir Central College Economic Society in Allahabad was in the form of a sermon on the Rich Young Ruler though its title was " Economic *vs.* Moral Progress."[132]   The Victorian sermon left an impress both on the ideas and the style of the Mahatma.

---

[129] An association for the sale of the Scriptures was formed in Manchester about 1846. See the *Jubilee Commemoration at Bombay* of the British and Foreign Bible Society, (Bombay, American Mission Press, 1854), pp. 10-11, for an account of Manchester's interest in the Scriptures.

[130] *Speeches and Writings of Mahatma Gandhi*, (Madras, G. A. Natesan & Co., 1922), p. 289.

[131] *Op. cit.*, p. 14.

[132] *Speeches and Writings of Mahatma Gandhi*, pp. 286-293.   In a letter to Fr. Lash (now Bishop of Bombay) in 1942 conveying greetings to " our English friends " the Mahatma wrote, " Has not an English divine said that ' duty will be merit when debt becomes a donation? ' "   See *Reminiscences of Gandhiji*, p. 167.

The Mahatma himself had said, " I yield to no Christian in the strength of devotion with which I sing ' Lead Kindly Light.' "[133] In 1921, Gandhi wrote an article entitled " Mists " which contained the lines, " We shall know each other better when the mists have rolled away;"[134] it was an echo from his student days in London when Dwight L. Moody and Ira D. Sankey gave a revivalist tinge to a growing democracy. Gandhi used those words several times in *Indian Opinion*.[135] Another hymn he liked in South Africa was " Take My Life, and Let It Be."[136] Towards the end of his life the Mahatma wrote to his Quaker friend, Carl Heath, " I am in the midst of a raging fire and often hum to myself: ' Rock of Ages cleft for me, Let me hide myself in Thee.' "[137] In addition to Newman's hymn and A. M. Toplady's " Rock of Ages," Gandhi loved " When I survey the wondrous Cross " by Isaac Watts. English hymns performed two services for the young Gandhi; they helped him in his spiritual struggle to maintain his integrity in London and led him later to appreciate the deep devotional note in Indian *bhakti* literature especially of the Vaishnava schools. A hymn which he liked during his student days was " Abide with me "; later on he found that Surdas, a Gujarati poet, had breathed the same spirit when he sang, " He is the help of the helpless, the strength of the weak."

The Mahatma, who was critical of Christian Missions throughout the 1920's, had moved even further away from the Christian influence of his London and South African periods by the 1930's. But the prisoner in Yeravada Jail still showed

---

133 *Speeches and Writings of Mahatma Gandhi*, p. 275.

134 *Young India*, April 20.

135 *Collected Works*, IV, p. 95.

136 M. G. Polak, *Mr. Gandhi: The Man*, (London, George Allen & Unwin Ltd., 1931), p. 140.

137 Pyarelal, *The Last Phase*, 2 Vols., (Ahmedabad, Navajivan Publishing House, 1956–1958), Vol. I, p. 103.

traces of those far-off days. When he called Yeravada Jail a "*mandir*" (a temple), the images in his mind were still mixed; echoes from the City Temple mingled with the chanting in the Vallabhachari *havelis*. The Mahatma emerged from his incarceration with a collection of his sermons in his *From Yeravada Mandir*[138] and a collection of Vaishnava hymns with a title suggestive of Kagawa—*Songs from Prison*.[139] The contents of both collections were now thoroughly Indian, but his desire to involve himself in these two literary forms was not unrelated to the inspiration, however weakened, which he had received before his return to his mother country. When the Mahatma was a prisoner in the Aga Khan's Palace in 1943 he asked Father Lash (later Bishop) to send him a volume of Christian hymns.[140]

The student who told the gathering in the Alfred High School, met to bid him farewell, that they should work for " big reforms "[141] would not fail to be struck by the interest of religious organizations in social service in England. Describing the great interest of the period in social problems MacCallum says, " A London docker, starving and miserable in mind and body, might find himself ready to be ' rescued ' by Salvationist or Protestant pastor, by an Anglo—or Roman Catholic priest, or by a social worker proceeding from rationalist and secular motives."[142] Methodism in the eighties, led by men like Hugh Price Hughes, was reaching the workers of the great industrial centres and the coalfields with its social services; and hundreds of Methodist lay preachers were active in trade unionism and labour politics. The

---

[138] M. K. Gandhi, *From Yeravada Mandir*, (trans.), Valji Govindji Desai, (Ahmedabad, Jivanji Desai, 1933).

[139] M. K. Gandhi, *Songs From Prison*, (New York, Macmillan & Co., 1934).

[140] W. Q. Lash, " Since 1932," *Reminiscences of Gandhiji*, p. 165.

[141] *Collected Works*, I, p. 1.

[142] *Victorian Years*, p. 439.

Salvation Army had been founded in 1878 by William Booth, a vehement man with the appearance of a prophet, who was unroofing " the slum to Victorian respectability " and " unveiling the dark places of civilization."[143] Christian writers were using the mission fields and travelogues of Asia and Africa for the titles of books[144] exposing the sufferings of the London poor. In 1883, *The Bitter Cry of Outcaste London* by Reverend Andrew Mearns, Secretary of the Congregational Union, was matched, in 1890, by William Booth's *In Darkest England, and the Way Out* written with the help of W. T. Stead. High Churchmen were not lagging behind their Non-Conformist brethren in their zeal for working in squalid industrial slums even if it was rather unkindly called " slumming." Many Anglo-Catholics were attracted by the University settlements that had sprung up bringing graduates from Oxford and Cambridge into the heart of the slums-Ruskin, who inspired Gandhi to found Phoenix Farm, had earlier inspired the founding of Toynbee Hall (1884).

An aspect of social reform which touched Gandhi personally was the Temperance agitation of the period. In the pause following the reforms of the early 1880's, Temperance came in for a good deal of discussion; it served to deflect attention from the demand for more serious social welfare measures which were being formulated. It was " keeping terms," the required attendance at a minimum of six out of the twenty-four dinners each term, which stimulated Gandhi's concern with the drink question. It surprised him to find that the cost of drink exceeded the cost of food. " The first revelation gave me a great shock, and I wondered how people had the heart to throw away so much money on drink." In one of his articles in *The Vegetarian* he describes alcohol as " that

---

143 " Booth, William," *Dictionary of National Biography*, 1912–1921, 3rd supplement, p. 52.
144 H. M. Stanley's book was entitled *Darkest Africa*.

enemy of mankind, that curse of civilization—in some form or another."[145] The same article contains the germ of his attitude to British rule: the British were ruining the health of Indians by introducing tea, coffee and alcohol, thus proving that Western civilization was not good for India.   The young Gandhi's capacious appetite had led him into some strange fields of exploration; he had found a radical kernel inside the curious shell of British Vegetarianism.   Gandhi's instinct was right when he went to history for the study of Indian foods; Indian history cannot be truly understood without insight into the feeding habits of the people of India.   Gandhi began to feel he could not stomach the British because he could not stomach their food or drink.   Gandhi taught Indians not to accept British rule because Western civilization had been a poison to them; they must remove the blight altogether. But his actions in relation to the British were ambivalent because he could not forget the bonds that gave him an affection for and an understanding of the religion of the British middle-class.

The Key to Theosophy

Towards the end of 1889 another dimension of thought and feeling was added to Gandhi's religious experiences in London when he came into contact with Theosophy.   The assaults of science on nature revived an interest in the supernatural; men, whose cherished beliefs were shaken, wanted to be assured that science could not explain everything.   Some scientists were attracted to Spiritualism and Theosophy even as some are attracted to the Fundamentalist creeds of Christianity today.   Thomas Alva Edison was a Fellow of the Theosophical Society of New York; Alfred Russel Wallace, Darwin's collaborator, and William Crooks, the discoverer of " radiant matter," were members of the London Lodge.

---

[145] " Indian Vegetarians," *Collected Works*, I, p. 29.

When Gandhi went to England, Theosophy was only fourteen years old and still in the vigour of its youth. The Theosophical Society was launched in 1875 in New York, and *Isis Unveiled*, the first gospel of the movement, was published two years later. The Theosophical venture to India paid golden dividends since India in 1879 was in just the right mood to welcome this new species of missionary. The proposed alliance with the Arya Samaj did not materialize; the Hindu Luther, Dayanand Saraswati, as much of a sectarian as the denominationalists of the West, could not appreciate the eclecticism of the Theosophists.[146] But the general response was good and Theosophy made converts both among the Indians and the British. After a spell in Bombay the world headquarters of Theosophy was established in 1882 at Adyar in Madras. India gave Theosophy both greater reality and a new depth of understanding of Eastern religions.

Since Theosophy had met with such an encouraging response when Gandhi was a schoolboy in Rajkot, why did he hesitate to join the Society as a student in London? The explanation lies not simply in the diffidence and modesty of the young Gandhi, but also in the subsequent history of the Theosophical Movement after 1884 and its repercussions in London. The London Lodge, organized by a group of students inspired by reading *Isis Unveiled*, led to the formation of the British Theosophical Society in June, 1878. The leadership felt that the London Lodge " had been a centre for discontent and trouble almost from its foundation " but many of its members had good reasons for the apprehensions they exhibited. After its halcyon beginnings and sunny Indian days, Theosophy was sailing into deep and stormy waters. The first rumblings of the blast began in 1883 with the " Kiddle incident " arising out of Sinnett's publication of his *The*

---

[146] Olcott, " Swami Dayanand," *op. cit.* See also " Early Days of the Theosophical Society," *The Theosophical Movement.*

Occult World. Serious charges of plagiarism were levelled at Sinnett by Henry Kiddle. But worse was to follow late in 1885 when the defection of the Coulombs from Adyar resulted in grave charges of fraud and chicanery against Madame Blavatsky. Fuel was added to the fire by the publication of the Report of the investigations of Ralph Hodgson into the Coulomb Affair on behalf of the Society for Psychical Research. The strain of these exposures began to tell on the London Lodge and dissensions broke out which led to the resignation of Dr. Anna Kingsford as President and the election of Sinnett in her place. Anna Kingsford founded the Hermetic Society and claimed that the occult in other great religions could be explained in terms of Christian esotericism.

Gandhi became linked to this now forgotten controversy when he was in South Africa. He corresponded with Edward Maitland, Anna Kingsford's eccentric collaborator, and became the representative of his Esoteric Christian Union. It is interesting that Anna Kingsford, who had corresponded with T. Subba Row, made a forlorn attempt to claim for Christianity what Hinduism was already claiming for itself, namely, that all religions could find shelter within its ample folds. Her reaction to Theosophy was similar to that of most Hindu leaders including Gandhi himself in later years.[147]

Though Madame Blavatsky continued to be a controversial figure, her last years in England were fruitful in many directions. The intellectual liveliness of London stimulated her literary bent; *The Secret Doctrine* appeared in 1887, *The Voice of the Silence* and *The Key to Theosophy*, in 1889. The interest in social reform she had gained in India was strengthened by the economic and political ferment in London. She began to discuss the applications of Theosophy to social problems in

---

[147] Her views were expressed in a joint letter with Edward Maitland circulated to the members of the London Lodge.

her books and tried to relate the activities of the Blavatsky Lodge to the social movement of the day by organizing the East London Club for Working Women. These new social interests helped Madame Blavatsky to score one of her greatest triumphs; early in the summer of 1889 Annie Besant became a convert to Theosophy. It was in the wake of this much discussed event that the young Gandhi found his way to the Blavatsky Lodge in November of the same year.

" Towards the end of my second year in England I came across two Theosophists, brothers, and both unmarried."[148] Who were they? While there is no documentary evidence to substantiate it, the men referred to may have been Bertram Keightley and his nephew, Dr. Archibald Keightley. They were known in Theosophical circles as " the two Keightleys "[149] and the young Gandhi may have been too shy to ask or had not bothered to find out their exact relationship. Alternatively, the Mahatma may have forgotten what he had known, remembered they were connected by their names, and put them down as brothers. Archibald Keightley was a bachelor; he married Julia Campbell Ver-Planck after Gandhi had left England.[150] Bertram Keightley is described as " a man of wealth, of good education and excellent abilities " —the sort of man who would be interested in Edwin Arnold and the study of Sanskrit. Both the Keightleys played a part in inviting Madame Blavatsky to London and actively supported her Lodge with their time and money. They were particularly active in 1889, the year in which Gandhi said he became interested in Theosophy.[151] Being close to Madame Blavatsky and certainly well-known to Annie Besant, the two Keightleys sound very like the " two brothers "

---

148 *Autobiography*, p. 90.
149 *The Theosophical Movement*, p. 103.
150 *Ibid.*, p. 420.
151 *The Theosophical Movement*, p. 442.

who took Gandhi to meet the two famous women.

The Blavatsky Lodge the young Gandhi went to had been moved in July from 17 Lansdowne Road in Notting Hill to larger quarters at 19 Avenue Road in Regent's Park. The garden was spacious enough for the building of a large hall decorated with symbolic paintings by R. W. Machell, a keen member. Students receiving advanced esoteric training were taught by Madame Blavatsky in a small room with a tiled floor and a coloured glass dome. Perhaps Gandhi had seen her seated in the favourite armchair in which she died in May, 1891, shortly before he left England.[152] Though the years had taken their toll of Helena Petrovna Blavatsky, (she was born in 1831), she was still a striking looking woman, her height contrasting with an obesity exaggerated by dropsy. The grey hair crowning " a massive Calmuk face " was crinkled to the roots.[153] What thoughts passed through the young Indian's mind as he looked into that broad face with the wide mouth and the large luminous eyes that made W. Q. Judge feel that he and she had known each other " in lives long passed away? "[154] As he watched her restlessly rolling cigarettes with her pudgy, beringed fingers and chain smoking them, perhaps he asked himself whether she was a saint or a charlatan, not knowing that men would speculate about him in the same fashion after he had become the Mahatma.[155]

We do not know what Gandhi thought about her as a student, but we know his actions; he politely refused to join the Theosophical Society. They were too different—the shrewd, worldly-wise old woman and the young Indian student with his stark simplicity of spirit. He liked putting in an occasional French expression into his early writings but

---

[152] Ryan, " Closing Years of H. P. Blavatsky's Life," *op. cit.*, *passim*.
[153] Olcott, *op. cit.*, p. 49.
[154] Ryan, *op. cit.*, p. 45.
[155] Olcott, *op. cit.*, p. 413.

he could not say, " Permettez moi, Madame," and light a cigarette for her as Olcott had done at their first meeting; Gandhi detested smoking. He was not an emotional type like Mohini K. Chatterjee who could throw himself at Madame Blavatsky's feet and kiss the hem of her robe.[156]

Many years later the Mahatma said of Theosophy, " What has been a bar to my joining the society is its secret side—its occultism. It has never appealed to me."[157] Madame Blavatsky could not draw him into the little room with the tiled floor and the coloured glass dome. It was just as well that, unlike Mavalankar, Mohini K. Chatterjee, Babaji, and J. Krishnamurti, the young Gandhi escaped the role of a Theosophical *chela*. " The Collapse of Koot Hoomi "[158] was not unconnected with the rise of Mahatma Gandhi, a real, flesh and blood Mahatma whose life and struggles are all the more attractive because of their lack of occult trimmings. Gandhi was attracted by the Universal Brotherhood preached by Theosophy, but was too down to earth to involve himself in any scheme for the good of mankind which involved such strange dabblings in the occult.

It is very difficult for an Indian to rid himself of all traces of any belief in the occult and Gandhi was no exception. Even today the young Indian who goes to the West finds that there are some types of people who have a romantic image of him as a man coming from the land of occultism and mystery. In Gandhi's student days it was even easier to conform to the exotic stereotype in the minds of some Westerners when Occultism occupied a position in the popular mind somewhat similar to that of Outer Space today. Gandhi read Christian and Theosophist esoteric literature

---

[156] Ryan, *op. cit.*, p. 176.
[157] *This Was Bapu*, p. 13.
[158] The Coulomb Letters were published under this title in *The Madras Christian College Magazine* beginning September, 1884.

during his South African days. There are traces of occultism in his faith in the "inner voice," in Satyagraha as "soul-force" and his attitude to dreams. An American admirer, Vincent Sheean, would see more of the occult in Gandhi than Gandhi saw in himself. The Mahatma was an intrepid voyager in the realms of the spirit but he always carried with him the sheet anchor of a sound common sense.

The Key to Theosophy[159] which Gandhi read was a textbook described as "a clear exposition in the form of question and answer, of the ethics, science and philosophy for the study of which the Theosophical Society has been founded." Some of the discursiveness had been disciplined by the time Madame Blavatsky wrote *The Key to Theosophy*, but her rambling familiarity with dead cults and ancient religions made the young Gandhi feel how meagre was his own knowledge of his ancestral faith.

There were many things Madame Blavatsky had to say about the contemporary situation which stuck in his mind and coloured his later writings. Two sections can be picked out of the book which struck immediate chords in the young Gandhi; they are what Madame Blavatsky had to say about "Pledges" and how "Prayer kills self-reliance." He must have read with joy the words she quoted from the *Path* of 1889: "A pledge, once taken, is forever binding in both the moral and occult worlds. If we break it once and are punished, that does not justify us in breaking it again; and so long as we do, so long will the mighty lever of the Law of Karma react upon us."[160] Madame Blavatsky was concerned with the loyalty of the membership to her and Gandhi with loyalty to his mother, but, as his account of his London days

---

159 The book was first printed by the Theosophical Publishing Company, London, in 1889. The quotations in this book are from the second edition of the Theosophical Publishing Company of New York published in 1896.
160 "On the Sacredness of Pledges," *The Key to Theosophy*, p. 46.

shows, words like these helped him to remain true to his pledge to Putlibai.[161] On prayer, however, he obviously found himself in disagreement with Blavatsky; the young Gandhi could not think of prayer as killing self-reliance. Recalling his moral struggles in London he wrote, " Supplication, worship, prayer are no superstition; they are acts more real than the acts of eating, drinking, sitting, or walking."[162]

The young Gandhi would see more of the other famous woman he met in Blavatsky Lodge—Annie Besant. She came to India in 1893, the year Gandhi left for South Africa, and died in the land of her adoption in 1933. Their relations were marked by an ambivalence compounded of mingled elements of dislike and mutual admiration. But in 1889 the young student was deeply interested in Annie Besant's conversion to Theosophy as a result of her being asked by W. T. Stead to review Blavatsky's *The Secret Doctrine* in the *Review of Reviews*. Gandhi, ever an admirer of courage in others, was impressed by the manner in which she stood by her new convictions amidst the dismayed groans of her friends and the galling jeers of her enemies. He read her pamphlet, *Why I Became A Theosophist*, in which she replied to attacks by *The Freethinker*, *Medium and Daybreak*, and the National Secular Society. The young Indian did not fail to note the able manner in which she turned the motto of the National Secular Society—" We seek for Truth "—against them. " That one loyalty to Truth I must keep stainless," she wrote, " whatever friendships fail me or human ties be broken."[163] It was a lesson Gandhi never forgot.

---

[161] *Autobiography*, pp. 78-79.

[162] " Prayer Kills Self-reliance," *The Key to Theosophy*, p. 64; also *Autobiography*, p. 96.

[163] This little pamphlet of thirty-one pages was printed in 1889 by the Free Thought Publishing Company of London. For an account of Gandhi's later relations with Annie Besant, see Eleanor Morton's *The Women in Gandhi's Life*.

206

Gandhi says *The Key to Theosophy* " stimulated in me the desire to read books on Hinduism, and disabused me of the notion fostered by the missionaries that Hinduism was rife with superstition."[164] Though his reading of books on Hinduism did not begin in a serious way till he got to South Africa, the Theosophists planted the desire to do so by introducing him to *The Song Celestial* and *The Light of Asia* by Edwin Arnold. As a student, the romantic, etherealized image of the Buddha by the professor turned poet appealed to him more than the *Bhagavad Gita*. Edwin Arnold was contributing to a process of cultural assimilation by which many old gods around the world would come to look like Jesus Christ rather than their original selves. It must also be remembered that the young Gandhi belonged to an organization of Muslim students called the Anjuman Islamia.[165] It had stimulated his interest in the Prophet Mohammed and he gladly read the chapter on " The Hero as a Prophet " in Carlyle's *Heroes and Hero-Worship*. The little boy who listened to the discussions between his father and his friends from many communities continued the debate within himself in London. *The Key to Theosophy* suggested that there are common threads running through all the great religions. In London, the young Gandhi found the particular thread he was looking for in renunciation. " That renunciation was the highest form of religion appealed to me greatly."[166] It was a first intuitive and unformulated realization of the path he would choose to tread.

What Gandhi came to value in Theosophy was not its teachings but the role it played in creating a new respect for Eastern religions and peoples and the development of Asian nationalism. The Theosophical movement was, in the

---

[164] *Autobiography*, p. 91.
[165] B. R. Nanda, *op. cit.*, p. 30.
[166] *Ibid.*, p. 92.

words of Olcott, " a sign of a world-wide acceptance of Eastern
philosophical ideas, which must work for the reinvigoration
and incalculable broadening of the spiritual sympathies of
mankind."[167]   But as a popular movement it was a humanistic
undercurrent below the placid surface of the intellectual
studies of scholarly philosophers and linguists.   In this sense
it became part of the revolt of the " external proletariat of the
Western world," in Toynbee's conception, against modern
civilization and white Imperialism.   When Gandhi agreed
to address the Theosophical Society in Johannesburg in 1905
he did so in the spirit of the Tibetan, Tsong-Kha-Pa, who
wanted to enlighten the " white barbarians."[168]

The Theosophists also achieved a larger measure of identification with Eastern peoples than the Christian missionaries,
partly by their acceptance of Vegetarianism.   Their praise
of Eastern religions, sometimes in terms of fulsome flattery,
appealed to the national feelings of suppressed peoples.
Blavatsky could, for example, describe Sanskrit as the
language of the gods.[169]   Their excessive adulation of Oriental
mysticism brought forth a mild protest even from Max
Muller.

Theosophy stimulated Gandhi without making him into a
Theosophist.   As a student the popular side of Hinduism
rather than the intellectual one remained uppermost in his
mind.   His picture of Hinduism, sketched with real ability,
emerged in " Some Indian Festivals," perhaps his best written
article in *The Vegetarian*.   His description of *Diwali* is particularly appealing.   The article shows the boy was a keen
observer of the colourful life of Rajkot and greatly enjoyed
the social aspects of Hindu festivals.   Yet his account of Holi
shows that he could pick out both the lighter and darker

---

[167] *Op. cit.*, p. 3.
[168] *Collected Works*, IV, p. 405.
[169] Ryan, *op. cit.*, p. 102.

shades in his Vallabhachari heritage. Gandhi may have read the account of Hindu festivals in B. M. Malabari's *Gujarat and the Gujaratis*; like the Parsi writer, he too was critical of some aspects of *Holi*.

There is real beauty in his " peep at one of the temples " when he makes you hear, feel and smell the scene. " Pious persons are sitting on the steps making garlands for *Thakorji*. Among the flowers you see beautiful roses, *chameli*, *moghra*... When the doors are flung open for *darshan*, you observe the fountains in full play. You enjoy soft and fragrant breezes. *Thakorji* has worn light costumes of delicate shades. Piles of flowers before him and garlands round his neck almost hide him from your view. He is swung to and fro. The swing, too, is covered with green leaves sprinkled with fragrant waters." And then a shadow falls across this vision full of light and colour. " Outside the temple the sight is not edifying. You here meet with nothing but obscene language during the fortnight preceding *Holi*...People form themselves into small parties. Then one party competes with another in using obscene language and singing obscene songs...They paint obscene words on your clothes...Whether you are in the house or out of it, obscene words are jarring on your ears." The young Gandhi used the language of a missionary rather than that of a dispassionate student of cultural anthropology when he commented, " It is a relief to be able to say that with the progress of education and civilization such scenes are slowly, though surely, dying out."[170]

The conflicting roles of reformer and revivalist in the young Gandhi survived in the Mahatma, but both he and India had changed greatly by the time Pandit Madan Mohan Malaviya read the *Bhagavata Purana* to him during his epic fast of twenty-one days. The obscenity the boy had deplored had receded

---

[170] *Collected Works*, I, pp. 37-44, *passim*.

after the fiery ordeal of The Maharaj Libel Case. Writers like Manilal C. Parekh could now go to the original sources of Vallabhachari philosophy which inspired deep *bhakti* and ignore the eroticism as an historical aberration. The Mahatma could not always resolve the tension between the Indian Renaissance and the need for Indian Reform; he stressed one or the other in empirical and pragmatic fashion. He was never really in doubt though that India needed a reformation in morals as much as she needed a renaissance of her culture.

" ...dear London "

Apart from London, the only other European capital visited by Gandhi before his brief Continental tour of 1931 was Paris. The young student spent a week in Paris drawn there by the great Exhibition in 1890, the year in which Walt Whitman greeted it with his " Bravo, Paris Exposition." Another young man destined to fame who visited it was Sigmund Freud. Bewildered and unimpressed by the Exhibition the young Gandhi preferred the atmosphere of the old churches. " I remember nothing of the Exhibition excepting its magnitude and variety...The ancient churches of Paris are still in my memory. Their grandeur and their peacefulness are unforgettable."[171]

In 1922, when the young Indian who tramped the streets of Paris had hit the newspaper headlines with his Non-Cooperation Movement, Lady Gregory, George Bernard Shaw and H. J. Massingham discussed the significance of the Mahatma. When they had concluded that he portended the end of the British Empire, G. B. S. playfully suggested that Gandhi should be locked up at the top of an Eiffel Tower

---

[171] *Autobiography*, p. 101.

to prevent him from rousing his people.[172] They did not know then that Gandhi had actually ascended to the top of the Eiffel Tower more than once. He had heartily agreed with Tolstoy's verdict that the Eiffel Tower was a monument to human folly brought about by the smoking of tobacco. Gandhi devoted a whole paragraph to the Eiffel Tower in his autobiography which suggested that it had become a Tower of Babel symbol to him even when he was a young man.[173] Had he gone to the Exhibition in 1889 he might have run into Max Nordau, the Zionist philosopher. Nordau, in a mood very different from that of a Hemingway, was nauseated by the Spanish bull-fighters he saw at the Exhibition,[174] even as Gandhi was sickened by the Eiffel Tower. A similar attitude, though derived from different aspects of the Exhibition, would endear Nordau's writings to Gandhi in the distant future in South Africa.

It was only London that the young Gandhi knew, and the Mahatma had a soft corner in his heart for that metropolis to the end of his days. The student has preserved for us his mood on that warm and sunny June 12, 1891, when his train steamed out of Liverpool Street Station. " I could not make myself believe that I was going to India until I stepped into the steamship *Oceana* of the P. & O. Company. So much attached was I to London and its environments; for who would not be? London with its teaching institutions, public galleries, museums, theatres, vast commerce, public parks, and Vegetarian restaurants is a fit place for a student and a traveller, a trader and a ' faddist '—as a Vegetarian would be called by his opponents. Thus, it was not without deep

---

[172] *This Was Bapu*, p. 62.

[173] *Autobiography*, pp. 101, 102. He did, however, appreciate French cooking, *Collected Works*, I, p. 51.

[174] Max Nordau, *Degeneration*, trans., from 2nd ed. of German work, (New York, Appleton, 1895), p. 8.

regret that I left dear London."[175]   Within the brief compass
of Gandhi's description lie not only some of the images of a
stimulating world he lived, moved, and breathed in for three
years, but also a good deal of the history of a London which
underwent a rapid transformation in the nineteenth century.

Many of the features of London he listed came into existence
only after the accession of Queen Victoria.   A visit to the
National or the Tate or the numerous art galleries around
Bond Street, Piccadilly, Regent Street, and the Mall became
popular after the introduction of cheap one-day excursion
tickets on the railways.   The British Museum in Bloomsbury
and the Victoria and Albert in Kensington (two localities
where Gandhi had lived), were built in the young student's
life-time.   E. J. Rapson was at the Indian section of the
Museum in Kensington making his contribution to the study
of Indian history.   Matinee concerts had been legalized by
the Public Entertainment Act of 1875.   Lydia Thompson
had opened the Strand Theatre under her own management
in 1886, and Dan Leno was the popular Pantomime star of
the period at Drury Lane.   Did Gandhi perchance take his
landlady's daughter to see Leno as the Wicked Aunt in *The
Babes in the Wood* which ran till the end of April, 1889?   Or
is there an echo of Leno's popular song, " Going to Buy
Milk for the Twins," in Gandhi's description of the little
milkmaids in an article for *The Vegetarian*?[176]   After all, the
young student did air his knowledge of the famous singer,
Patti.[177]   Gandhi had a keen eye for some of the buildings
he saw as he walked the gas-lighted streets or travelled on a
horse-drawn tram.

The injustice of the colour bar in South Africa recalled to
his mind the figure of Justice he had often seen in London.

---

[175] *Collected Works*, I, p. 64.
[176] *Collected Works*, I, p. 40.
[177] *Ibid.*, p. 67.

A Young Indian as a Late-Victorian

The symbol of a Court of Justice is a pair of scales held evenly by an impartial and blind but sagacious woman. Fate has purposely made her blind in order that she may not judge a person from his exterior but from his intrinsic worth."[178] Gandhi remembered the figure of Justice on the Law Courts in the Strand built in 1882; he wished the members of the Law Society of Natal, who opposed his admission as an advocate, knew what she really stood for.

What was the young Gandhi of twenty who lived in London really like? His father had predicted that Mohandas would bring credit to "the family"—that little unit immersed in the local history of Kathiawad. But what of those who met him in London at twenty? There is not a breath of suspicion that the young man of twenty is destined for greatness—not even in one of his closest friends, Josiah Oldfield. When Oldfield wrote "Gandhi as I Knew Him" in 1930, the overpowering image of the Mahatma has overlaid the picture of the "young, shy, diffident youth, slim and a little weakly" who called on him when he was Editor of *The Vegetarian*.[179] Oldfield outlived Gandhi and his article entitled "My Friend Gandhi" does not tell us any more than his previous fragment about the young Indian with whom he shared "digs" in St. Stephens Square, Bayswater, and with whom he founded the West London Food Reform Society.[180] "We lived in the same diggings, shared the same table, sat on the same committees, wrestled with the same social problems and were faced with the same temptations of youth.."[181]

---

[178] *Autobiography*, p. 181.

[179] *John O' London's Weekly*, March 29, 1930. See Joseph John (ed.), *Gandhi As Others See Him*, (Colombo, W. E. Bastian & Co., 1933), pp. 16-24.

[180] *Reminiscences of Gandhiji*, pp. 187-189, dated October 10, 1948.

[181] *Gandhi As Others See Him*, p. 19.

Oldfield was a prolific author himself.[182] Why does he content himself with a few enthusiastic generalizations about the youth of the Mahatma? Is it because he could never really get over his surprise that the friend of his youth, " a man of comparatively obscure birth, of no great family influence, of small financial means, and of delicate constitution " had reached such a pinnacle of fame?[183] Or is his diffidence symptomatic of what would happen to most of Gandhi's biographers? " There is no Saint that has been placed in Christian hagiology since the time of the Apostles who could be invoked to mould men's actions today to the same extent that Mahatma Gandhi can influence devout and superstitious Hindus of certain classes," wrote Oldfield.[184] Why did Oldfield do little more than add a small bit to the spate of hagiography about Gandhi when he could have done so much to help in tracing the development of a great man? Gandhi accused modern civilization of mesmerism and hypnotism in its effects on the minds of men just as Tolstoy had done before him. Perhaps even Oldfield had succumbed to that mesmerism and hypnotism which mass adoration built up around a very human Mahatma, so that the writing of objective biography became impossible.

There is one keen insight, however, which Oldfield did provide for understanding those London days. The Mahatma had suffered martyrdom when he wrote, " I have always felt since, that the Indians coming to England have to face the same great testing examination. If they fail, they prove that they have commonplace minds and they drop into the ordinary

---

182 One of Oldfield's books was titled *The Beauty Aspect of Life*. It suggests that one of Gandhi's expressions (as recalled by Millie Graham Polak) which he frequently used in South Africa—" That is the beauty of it "—was a vestige of his London friendship. See *Mr. Gandhi: The Man*, p. 157.

183 *Gandhi As Others See Him*, p. 18.

184 *Gandhi As Others See Him*, p. 18.

run of English diet, English habits, and general mediocrity. If, on the other hand, they can stand firm in their faith and be prepared to die for it, they prove themselves men indeed. Upon this class of men does the mantle of Gandhi still fall and the future of India depend."[185] Oldfield was right and yet the claim requires a historical setting. The struggle for integrity was more intense in the young Gandhi's case partly because he came from Kathiawad, a long-isolated region rich in regional history which had only recently come under effective British rule.

In 1945, Gandhi described the young Mohandas, who set off for London, to Gope Gurbax Gurbaxani: " I was only a matriculate when I left for England. I saw Bombay then for the first time. I had once been to Ahmedabad to appear at the Matriculation Examination. Otherwise I had remained in Kathiawad all the time, and had roamed about the villages in a bullock cart. As I was the son of a dewan, the people fed me on the way with *jowar roti* and curds, and at times they paid me an eight anna piece. When I remember those days my mouth begins to water even now."[186] Would the Mahatma's mouth, symbolic of his archaism, his taste for the past, have watered any less had he grown up in Ahmedabad or Bombay? Or is there something in a great man that defies historical analysis—something inborn and inherent which will make him a great man despite all outward circumstances? " Like Socrates he is guided by his Daimon..."[187] So says Oldfield who helped him to cook lentils and rice before the spirit of his destiny took full possession of him.

Oldfield is both right and wrong about Indian students who go abroad. They have to struggle for integrity but it is not a simple process of isolating themselves in the castle of their

---

[185] *Reminiscences of Gandhiji*, p. 188.
[186] *Reminiscences of Gandhiji*, p. 110.
[187] *Gandhi As Others See Him*, p. 18.

skins. They also have to decide what can get underneath their skins, what can get in and mix with their own spirits as they try to find a new meaning, a new synthesis with which to shape their lives. The process of rejection and assimilation in the young Gandhi continued in the Mahatma; the war of the worlds in him was endless. The returning student who writes so vividly and breezily about his return voyage to India had become something of a Late-Victorian gentleman. The account of the homeward journey, so full of vitality and confidence, is in striking contrast to the venturesome timidity of the outward pilgrimage.[188]

" Can it be said of a man of fifty that he is the same being that he was at twenty? " The Gandhi who returned to India from South Africa when approaching his fifties seemed an extremely strange being to many, but had he really divested himself of all the traits of a Late-Victorian gentleman with his clothes? He was still reacting to that top-hatted young student carrying his silver-topped cane jauntily as he wended his way through Piccadilly Circus but he could not shake off that " inner man " fashioned by the Late-Victorian era quite so easily. There was his terrible earnestness and Gladstonian moral fervour which went along with a punctiliousness that could make him give a young man a lecture on how to fold and cut paper properly with a paper knife.[189] Carlyle would have been delighted with the Mahatma's love of hard work in which the energy of the Bania had fused with a very Victorian emphasis.

A quotation from Carlyle in *The Key to Theosophy* read, " The end of man is an action and not a thought, though it were the noblest."[190] Action so dominated the life of the

---

[188] " On My Way Home Again To India," *Collected Works*, I, pp 64-70.
[189] Kishorlal Mashruwala, " Small Things I Learnt from Him," *Reminiscences of Gandhiji*, pp 172-173.
[190] *Op. cit.*, p 205.

Mahatma that, apart from the times when he was in jail, books had little claim on his attention. It is doubtful whether the Mahatma read a single book by any author of repute who belonged to the twentieth rather than the nineteenth century. His mind was coloured by Victorian literature with which he had a wider familiarity than is generally known; his knowledge extended from " shilling shockers "[191] to Victorian novelists and poets. The young Indian speaker who addressed the Band of Mercy in Upper Norwood ended by quoting Shakespeare.[192] Later, he could still illustrate a point with a reference to Thackeray, (" We know that Becky lived on nothing a year in Vanity Fair ")[193] or turn a line from Tennyson into the title of an article (" Ring out the old, ring in the new ");[194] his knowledge of the Poet Laureate ranged from " In Memoriam " to " The Charge of the Light Brigade."[195] His English vocabulary not only gave him away as a Late-Victorian but sometimes brought him much misunderstanding. A generation of Englishmen, who had forgotten how frequently the adjective " satanic " had been employed by a host of Victorian writers from Blake to Blavatsky, were furious with the Mahatma when he used it to describe British rule in India in the 1920's. Even some of the expressions the student read in the British newspapers stuck in the Mahatma's mind; a phrase he often employed—" a union of hearts "— can be traced back to the speeches of Gladstone.[196]

The main impress of Victorian literature on Gandhi's mind

---

[191] See Gandhi's Introduction to K. M. Munshi's *Gujarat and Its Literature*, p. 6, for an example of his use of it. Catherine Mayo's *Mother India* was dismissed by him as a " shilling shocker."

[192] *Collected Works*, I, p. 52.

[193] *Ibid*, I, p. 76.

[194] *Collected Works*, IV, p. 216.

[195] *Young India*, November 5, 1919.

[196] G. P. Gooch cites Gladstone's use of it in *History of Modern Europe* 1878–1919, (London, Home University Library, 1923), p. 4.

is the anarchism with which so much of it was saturated, particularly during the last three decades of the nineteenth century. The young Gandhi had only to walk down the Strand to be reminded of movements like the Land Nationalisation Society presided over by Alfred Russel Wallace, formed " To restore the Land to the People and the People to the Land." In the windows of the bookshops he would see publications in the Social Science Series put out by Swan Sonnenschein and commended by the *Westminster Review*. The Anarchistic writers appealed most to the young Indian whose Bania heritage would incline him towards a philosophy which had its roots in those institutions evolved by the European masses—the clan, the village community, the guild, the free medieval city. This philosophy would allow him intellectually to oppose hierarchically structured conceptions of government. If Gandhi had been projected into Medieval Europe, he would have found much that he could understand.

The International Working Men's Association founded in 1864 showed a distrust of parliamentary legislation from its very inception. Anarchist influence developed rapidly with the reorganization of the Anarchist International in 1881 in London. By the second half of the eighties, the Anarchists were fomenting strikes and leading May Day demonstrations in many countries. Their advocacy of a general strike for an eight-hour day and their attempt to infiltrate armies with anti-militarist propaganda met with violent opposition particularly in Spain and the United States. Anarchists were tortured in Barcelona Castle and executed in Chicago in 1887. Anarchism retaliated with waves of violence that lapped the shores of India and led to a period of Terrorism.

When Gandhi was a student in London, Prince Peter Kropotkin, who had settled there since 1886, was doing much to rid Anarchism of its evil reputation by his lectures to bodies like the Ancoats Brotherhood of Manchester and the London

Ethical Society. Kropotkin's *The Conquest of Bread* appeared in French in 1888 and articles by him appeared in *The Nineteenth Century*. The wider influence of Anarchism is seen in the revived interest in Godwin, Shelley, and Thoreau, in which H. S. Salt played a part, and in a host of writers including Herbert Spencer, Nietzeche, Alexander Herzen, Edward Carpenter and Ibsen. The work of Proudhon, who first used the term "Anarchism" in his *Qu'est-ce que la Propriete?* in 1840, was reflected in William Morris and Zola. A Russian element was introduced with the writings of Mikhail Bakunin and the Christian Anarchism of Tolstoy. The sociological roots of Gandhi's anarchism are in the economic and social history of Kathiawad which we have outlined; its intellectual roots were in the Late-Victorian Era symbolised by his fondness for Shelley's "Masque of Anarchy." Gandhi's anarchism was summed up in Victorian images borrowed from Fitzgerald and Blake.

"...dear London." The warmth in those two words stayed with the young lawyer drinking the bitter cup of racial prejudice in South Africa and stayed with the Mahatma in the heat of the Civil Disobedience movements. Something of the magic of a Mahatma, transforming mutual dislike and mistrust into the bonds of understanding and co-operation within a great Commonwealth, was derived from this fond association with London. Could Gandhi have become a Mahatma if he had never gone to England, never walked the streets of London? It is doubtful whether he would have been a Mahatma with such universal appeal if his road had not led through to London and Johannesburg. Gandhi was no Walt Whitman in love with the very pavements of the great cities created by the industrialism and commerce of the nineteenth century. But "...dear London" is the point at which the spirit of Gandhi, so disillusioned with modern urban civilization, and the spirit of Whitman, so much in love with it, meet in the embrace of a common humanity.

Gandhi went to London soon after the passing of the Reform Bill of 1884; he caught the note of deep pessimism in a period of transition, but missed the fact that the Welfare State was just around the corner. The young Nehru, a student at Harrow and Cambridge in Edwardian England, saw the growth of Labour and the development of British Socialist thought. Each of these leaders brought to Indian affairs an understanding of the world which had its roots both in India and in England. A host of incidents and images symbolise that relationship of two cultures, but one of the most touching is the picture of the aged Mahatma concerned about what he should send Princess Elizabeth, the great great grand-daughter of Queen Victoria, for a wedding present. In the end he decided to send her " a small lace cloth made from the yarn he had himself spun."[197] That small lace cloth was symbolic of a significant process in which a shuttle plied by many hands had moved to and fro between India and England, weaving a pattern in which there was much evil and much good.

---

[197] *Reminiscences of Gandhiji*, p. 183.

CHAPTER FIVE

The Birth of a Fighter

The same sun that shone so brilliantly when Gandhi left England was wrapped in monsoon clouds when the *Assam* lurched through misty rain into the choppy waters of Bombay Harbour on July 5, 1891. A good sailor, his feet were steady on the swaying deck, but his mind sought for some safe anchorage.[1] Coleridge would have found in Gandhi an apt illustration of his point that Nature clothes us with her moods. He liked the stormy surge and the splash of the waves, but his thoughts veered between hope and despair. " The outer storm was to me the symbol of the inner."[2] The returning student knew instinctively that he would not find it easy to readjust to a family and a country he had not seen for three years. He looked the same but the inner man had changed.[3]

The brief interlude between his return to India and his departure for South Africa was stamped with the restlessness that Durkheim calls *anomie*; Gandhi felt uprooted and out of touch with his surroundings whether he was in Bombay,

---

[1] *Collected Works*, I, p. 70.
[2] *Autobiography*, p. 111.
[3] For a study of the problems of Indian students who return from abroad see John and Ruth Useem, *The Western Educated Man in India*, (New York, Dryden Press, 1955).

Rajkot or Porbandar. The exile longs for home, and, when he is home, longs for exile. At the end of a year he was looking for some means of escape. His letter to Patwari shows that he was thinking of going abroad again.[4] Despite Haridas Vakhatchand Vora's courageous stand on his behalf,[5] his caste, including near relatives, remained unfriendly; his relations with Kasturba were strained by an added dimension of unshared experience; the desire for a higher standard of living only emphasized the hopelessness of his financial circumstances. The legal profession had already become overcrowded and Gandhi, with his British notions of professional conduct, could not compete successfully in the scramble after every potential client. When a Meman business firm of Porbandar sounded him out about going to South Africa he accepted their offer with alacrity and a sense of relief.[6]

If Gandhi's preparation for going to England was inadequate he was even less ready for what he would experience in South Africa. Sheth Abdul Karim Jhaveri, a partner of the Durban firm of Dada Abdulla and Company, gave him a rather rosy picture of conditions in Natal coloured by the business rather than the social aspects of life in that British colony.[7] The Gandhi who " set forth full of zest to try my luck in South Africa "[8] was in an adventurous frame of mind: " I was fond of novel experiences. I love to see fresh fields and pastures new."[9]

After a leisurely voyage, Gandhi's ship arrived off Durban towards the end of May, 1893. It was the winter season in Natal. The air was fresh and crisp as the young Indian saw the famous promontory sheltering the harbour, the steep and

---

4 *Collected Works*, I, p. 71.
5 *Ibid.*, III, p. 71.
6 *Autobiography*, pp. 111-129, *passim*
7 *Satyagraha in South Africa*, p. 41.
8 *Autobiography*, p. 131.
9 *Satyagraha in South Africa*, p. 41.

A view of the old harbour, Durban.

Gandhiji in Kathiawadi dress.

wooded Bluff, as well as the outline of the hill behind the town called the Berea, which rose out of the sea. When the ship anchored outside Durban Harbour—a land-locked lagoon with a sandbar at its mouth which prevented the entry of ocean-going steamers at that time—he may have watched " the huge jelly-fish, shaped like open umbrellas and exquisitely coloured "[10] or admired the trim-looking bungalows on the Berea. Durban was lovely and Gandhi was glad he had launched on this adventure. Then there was all the familiar excitement of disembarking—the little steam launches bouncing over the waves towards the ship, the white handkerchiefs fluttering, the shrill cries of greeting. Here was Dada Abdulla coming towards him in the flowing robes and turban of a Meman merchant; but the whites boarding the ship brought a chill wind with them. Apprehension and anger surged through Gandhi as he observed the slightly obsequious manner of Dada Abdulla towards the whites and the reluctant or patronising familiarity with which they greeted him. Some of them looked at the young Indian dressed in a morning coat like a London barrister with barely concealed surprise ("Aren't these coolies getting uppish!"). Here Gandhi had his first whiff of awareness that though Natal was a British colony, Durban was not Tilbury.

The landing was a novel and thrilling experience. Like all passengers going ashore, he and Dada Abdulla got into the basket cage which was then swung over the ship's side by a crane and lowered into a waiting tender that bucked sometimes " with all an untamed broncho's devilry."[11] The tender chugged away in the lee of the Bluff to the landing place called the Point. Gandhi was soon taking in all the

---

[10] H. Hamilton Fyfe, *South Africa Today*, (London, Eveleigh Nash, 1911), p. 173.
[11] Stuart Cumberland, *What I Think of South Africa: Its People and Its Politics*, (London, Chapman & Hall Ltd., 1896), pp. 171-172. See also Lady Sarah Wilson, *South African Memories*, (London, Edward Arnold, 1909), p. 34.

223

sights and sounds of a town which, because it lies so bright and sparkling beside the Indian Ocean, has reminded many travellers of Colombo. He spent his first week there getting to know Dada Abdulla and Durban.

In 1893, Durban was only a fair-sized town with a population of 27,492 (Whites 13,293, Africans 7059, Indians 7140)[12] but it had changed greatly since the days when it was a straggling settlement of adventurous ivory-hunters unrecognized by either the Imperial or the Cape Governments and dependent on the goodwill of the war-like Zulus.[13] In 1851, the total population was only 1,694. A decade later Natal was being rapidly transformed into the Garden Colony of South Africa by cheap indentured labour from India. The rich and fertile soil of Natal produced sugar harvests of colonial wealth for the whites and bitter rice of racial hatred for the Indians.[14]

But of all this Gandhi would learn in time. At the moment he was just a young Indian wandering about the streets of a strange and fascinating town. He noted the fine bodies of the Zulus as he watched the rickshaw pullers in their resplendent headgear and strapping girls wrapped in coloured "blankets" swinging through the streets on their way back to their beehive-shaped homes on the hillsides around Durban. They may have recalled to his mind J. K. Lavater's *Essays on Physiognomy* which he had read in London. He felt a slight distaste for the discarded European clothes worn by some of the Negroes lounging about, apparently with nothing to do.[15]

---

[12] *Brown's South Africa*, (Cape Town and Johannesburg, J. C. Juta Co., 1893); see section on " Durban."

[13] George McCall Theal, *Progress of South Africa in the Century*, The Nineteenth Century Series, (London, W. R. Chambers, 1902), p. 233.

[14] C. J. Ferguson-Davie, *The Early History of Indians in Natal*, (Johannesburg, South African Institute of Race Relations, 1953); see " The Effect of Their Work in the First Ten Years."

[15] *Satyagraha in South Africa*, pp. 8-20, *passim*.

He did not then know that the fine plumes on the heads of the rickshaw pullers were the crest-fallen reminders of a manly race that once struck terror into the whites with the names of Shaka and Dingaan.

Perhaps Gandhi took a three-penny tram ride (two horse-trams were first introduced in 1885)[16] from the Point or Field Street up to the Berea.   From this spot one could get a glorious view of the Bluff and the sea.   Here was the suburbia of the wealthy, a cluster of bungalows with long shady verandahs and gardens a riot of colour, the grenadillas and magnolias contrasting with the dark green foliage of the trees. It was a form of gracious living made possible by indentured Indian servants. Gandhi may have seen one here tying up the mosquito curtains over a bed, another busy in the garden.   There were two hotels on the Berea—the Grand and the Fairholme.[17]

The town below the Berea was a blending of East and West, of Calcutta and London.   The Town Hall in West Street with its fine Corinthian pillars and the Public Gardens in front of it were English, the Market behind it and the mosque in Covey Street were Indian.   The deeper one went into the commercial areas the more intense the mixture became.   The British firms and Indian shops stood side by side as they had sprung up in a developing Colony catering to Natal farmers and planters, the diamond miners of Kimberley and the gold diggers of Johannesburg.   In the same streets were many law firms; for the British lawyers throve on the commerce of English and Indian merchant alike.   The news of the world was brought to the merchants and lawyers by two newspapers—the *Natal Mercury* and the

---

[16] Alan F. Hattersley, *Later Annals of Natal*, (London, Longmans Green & Co., 1938), p. 13.

[17] For a description of Durban in the early 1890's, see *Brown's South Africa* and H. Lincoln Tangye, *In New South Africa*, (London, Horace Cox, 1896), pp. 137-138.

15

Natal Advertiser. Pietermaritzburg with its Anglo-Indian atmosphere was the capital, but Durban was the real heart of Natal. Here lived the true colonials, a first generation of Britishers born in the Colony. The young Gandhi did not know it during those few days in Durban but the colonials were on the verge of fulfilling their own dreams for Natal. These white planters and merchants, lawyers and journalists had a fair dream of what they would do with responsible government. This was to result in a dark nightmare for the Indians—one so dark that they have not yet emerged from it.

On the second or third day after Gandhi arrived, Dada Abdulla took him to see the Circuit Court. The young lawyer was naturally anxious to know how the courts functioned in Natal if he was to be useful to the Meman merchant who had brought him to South Africa in connection with a complicated commercial case. Dada Abdulla, who knew the Court well, introduced him to some of the white barristers and seated him at the horse-shoe next to his attorney, Harry Escombe, a well-known and popular figure in the Colony. Suddenly, Gandhi was aware that the Magistrate was staring at him. The duel of the two pairs of eyes ended with the Magistrate's asking him to remove his turban—a boat-shaped, cardboard turban covered with black muslin. A poor indentured Indian would have done so hastily—but not Gandhi. For the second time he felt a wave of anger pass over him. He refused and left the Court. Dada Abdulla felt a warm glow inside him; for the first time in his long experience he had seen an Indian in South Africa show some spirit when insulted by a white man. For this alone it was worth bringing this Anglicised youth all the way from Porbandar. A turban had bound a shrewd old Muslim to a young Hindu; Gandhi had won his first loyal supporter. When his anger cooled, he realized that the Magistrate had not asked the Indian merchant to remove his turban. Dada Abdulla explained that the Meman merchants had succeeded in exempting themselves from two humiliating measures imposed on Africans and indentured Indians. Indians dressed in the Meman clothes were not to be arrested if they were out after 9-00 p.m. (all other coloured persons out at night had to carry a special pass). They had also won the right to wear their turbans in Court. Gandhi's surprise and indignation were mingled with feelings of admiration for the Indian merchants. This marked the beginning of his realization that a man did not have to be a graduate of a university or wear European clothes, or speak good English in order to fight for his rights.

During the week he lived with Dada Abdulla another thought began to take shape in his mind. The Meman merchant was practically unlettered, but he was not illiterate. He had built up one of the largest commercial enterprises in Natal despite his broken English. He had a deep love for Islam and could talk interestingly about it. Gandhi found talking to him about Islamic philosophy much more worthwhile than the polite tea-party discussions he had participated in as a member of the *Anjuman Islamia* in London.

When Gandhi walked out of the Magistrate's Court he did not realize the full import of the demand that he remove his turban. Enlightened by Dada Abdulla as to the significance of the incident, he immediately wrote a letter of protest to the papers which led to a spate of correspondence for and against him. Gandhi came to have quite a sentimental attachment to that bit of cardboard and black muslin—an imitation of the Bengali *pagri*. He learned many valuable lessons from his turban. In 1893, it taught him the value of human dignity. In 1894, he had to agree not to wear it in Court when he won his battle for enrolment as a barrister in Durban, but his turban had taught him " to appreciate the beauty of compromise."[18] In 1897, it taught him courage because he

---

[18] *Autobiography*, p. 184.

wore it knowing it would help the Durban mob to recognize him; a ruffian snatched it off his head. In 1912, Gandhi sent an urgent note to Maganlal asking for his turban which he had not worn for sometime. Kasturba managed to find the frayed old turban among his discarded clothes and it was posted to Cape Town where Gandhi had gone to receive Gokhale.

Was it showmanship? Had he realized that his turban had become part of his public identity? " But newspapers had made it quite famous. I had seen many pictures and cartoons of Gandhiji wearing a turban,"[19] says Prabhudas Gandhi who was a youngster on the Tolstoy Farm when Kasturba searched for the battered, old headgear. Possibly there was a mixture here of conceit and love of old battle-dress, something like Garibaldi sticking to his colourful uniform in London or Montgomery wearing his greasy, old beret. But there was more to it than just that; it was some-thing deeply rooted in the psychology of the Mahatma—that proud wearing of the badge of suffering. Gandhi was adept in the use of symbols for transforming humiliation into triumph. The young student in London had been taken by a friend to the Holborn Restaurant in the hope that its palatial appearance would awe Gandhi into eating meat without asking any questions. When Gandhi was about to ask the waiter whether the soup contained any meat the friend lost his temper and told him to get out if he could not behave like a gentleman. " This delighted me,"[20] recorded the Mahatma bringing out that strain of masochism latent in him. Actually the young man was cold and hungry; the vegetarian restaurant he went to was closed, and he accompanied his friend to the theatre on an empty stomach. On the eve of his departure from London, Gandhi arranged a farewell

---

[19] P. Gandhi, *op. cit.*, pp. 95-96.
[20] *Autobiography*, p. 69.

dinner for his vegetarian friends in that very same non-vegetarian Holborn Restaurant. The humiliating memory of the night he had walked the streets while his friend gorged himself inside was wiped out by the happiness of the young Indian listening to the gay sounds of his party in the Holborn. More than twenty years later, in 1914, when Gandhi was in England, Sarojini Naidu, who had heard much about him from Gokhale, " went wandering around in search of his lodgings in an obscure part of Kensington and climbed the steep stairs of an old, unfashionable house to find an open door framing a living picture of a little man with a shaven head, seated on the floor on a black prison blanket and eating a messy meal of squashed tomatoes and olive oil out of a wooden prison bowl."[21] The famous " Gandhi cap," now sometimes detested as a symbol of insolence and power, was nothing but the headgear African prisoners were forced to wear in Transvaal jails. One of the Mahatma's great abilities was this agile exploitation of the symbolic drama latent in what was ostensibly a commonplace. He could change a battered tin badge into an inspiring silver escutcheon.

Mutual trust and confidence having been established, it was decided that Gandhi should go to Pretoria where an English attorney was handling the case in which Dada Abdulla was involved. Before he set off on the journey, it is more than likely that he bought a copy of *Brown's South Africa*, published earlier that year and described as " A Practical and Complete Guide for the Use of Tourists, Sportsmen, Invalids and Settlers."[22] Gandhi was young and resilient. He had apparently forgotten the humiliation of the preceding week's experience in court, for he ignored both Dada Abdulla's advice to make a bed reservation from Pietermaritzburg and

---

[21] Quoted in H. L. Polak, H. N. Brailsford and H. Pethick Lawrence, *Mahatma Gandhi*, (London, Odhams Ltd., 1949), p. 7.
[22] See footnote 11, *supra.*

the information in Brown's Guide which stated that " passengers on night trains can obtain tickets entitling them to sleeping accommodation on payment of 5 s. extra."[23] The young lawyer settled down comfortably in his First Class compartment and was soon absorbed in admiring a series of beautiful views from his carriage windows. After the first fifteen miles through lush tropical vegetation the line climbs in a series of ascending curves to a height of 3,700 feet at a point twelve miles outside Maritzburg and then descends, like the run from the Kadugannawa Pass to Kandy, to the capital which is 2200 feet above sea level. The waving banana fronds, the spreading fields of sugarcane and the date-palms rising out of a tangle of shrubbery reminded Gandhi of India.[24] After leaving the level stretch there were times when Gandhi could see the engine for long periods on the opposite sweep of a curve. The train alternately ascended and descended steep hills and skirted some blood-curdling ravines. It also passed through the farms and fruit gardens, the sugar plantations and tea estates that Indian labour had created.[25]

It was afternoon when Gandhi left Durban; night had fallen when the train pulled into the dimly-lighted station at Maritzburg six hours later. A man came down the platform and asked Gandhi if he wanted a bedroll; the careful young Bania refused. At this stop a white passenger appeared, who looked at him with obvious distaste, then disappeared only to return with two railway officials. A third official joined the group, who were staring at the young Indian, and asked

---

[23] *Brown's South Africa*, p. 29.

[24] Doke, *op. cit.*, p. 34.

[25] For descriptions of the train journey from Durban to Maritzburg in the 1890's see *Letters from South Africa*, by the *Times* special correspondent, reprinted from the *Times*, July—October, 1892, (London, Macmillan & Co., 1893), p. 116. Cf. *Brown's South Africa*; H. Hamilton Fyfe, *op. cit.*, p. 155; *Letters of Major-Gen. Hart-Synnot*, (London, Edward Arnold, 1912), p. 182.

Interior of Railway Station, Maritzburg, in the 1890s.

A South African coach.

him to get out and go to the luggage van. Gandhi refused. A constable was called who pushed him out of the compartment. He refused to get in anywhere else, and the train steamed off leaving him on the platform shivering in the cold night air. Gandhi later regretted both his failure to purchase a bed reservation and his parsimony, because this shortsightedness was used as an excuse for ejecting him.

The Mahatma never forgot the bitter cold of that night as he sat and shivered in the waiting room. What had happened to Gandhi's additional clothing? He did not know. He was too frightened to ask. " My overcoat was in my luggage, but I did not dare ask for it lest I should be insulted again."[26] Gandhi's luggage was safely restored to him in the morning. The Natal Railways were certainly efficient. But it is also probable that his baggage received special attention from the railway porters who were indentured Indians. It was the least that these silent witnesses to a compatriot's humiliation could do for him.

The officials who were so uncivil to Gandhi knew no Indians other than traders and coolies. If they were local officials living in the town they were only reflecting the social situation in Pietermaritzburg itself. Rosamund Southey has described Indian life in the capital of Natal as she knew it in the 1890's.[27] The town named after Pieter Retief and Gerit Maritz stands on the banks of the muddy Umbindusi. There were a large number of Indian coolies who lived at this time in shanties close to the river cultivating their little vegetable gardens. The Indian shanties stretched for a mile along the river and included a bazaar with a few gold and silversmith shops. These humble labourers were treated with contempt, and no

---

[26] *Autobiography*, p. 141.
[27] Rosamund Southey, *Storm and Sunshine in South Africa*, (London, John Murray, 1910), pp. 167, 206-210.

one was concerned with their education or their social and moral welfare.

Perhaps Gandhi heard the sound of Indian tom-toms drifting up from the valley as he struggled with his thoughts and feelings that night in the cold waiting room. He could not understand why these whites should be so different from the people he had met in the London he loved. Did he think of Frederick Pincott? " His smiling, open face stayed in my memory..." What is human nature? Why should it be different in Maritzburg and in London? The old British lawyer had told the budding, young *vakil* that he should try to understand human nature, and had recommended that he read the works of Mary Anne Schimmelpenninck and John Caspar Lavater. The dutiful young law student had gone to a bookshop the very next day and bought a copy of Lavater's *Essays on Physiognomy*.[28] Lavater exhorted his readers to peruse his work " to improve in the necessary knowledge of yourself, of your fellow creatures, and of the great and all-wise Creator."[29] Why didn't these whites treat their fellow creatures as the all-wise Creator had intended them to—or even like old Pincott? " He greeted me as a friend...his face beamed with a pleasing smile," Gandhi remembered. And Lavater had written, " An eye, which welcomes you with a generous, engaging and gracious look, and a heart frank, honest and expansive, and which seems gratefully to meet you, are not to be found united by chance only. Wherever this is the case, the cause has a relation to effect, and the eye denotes the open generous temper of the mind."[30] What was wrong with the eye of the white man,

---

[28] John Caspar Lavater, *Essays on Physiognomy Calculated to Extend the Love of Mankind*, (trans.) C. Moore, 3 Vols., (London, H. D. Symonds, 1797).

[29] *Ibid.*, I, Preface, p. 5.

[30] *Ibid.*, I, p. 21.

this dark eye in Africa as Laurens Van Der Post called it many years later?

South Africa is still noted for its fruit which Gandhi had already begun to enjoy. Perhaps they judged men as they judged their fruit, for had not Lavater written: " What determines our choice when a basket of fruit is presented to us? Why do we fix upon one and reject another? The exterior is the principal cause, and the appearance decides it."[31] But why judge men by their exterior? What is this colour prejudice for are not all men coloured and none transparent? Perhaps it is a disease which comes with civilization. A white man came into the waiting room about midnight and appeared willing to talk. But the sleepless young Indian did not open his mouth; how could he tell whether the man was not suffering from the disease?

Cold and miserable, angry and frightened, Gandhi debated within himself whether to go on or to turn back. He seemed to be back in the basket cage swinging over a black sea, back on the train looking down into the terrifying depth of a ravine. The cowardly desire to run fought with the determination to stay and fight. When dawn streaked the hills his decision had been made—he would go on to Pretoria come what may. He found his way to the post office, and the telegraph wires between Durban and Maritzburg were soon humming with messages from a defensive but cooperative General Manager, David Hunter, and a doughty Indian merchant. Dada Abdulla was not going to let him down; Indian merchants came flocking to the station and kept him company till the evening train from Durban pulled into the station again. Gandhi climbed aboard armed with a bedding ticket and the light of Maritzburg faded as the train made for Charlestown

---

[31] *Essays on Physiognomy Calculated to Extend the Love of Mankind,* I, p. 26; *Satyagraha in South Africa,* p. 5.

on the Natal border where the line ended. The Boer Republic of the Transvaal had not yet agreed to the building of the railway from Charlestown to Johannesburg—the Golden City high up on the Rand; that part of the journey would have to be completed by coach.

When the train reached Charlestown the next morning the young Indian became involved in an argument with the Coach Agent and the " leader," a rough looking Boer, who refused to let him sit by the side of any white passenger. He was forced to clamber up to the box where there was room for him next to the Hottentot driver. There were three seats up there. The Hottentot driver sat in the middle, with the " leader " usually on one side and another Hottentot with a whip on the other. Gandhi, determined not to be left behind again, occupied the leader's place on the box while the guard occupied his First Class seat inside. The coach started with a wild whoop from the Kaffir who held the heavy reins in his hands and steered the team. Charlestown, which had many Indian shops, was to see the young lawyer perched precariously on the box of that coach again under very different circumstances. He would reappear in 1913 as a new kind of John Burns leading a ragged army of thousands of indentured Indians into the Transvaal.[32] But on this cold and frosty morning he was only an unhappy and upset young man determined to get to Pretoria—and Pretoria was still far away. It was not easy riding on the coach box with the yells of the Hottentot and the ferocious crack of the whip splitting his ear drums. The Kaffir on the other side of the driver wielded a bamboo twelve feet long which he grasped with both hands; he curled and unwound the snake-like thong attached to it with a crack like a revolver shot.[33]

---

[32] *Satyagraha in South Africa*, p. 294.
[33] Tangye, *op. cit.*, p. 104.

The Birth of a Fighter

Gandhi's coach was travelling in the historic area of Laing's Nek and Majuba, but his thoughts were elsewhere and he hardly noticed the typical South African scenery, through which he was passing.[34] The morning cold had given place to the hot, burning sun of afternoon as the coach, which had been climbing steadily, approached Pardekop. The coach had come through Volksrust and twisted through a land of undulating meadows dotted with prosperous farms as it drew nearer to the mountain over six thousand feet high which gave its name to Pardekop; its summit was said to be free of horse-sickness and farmers brought their best breeding animals to pasture there during the summer.[35] There was a short halt at Pardekop. Before the coach started again the Boer " leader " came up to Gandhi, threw a dirty piece of sackcloth on to the foot-board, and asked him to sit on it as he wanted to sit up on the box in order to smoke. The insult was more than Gandhi could bear. His whole body trembled and his lips quivered as he desperately jerked out sentences of indignant refusal. The tall Boer grabbed Gandhi, boxed his ears and tried to drag him off the seat. The young Indian held on grimly to the brass rails of the coach as the Boer, swearing fearfully, continued to hit him. In the end, some of the more decent white passengers intervened and put an end to the unequal contest.[36] Later on Gandhi found that Indians were charged with being able to " live on the smell of an oiled rag." The rag he was asked to sit on became an insulting symbol to which he referred many times during his early days in South Africa.[37]

---

[34] James Bryce, *Impressions of South Africa*, (London, Macmillan & Co., 1899), pp. 50-57.

[35] T. V. Bulpin, *Storm Over the Transvaal*, (Cape Town, Howard Timmins, 1955), p. 17.

[36] *Autobiography*, pp. 143-144.

[37] *Collected Works*, I, p. 97.

The whistle was given and the coach rattled away with the
Boer sitting on the other side of the driver with the second
Hottentot at their feet. Every now and then he leaned
forward and growled threats at Gandhi who was really
frightened: " My heart was beating fast within my breast,
and I was wondering whether I would reach my destination
alive...I sat speechless and prayed to God to help me."[38]
Years later Gandhi would realize that there was another
scared man sitting on that box with him. That Boer was an
insecure man working off his own frustrations through physical
brutality; he was already a bit of an anachronism—a man
threatened with extinction by the coming of the railways and
the growing power of the Uitlanders, like some of the *rooineks*
who had stood up for this Indian. The coach was jolting
over one of the Great Transport Roads of South Africa—a
road that had seen hundreds of great, lumbering waggons,
each drawn by sixteen oxen, going up and down between
Durban and Johannesburg. The *voorloepers*, as the waggoners
were called, looked to Kruger to save them from the railway—
the railway that had now come as far as Charlestown.
Stanley Portal Hyatt would write of the Road with nostalgia,
" It was all Romance, the finest form of Romance..."[39] The
romance was fading all over South Africa, however, and the
cities were filling up with poor whites, small bitter men who
were finding an outlet for their misery and insecurity in a
growing hatred of the blacks—coloured, African or Indian.

Great clouds sailed overhead as the coach reached the upper
Vaal River, twenty-five miles from Pardekop.[40] The coach
forded the river at Stander's Drift and rolled on towards
Standerton as night was falling. When they entered the

---

[38] *Autobiography*, p. 144.
[39] S. P. Hyatt, *The Old Transport Road*, (London, Andrew Melrose Ltd., 1914),
p. 10.
[40] Bulpin, *op. cit.*, p. 18.

small town set in the midst of a grassy plain, Gandhi was relieved to find friendly Indian faces in the crowd waiting for the coach; Dada Abdulla had wired to Isa Sheth to meet him. The next morning he was on his way again. The road to Johannesburg ran for sixty-five miles to the north-west through long miles of open veldt. Gandhi was passing through country he would make historic by his own march twenty years later. He would be arrested in Standerton in 1913 while his " army " rested in the next town the coach came to—a small but beautiful settlement called Heidelburg within the rocky gorge of the Sinkerbosrand Hills.[41] The Blesbok River swept through Heidelburg, its banks festooned with weeping willows. The coach rolled on through typical stretches of high veldt scenery with patches of green and a clear blue sky overhead drawing nearer and nearer to one of the most coveted spots on the face of the earth—Johannesburg. The problem of accommodation for a night was uppermost in the mind of Gandhi, for no Indian had met him at the coach stop in Johannesburg. After the emptiness of the veldt, the streets seemed full of bustling people, though the population of the city was only about 40,000 in 1893.[42] The hurrying crowds, the brightly-lighted shop windows with ball-dresses and silver plate in them, the well-dressed women in their furs, the smart carriages and the horse-tram cars—all reminded him of London.[43] And thoughts of London reminded him especially of the Victoria Hotel and the Holborn Restaurant. " So I decided to go to a hotel. I knew the names of several." They were all listed in *Brown's South Africa*. Having chosen the Grand National, Gandhi took a cab (probably a Cape cart), drove to the hotel, and asked for the manager. He had learned to expect rudeness from

---

[41] *Satyagraha in South Africa*, p. 307.
[42] *Satyagraha in South Africa*, p. 4.
[43] *Letters from South Africa*, pp. 28-29, 42-43.

white servants and minor officials by now. The manager came. " He eyed me for a moment..." In South Africa the eye is an efficient little machine; it requires only a moment to classify, accept or reject and file away a man in the compartments of one's memory. The speech was polite. " I am very sorry, we are full up." The dark stranger with a surprisingly good English accent was forgotten. Gandhi turned away not fully realizing as yet that most hotels in South Africa would always fill up a moment ahead of his request for accommodation.

His cab was still waiting, so Gandhi went to the shop of the Indian merchant who should have met him. Abdul Ghani Sheth was awaiting his arrival; his servant had missed him at the coach stop. Neither the merchant nor his servant, however, had expected a young Indian in a smart London overcoat but rather someone in Gujarati or Meman dress. The Sheth was amused to hear that this youngster had walked into the Grand National asking for accommodation. He also looked at him with pity, for this young lawyer would have to be disillusioned quickly about conditions in the Transvaal before he hurt himself any more. The Sheth told him that conditions were, if anything, even worse for Indians here than in Natal. You could buy a First Class ticket in Durban but not in Johannesburg; Indians were only allowed to travel Third Class along with the natives. Gandhi startled the merchant, who had learned to pocket insults, with a volley of questions. Why had the Indians not protested? Why did they tamely put up with the discrimination? The Sheth shook his head sadly. Nothing could be done and Gandhi would have to travel Third Class to Pretoria. At Gandhi's insistence a copy of the railway regulations was procured, and he found a loophole in its vague language as his grandfather had done in the mortgage deeds of Porbandar State. He was determined to travel in a class of his choice. If he could not, he would take a cab to Pretoria which was thirty-seven miles away. The Sheth listened with growing astonishment, but agreed to send the Station Master Gandhi's note stating he was a barrister trained in London who always travelled First Class, that he was going to Pretoria on urgent business, and that he expected to get the ticket he wanted when he presented himself personally the next morning. It was a carefully worded letter. Gandhi was not giving the Station Master a chance to refuse him First Class accommodation. The harsh treatment he had experienced was making a subtle lawyer out of Gandhi. After all, he belonged to a profession which had supplied both architects of oppression and builders for freedom. [44]

The next morning, Gandhi appeared in " faultless English dress " with a morning coat and a necktie. He was playing the English gentleman again, but in a different key. The student who studied the faces of Londoners after reading Lavater's book had taken a good look at the people in the streets of Johannesburg. Their features belonged to White-chapel (later he would learn that Barney Barnato had come from there with a capital of fifty boxes of cigars) but the clothes were stamped with Bond Street. The *nouveau riche* of the Rand were flashy dressers and even barmaids could rise to furs. It was the young dandy who had strolled through Piccadilly Circus who now walked into the Park Station of Johannesburg, placed on the counter a sovereign (for gold talked like nothing else could do on the Rand) and asked for a First Class ticket. Gandhi's bit of play acting was as good as anything in the old Searelles Theatre of the town's early mining days, and it worked—but only because the man behind the counter was a Hollander and not a Boer.

Gandhi was learning that although they looked alike all white men in South Africa were not the same. A Boer would have looked like that Hollander but he would not have been

---

[44] *Autobiography*, pp. 145-146.

truly European. The Boer's roots were in South Africa and the Dutchman's in Holland. Even the Dutchman's eye was different. He smiled at Gandhi, sensed his predicament immediately, and gave him both sympathy and a ticket on condition that the young Indian would not involve him in any litigation should he run into trouble. " I can see that you are a gentleman,"[45] said the Dutchman. South Africa could not or would not recognize the cultural status of India but Europe could. It was fortunate that a Dutchman stood behind that counter. His presence could be explained historically; the first train from Cape Colony had entered the Park Station just the previous September and the Boers could not run a railway themselves—nor did they want to. They saw railways as steel nooses flung from Durban and Cape Colony to catch the Golden Calf on the Rand, worshipped by the Uitlanders. They saw railways as a threat to their independence and hated them. A day would come when the young Indian putting down his sovereign on the counter would come to see this imperialist aspect of the railways through the eyes of the Boers.

Sheth Abdul Gani was happily surprised, but still sceptical, when Gandhi emerged with a First Class ticket. He was full of gloomy forebodings as to what might happen to his young compatriot between Johannesburg and Pretoria right up to the moment the train left the platform. When the Sheth turned homewards though, there was a warm glow inside him as there had been in Dada Abdulla only a week before in Durban. The young Hindu had courage—the kind of courage the Indian merchants would need in the explosive situation developing in the Transvaal. Gandhi had won another friend. Sheth Abdul Gani was Chairman of the

---

[45] *Autobiography*, p. 147.

240

The Birth of a Fighter

Transvaal British Indian Association when Satyagraha was launched in Johannesburg in 1906.[46]

Three days had gone by since Gandhi left Durban, though it seemed to him like three years. Would he have any more trouble before he reached Pretoria now only a few hours away? The train came to a halt at Germiston and the guard entered the compartment. Gandhi braced himself to meet his look. Anger was plainly written on his face and in his gestures. Of gestures Lavater had written, "O did man but know how many languages he speaks at once, in how many forms he exhibits himself at the same instant, by what variety of expression he makes himself known to his fellow-creatures—with what dignity, with what wisdom would his words and actions be clothed?"[47] Lavater had once tried to explain why a Negro's hair is different, using the limited scientific knowledge of his day. In doing so, however, he was not conscious of colour. He did not know in how many languages men could speak to express their colour prejudice without either dignity or wisdom. Here was this guard with an ugly look on his face gesturing and signalling him to go to a Third Class compartment. Then, the only other occupant of the compartment where this clash of colour was taking place spoke, and Gandhi knew from his language that he was an Englishman. He was the kind of Englishman the Mahatma always respected—the Englishman with an honest voice raised in indignant protest against injustice. He sent the guard about his business. After the guard had left, muttering about "coolies," the Englishman turned to Gandhi and said, "Make yourself comfortable where you are." The young Gandhi believed that the decency of that plain spoken Englishman was in every Briton. Again and again, throughout the remainder of his long life, Gandhi would appeal to

---

[46] *Satyagraha in South Africa*, p. 102.
[47] Lavater, *op. cit.*, III, Ch. III, "Of Gestures."

the British sense of fair play demonstrated by his companion in the compartment on the Pretoria-bound train.

It was a quiet Sunday night when at last the train drew to a stop in Pretoria. There was no one to meet him. The experiences of the past few days had reduced him to a bundle of nerves. What was he to do? Where was he to go? He stood watching the few passengers alight on the dimly-lit platform. He decided to wait until they had all filed past the ticket collector. Perhaps the ticket collector would not be rude if there were no white passengers about. Gandhi approached the man nervously with his ticket conspicuously held in his hand to show he too was a passenger. If the ticket collec:or could not suggest a place to stay, Gandhi wanted to ask him whether he could at least spend the night on the platform. He was mustering up the courage to ask that simple question. " I must confess I shrank from asking him even this, for I was afraid of being insulted."[48] Gandhi was extremely relieved to find the man courteous.

The ticket collector could not help him but an American Negro who happened to be standing close by came to the rescue of the Indian stranger. The presence of an American Negro on the platform of the Pretoria station in 1893 is quite startling, and cannot be exactly explained; he may have been connected with the Ethiopian Church movement, a body of seceded Christian Bantus later linked to a Negro denomination in America. It was fitting, however, that he should be there—that he should form part of this picture of Gandhi's first encounter with colour prejudice. In 1903, the young Indian (who had been led to his Pretoria hotel by an American Negro, a decade before) was to write an article for *Indian Opinion* on Booker T. Washington under the caption " From Slave to College President." He would tell the story of his

---

[48] *Autobiography*, p. 149.

life, describe the achievement of Tuskegee College, note the honour conferred on him by Harvard University and conclude by saying, " a contemplation of lives like this cannot fail to do good."[49] Half a century later, American Negroes would contemplate the life of the Mahatma and draw inspiration from it.

The two men arrived at Johnston's Family Hotel which was run by an American. While the American Negro spoke to Mr. Johnston, Gandhi anxiously waited for the verdict. Would he be accepted as a member of the human family in Johnston's Family Hotel? Yes, he would, but not as a full member of the family. Mr. Johnston had no colour prejudice but he was not sure about his European customers. He could stay if he agreed to eat in his own room. Tired and hungry, Gandhi readily agreed. " I was shown into a room, where I now sat waiting for the dinner and musing, as I was quite alone."[50] Mr. Johnston was back in a moment to announce that his customers had no objection to Gandhi's being served in the dining room. The human family, perhaps, then, was never totally wicked. The knowledge that the feeling of humanity still existed even in racist territory gave an edge to Gandhi's appetite and he had a hearty meal. As long as he lived in South Africa, however, hotels would always give Gandhi an uneasy feeling in the pit of his stomach. Back in India in 1896, he was only going to Madras when he wrote to a friend, F. S. Taleyarkhan, "I do not know at which hotel I shall put up there. The Natal hotels have made me quite nervous."[51]

The next morning he met A. W. Baker, Dada Abdulla's attorney in Pretoria, who found lodgings for him in the friendly home of a struggling English family. Gandhi found the personality of the attorney, with whom he would have to work, rather overwhelming. The friendly, warm-hearted

---

[49] *Collected Works*, III, p. 437.
[50] *Autobiography*, p. 150.
[51] *Collected Works*, II, p. 85.

English lawyer was a passionate Evangelical, a lay preacher, and an enthusiastic supporter of the South Africa General Mission. Before he had time to think, Gandhi found himself agreeing to attend a little prayer meeting every day at lunch time. He knew that Baker's missionary zeal had kindled when he learned Gandhi was a Hindu but he liked the genial good nature of the man.

At the end of his first day in Pretoria, Gandhi went to his room after dinner " and lay there absorbed in deep thought." All the scenes of his nightmare journey passed through his mind. How could the mere colour of his skin have evoked such brutality? Perhaps it was all due to ignorance, for these men knew nothing about Indian civilization or the Hindu religion. Yet how could he blame them when he was so ignorant himself about Indian culture and religion? He must get some books on Indian history and Hinduism. Was there a library in Pretoria or would he have to write to India for books? The blame, however, was not one-sided. The Indian merchants ought to keep their shops in better condition and provide better accommodation for their Gujarati clerks. How curious these white men are! One slaps and beats you, and another wants to make a good Christian out of you. There must be something wrong with their whole idea of civilization. "Thus musing I feel asleep.."[52]

The young man who fell sound asleep after his trying journey had not completed his twenty-fourth year. He had a friendly boyish smile that could win him a place in the British Captain's cabin, when no other accommodation was available, on the ship that had brought him to Africa.[53] He was still a bit indisciplined; for instance, on his voyage to Durban he had disregarded the Captain's warning that he

---

[52] *Autobiography*, pp. 149-152.
[53] *Ibid.*, p. 131.

should be back in good time when the ship was in the port of Lamu. The ship left the dock without him. Racing after it in a dinghy, Gandhi managed to get alongside the moving ship, and had to be drawn up onto the deck dangling from the end of a rope.[54] When he arrived in Durban, Gandhi was still so ignorant even of his profession that he did not know what a promissory note was.[55] Sensitive and quick to anger, he was easily hurt or stunned. He knew what it was to lose his temper, he could be nervous, timid, frightened. He was like most young men of his age.

Gandhi knew, his family knew, his wife knew, that he had always had a kind of dogged persistence and determination. On the way to England in 1888, he had written in his diary, " But I am not a man who would, after having formed any intention, leave it easily...But, as all of them knew it that I should not leave off anything having first begun it, they were silent."[56] The silent veldt had witnessed his determination to get to Pretoria. " The Almighty Searcher of all hearts put my determination to a full test. . But all this only confirmed me in my determination,"[57] are the words of the Mahatma thirty years later, looking back on that journey. He had come to a land of which it has been written, " There are more problems to the square mile in South Africa than any other country in the world."[58] Every problem he faced in South Africa would further strengthen Gandhi's determination, and from that tried and tested determination would come the Mahatma.

Pretoria

Pretoria, once described by Rider Haggard as the prettiest village in South Africa, was still a picturesque town when

---

[54] *Autobiography*, pp. 131-132.
[55] *Ibid.*, p. 139.
[56] *Collected Works*, I, pp. 5, 9.
[57] *Satyagraha in South Africa*, p. 43.
[58] Hamilton Fyfe, *op. cit.*, p. 34.

Gandhi took up residence there from the winter of 1893 to the middle of 1894. Built by Marthinus Pretorius and named after his father, Andries, the town nestled in a hollow 4,500 feet above sea level, at the foot of the Johannesburg slopes. The streets ran in parallels and every *kopje* was dotted with quaint houses painted orange or white. The town was full of cool shade trees, and most houses were surrounded by hedges of roses. In the centre of Pretoria was a large square with the Raadzaal, the Parliament building of the South African Republic, on one side of it. This open space was known as Church Square because it also contained a little Dopper church where President Kruger worshipped every Sunday.[59]

The young Indian, who had arrived after such a nightmare journey, might well have asked himself:

> " Ah, what shall I be at fifty
> Should Nature keep me alive,
> If I find the world so bitter
> When I am but twenty-five? "[60]

Gandhi was well below twenty-five, and nature, so beautiful in the region of Pretoria, certainly helped to keep him alive. He walked about a good deal, as he had done in London, and enjoyed surveying the landscape with its magnificent hills, its snug little farms, the streams caught in the rays of the sun, and the rich green pasture lands with browsing herds of fat cattle. The winter, which had made the veldt brown and

---

[59] K. E. Cross, *Pretoria: A Bibliography*, (Cape Town, School of Librarianship, University of Cape Town, 1948). For descriptions of Pretoria in the 1890's, see *Brown's South Africa*, p. 53; Cumberland, *op. cit.*, p. 152; Wilson, *op. cit.*, p. 45; Southey, *op. cit.*, pp. 106-108; Bulpin, *op. cit.*, p. 29.

[60] Alfred Tennyson, " Maud," *The Selected Poetry of Tennyson*, Douglas Bush, (ed.), (New York, The Modern Library, 1951), p. 264.

dry, was fresh and invigorating in Pretoria, though the sun could be hot at midday. The rains were heavy that year and the town became swampy and wet,[61] but nature helped Gandhi even through the summer rains; he stayed indoors trying experiments with " vital foods " and reading incessantly. He told his first biographer, Joseph Doke, that he read more than eighty books in Pretoria.[62] It was a germinal year in the long period of gestation which gave birth to the Mahatma. When in his fifties, the Mahatma appropriately recorded that the year's stay in Pretoria was a most valuable experience in his life.

His autobiography, however, does not bring out all that he gained from that quiet but memorable year. The Mahatma obscured its value to some extent, like the heavy mists that obscure Pretoria during the rainy season, with too much emphasis on the development of his religious life. We have to recreate the atmosphere and probe his thought and activities immediately after he left Pretoria to gauge how much he derived from his stay in the capital of the Boer Republic.

The boy who had seen a period of rapid change in Kathiawad was destined to watch with the heightened awareness of a thoughtful young man a similar process at work in Pretoria. An old Transvaal was passing away and the new order taking its place was visible in the changing face of Pretoria. Gandhi saw the old Transvaal on market days as he watched the huge, lumbering waggons loaded with the produce of the farms, *outspanning* in Church Square in the shadow of the Raadzaal with its modern facade. He watched the Boer *vrows* in their large cuckoo bonnets called *kappjes* and the men in their big cloth hats with wide, flapping brims. An American traveller, Poultney Bigelow, who visited Pretoria on May 30, 1896, described the sight which Gandhi must

---

[61] Bulpin, *op. cit.*, p. 199.
[62] Doke, *op. cit.*, p. 36.

have observed many times: " It was about noon; the sun was broiling down as it does in Texas; the broad, dusty streets reminded me of an average prairie town west of the Mississippi, and this impression was further heightened by noting great freight wagons drawn by sixteen oxen, and scrawny mustangs galloping about, with sunburnt, shaggy-bearded Boers astride them. There was a flavour of cowboy and sombrero to the scene."[63] Gandhi also saw the old Transvaal in the members of the Volksraad going in and out of the Raadzaal, sober-looking men, thickly bearded, and awkward in their silk top-hats and black frock coats.

The agricultural scene in Church Square was re-enacted every Market Day in a Pretoria which had changed since 1890 when the discovery of gold on the Rand had cleared away the depression of the previous years. A sign of the times was the new National Bank, opened by Kruger in April, 1891, and operated by Labouchere Ozens and Company of Amsterdam. The streets had been lighted by electricity only since September 8, 1892. The train which brought Gandhi from Johannesburg had been running for a little more than six months. The first engine, pulling a ballast train, had arrived in Pretoria on a Saturday afternoon in December, 1892. Gandhi probably heard the event described. The townsfolk had spent most of that night inspecting the engine which kept blowing its whistle " as though it were a hen cackling with pride at having at long last laid the desired railway egg."[64] The first train from Delagoa Bay, on the eastern seaboard, had arrived as recently as January, 1893. Gandhi would also hear talk about the approaching rail link between Pretoria and the Cape.

---

[63] Poultney Bigelow, *White Man's Africa*, (New York, Harper & Brothers, 1898), p. 20.

[64] Bulpin, *op. cit.*, p. 187.

The Birth of a Fighter

In Pretoria, Gandhi was at the centre of a developing storm that would burst over South Africa before the end of the century.[65] Here Gandhi began acquiring a knowledge of the history and problems of the land he had come to. The Transvaal was changing, and, with it, a whole continent. He had come to a vast land only recently opened up by traders, hunters and missionaries of many nationalities. The grab for Africa had begun and the European powers were carving the country up between them. The Matabele War would add Southern Rhodesia to the British Empire while Gandhi was still in Pretoria. Africans drawn from many tribes were stepping over the threshold of history as they entered the mines on the Rand, as they delved for the gold the white men coveted. The Arab slave-dealers and the ivory-hunters had given place to city-bred scum from many parts of the world—land speculators, confidence sharks, remittance men, and plain desperadoes capable of waylaying and robbing the black miners of their hard-earned money intended for hut or poll tax. The simple farmers sitting in the Volksraad were harassed or tempted with offers of large sums of money by hordes of speculators seeking concessions or promoting railway schemes. When Gandhi arrived in 1893, " the sunny veld had become the most famous and desirable piece of country on earth,"[66] and " Kaffirs " meant gold shares wherever there was a stock exchange.

Pretoria was once described by Sir Arthur Lawley as "an ice maiden," Mrs. Leonard Phillips referred to it as "that Sleepy Hollow " and the Mahatma spoke of it as " a comparatively

---

[65] See H. Rider Haggard, *A History of the Transvaal*, (London, Kegan Paul, Trench, Trubner Co., Ltd., 1899), and A. H. Keane, *The Boer States*, (London, Methuen & Co., 1900).

[66] T. V. Bulpin, *The Golden Republic*, (Cape Town, Howard B. Timmins, 1957), p. 230.

quiet place."[67] Yet Pretoria was the capital of a beleaguered Republic, a town full of raging, bitter memories beneath its placid surface. Gandhi spent most of his time in Pretoria in Uitlander company, praying with them, lunching with Baker or having tea on Sundays with two elderly maiden ladies, Miss Harris and Miss Gabb, listening to "their sweet experiences and the peace they had found."[68] Elderly British spinsters, however, are often unconscious propagandists for the prejudices of their race, and Gandhi, as his later writings show, acquired a picture of the grievances of the Uitlanders which stood him in good stead as he argued the case of the Indians. With their usual nonchalance, the British had taken over a good deal of the life of Pretoria. English had appeared on the name boards of the shops at a time when an able Hollander, Dr. Mansvelt, the Superintendent of Education, was trying to promote the Taal spoken by the Boers. The Uitlander outlook cropped up conspicuously in the capital of the Boer Republic; Gandhi could hardly avoid coming into contact with it. Even the friendliness shown to Gandhi by the English in Pretoria was tinged with Uitlander feeling. After all, the young Indian barrister had been in London, spoke English fluently, and *was* a British subject.

It is significant that Gandhi arrived in Pretoria when the Uitlander agitation for the franchise was at its height. The Uitlanders had succeeded in getting an extremely limited form of franchise from the Volksraad in 1890, the year in which the Political Reform Association was formed. The Imperial Government had helped them to wrest those very limited concessions from Kruger by using the Swaziland

---

[67] H. R. Abercrombie, *The Secret History of South Africa*, (Johannesburg, The Central News Agency, Ltd., 1951), p. 180; *Some South African Recollections*, p. 144; *Satyagraha in South Africa*, p. 4.

[68] *Autobiography*, p. 153.

issue as a lever. In April, 1893, with the presidential election just a month away, Lord Ripon, the Colonial Secretary, had brought about a wasted meeting between Kruger and Loch, the British Agent, in an attempt to settle the franchise question. Disappointed, the Uitlanders redoubled their efforts to get Kruger defeated by one of his two rivals, Christian Joubert or Chief Justice Kotze. Concession scandals, corruption among civil servants, dissatisfaction with railway policies, and the dynamite monopoly made the election a hard fight for Kruger. Emotion ran high—an English shopkeeper was fined severely for merely saying he was going to throw rotten eggs at the old Dopper. Kruger was re-elected for the third time, amidst great excitement, on May 12, 1893.

When Gandhi arrived about three weeks later, Pretoria was still bubbling with the aftermath of the election. Gandhi, whose interest in the Uitlander agitation was stimulated in Pretoria, would continue to watch its progress closely from Durban. The Uitlanders would bombard the Colonial Office with memorials and organize monster petitions. When petitioning seemed to fail, the Uitlanders would resort to intimidation by the abortive Jameson Raid of 1895. This rash adventure led to the fall of Rhodes as Prime Minister of the Cape, and proved to be the prelude to the Boer War.

All these dramatic events would make a deep impression on Gandhi and create images in his mind which were to influence his own development and the character of the Indian agitation in South Africa. The drama of Gandhi's career was to be, in a sense, a re-enactment using lessons learned from both sides—of different phases in the protracted and grim struggle of Boer and Uitlander. As leader of the Indians in Natal from 1894–1901, he was to recast the Uitlander struggle in the Transvaal; returning from India to South Africa in 1902, he would settle in Johannesburg to lead the Indians in the Transvaal against the combined forces of Boer and Briton who by this time would have closed their ranks as far as

Asiatics were concerned. His first Passive Resistance campaign in 1906, though conceived in a different spirit, would be like the Jameson Raid—an indication that he was tiring of petitions and prepared to resort to unconstitutional methods as the Uitlanders had done. The failure of that first struggle was to lead to further skirmishes. When there was no real response from the Government in Pretoria, Gandhi would declare " war " on the Transvaal, and a former Boer commander, Jan Christian Smuts, then Colonial Secretary, would oppose him. The image of the British generals who conducted the Boer War would be in his mind as he marched his " army "[69] into the Transvaal from the Natal border in 1913. "Only the general who conducts a campaign can know the objective of each particular move,"[70] the Mahatma would write in his memoirs of the battle, *Satyagraha in South Africa*.

During his year in Pretoria, Gandhi tended to see the Boers through the eyes of his British friends and the Indian merchants in Primsloo and Church Streets. He knew Jacobus de Wet, the British Agent, and Krause, the State Attorney, but these men represented a liberal point of view unlike that of the Doppers. The oppressive treatment of the Indians, combined with his own experience (he was roughly pushed off the pavement in front of Kruger's house), did not give him much sympathy with the Boer case at this time. The Boers, however, were a simple people whom Gandhi could understand. Like the Kathiawadi peasants, they measured distance by the amount of time it took to travel from one place to another and considered natural calamities, such as drought, to be punishments from God. He admired their rugged faith although he knew it rested on too literal an interpretation of the Old Testament.[71] The young Indian from a land of Rajputs

---

[69] *Satyagraha in South Africa*, p. 224.
[70] *Ibid*., p. 11.
[71] *Ibid*., p. 16.

heard stories of the Boers' fighting qualities, and may have learned that seventeen out of the twenty-four members of the Volksraad bore bullet wounds.[72]

Gandhi's appreciation of President Kruger, however, was largely free of ambiguity even at this period. Mrs. Leonard Phillips said of Kruger that " once seen he is not easily forgotten."[73] Kruger's familiar figure certainly made an indelible impression on the young Indian's mind. Then in his sixties, the indefatigable old President worked in his office from 5 a.m. to 5 p.m. Gandhi may have seen him emerging from his office for his midday meal, a stout figure in an old frock coat with a frayed silk hat perched above a penetrating pair of eyes and a venerable white beard. Or he may have caught a glimpse of Kruger sitting on the *stoep* of his house in President Street in an upright armchair, smoking his pipe and spitting frequently and noisily. The President was easily accessible to his people; the poorest citizen was welcome to sit with him on the *stoep* of his unpretentious house, drink coffee and pass the time of day.[74] " Indeed President Kruger's simplicity was proverbial,"[75] the Mahatma later recalled. When Kruger died in 1904, Gandhi paid tribute to him as " one of the most striking personalities of the nineteenth century " in the obituary in *Indian Opinion*.[76] By then Gandhi's perspective on South African problems would be changing; influenced by Tolstoy and Ruskin and their idealization of rural life, he moved away from the urban Uitlander outlook and closer to that of the simple Boer farmers. He sounded rather like a Dopper in his rejection of railways, doctors and lawyers in *Hind*

---

[72] F. E. Younghusband, *South Africa Today*, (London, Macmillan & Co., Ltd., 1898), p. 23.

[73] *Op. cit.*, p. 19.

[74] Millin, *op. cit.*, pp. 77-78.

[75] *Autobiography*, p. 163.

[76] *Collected Works*, IV, p. 225.

Swaraj. When the Mahatma returned to India, he opposed the machine age even as Kruger and his Boers had tried vainly to stem the dark tide of modern civilization spilling over from Johannesburg on to the virgin soil of the veldt.

Though Gandhi enjoyed good social relations with many European residents of Pretoria, he realized, rather painfully that his status in the eyes of most whites was no higher than that of the African servants and Cape Coloured cabmen and cigar-makers in the town. He escaped the Pass Law (by which all Africans were expected to be indoors by 9 p.m.) only because of a special letter of identification given him by the State Attorney.

His personal experience of the Footpath Law was a shocking lesson in the disabilities to which any coloured person in the Transvaal was subjected. One of Gandhi's favourite walks in Pretoria took him past Kruger's house in President Street to an open plain. In his description of Kruger's well-known house, Poultney Bigelow says, " A verandah ran along the front, and perhaps six feet of shrubbery separated the *stoep* from the sidewalk. It was a typical farmhouse, such as a prosperous Boer farmer would be inclined to build, and was almost concealed by lofty shade trees. There was no drive way to the front door, no sign that the house contained any but an average citizen of Pretoria. But at the wicket-gate were two soldiers with rifles, who challenged us as we attempted to pass."[77] For a long time Gandhi had no difficulty in passing the famous house which he described as " a very modest, unostentatious building, without a garden, and not distinguishable from other houses in its neighbourhood."[78] On the day of the incident, the two guards who knew Gandhi by sight had been changed; as he was walking past Kruger's

[77] Bigelow, *op. cit.*, p. 23.

[78] *Autobiography*, p. 162.

house as usual, one of these new soldiers suddenly pushed and kicked him off the footpath into the street. Coates, a Quaker friend of Gandhi, happened to ride by at that moment and came to his rescue. The incident ended on a decent note with the Boer soldier apologizing to Gandhi after a reprimand from Coates. The young Indian had forgiven the soldier even before he apologised, but he was not so sentimental that he would forgive the Transvaal Government for passing a law forbidding coloured people to use the footpaths. " I saw that South Africa was no country for a self-respecting Indian, and my mind became more and more occupied with the question as to how this state of things might be improved."[79] The Mahatma thus gave a truer indication of his mood, in these words after the incident, than in his account of how forgiving he had been.

In 1904, Gandhi wrote an editorial entitled " Footpaths in the Transvaal " showing that the problem had become worse, and that even small towns like Boksburg were trying to enforce the law. One of the reasons given for the footpath legislation was that no African when drunk would move aside for a white woman. Liquor, however, had been forbidden to the Africans and there were penalties for selling it to them. Thus, the footpath issue and the temperance question became connected in curious fashion. Many poor whites in Johannesburg lived by selling illicit liquor to the African miners, and the Native Locations hid illegal stills which produced powerful and poisonous brews. Coloured men were not permitted to walk past white girls on a footpath, but they could sell them skokian, a concoction calculated to stiffen greatly the cocktails some of the same young women served at cozy, private parties in Johannesburg.

Gandhi knew practically every Indian trader, shop-keeper's

---

[79] *Ibid.*, p. 164.

assistant, hawker, cook, waiter and labourer in Pretoria.
He was soon familiar with all the recent discriminatory
legislation against the Indians both in the Orange Free State
and the Transvaal.[80] He also learned of the efforts of the
Indian merchants to fight the discrimination through petitions
and memorials to the Colonial Office in London.[81] Gandhi
later recalled his meeting in England with Dadhabhai Naoroji
when he found that leader's name to be familiar to the Indians
in Pretoria as the one who presented their case to the Imperial
Government. Underlying all the knowledge he acquired
about the plight of the Indians in South Africa, however, was
a growing concern in Gandhi's mind that his people were
classified among the uncivilized races of the world. How
could he convince these ignorant Boers and the artisan class
of Englishmen that India was not an uncivilized country?
Even an educated man like his Quaker friend, Coates, thought
of Hinduism as superstition; for example, Coates asked him
to discard the Vallabhachari *kanthi*, a chain with a religious
significance, which he wore round his neck—a request Gandhi
gently refused. Gandhi was attached to the young Quaker
who had made him read many books on Christianity. He
reminded Gandhi of Frederick Pincott who had also urged
him to read more.

As Gandhi read steadily and purposefully through the
rainy summer months, one of his objectives was a better
knowledge of Indian civilization. It was in Pretoria that he
stumbled upon Max Muller's *India—What Can It Teach Us?*[82]

[80] See W. A. Macfayden, (tran.), *The Political Laws of the South African Republic*
(with the Constitution of the Orange Free State),(London,William Clowes &
Sons, Ltd., 1896).

[81] Masani, *op. cit.*, " Indians in South Africa."

[82] *A Course of Lectures Delivered Before the University of Cambridge*, (London, Longmans, Green & Co., 1883). Gandhi stated that books by Max Muller and
Morris were easily obtainable in Pretoria, *Collected Works*, III, p. 8. His
autobiography, however, is not very clear as to exactly when he read the book.

As Gandhi read it avidly, new images of India rose in his mind—India the Mother of cultures, India the Teacher of nations. The young Indian walked the streets of Pretoria a little less dejected than before. Gandhi called together a meeting of the Indians in the town, gave them a new vision of their own country and pleaded with them to win respect for their motherland by their mode of life and behaviour. His desire to be a teacher thus found a useful outlet.

Gandhi's Christian contacts in Pretoria involved him in some tough reading. He probably told Coates he had enjoyed going to the City Temple in London with the result that Parker's *Commentary* was thrust on him. *The Peoples' Bible: Discourses upon Holy Scripture*[83] by the Reverend Dr. Joseph Parker left Gandhi unmoved, but a spate of other equally difficult books followed until his shelf was filled with them. The book the Mahatma would remember as *Many Infallible Proofs* was J. R. Pearson's *Remarkable Providence and Proofs of Divine Revelation.*[84] Butler's *Analogy* struck Gandhi as " a very profound and difficult book, which should be read four or five times to be understood properly."[85] This was *The Analogy of Religion, Natural and Revealed, to the Constitution and Course of Nature* published in 1736 by Joseph Butler, who was successively Bishop of Bristol and Durham. Butler had exercised an influence on the mind of Gladstone, who edited his collected works.[86] Gandhi waded through this book— one that Annie Besant dismissed in 1909 with, " Who now dreams of troubling himself much about Butler's analogy? "[87]

---

[83] Joseph Parker, *The Peoples' Bible: Discourses upon Holy Scripture*, (London, Hazell & Co., 1889).

[84] J. R. Pearson, *Remarkable Providence and Proofs of Divine Revelation*, (London, Partridge, 1876).

[85] *Autobiography*, p. 154.

[86] Joseph Butler, *The Analogy of Religion, Natural and Revealed, to the Constitution and Course of Nature*, (London, J. J. & P. Knapton, 1736).

[87] Annie Besant, *The Changing World*, (Chicago, The Theosophical Book C 1909), p. 9.

Colonial libraries were notoriously out of date and the young Indian was given some unappetising and irrelevant fare. Coates insisted on his maintaining a religious journal and had weekly discussions with Gandhi on the books he had read. If it did nothing else, the reading and discussion of these heavy works provided a rigorous discipline which sharpened and stimulated Gandhi's mind.

The main result, however, of the attempts of well-meaning Christian friends to convert Gandhi was to make him adept at marshalling arguments against Christianity and defenses for Hinduism. The efforts of these Christian Evangelicals ultimately converted Gandhi into a vigorous Evangelical Hindu. He has put forward four strong arguments as to why he could not accept Christianity, illustrating the genuine differences as well as the misunderstandings between the two religions. First, an ethical problem was raised by his contact with a Plymouth Brother in Pretoria. (He later met another, the Captain of the *Pangola*, on his way back to India in 1896.) The Plymouth Brother advocating the *pecca fortiter* of Martin Luther, urged that man, being a sinner, was only justified by faith. The redeemed man will never cease to be a sinner because the more saintly he becomes the more aware he is of subtle sins yet to be conquered. This point of view proved obnoxious to Gandhi who stood by the *tat tvam asi*, the " thou art that " of the Vedanta. The divine Brahman dwelling in man makes perfection in this life possible.

Gandhi had misunderstood the Plymouth Brother to mean that a man can sin cheerfully so long as he holds the correct beliefs; actually, however, the issues involved went much deeper. Perhaps Gandhi might have benefited had he understood what the Plymouth Brother really meant. George Catlin expressed it more clearly when he wrote, " Let us admit that the Indian Vedantist belief that, if one can discover one's true self, one discovers it to be identical with the spirit of all being to be a god, is a dangerous belief, encouraging vanity and spiritual arrogance."[88]

George Orwell, in his thoughtful little essay on Gandhi, doubts that the Mahatma was never moved by vanity.[89] Perhaps the Mahatma was not guilty of spiritual arrogance, but is there not an occasional touch of megalomania in his writings in the 1920's? Speaking of his earlier allegiance to the British, the Mahatma later wrote, " Never in my life did I exploit this loyalty, never did I seek to gain a selfish end by its means. It was for me more in the nature of an obligation, and I rendered it without expecting a reward."[90] Who was speaking then—the saint or the politician? Was this true even when the young man in Kathiawad traded on his father's loyalty to the British in an effort to get a scholarship for his studies in England? The Mahatma was also to write, " ...I do not remember to have ever resorted to cunning during all those years I lived in South Africa. I may now go even further and say without the least hesitation that I have never had recourse to cunning in all my life."[91] Some accepted the Mahatma as a superman. J. B. Kripalani wrote that " Gandhiji in his life and teachings discards all double standards of morality."[92] A man, however great, may try to discard all double standards, to reach perfection in this life, but Gandhi's perfectionist ethics were to prove unworkable in many situations.

Gandhi and the Plymouth Brother joined a debate which has not ended yet. Similarly, that simple Christian group in Pretoria had very little conception of the intellectual and philosophical issues involved in the three other grounds on

---

[88] *Op. cit.*, p. 75.
[89] George Orwell, *A Collection of Essays*, (Garden City, New York, Doubleday Anchor, 1954), p. 177.
[90] *Autobiography*, p. 212.
[91] *Satyagraha in South Africa*, p. 208.
[92] " Unity—Gandhiji's Conception," Gandhi Memorial Number, p. 21.

which Gandhi rejected Christianity—namely, his unwillingness to accept any uniqueness about the Christian revelation,
his feeling that renunciation was better exemplified by
Hinduism, and his belief in metempsychosis or the transmigra-
tion of souls. Gandhi objected to Tolstoy's views on reincarnation expressed in his *Letter to a Hindu*.[93] He made good
use of the books sent to him by Raychand, a wealthy Jain
jeweller, whose religious philosophy had impressed Gandhi
in Bombay. Gandhi was winning his spurs on behalf of his
religion in intellectually backward Pretoria at a time when
Hinduism was becoming better known in other parts of the
world. It was also in 1893 that Swami Vivekananda was
to have an impact on audiences made receptive by Edwin
Arnold's poetry and Lew Wallace's novels at the World
Parliament of Religions in Chicago.

Gandhi's trip to Wellington in the company of Baker to
attend a revivalist meeting patterned after the Keswick
Convention in England gave him further education in racial
prejudice and more experience with a particular type of
Protestant Christianity. Baker had a hard time protecting
the young Indian from the slights and affronts that his colour
attracted. At the Convention itself Gandhi enjoyed the
hymns and met the Reverend Andrew Murray, well-known
in South Africa. The son of a Presbyterian minister who
had come from Scotland to serve in the Dutch Reformed
Church, the junior Andrew Murray had made Wellington a
famous missionary centre. The Convention itself must have
been held either at the Huguenot Seminary or the Mission
Training College, both founded by Andrew Murray himself.
At Wellington, Gandhi met several Americans who had come
as teachers to those institutions.[94] Baker's hopes that the

---

[93] Marc Semenoff, (ed.), *Gandhi et Tolstoi*, (Paris, Editions Denoel, 1958). See
Gandhi's letter to Tolstoy dated October 1, 1909.

[94] Theal, *op. cit.*, p. 320.

young Hindu would accept Christianity by attending the Convention were disappointed.

The difficulties Gandhi experienced with regard to Christianity were not all intellectual. He could not reconcile the professions of Christianity with the practice of colour prejudice. It pained him to find that good Christians could go to a meeting like the Wellington Convention to listen to stirring addresses with no relevance to any of the pressing social problems of the time. Gandhi was in search of a social gospel, a gospel of applied religion. It was this pressing need which explains the immediate attraction Tolstoy had for him. *The Kingdom of God is Within You, or, Christianity Not as Mystical Teaching but as a New Concept of Life*,[95] completed by Tolstoy in May, 1893, was probably sent to Gandhi by one of his friends in London. He was still in touch with Josiah Oldfield and other members of the Vegetarian Society. The Mahatma later described how the book overwhelmed him, but the young man in Pretoria was more likely impressed by those parts of it which struck immediate chords in him. Gandhi was overwhelmed by Tolstoy, but not all at once.

The Gandhi of those Pretoria days found one paragraph in the book immensely relevant to his own mental condition. " I think it is Max Muller," Tolstoy wrote, " who tells of the surprise of an Indian converted to Christianity, who, having grasped the essence of the Christian teaching, arrived in Europe and saw the life of the Christians. He could not recover from his astonishment in the presence of the reality, which was the opposite of what he had expected to find among the Christian nations."[96] Gandhi had not been converted to Christianity like Nehemiah Goreh, whom Max Muller knew,

---

[95] Count Leo N. Tolstoy, *The Kingdom of God is Within You*, Christianity and Patriotism, Miscellanies, (trans.), Leo Wiener, (London, J. M. Dent & Co., 1905).

[96] *Ibid.*, p. 207.

but he was suffering from the same surprise and astonishment—emotions he had not felt to the same extent in England
as he did in South Africa. Beside the burning sincerity, the
scorching indictments of hypocrisy, the challenges to higher
ethical living which Gandhi found in Tolstoy's work, the
books lent to him by Coates " seemed to pale into insignifi-
cance."[97]

" I have remained forever indebted to them for the religious
quest that they awakened in me,"[98] was the Mahatma's
tribute to his Christian friends in Pretoria. There were two
more services rendered by those pious Christians to Gandhi.
First, they not only forced him to study Hinduism by making
him the object of their missionary zeal, but also created in
him an awareness of the need for a reformation of his religion
from within. Although the reform of Hinduism began
early in the nineteenth century, Gandhi was destined to play
the role of one of the greatest of Hindu reformers by his
attack on untouchability. The treatment of Indians as
pariahs in South Africa quickened Gandhi's conscience about
the caste system in India. Gokhale reflected Gandhi's
feelings based on his experiences in South Africa when he
delivered a lecture on April 27, 1903, to the Indian Social
Conference at Dharwar entitled " Treatment of Indians by
the Boers and Treatment of Low Castes in India by their own
Countrymen." It was published as a pamphlet " with
additional remarks showing the Selfishness, Injustice, Cruelty
and Fraud of the Caste System, which is also the Chief Cause
of India's stationary semi-civilization."[99]

Second, his Christian friends in Pretoria helped him to
understand the " Colonial " as opposed to the " English "

---

[97] *Autobiography*, p. 172.
[98] *Autobiography*, p. 172.
[99] *Great Indian Questions of the Day Series*, (London and Madras, The Christian
Literature Society, 1903).

mind. Gandhi's experiences in Pretoria would be a great help to him in the very British Colony of Natal where there was an older generation of settlers whose liberal and Christian outlook had not completely faded away in a tropical climate. Speaking of the role of African leadership twenty years ago, Malinowski wrote, "The chief who adopts Christianity becomes the religious leader of his tribesmen in a new guise, but above all he gains the support of a powerful section of the European community."[100] Though a Hindu, Gandhi could appeal to the Christian conscience of that generation, and, in turn, he appealed to them as a man of an essentially Christian spirit. However, when Gandhi settled in Johannesburg, a polyglot city with a large Jewish population, he would find that in some respects Theosophy, rather than Christianity, would have the greater appeal.

A. W. Baker failed to make Gandhi into a church-going Christian, but he succeeded in making him into a good lawyer. The most significant change in Gandhi at the end of his year in Pretoria was not that he had become more religious, but that he was more able as a barrister. What Gandhi had missed most since he left London were "the things that a junior barrister learns in a senior barrister's chamber". Gandhi made it abundantly clear that his primary interest in Pretoria was in Dada Abdulla's case. Religion was an avocational interest and the main objective of his extensive reading was a better knowledge of the law. He was continuing the studies begun on the boat trip to Africa by familiarising himself with the Indian Evidence Act. When Gandhi emerged from Pretoria his legal education had been completed in Baker's chambers, and Dada Abdulla's case had tested his "powers of comprehension" and his "capacity for

---

[100] Bronislaw Malinowski, *The Dynamics of Culture Change*: *An Inquiry into Race Relations in Africa,* (New Haven, Yale University Press, 1961), p. 38.

marshalling evidence."[101] His legal abilities would be displayed to the full as he fought the Natal Legislature over the Indian Franchise.

In analysing Gandhi's career in South Africa, it may be said that the law dominated the period in Natal from 1894 to 1901, and religion, in the Transvaal period from 1902 to 1914. There were signs of disillusionment with legal and constitutional procedures even in Pretoria but they remained largely dormant in Gandhi until the middle of his Johannesburg period when he gave up his law practice—a decision which can be traced back to his reading of *The Kingdom of God Is Within You.*

A by-product of his handling of Dada Abdulla's case was the beginning of a serious interest in Gujarati, Gandhi's mother tongue. A long-forgotten case in Pretoria would ultimately result in a Gandhian Era in the revival of Gujarati language and literature.[102] Gandhi's interest in Gujarati had been stirred from time to time without any practical results. The little boy in Porbandar was moved by the drama of *Harischandra,* but not by its literary style. The young student in London knew that Narayan Hemachandra was aspiring to be another B. M. Malabari by translating many books into Gujarati. The briefless lawyer in Bombay knew that his friend, Raychand, was making a name for himself with his books in Gujarati. It was only in Pretoria that Gandhi began to discover Gujarati literature—through the humble process of translating legal documents. The books Raychand sent him from Bombay stimulated not only a religious, but also a literary, interest. Another man whose deep devotion to Gujarati would make an impression on Gandhi was Pestonji Padshah, the Vegetarian Parsi whom

---

[101] *Autobiography*, pp. 165-168.
[102] Mansuklal Jhaveri, " Gujarati Literature," *Contemporary Indian Literature: A Symposium,* (Delhi, Sahitya Akademi, 1959), p. 61.

Gandhi first met in a restaurant in London. In 1896, Gandhi would meet him again; at this second meeting in Bombay, Gandhi found him busy contributing to a Higher Gujarati Dictionary. Pestonji tried at that time to persuade Gandhi to stay in India to work for the development of Gujarati.[103] Before he finally left South Africa, Gandhi would be familiar with a body of literature extending from the poetry of Narsi Mehta and Mirabhai in the fifteenth century to the writings of Narmadshankar (1833–1886), the father of modern Gujarati. The young barrister in Pretoria would have progressed from the translation of legal documents to the translation of books like Ruskin's *Unto This Last*, and then to the writing of Gujarati prose. Eventually K. M. Munshi would include " the literary output of Mahatma Gandhi "[104] among the achievements of modern Gujarati.

Busy and reasonably happy though he was, Gandhi had not really forgotten his nightmare journey to Pretoria. " Suffice it to say, all those experiences sank in me..."[105] The recollections of the journey from Durban sank into the subconscious mind of Gandhi, but, far from dissolving, they were acting as the leaven in his religious and intellectual ferment. " Speaking generally," wrote William James, " our moral and practical attitude, at any given time, is always a resultant of two sets of forces within us, impulses pushing us one way and obstructions and inhibitions holding us back."[106] During his year in Pretoria he was, like Olive Schreiner, lost in a dream. (Gandhi would meet her later and read her *Dreams*.) He also resembled a character in one of the romances of William Morris (of whose work he read in Pretoria) who

---

[103] *Autobiography*, p. 218.
[104] *Gujarat and Its Literature*, p. 10.
[105] *Satyagraha in South Africa*, p. 42.
[106] *The Varieties of Religious Experience*, (New York, The Modern Library, n. d.), p. 256.

lived between action and inaction until he found a solution: " Even though he half saw it he began to dream about it, as his was about everything, to make it different from what it was."[107]

Behind the seeming passivity, however, Gandhi's mood was keyed to a high pitch of intensity. He was tuned for action but there was no emotional impulse strong enough to make him act. The pent up forces gathering strength within Gandhi would be liberated the moment he returned to Durban. The issue of the Indian Franchise in Natal would provide the overmastering impulse which swept Gandhi's inhibitions aside as he plunged into feverish activity after that quiet year in Pretoria. " During the first year...I was merely the witness and the victim of these wrongs...I then awoke to a sense of my duty."[108] A nightmare had been followed by a thought-filled dream that was to lead to an awakening and an intense period of action in Natal.

Barrister Gandhi

Dada Abdulla's case was a dispute over a large sum of money owed to him by Sheth Tyeb Haji Khan Muhammed, the leading Indian merchant in Pretoria. Disgusted by some of the pettifogging aspects of a case involving two merchants who were relatives, Gandhi probably recollected the methods of the Rajasthanik Court on which his father had served. He appealed to the common sense of both parties and effected an agreement satisfactory to all concerned. When Gandhi returned to Durban about the middle of May, 1894, he had earned the gratitude of Dada Abdulla who received him much more warmly than he had the previous year. The young barrister had proved his worth, but there seemed to be nothing

---

[107] J. W. MacKail, in his biography of Morris, quotes these lines, Vol. I, p. 20; cited by Brinton, *op. cit.*, p. 253.

[108] *Satyagraha in South Africa*, p. 42.

more he could do; the date was set for his departure to India.

Gandhi, however, was not to leave without a fitting fare-well. The hospitable merchant, accompanied by his friends, took Gandhi to Sydenham, a village in Durban County, where they could relax in congenial surroundings. The greater part of the day had passed in pleasant idleness when Gandhi chanced to pick up a copy of *The Natal Mercury* in the home of the Indian merchant who was host to the party from Durban. His eyes lighted on a paragraph captioned " Indian Franchise " which stated that a bill to disenfranchise his fellow countrymen had passed its second reading in the Natal Legislature. All that he had learned of the Uitlander agitation for the franchise in the Transvaal leaped into Gandhi's mind. The year in Pretoria had taught him the value and significance of the franchise. He controlled his excitement as he realised that here at last was an issue on which the Indians could take a stand. Within the next hour, Gandhi had transformed a picnic into a political meeting, organized his hosts into an *ad hoc* committee and decided to cancel his passage to India. A leisurely day ended on a hurried note since there was no time to be lost if the discriminatory bill was to be prevented from becoming final at its third reading. It was not Dada Abdulla but Gandhi who controlled the party that returned to Durban after a hasty dinner.

The Mahatma later felt a deep sense of gratitude whenever he recollected that light-hearted outing which had turned into a momentous occasion; he attributed the happenings of that day to Providence. " Thus God laid the foundations of my life in South Africa and sowed the seeds of the fight for national self-respect."[109] He had decided at Sydenham to stay a month longer; South Africa claimed him for twenty-one years more. The Mahatma recalled the element of

---

[109] *Autobiography*, p. 175.

chance that altered the nature of that day when he described the technique of political struggle he had evolved. " That is the beauty of Satyagraha. It comes up to oneself, one has not to go out in search of it."[110]   Gandhi had not gone out to Sydenham looking for trouble.   Yet when that paragraph in *The Natal Mercury* leaped to his eye he had realized that life poses some challenges which cannot be evaded without loss of self-respect.

Looking back, the Mahatma said he knew the Indians "should strenuously resist this attack on their rights" though he was " not in possession of all the facts " at that time.[111] Like Gandhi in 1894, we need some knowledge of the background of events leading to the bill in the Natal Legislature to disenfranchise the Indians.   This bitter pill for the Indians had a lot to do with sugar.   For a period in 1906, (Gandhi lived with the Polaks, a British couple, at the time) sugar was banned from the table because it was a product of Indian indentured labour.[112]   As we have seen, the story of cotton in Western India played a part in shaping the future of the young Gandhi.   In Natal, his life became part of the story of sugar.

In the early days of the Colony, the settlers in the coastlands had experimented unsuccessfully with a few export crops like arrowroot and indigo.[113] The outlook for the settlers had remained bleak until about 1851, when Morewood, a pioneer like Drennan who had brought the cotton industry to Kathiawad, proved that sugarcane could be cultivated in Natal.   The Colonists realized that sugar could become a source of great prosperity; only the lack of good and cheap

---

[110] *Satyagraha in South Africa*, p. 14.

[111] *Satyagraha in South Africa*, pp. 43-44.

[112] M. G. Polak, *op. cit.*, p. 82.

[113] N. Hurwitz, *Agriculture in Natal* 1860–1950, Natal Regional Survey, (London, Oxford University Press, 1957), p. 36.

labour stood between them and their dreams of wealth. With a few exceptions, such as the Wesleyan missionary Holden, the settlers had convinced themselves that the native African was not suited to the regularity required of the plantation and agricultural labourer. Every possible source of immigrant labour was discussed—English agricultural labourers and orphan boys from Lord Shaftesbury's Homes, freed slaves from the Northern States of America, coolies from India or China. Sir George Grey, Governor at the Cape, favoured the importation of coolies from India (indentured Indians were then already at work in the cane fields of Mauritius[114] and the West Indies), and addressed the first letter on the subject to the East India Company in 1855. The Colonists remained undecided about the wisdom of the move, however, and their vacillations were reflected in the elections to the first legislature when Natal became a Crown Colony in 1856. The planting interests fared better in the elections to the reformed Legislative Council of 1859; a unanimous resolution welcomed the importation of labour from India. The stage was thus set by the planters for the drama of Natal's Indian Question in which Gandhi was destined to play a notable role.

The first batch of coolies arrived from Madras on November 16, 1860. A young colonist of twenty-one who watched the arrival of the Indians described the event in his autobiography written forty years later. "I well remember one evening late in 1860," he wrote, "watching, from a height overlooking the sea, the ship *Truro* sail up to the anchorage. Her white canvas towered over the blue sea-line, and we all regarded her as the harbinger of a new dispensation. And so she proved to be, though in a sense far wider than we

---

[114] S. B. De Burgh-Edwardes, *History of Mauritius* 1507–1914, (London, East & West Ltd., 1921), p. 72; P. J. Barnewell and A. Toussaint, *A Short History of Mauritius*, (Longmans, Green & Co., 1949), pp. 157-158.

expected."[115]   That young man was John Robinson, destined to be the first Prime Minister after Natal's achievement of Responsible Government in July, 1893.   Now in May, 1894, Robinson's friend, the new Attorney General, Harry Escombe (twenty-two at the time the first Indians arrived), was pushing through the bill which caught Gandhi's eye in a newspaper at Sydenham.   *The Natal Mercury*, which contained the paragraph Gandhi read, had been owned by the Robinson family since 1852.   A lot of water had flowed down the Umbilo and Umhlatuzan into the bay at Durban where the *Truro* had anchored.   Within a decade of their arrival, the Indian indentured labourers had ensured the prosperity of the sugar and tea estates and turned Natal into " the Garden Colony." There was also a marked change in the amenities of life since indentured Indians made good household servants and gardeners, and provided the municipalities with sanitary workers.   In 1870, however, the discovery of diamonds at Kimberley[116] altered the economic structure of Natal and released the Colony from excessive dependence on the sugar barons with their palatial homes on the Berea.   Natal was drawn into a wider economic orbit, and plans were initiated for the development of Durban Harbour and the extension of the railways to the borders of the Colony to take advantage of the growing import trade.   This process was further accelerated in 1886, when gold was discovered on the Rand. The merchants of Durban prospered as they supplied the apparently insatiable needs of Kimberley and Johannesburg.

The economic developments of the 1870's and 1880's obscured the earlier service rendered by indentured labour in putting the Colony on its feet and sowed the seeds of a growing

---

[115] John Robinson, *A Life Time in South Africa*, (London, Smith, Elder & Co., 1900), pp. 75–77.
[116] G. F. Williams, *The Diamond Mines of South Africa*, (New York, B. F. Buck & Co., 1905).

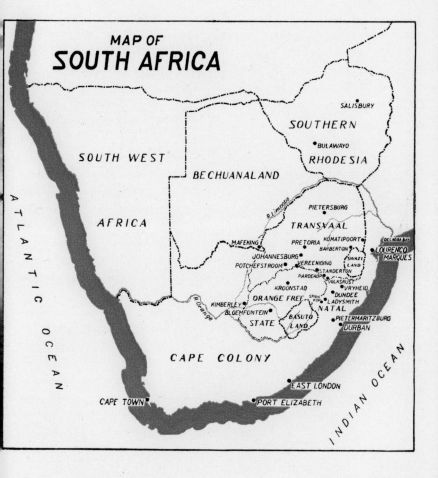

MAP OF
SOUTH AFRICA

racial hatred towards the Indians. By the 1890's, the attitudes towards the different classes of Indians in the Colony were beginning to crystallize. The indentured Indians were regarded with contempt, but the planting interests took good care to see that their indispensability was recognized. The official Railway Guide published in 1895 reflected the prevailing attitude: " The Indians are taken, generally speaking, from the labouring classes of their own country. There are, of course, exceptions, but the bulk, while useful, and in fact almost indispensable as regular, steady labourers, have amongst them a proportion who produce more crime than the whites collectively. The sale of intoxicating liquors to them, and its prohibition from the natives may account for this...In the earlier days, for lack of reliable labour, many an industry was wrecked, and many a failure, as the Insolvency Courts will attest, can be justly laid to this cause...Taken on the whole, the Indians have proved their value, and but little is now urged against them."[117]

If the dislike of indentured labour was still subdued, the tide of racial feeling against the " free " Indians was rising. The indentured labourer was bound by his contract to serve for five years. At the end of this period, he became a " free " Indian and the Immigration Laws permitted him either to settle in Natal or return to India. The majority of the " free " Indians, like most immigrants in similar circumstances, chose to stay. As successful market-gardeners, many of them cultivated small plots and ensured a cheap and plentiful supply of vegetables.[118] Others took to fishing or started small business ventures. Some who had received a smattering

---

[117] *The Colony of Natal*, pp. 17-18.
[118] Lionel Phillips, *Transvaal Problems: Some Notes on Current Politics*, (London, John Murray, 1905), p. 36. Phillips disagreed with Owen Thomas's good opinion of Indian market gardeners in the latter's *Agricultural and Pastoral Prospects of South Africa*, p. 210.

of English education became clerks or interpreters in the courts; this was especially true of those who were Indian Christians. The growing numbers of "free" Indians were particularly distrusted (as potential rivals) by the white artisan class of skilled labourers and railway workers.

The first group discriminated against after the coming of Responsible Government, however, were the "Arabs," as the Indian merchants were collectively known because of the flowing robes worn by the Meman Muslim merchants. Indian traders had followed indentured Indian labour to Mauritius as suppliers of rice, the staple diet of the plantation workers. The first Indian merchants to arrive in South Africa were welcomed and respected, such as Sheth Abubakar Amad,[119] who settled in Durban about 1870, and a Parsi, Dorabji Dhunjibhoy,[120] who opened a store at Komatipoort. By the 1890's, the Free Trade spirit of the old Colonial days had disappeared; ruthless competition was taking its place as the four states of South Africa manoeuvred against each other in the struggle for the riches on the Rand. The large number of Indian merchants who had prospered were becoming an eye-sore to the petty white traders and shopkeepers in the country districts. In Durban, the flourishing Indian shops in Grey Street, Pine Street and West Street were no longer regarded with friendliness by white businessmen. The Indian merchants, however, were still patronised by many whites who found them cheaper—another reason for their rivals' animosity.

The commercial interests were well represented in the Legislature elected immediately after the coming of Responsible Government. Their first move, the abolition of the grant-in-aid for assisting Indian immigration, was aimed at the planters

---

[119] *Satyagraha in South Africa*, p. 23; Ferguson-Davie, *op. cit.*, p. 21.
[120] *Storm Over the Transvaal*, p. 43.

who were still clamouring for more indentured labour. Their trade rivals, the Indian merchants, were the next target of attack. The number of Indians registered as voters was only a little over two hundred, but, as Gandhi rightly surmised, the disenfranchisement bill was part of a calculated move to ensure white supremacy in Natal.

The role of the Durban barristers (many of whom were to become friends, and even admirers, of Gandhi) in fostering anti-Indian legislation deserves careful study. The older generation of lawyers in the Colony had begun their careers by serving the sugar and tea planters and the Indian merchants, who were allied commercially with the planting interests. "Our eyes and ears are the European attorneys here,"[121] Dada Abdulla told Gandhi. One of the lawyers most closely associated with the Indian merchants was Harry Escombe. In fact, many of the Indian merchants had registered themselves as voters at the request of Escombe at a time when he needed their help in his struggle with the Wharf Engineer.[122] This had enabled Escombe as a member of the old Legislative Council to push through the development of Durban Harbour and had earned him the title of "Father of Port Natal."[123] Lawyers like Escombe and Binns had given invaluable help to the planters during the sittings of the Wragg Commission (1885–1886) which inquired into the problem of Indian labour. At that time, Escombe had defended the right of "free" Indians to settle in Natal. It was this same Escombe, caught in a changing political atmosphere, who was responsible as Attorney General for drafting the first piece of anti-Indian legislation in 1894.

Men in their fifties like Robinson and Escombe could remember the difference the coming of the Indians had made

---

[121] *Autobiography*, p. 173.
[122] *Ibid.*, p. 174; *Satyagraha in South Africa*, p. 29.
[123] Bigelow, *op. cit.*, p. 228; See Hattersley, *Later Annals*, p. 16.

18

to the Colony, but this was not true of the large number of white immigrants who came to Natal after 1860. The old Colonials who were elected to the first Legislature under Responsible Government now depended on these new immigrants for their votes. Many of the newcomers were white artisans with no interests allied to those of the planters. Both old Colonial and newcomer were also oppressed by their consciousness of the Colony's changed racial character. In 1895, the population statistics showed that there were 45,000 whites and 40,000 Indians; still in the background, largely inarticulate but an ever present reality, was the mass of 450,000 native Africans.[124] The whites were becoming uneasy in the 1890's, and frightened men act hastily and emotionally. The Mahatma later wrote, " The Europeans had no solid grounds for their apprehensions, but it is impossible to convince by argument men who have been seized by vague terrors."[125]

The old Colonials never completely succumbed to the racist madness; but the new immigrants who displaced them politically before the turn of the century did just that. Escombe himself, and other barristers like Binns, Labistour and Laughton, never completely lost their sense of fair play and justice. When they moved to disenfranchise the Indians, both Robinson and Escombe made speeches showing they hoped the whites would feel a concern and a paternal sense of responsibility for the entire coloured population of the Colony. They failed to bequeath their heritage of liberalism (sincere, but weakened by a difficult racial situation) to their posterity in Natal. Gandhi never forgot that Harry Escombe had had the courage to enrol him as a barrister in the face of opposition from a colour-conscious Natal Law Society. The relations between Gandhi and the old Colonials were at their

---

[124] *The Colony of Natal* (Railway Guide), p. 16.
[125] *Satyagraha in South Africa*, p. 30.

best during the Boer War; many of them appreciated deeply Gandhi's gesture in organizing an Indian Ambulance Corps to serve at Colenso and Spion Kop. Gandhi knew Escombe almost from the day he first landed in Durban; he won the friendship of Sir John Robinson during the Boer War.

The Mahatma later recalled that even before he started for Durban from Sydenham he had " an outline of the campaign " in his mind.[126] Actually, many aspects of the campaign had been maturing in his mind as a result of his experiences in Pretoria. He had watched the Uitlander campaign take shape while he studied the grievances of the Indians. The campaign he outlined to himself that evening in Sydenham was to dominate his life until he discarded it in favour of Passive Resistance in the Transvaal in 1906. Until then, Gandhi showed impressive industry and great forensic skill as he marshalled all the facts of the Indian case in a series of memorials and petitions to the Natal Legislature and the Colonial Office in London. He also worked hard to enlist the support of the Imperial authorities and the Government of India. This part of Gandhi's work belongs to British Colonial and Empire history; it is recorded in documents preserved by the South African, Imperial, and Indian archives.

It is more meaningful and valuable here to study Gandhi's activities in South Africa against the wider background of world immigration.[127] The campaign led by Gandhi against the attempt to disenfranchise Indians in Natal forms part of the unfinished story of Asiatic migration to different parts of the world. Today it is no longer true that Asians are discriminated against only in countries dominated by Anglo-Saxon peoples. The absence of a colour bar cannot conceal

---

[126] *Autobiography*, p. 175.
[127] See Maurice R. Davie, *World Immigration*, (New York, The Macmillan Co., 1936); Oscar Handlin, (ed.), *Immigration as a Factor in American History*, (Englewood Cliffs, N.J., Prentice Hall, Inc., 1959).

the fact that Asians are discriminating against other Asians who have migrated to their countries. There is also growing evidence that increasingly Asians will be discriminated against by African peoples. The clash of colour is no longer just between black and white; it has become many-hued. All these tragic developments give both poignancy and greater significance to Gandhi's struggles against racial prejudices in South Africa. Satyagraha was not conceived originally as a method of national struggle. Born in the midst of colour prejudice, Satyagraha remains relevant to every unresolved racial situation in the world.

The first step any immigrant community takes in the face of discrimination is to unite. At the meeting of Indians he had organized in Pretoria, Gandhi had stressed the need for unity. It had become clear to him by then that the Indians were hopelessly disunited and out of touch with each other. The Indian merchants considered themselves superior to the indentured labourers; they had allowed themselves to be called " Arabs " in order to be on a better social footing with the whites. The Colonial-born Indians, ashamed of their humble coolie origin and yet contemptuous of the more glaring crudities of the unsophisticated Indian merchants, were a group apart. In the franchise bill, Gandhi found an issue which could bring together the merchants and " free " Indians. The young Gandhi's enthusiasm was infectious as he worked through the remaining months of 1894 with tremendous energy to unite the Indians. He was both tireless and happy—he had found a cause which absorbed him completely.

When an immigrant community finds leadership, the next step it usually takes is to set up an organization. In August 1894, the Natal Indian Congress came into being with Gandhi, as its honorary secretary. While it is true that this body owed its name to what Gandhi knew of the Indian National Congress and that, as Mrs. Polak put it, he played David to

Dadhabhai Naoroji's Saul,[128] the new organization was much more like some of the other immigrant organizations in South Africa. The Indian National Congress was the parent of the Natal organization only in a limited sense; the younger association was more analogous to the National Union of the Uitlanders or the Irish Association of Natal, for the Natal Indian Congress was not a nationalist body, but an immigrant organization struggling for minority rights. As the Indians struggled for status and acceptance, they would find they were sometimes helped, sometimes opposed, by other immigrant groups such as the Irish and the Jews. After the Boer War, racial prejudice was a useful lever for hastening the union of the four states of South Africa. The closing of their ranks by the different ethnic groups among the whites contributed to Gandhi's decision to launch Passive Resistance.

The similarity of the Natal Indian Congress to immigrant organizations elsewhere became more clear when Gandhi induced that body to purchase a building in Durban. The Congress Hall in Grey Street was like other immigrant centres (Butt Hall of the Hibernian Society in Boston, for example) where the Indian community met for both political and social purposes. Gandhi's reports of the activities of the Natal Indian Congress are interesting from this point of view. Gandhi's second " Report " contained the following item: " The birth of a son to Mr. Abdul Kadir in the month of March, 1896, deserves a special paragraph. At the ceremony performed in the Congress Hall to commemorate the event, over five hundred people gathered together. The Hall was brilliantly lit up, Mr. Abdul Kadir made a present to the Congress of £ 7. This was followed by others and the donations given on the occasion amounted to £ 58."[129]

---

[128] *Op. cit.*, p. 40.
[129] *Collected Works*, III, p. 101.

Wherever white immigrants have gone they have taken their churches with them. The Mahatma often regretted the fact that the Indian immigrants had no religious organizations of their own (the Ramakrishna Mission had not yet come into existence) to help them socially and educationally. He found a useful ally, however, in the Church Missionary Society which had been working among indentured Indian labourers for some time. Gandhi was particularly drawn to the Reverend Dr. L. P. Booth of St. Aidan's Hospital who was a warm friend of all classes of Indians. Gandhi was grateful for the support his C. M. S. missionary friends gave to the humanitarian aspects of the work of the Natal Indian Congress.[130] The other missionary bodies at work in Natal, like the Zulu Mission of the American Board of Boston, were primarily interested in the native Africans. The Church Missionary Society, however, had been very successful in some of the Tamil districts of South India with the result that its workers were to be found wherever there were Tamil people. Booth was Superintendent of the Indian Mission of the Diocese of Natal.

Gandhi became interested in the problems of Indian Christians in Natal through Subhan Godfrey, the headmaster of the C. M. S. school in Durban. Many of the Colonial-born Indians were Christians. Partly westernized, the Colonial-born youth felt the racial discrimination more deeply than any other section of the Indian population. Gandhi started the Natal Indian Educational Association and the Diamond Jubilee Library largely to give these young men a useful outlet for their energies. We get an interesting picture of some of their activities in Gandhi's "Reports." In 1897, for example, Dr. Booth and his wife organized two benefit shows on behalf of the Educational Association in the

---

[130] *Ibid.*, III, p. 145.

Congress Hall when " an improvised stage was erected and the members with some non-members played ' Ali Baba and the Forty Thieves', the Hall being packed full on both occasions and the proceeds amounting to £ 40."[131]

The interest in nursing which Gandhi had developed as a boy attracted him to the medical work of the C. M. S. The example of Dr. Booth and St. Aidan's Hospital influenced the establishment of the Indian Hospital in 1898, through a generous donation from Parsi Rustomji. The young lawyer then found time to attend to minor injuries and dispense drugs in the Indian Hospital in the mornings before other activities claimed him. Both his friendship with Booth and his experience of serving in the Indian Hospital were to prove useful to Gandhi when the Boer War broke out. At that time, Booth helped Gandhi to organize the Indian Ambulance Corps, and accompanied the volunteer stretcher-bearers to the front as their medical officer.

In an interview with the editor of *The Statesman* of Calcutta during his first holiday in India in 1896, Gandhi summed up his attitude to the legal aspects of the struggle against racial discrimination. " We hope," he said, " that when the legal disabilities are removed the social persecution will gradually disappear."[132] Indian associations had been formed at the Cape and in Transvaal when Gandhi first arrived, but not in Natal. The presence of the young Indian lawyer and the establishment of the Natal Indian Congress enabled the community to give organized support to individuals courageous enough to fight discrimination through the law courts in a Colony which prided itself on its British legal traditions. One of these early " test cases " was that of *Vinden* v. *Lady-smith Local Board* in 1896. Mrs. David Vinden, an educated Indian Christian woman, was treated roughly by the police

---

[131] *Collected Works*, III, pp. 105-106.
[132] *Collected Works*, II, p. 127.

when she was on her way home from church on a Sunday night because she was not carrying a pass. Mrs. Vinden and her husband had not immigrated to Natal as labourers, and they took legal steps to establish their claim that she could not be compelled to carry a pass. The Magistrate of Lady-smith supported Mrs. Vinden. Three years later when that Magistrate, G. M. Rudolph, retired, the Indians gave him a farewell. Gandhi was present, as secretary of the Natal Indian Congress, to light " the lamp of gratitude and affection in the Indian heart " as he thanked Rudolph for adding lustre " to the British Constitution, so worthily represented by you for so long in Ladysmith."[133]

Gandhi became adept at fighting " test cases " but felt overburdened by all the legal work involved. During his visit to India in 1896, he would try to persuade law students he had known in London like Taleyarkhan and Pestonji Padshah to join him in Natal. H. M. Nazar, a lawyer who had arrived on his own volition in Natal, proved very helpful, but for most of his time in South Africa, Gandhi was a one-man "Immigrant Legal Aid Society." Gandhi's early legal struggles on behalf of the Indian community were impressive, but he was fighting a losing battle against a rising tide of racial prejudice; the legislation in South Africa resembled anti-Asiatic enactments in other parts of the world. After a decade of failure in Natal, Gandhi became dis-illusioned with legal processes; his weariness of law courts was evidenced in his vehement attack on lawyers in *Hind Swaraj*. Yet, had Gandhi not been a lawyer himself, his usefulness in Natal would have been severely limited. His standing as a barrister gave him status in the eyes of the whites which he would not otherwise have possessed; after all, the young Indian had been a back bencher in the Inns of Court like

---

[133] *Ibid.*, pp. 10, 79.

their Governor, Sir Walter Hely-Hutchinson.[134] The Indians could never forget him in his role as " Barrister Gandhi." He was more approachable than the white lawyers. The indentured labourer, Balasundaram,[135] assaulted by his white employer, could not have found redress for his injuries without Gandhi's presence in Natal as a lawyer.

An immigrant community usually runs into problems regarding the education of their children; the Indians in Natal were no exception to this general rule. The employers of indentured labour were considered responsible for the education of the children of the coolies. A not very satisfactory primary education was provided by the sugar and tea estates, the railways, and the Durban Corporation. The Church Missionary Society schools were attended mainly by Indian Christian children; their evangelical character deterred the Hindu and Muslim traders from sending their children to them. The economically well-placed Indian classes faced a problem, especially regarding higher education. A few Indian children had been admitted to the public schools but the Government of Natal refused to admit any more after 1899. In an article for *The Times of India*, Gandhi later cited the Godfreys, a well-known Christian family, as an example of the type of Indians affected by the discrimination. He also described the move of the Government to establish a higher grade school for Indian children separate but equal to the white public schools, as " a sop to their conscience..."[136] Gandhi would continue to agitate for the improvement of this school which proved to be separate but

---

[134] *The Argus Annual and South African Gazetteer of* 1895, (Johannesburg, Cape Town and Pretoria, The Argus Printing and Publishing Co., Ltd.) p. 47.

[135] *Autobiography*, p. 191; *Collected Works*, II, p. 20, III, p. 173.

[136] *Collected Works*, III, pp. 82-84.

far from equal.[137] The school issue in Natal was the beginning of his interest in the problems of education. The difficulties experienced by Indian children led him to make his own educational experiments in the Phoenix Settlement.

Another problem an immigrant community faces is the distressing image of themselves which they find mirrored in the prejudices of the dominant group in the country to which they have ventured. Since the majority of the members of the immigrant community usually come from the poorer strata of the population of their own country, the stereotypes established at the time of their arrival are hard to remove even after the incoming group has improved itself educationally and socially. Throughout his stay in South Africa, Gandhi fought hard to remove the stereotyped images of Indians and India in the minds of the whites. In addition to his political, social, and legal work, Gandhi found time to write numerous letters to the press and published articles and pamphlets in order to remove misconceptions about the Indian community. He felt the need for a journal through which to express the views of his community; but this was not established until 1903 when he founded his multi-lingual newspaper, *Indian Opinion*.

The dominant stereotype in the minds of the whites was the image of the Indian as a coolie and the country from which Indians came as a land of coolies. As we have seen, Gandhi himself was known as " the coolie lawyer " or " the coolie barrister,"[138] while the Indian merchants were sometimes referred to as " coolie traders." During his first decade in South Africa, when Gandhi laboured mainly on behalf of the Indian merchants, he tried to disassociate in the minds of the whites the image of the coolie from that of the better class of Indians. Later, his attitude to the coolie changed

---

[137] *Ibid.*, III, pp. 171, 198.
[138] *Autobiography*, p. 136; *Satyagraha in South Africa*, p. 40.

from one of separation to one of identification; he regretted his own unconscious assimilation of the feelings of superiority towards the indentured labourers entertained by the Indian merchants. The Mahatma was to carry his attempt to identify with the poor even further after he returned to India. He would also popularize a new name for the coolies by calling them " Harijans " or " God's people." When this name was first suggested to him by a humble outcaste after his return to India, perhaps the Mahatma remembered that the people whose fine build he had admired when he landed in Durban called themselves the Ama-Zulu—" the people of heaven."

In the 1890's, when the feeling against the Indian merchants in Natal was growing, anti-Semitic stereotypes were being transferred to " the sons of Ishmael,"[139] as Kruger had once referred to these Muslim traders. Sarah Gertrude Millin wrote of the Jews, " In Durban, they could not compete against the Indian traders and were not socially acceptable to the British."[140] Anti-Semitic images, however, were useful in the campaign against the Indian merchants. Macnab's anti-Semitism in her descriptions of Johannesburg reappears as violent anti-Indian prejudice in her account of Natal. *On Veldt and Farm* appeared in 1897. Poultney Bigelow's *White Man's Africa*, published the following year, made the connection between anti-Semitism and anti-Indian feeling much more explicit. Describing the Indians of Natal, this American racist wrote, " Their forbidding features haunted me wherever I went. They appeared to do for this country what the Jews of Hungary and Poland do for those two generous and unsuspecting nations. They traffic with the natives by wily ways, which Westerners can only emulate at a distance. If they have not already, they will soon have

---

[139] *Satyagraha in South Africa*, p. 33.
[140] *Op. cit.*, p. 215.

283

the blacks of Natal in a bondage similar to that in which the Jews today hold the improvident emancipated slaves of the United States...The Natal Shylock asks only a promissory note or a mortgage, along with a stipulation that his debtor shall trade with no one excepting himself."[141]

Gandhi encountered a racialism in South Africa which was articulated openly and forcibly. Cumberland, a travelling showman and mind reader, could write, " The way in which the dirty coloured people jostle the white man on the pavements in Cape Town is simply disgusting. A black man is a black man, and a dirty coloured man is a dirty coloured man, but I have never yet succeeded in looking upon him as a brother. I object to knocking against him, and I resent his knocking against me."[142] Macnab could argue that native policies should be based on " stern and terrible necessity " since " our conquest of Africa has taught us that if there is a supreme question between the black man and the white, the black man must be shot."[143] To imagine that this atmosphere of racial prejudice did not ruffle Gandhi's feelings or make him angry is to turn him into an Uncle Tom or a stained-glass-window saint. Within three months of his arrival in Pretoria, Gandhi wrote an indignant letter to *The Natal Advertiser* about the racial situation in which he asked, " Is this Christian-like, is this fair play, is this justice, is this civilization? I pause for a reply."[144] Gandhi would pause for a reply for twenty years before answering the question he had asked with a total rejection of Western civilization in *Hind Swaraj*.

During his stay in South Africa, Gandhi marshalled an array of Western writers in support of his contention that Indian civilization is not inferior to that of the West. In his

---

[141] *Op. cit.*, pp. 236-238.
[142] *Op. cit.*, p. 12.
[143] *Op. cit.*, p. 274.
[144] *Collected Works*, I, p. 76.

Open Letter of 1894 addressed to the members of the Natal Legislative Council and Assembly, for example, he either quoted from their writings or cited the authority of Sir W. W. Hunter, Max Muller, Schopenhauer, Sir Henry S. Maine, Andrew Carnegie, Bishop Heber, Sir Thomas Munro, Sir George Birdwood, Sir Charles Trevelyan, Frederick Pincott, M. Louis Jacolliot, Victor Hugo, Macaulay, Mill, Burke, Bright, Fawcett, Bradlaugh, Gladstone, Lord Ripon, Lord Reay, Lord Northbrooke, and the Marquis of Dufferin.[145] Indian civilization was on trial and the twenty-four-year old lawyer was conducting the case for the defence assisted by the witnesses he had summoned. The quotations, which were the statements of his witnesses testifying to the character of Indian civilization, would appear again and again in his writings. Gandhi seems to have carried the quotations around with him almost like a research student with his cards. This habit had not left Gandhi when he added a second appendix to *Hind Swaraj* entitled " Testimonies by Eminent Men," consisting of extracts from the " valuable collection " of the Irish M. P., Alfred Webb, showing that " the ancient Indian civilization has little to learn from the modern."[146] The quotation from Max Muller in Webb's collection was an old favourite with Gandhi; already rather shop-soiled by the time it found its way into *Hind Swaraj*, that famous passage from *India—What Can It Teach Us*? would be used repeatedly in Indian nationalist writings of the twentieth century.[147]

Before he left South Africa, Gandhi would be prosecuting Western civilization in the same manner in which he had defended Indian culture. The witnesses summoned and the authorities cited would testify to the immoral character of the West. Tolstoy would be the chief witness for the prosecution.

---

[145] *Collected Works*, I, pp. 142-165.
[146] Webb, *op. cit.*, pp. 77-80.
[147] *Ibid.*, p. 78.

Damaging evidence would be supplied by other witnesses like Ruskin, Thoreau, Max Nordau, Edward Carpenter, R. H. Sherard, and minor writers like Godfrey Blount and T. F. Taylor, whom Gandhi included in the first appendix to *Hind Swaraj*.[148] All his witnesses agreed that the immoral character of the West was due to the " disease " of modern civilization.

The profile Gandhi drew of Western civilization, based on its distorted image in South Africa, was a caricature rather than a true likeness of European culture. It was as un-complimentary as the profile of Indian civilization in the minds of the whites. The level of this inter-cultural debate was a depressing clash of stereotypes in which each side was trying to prove the inferiority of the other. This battle of stereotypes resounds in one of the earliest of Gandhi's letters to the press in defence of Indian merchants: " But you say these wretched Asiatics live a semi-barbaric life. It would be highly interesting to learn your views of a semi-barbaric life. I have some notion of the life they live. If a room without a nice, rich carpet and ornamental hangings, a dinner table (perhaps unvarnished), without an expensive table cloth, with no flowers to decorate it, with no wines spread, no pork or beef *ad lib*, be a semi-barbaric life; if a white comfortable dress, specially adapted to a warm climate, which, I am told, many Europeans envy them in the trying heat of summer, be a semi-barbaric life; if no beer, no tobacco, no ornamental walking stick, no golden watch chain, no luxuriously-fitted sitting room, be a semi-barbaric life; if, in short, what one commonly understands by a simple frugal life be a semi-barbaric life, then, indeed, the Indian traders must plead guilty to the charge, and the sooner the semi-barbarity is wiped out from the highest Colonial civilization, the better."[149]

---

[148] Webb, *op. cit.*, p. 77.
[149] *Collected Works*, I, pp. 75-76.

The Birth of a Fighter

The young Gandhi had begun contributing to the development of a vast cultural mythology which the conflict of races and civilizations nurtured. The fiery ordeal of race prejudice led the Mahatma later to assert that Indian civilization, based on simple living and high thinking, is essentially spiritual and to characterize Western civilization as brutal, materialistic, and wedded to the pursuit of pleasure.

During his early days in Natal, however, Gandhi saw himself in the role of " a humble interpreter " between the Indians and the whites. While opposing stereotypes which condemned a whole people, he was quick to acknowledge the elements of truth in the criticism levelled against the Indians. Mrs. Polak would say of Gandhi that " one of his cherished roles has always been that of super-scavenger."[150] He was indefatigable in his attempts to educate the Indians on the need for more sanitary ways of living. He contrasted Zanzibar with Durban as an object lesson to the Indian merchants; the success of the Indian mercantile community in Zanzibar had not made it a clean town like Durban, which owed its elegance " to European enterprise and English taste."[151] Gandhi also insisted on truthfulness and honest business dealings to the point of opposing even " the habit of exaggeration."[152] The young Indian became the self-appointed censor of the morals of the community; no moral lapse on the part of an Indian would go unnoticed by him. A streak of censoriousness was one of the marks left on the Mahatma by his puritanical role as the young moral preceptor and guide of a community freed from traditional restraints.

Gandhi had told Kasturba he would see her again at the end of a year. Three eventful years had sped by before he felt he should return to India to fetch his wife and two little

---

[150] *Op. cit.*, p. 50.
[151] *Collected Works*, III, p. 355.
[152] *Satyagraha in South Africa*, p. 48.

287

boys to Durban. The long separation had been harder for
Kasturba than for him. Absorbed in his work on behalf of
the Indian community, Gandhi had temporarily sublimated
the strong desire her presence could arouse in him. He had
grown and matured into a leader of men. Gandhi thoroughly
enjoyed being a leader, as he always would. He had played
the arbiter (in the disputes of the little boys playing in Shitla
Chowk in Porbandar),[153] the husband in Rajkot, the English
gentleman in London—now he had learned to play the
dewan like his father and grandfather. Gandhi had a dewan's
memory for people and faces. " I had got to know the
people and they had got to know me,"[154] said the Mahatma
recollecting those three years in Natal. He had admired
Raychand's phenomenal memory and would appreciate the
same gift in Gokhale. Yet his own ability to remember
names and faces was already outstanding. He was primarily
interested in people rather than in ideas. He ran the Natal
Indian Congress like a dewan, instituting the familiar Kathiawadi system of fines and levies. Thus, every truant was
either fined for his absence from meetings or a levy was placed
on every package of salt imported by the absentee Indian
merchants.[155] " Gandhibhai," as he was affectionately
called, could be a young tyrant; he had kept an Indian
merchant of Tongaat awake for the best part of the night
until the old miser parted with a substantial donation.[156]
Youthful as he was, he could turn any group into a *durbar*
with himself as its central figure. The Mahatma was to play
the dewan even better; whether he was giving *darshan* to
thousands or sitting on the mud floor of his hut in Sevagram,
the atmosphere would always be that of a *durbar*. Natal had

[153] P. Gandhi, *op. cit.*, p. 28.
[154] *Autobiography*, p. 205.
[155] *Collected Works*, III, p. 109.
[156] *Autobiography*, p. 187.

helped Gandhi to discover himself as the grandson of Ota Baba, the last great dewan of Porbandar.[157]

The Anti-Indian Demonstration Crisis of 1897[158]

It was late in the evening of the last day of November, 1896, when a small steamer, the *Courland* (760 tons) steamed slowly out of Bombay Harbour and headed into the setting sun. Her Captain, Alexander Milne, was glad his ship was moving out to sea. He had feared that the outbreak of plague in some districts of Western India might have led to delays causing extra expense to her owners, Dada Abdulla and Company of Durban. The port health authorities, however, had given the *Courland* a clean bill of health after an inspection of the crew and her two hundred and fifty-five passengers who were bound for Natal, the Transvaal, and Delagoa Bay. Most of them had been in South Africa before; only a few were new emigrants. Captain Milne set his course directly for Durban and hoped his supply of water would last, since he had a consignment of horses in the hold. The Indian Ocean could be stormy in December, and the *Courland* might take longer than usual to reach her destination.

Among the saloon passengers were four Europeans and a young Indian lawyer and his family. Captain Milne was soon on friendly terms with this likeable barrister whom he knew to be a close personal friend of the ship's owner, Dada

---

[157] For an account of the events covered by this section, see Mabel Palmer, *The History of the Indians in Natal*, Vol. X, Natal Regional Survey, (London, Oxford University Press, 1957); Bhaskar Appasamy, *Indians of South Africa*, (Bombay, Padma Publication, 1943).

[158] Most of the information on which this account is based comes from the Memorial to Mr. Joseph Chamberlain, dated March 15, 1897, drafted by Gandhi and the documents appended to it, *Collected Works*, II, pp. 184-283. The incidents described are referred to as " The Anti-Indian Demonstration Crisis " in the letter of thanks to Mrs. R. C. Alexander, March 24, 1897, *Collected Works*, II, p. 285.

19

Abdulla. The Indian in question, M. K. Gandhi, had not expected to find himself and his family on board the *Courland*; it was a sudden arrangement necessitated by a cable from the Natal Indian Congress asking him to return immediately. The Transvaal Government was moving to segregate Indians into "locations." If this discriminatory legislation passed through the Volksraad unopposed, it could lead to further difficulties for Indian merchants in all four Colonies.

Gandhi had spent a busy six months in India dividing his time between his family in Rajkot and his campaign in the major Indian cities on behalf of his fellow countrymen in South Africa. The *Green Pamphlet* he had begun writing on the voyage to India the previous June contained the substance of the speeches he had delivered in Bombay, Poona, and Madras. During this period he had met all the important leaders of the Indian National Congress and the editors of the leading British and Indian newspapers. Despite the brevity of his stay in India, Gandhi had succeeded in arousing some concern for the plight of the Indians in South Africa. Now he could pay undivided attention to his family, helping Kasturba (who was pregnant)[159] to look after their two boys and the young son of his widowed sister whom he was taking as well. Kasturba and the boys felt uncomfortable wearing socks and shoes and using the crockery and cutlery in the ship's dining saloon—both of which Gandhi insisted on.

Four days out of Durban, the *Courland* ran into a terrible storm. Lashed by the tempest, the small steamer pitched and rolled alarmingly. The passengers were thoroughly frightened; Hindus, Muslims and Christians joined together in common prayers for their safety. The Captain and Gandhi, who was always a good sailor, worked together to calm the nervous passengers. The *Courland* was out of the storm the

---

[159] *Collected Works*, II, p. 313.

next day. The sky cleared and the sun made its welcome appearance.

The singing and the merriment with which the ship resounded again jarred Gandhi's nerves, which had been steady during the storm. That squally day, so quickly forgotten by his fellow passengers, was a reminder to the young lawyer that "the real storm was still to come."[160] Disturbing reports had reached Gandhi while in India that serious trouble had been brewing in the Colony for which he and his family were bound. His uneasiness increased as the *Courland* sailed closer to the coast of Natal. He looked cheerful but felt a twinge of anxiety when he looked at his wife and the boys. He had not spoiled the enjoyment of their first voyage together as a family by sharing with them his thoughts of impending danger.

The genesis of the disturbances in Natal could be traced back to an event in April, 1896, the year Gandhi left Durban. Early in that month, the Tongaat Sugar Company had applied to the Immigration Trust Board for permission to bring in twelve skilled artisans from India as indentured labourers. When the news that permission to do so had been granted leaked out in the press, it enraged the white artisan class of the Colony. By August, the storm of protest had led to meetings in Pietermaritzburg and Durban. There was no mistaking the angry mood of the white skilled workers, and the Tongaat Sugar Company withdrew its application. The anti-Indian feelings had not subsided when Reuters unfortunately cabled a few sentences to London from India summarizing the contents of Gandhi's *Green Pamphlet*: " A pamphlet published in India declares that the Indians in Natal are robbed and assaulted and treated like beasts, and are unable to obtain redress. *The Times of India* advocates an

---

[160] *Autobiography*, p. 231.

inquiry into these allegations."[161] A wave of anger had passed over the Colony when this cable received wide publicity in the Natal press on September 14th.

Four days later, *The Natal Mercury* and *The Natal Advertiser* tried to undo the damage, since copies of the offending pamphlet had reached them. They carried editorials pointing out that Gandhi had not done more than repeat what he had frequently and openly stated in Natal itself in defence of the Indians. As a British citizen, he was entitled to his opinions, and his agitation on behalf of his community was quite legitimate. The anti-Indian feeling, however, had become so strong that some groups of the Colonists had determined to organize. A body called the European Protection Association had been formed in Pietermaritzburg in September. Another, the Colonial Patriotic Union, had come into being in Durban in November.

Gandhi had been aware of all these developments. When addressing a large gathering in Madras in October, he had quoted excerpts from the angry speeches made in Durban two months earlier.[162] He was in Calcutta in November when the cable from Natal reached him asking him to return. Gandhi had written a letter to *The Englishman* (the editor, Saunders, was friendly to him) explaining the reasons for his sudden departure from Calcutta and outlining the most recent developments in South Africa. He had mentioned that the premier of Natal, Sir John Robinson, had gone to England to confer with the Colonial Office regarding the problem of Indian immigration into Natal.[163]

Two days before the *Courland* sailed from Bombay, a larger steamer, the *Naderi* also set out for Durban carrying general merchandise and three hundred and fifty passengers. Dada

---

[161] *Collected Works*, II, pp. 187-188.
[162] *Collected Works*, II, p. 97.
[163] *Ibid.*, II, pp. 127-130.

Abdulla and Company were agents for the Persian Steam Navigation Company of Bombay, the owners of the *Naderi*. On December 18, 1896, " the two ill-fated steamers "[164] (as Gandhi later described them) sailed into Durban Bay flying the quarantine flag.   There had been no illness aboard either ship, but it was a necessary precaution because of the outbreak of bubonic plague in Western India. The port health authorities asked the two steamers to remain in the outer anchorage for another five days until the normal quarantine period for plague had elapsed.   The outer anchorage was " an open roadstead very much exposed to the winds."[165] Since it was the rainy season, the passengers felt cold and wet as they wandered about the decks.   Sometimes they could see Durban clearly; at other times it was hidden by a haze.   They consoled themselves with the thought that the quarantine was only for a short period.   Actually, the passengers of the *Courland* and the *Naderi* did not set foot on land for another twenty-three days.

The arrival of the two Indian-owned ships in the Bay set the wildest rumours afloat in Durban.   Gandhi was said to have planned " an invasion " of Natal with " 800 Indians " he had brought with him.   The passengers, it was wrongly believed, consisted largely of skilled labour, including fifty blacksmiths and thirty compositors.   The *Courland* was supposed to have a whole printing plant on board.   Gandhi was also accused of having ".organized an independent immigration agency in India to land his countrymen here at the rate of 1,000 to 2,000 per month."[166]   More fuel was added to the fire with an allegation that Gandhi, and the lawyers he was supposed to have brought with him, were inciting the passengers to sue the Government of Natal for illegal detention in quarantine.

---

[164] *Ibid.*, II, p. 192.
[165] Cumberland, *op. cit.*, p. 174.
[166] *Collected Works*, II, p. 211.

The result of this explosive situation on land was to turn the detention of the *Courland* and the *Naderi* at sea into a political issue. The Government of Natal found itself in a quandary. "The men of Durban," as the agitators now referred to themselves, demanded that the ships be placed in indefinite quarantine in the hope that it would scare the Indians away. Their leaders were in constant touch with Pietermaritzburg and Harry Escombe, the Attorney General, as Sir John Robinson was away in London. At the same time, Dada Abdulla, a stubborn fighter, was bringing pressure to bear on the Government through his solicitors, Messrs. Goodricke, Laughton & Cooke, to lift the quarantine. The first victim of this political struggle was the Port Health Officer; this brave man was dismissed for refusing to extend the quarantine beyond the normal period he had previously fixed. Dr. MacKenzie, a strongly anti-Indian member of the Natal Medical Board, saw to his dismissal.

The new Port Health Officer, Dr. Birtwell, extended the quarantine period of the two ships for another twelve days. Birtwell, a political tool of "the men of Durban," was out to make the lives of the weary passengers as miserable as possible. The steamers smelt of carbolic acid from one end to the other. Most of the clothing and all the blankets used by the passengers found their way into the donkey furnaces of the ships. The two British captains, Milne and Raffin, were staunch in their loyalty to the owners of their respective vessels; their patience and firmness did much to encourage the passengers. They waged a daily battle with the port health authorities with the signals they hoisted. Captain Milne added a touch of humour to the struggle by his message signalled to the shore on December 31: "Do you intend *this year* to answer my signals of Tuesday and yesterday?"[167]

---

[167] *Collected Works*, II, p. 249.

Deck games and sports were organized to keep the passengers entertained.

In spite of the threat to their own safety, the Indian community in Durban rallied to the support of their compatriots marooned in the Bay. Led by dour old Dada Abdulla and H. M. Nazar, a plucky Gujarati lawyer who had recently arrived in the Colony, they started a Quarantine Relief Fund and supplied the passengers with food and blankets. Dada Abdulla and Company waged ceaseless warfare with the tardy port authorities to see that the ships were supplied with water. Milne frequently signalled for permission to land the horses and for supplies of hay.

If the Indians on shore showed calmness and courage, so did the passengers on the two ships. Neither the hardships of the quarantine period nor the news of the strong feelings in Durban succeeded in intimidating them. While expressing sympathy with the agitators, the Government in Pieter-maritzburg made no move beyond sanctioning the extension of the period of quarantine. Frustrated in their attempt to get rid of the Indians through the quarantine, some of the Colonists were in an ugly mood. A local butcher, Harry Sparks, now became the leader of the anti-Indian agitation. On December 30th, Sparks inserted an advertisement in *The Natal Advertiser* which read: " Wanted every man in Durban to attend a meeting to be held in the large room at the Victoria Cafe, on Monday the 4th January at 8 o'clock for the purpose of arranging a demonstration to proceed to the Point and protest against the landing of Asiatics."[168] The proposed demonstration became the talk of the town.

The excitement in Durban during the first week of January, 1897, was intense. A series of meetings was held at which large gatherings of white workers were treated to the " stump

---

[168] *Collected Works*, II, p. 197.

oratory of Dr. MacKenzie, and the inciting diatribes of Mr. Sparks and his neophyte Dan Taylor."[169] It became clear at these meetings that Gandhi himself was the main target of attack; the mere mention of his name was sufficient to elicit " prolonged hissing and hooting." At the meeting in the Town Hall on January 4th, Dr. MacKenzie, a Captain in the Naval Carabineers, said that " Mr. Gandhi had returned to India and dragged them (the Natalians) in the gutters, and painted them as black and filthy as his own skin." A resolution was passed calling upon the Government to repatriate the Indians on board the *Courland* and the *Naderi*. A Demonstration Committee was also appointed.

The threat of direct action by " the men of Durban " was now used to bring further pressure on the Government. The resolutions passed by the meeting on the 4th were wired to Pietermaritzburg, and a delegation interviewed Escombe. The Government's attitude seemed to be firm. The Demonstration Committee was informed that " the Government has at present no power apart from such as may be conferred by the Quarantine Laws, to prevent the landing in the Colony of any class of Her Majesty's subjects."[170] The Government apparently tried to discourage the proposed Demonstration at Durban Point as unnecessary and unhelpful. The Government communiqué, however, promised speedy legislation to prevent " the overrunning of the Colony by Asiatics." Escombe reiterated the same point of view to the deputation that awaited him; he even hinted that the Government might be forced to resign and the Governor asked to take over the Colony in case there were any serious disturbances.

The leaders of the Demonstration were now on the horns of a dilemma. Despite Escombe's personal affability, he had made it clear that the Demonstration might only serve to

---

[169] *Collected Works*, II, p. 225.
[170] *Ibid.*, II, p. 199.

embarrass the Government. On the other hand, the leaders had themselves aroused the artisan class by their fiery speeches. Sparks and MacKenzie hesitated to clash with the Government, but they had committed themselves too far to withdraw the idea of a demonstration. If we read between the lines, the predicament of the leaders is clear from their speeches at the second mass meeting (adjourned from Market Square to the Town Hall owing to rain) on the 7th. The white workers were in no mood to listen to the promises of the Government or appeals for calm; it was clear that they were solidly behind the proposed Demonstration. A naval volunteer reflected their feelings when he said " he would give a month's pay for a shot at that ship..."[171] The " men of Durban " were now leading their leaders through their noisy interjections at the meetings. Dr. MacKenzie succumbed to the atmosphere and played to the gallery. Gandhi was again the focal point of attack. When J. S. Wylie, a member of the Demonstration Committee, referred to Gandhi in a speech there were cries of, " Have you the tar ready for him? Is he going back? "

The upshot of the meeting on the 7th was that the Government seemed in danger of losing control of the situation. The Demonstration Committee, backed by the white workers, began to throw its weight about. On the 8th, a delegation boarded the *Courland* and handed a letter to Milne from Harry Sparks asking him to inform the passengers on both ships that they would be wise to return to India. " We shall, therefore, be glad to receive an answer from you before the ship comes alongside the wharf," the threatening letter concluded, " whether the passengers elect to return to India at the Colony's expense, or to endeavour to force a landing against the thousands of men who are ready, and waiting to oppose their landing."[172] After Gandhi had read and

---

[171] *Collected Works*, II, p. 201.
[172] *Collected Works*, II, p. 252.

explained this letter to the Indians aboard the *Courland*, Milne signalled a laconic reply telling the Demonstration Committee that the passengers were unwilling to return to India.

On the 10th, F. A. Laughton, one of Dada Abdulla's attorneys and an outspoken man, met Escombe who happened to be in Durban, and made it clear to the Attorney General that the Demonstration Committee claimed to have the backing of the Government. Escombe denied any connection between the Government and the agitators. The events of the following day, however, showed the Government the need for assuming control of the situation if mob rule was to be avoided. On the 11th, the *Greek*, a ship owned by the Union Steamship Company, arrived in Durban from Delagoa Bay with some Indian passengers aboard. The Demonstration Committee compelled the management of the Union Steamship Company to enter into negotiations with them regarding the Indian passengers aboard the *Greek*. Merchants were informed that their shops must close when " the men of Durban " were summoned to muster at the Point. Signatures of volunteers prepared to participate in the Demonstration were collected. The Government hesitated for another day while the situation steadily deteriorated.

Dada Abdulla had proposed, in a letter to Escombe on the 11th, that the passengers should be landed quietly at night. The Attorney General felt unwilling to take the risk involved. It was costing the Indian merchant £150 a day to keep both ships in the outer anchorage and the stalemate had lasted long enough. Dada Abdulla and Laughton decided to force the Government's hand. On the 12th, Escombe was informed that the ships would land their passengers on the following day, " relying on the protection which we respectfully submit, Government is bound to give us."[173] The daring move

---

[173] *Collected Works*, II, p. 205.

succeeded. On the 13th, Escombe sent a reply, at 10-45 a.m., which read: "The Port Captain has instructed that the steamers shall be ready to cross the bar inwards at 12 o'clock today. The Government needs no reminder of its responsibility for the maintenance of order."[174]

The whole town knew that Wednesday the 13th would be the day of the battle of Durban Point. Fifteen minutes before Escombe wrote his note, troopers were galloping through the town blowing their bugles to announce that the two ships were preparing to come into the Port. The shopkeepers put up their shutters hastily and people began to flock to the Point. Shortly before noon, the "volunteers" mustered in military array on Alexandra Square. Harry Sparks, a captain in the Volunteer Reserve of the Natal Mounted Rifles and J. S. Wylie, a captain in the Durban Light Infantry, had done their work well. The men were drawn up in lines according to their trades and professions under "leaders." *The Natal Advertiser* later gave full details of the battle order which consisted of the following sections: railway men, nine hundred to one thousand; Titheridge Yacht Club, Point Club, and Rowing Club, one hundred and fifty; carpenters and joiners, four hundred and fifty; printers, eighty; shop assistants, about four hundred; tailors and saddlers, seventy; plasterers and bricklayers, two hundred; general public, about one thousand.

A "Native section" had also been organized. A dwarf was appointed as their leader and "they were highly amused with this diminutive chap, who marched up and down in front of their ranks officering them, while they went through a number of exercises with their sticks, and danced and whooped."[175] The Africans were kept amused in this fashion

---

[174] *Ibid.*, p. 205.
[175] *Collected Works*, II, p. 208.

on Alexandra Square while the white demonstrators proceeded to the Point. An enterprising member of the Demonstration Committee had " taken advantage of the occurrence to advertise his firm by sending down his store boys, each armed with two or three sticks, with his firm's name appearing in glaring letters on their backs."[176] When the whites had left Alexandra Square, the Superintendent of Police arrived on horseback and quietly dispersed the Africans. Some of these " togt boys," however, drifted towards the main wharf of the harbour.

Let us turn from the happenings on land to the way the day began for the passengers on board the two ships. Shortly before 7 a.m., a tug was seen making towards the *Courland*. It turned out to be the *Churchill*, not loaded with more carbolic acid and sulphur, but with Pilot Gordon aboard bringing orders from the Government that both ships should prepare to enter the harbour at 10-30 a.m. Everyone aboard the ships knew there was going to be a " demonstration " but were not aware of the form it was likely to take. Captain Raffin of the *Naderi* was a little nervous; Captain Milne, therefore, decided to lead the way, though the *Courland* lay further up the coast. Gandhi had some acquaintance with British sea captains; one had taken him to a brothel in Zanzibar, another had preached Christianity to him. During the long wait in the outer anchorage the young lawyer and the sea captain had gotten to know each other well; they felt like comrades in arms. Milne prepared to sail the gallant little *Courland* into Durban Harbour with a fighting spirit. The Union Jack fluttered at the forecastle head, a red ensign flew above the ship's house flag on the main mast, and another red ensign flapped at her stern. Milne's orders to his officers were that demonstrators should be kept off the ship; if they

---

[176] *Collected Works*, II, p. 233.

tried to board her the Union Jack was to be hauled down and presented to them. The gesture would help to remind the attackers that his passengers were British subjects.

At 11-50 a.m., a pilot boarded the *Courland* and steered her across the bar, with the *Naderi* following. The passengers on deck could see a row of people stretched out in a long line from the south end of the main wharf to the north pier. *The Natal Advertiser*, describing the scene, reported that " the Indians on board did not seem much scared, and Mr. Gandhi and a few others who were on deck, looked on with an unperturbed expression."[177] Actually, the passengers on the ships and the main body of demonstrators could not see each other because of the other ships in the harbour. The demonstrators and their leaders were waiting on the main wharf while the two ships steamed down the Bluff channel. The vessels had been safely moored there at 12-45 p.m., before the demonstrators even realised that the steamers would not berth at the main wharf. Confused by the unexpected turn of events, the demonstrators spent some time dashing about aimlessly until their leaders summoned them to a meeting on Alexandra Square.

Half an hour later, a row boat made its way towards the ships in the Bluff channel. When the boat drew alongside the *Courland*, Captain Milne was surprised to find the Attorney General in it. Escombe, " the Father of Port Natal," had with him the Port Captain, the Wharf Master and the Mooring Master. " Captain Milne," shouted Escombe, " I want you to inform your passengers that they are safe under the Natal Government laws as if they were in their own native villages."[178] Having advised the Captain of the *Courland* to await further instructions before landing his passengers, Escombe was rowed to the *Naderi* to deliver a similar assurance to Captain Raffin.

---

[177] *Collected Works*, II, p. 208.
[178] *Ibid.*, p. 209.

In the meantime, a rowdy meeting was in progress on Alexandra Square. Cries of " Send these Indians back," " Why don't you bring Gandhi ashore? " and " Get the tar and feathers ready,"[179] rent the air. MacKenzie and Dan Taylor outdid themselves as rabble rousers, suggesting that Gandhi should be beaten up and spat upon. The angry speeches were interrupted by the arrival of Harry Escombe. The Attorney General was a persuasive speaker.[180] He reiterated his assurance given a week previously, that the Government would look into the whole question of Indian immigration. In the end he succeeded in getting the men to disperse. The Demonstration seemed to have concluded rather tamely.

By 3 p.m., the Indians were able to land; they were ferried from the two ships in small groups. Gandhi and his family, however, remained aboard the *Courland*; Escombe had sent word to Gandhi that the Water Police would take him ashore at night. About 5 p.m. that same evening, F. A. Laughton came aboard to see Gandhi. Dada Abdulla's attorney did not like the charges of cowardice that had been made by the leaders of the Demonstration against the young Indian. He therefore suggested that the two of them should proceed to the town together and Gandhi readily agreed. Separate arrangements had already been made to have Kasturba and the boys driven in a cab to Parsi Rustomji's house.

The evening sky was cloudy as Gandhi (with his turban on his head) and Laughton were rowed to the shore. As the boat approached the landing place at Cato's Creek in Addington, the Indian lawyer was recognized by some boys; the familiar turban had helped them to spot him. The white youngsters raised cries of " Gandhi! " " Thrash him! "

---

[179] *Collected Works*, II, p. 209.
[180] Robinson, *op. cit.*, p. xxix.

"Surround him!"[181]   As Laughton pointed out later, Gandhi could have had himself rowed back to the *Courland*, but he decided to land in spite of the hostile attitude of the people waiting to receive him.   The boys began throwing pebbles as Gandhi stepped ashore.

Parsi Rustomji's house was two miles away; it would take Gandhi and Laughton at least an hour to walk the distance. The crowd had become so menacing that Laughton decided it would be safer to take a rickshaw.   A young Zulu, in the standard white linen tunic, loose white shorts, and a magnificent head-dress of horns and feathers,[182] happened to pass by with his rickshaw.   Laughton hailed him.   The white men and boys, however, frightened the Zulu away by threatening to smash his rickshaw; Gandhi was spared the only ride he might have had in a form of transport he deplored.   The two lawyers had   no   alternative   but   to   walk   the   entire distance.

The mob following them increased with every step Gandhi and Laughton took; it had swelled to enormous proportions by the time they reached West Street, the main thoroughfare of Durban.   Laughton, "a brave and powerfully built man,"[183] had done his best to protect his friend.   In West Street, however, the pushing, jostling crowd managed to separate him from Gandhi.   The mob now became violent. Gandhi kept walking, his ears filled with jeers and catcalls and his clothes bespattered with the mud, stale fish and rotten eggs thrown at him.   A man snatched off his turban, another hit him with a riding whip.   A burly fellow, shouting, "Are you the man who wrote to the Press?" kicked him from behind.[184]   Shoved to one side of the street, Gandhi

---

[181] *Satyagraha in South Africa*, p. 58.
[182] Bigelow, *op. cit.*, p. 224.
[183] *Satyagraha in South Africa*, p. 57.
[184] Doke, *op. cit.*, p. 49.

held on desperately to the railings of a house.   He was bleeding
and out of breath as the crowd continued to batter him.

Then, as Joseph Doke put it, " a beautiful and brave thing
happened, which throws some glory over this wretched
scene."[185]   Mrs. R. C. Alexander, wife of the popular
Superintendent of the Borough Police came walking down
West Street from the opposite direction.   She knew the
Indian lawyer well.   The sky being overcast, she had a
parasol which she opened immediately to protect Gandhi
from the flying missiles thrown at him.   The brave woman
walked down West Street at his side, her parasol held over
his head.   In the meantime, an Indian boy had run to the
police station; constables arrived and formed a protective
cordon around the Indian lawyer.   The police station lay
on Gandhi's route; as the wild procession passed it, Superintendent Alexander came out and offered him asylum.
Anxious about his wife and children, Gandhi preferred to go
on to Parsi Rustomji's house.   Before they parted, Gandhi
thanked the Superintendent for the kindness and courage
shown by Mrs. Alexander.   Her descendants may yet have
the gold watch, chain and locket a grateful Indian community
later presented to her.

Escorted by the police, he reached Parsi Rustomji's house
in safety.   As night fell, however, the house in Field Street
was surrounded by a white mob.   The hooligan element
sent threatening messages to Parsi Rustomji that the house
would be burned if he did not hand Gandhi over to them.
Superintendent Alexander, however, was equal to the
occasion.   Plain-clothes detectives were sent to mingle with
the crowd and occupy strategic positions around the house.
Alexander had a bench placed in front of the house and stood
on it, thus blocking the entrance himself.   The Superintendent,

---

[185] Doke, *op. cit.*, p. 49.

a familiar and respected figure, knew how to deal with " the men of Durban." He put the crowd in a good humour by his banter and got them to sing community songs. Alexander caused considerable amusement by teaching them to sing:

> " Hang old Gandhi
>   On the sour apple tree.."[186]

While the crowd was singing, detectives entered the house with a message from Alexander offering to help Gandhi to escape. Years later the Mahatma wondered whether he had been right in accepting the friendly Superintendent's offer. But just then, with a huge mob about the house, there was no time to think. Gandhi was quickly disguised as an Indian constable, with a metal saucer for protection under his turban. Accompanied by a detective disguised as an Indian merchant, Gandhi wended his way through the still singing crowd. The lawyer and the detective jumped fences, squeezed between railings, and passed through a store before they reached the safety of the police station.[187]

A constable whispered the news to Alexander, who good-humouredly informed the crowd that their prey had escaped. He got the whites to promise they would disperse peacefully to their homes if Gandhi could not be found in the house. A committee appointed by the crowd searched the Parsi merchant's house and reported that the Indian lawyer was missing. When the disappointed whites had melted away, Kasturba heaved a sigh of relief. Thank God, her boys were safe. Thank God, her husband had escaped being lynched. What savage land had he brought her to? Was the father of her children really lodged safely in a police station? So

---

[186] *Autobiography*, p. 239.
[187] Doke, *op. cit.*, p. 49.

thinking, Kasturba tried to find some sleep on her first night in South Africa.

A few days after that night of terror, Kasturba was surprised to find that her husband could walk freely through the streets of Durban. Natal was still a British Colony; it had not yet turned completely into a blindly racist South African state. There had been courageous men who deprecated the idea of the Demonstration from its very inception; MacKenzie had referred insultingly to them as " old women." The Natal press, while sympathising with the agitators, had been practically unanimous in criticizing the proposed Demonstration. The Transvaal press, more conscious of the Imperial issues involved, had been even more strongly opposed to the whole idea. *The Johannesburg Times* had charged that " the present Demonstration resembles more the Knight of La Mancha's mad tilt against the windmill, than the action of sober-minded Englishmen."[188] When the Demonstration failed and the excitement died, the post-mortem which followed showed the more sober sections of the population to feel a healthy sense of shame as they reflected on all that had happened.

The personal attack on Gandhi was particularly regretted. Even a week earlier, *The Natal Advertiser* had pointed out that Dr. MacKenzie " did not exercise as much discretion as he might have done, and his dark hints regarding the treatment of Mr. Gandhi were extremely incautious."[189] After the assault on the Indian lawyer, there was a chorus of disapproval from individuals as well as the press. The sober criticism of his assailants by *The Natal Mercury* was matched by the pungency of *The Johannesburg Times*. This paper said the Demonstration had looked like " a Christmas pantomime "

---

[188] *Collected Works*, II, p. 220.
[189] *Ibid.*, II, p. 219.

until "matters took a barbarous turn" when "Mr. Gandhi was surrounded by a jeering crowd of hydrocephalous entities..." The same paper then described the indignities to which he had been subjected and concluded, "No doubt, all this proved grand fun for the canaille, but apart from the morals of law and order, the British love of fair play must be rapidly on the wane, when Englishmen resort to such ungentlemanly behaviour and brutality towards an un-convicted free man."[190]

There was also a horrified realization that Durban had escaped narrowly from the dangers of mob rule and a complete breakdown of law and order. Fears that the anti-Indian agitation might take a wrong turn had been expressed immediately after the first mass meeting in the Town Hall on January 4th. *The Natal Advertiser* had said, "We regard the proceedings as, to say the least, premature, and we cannot regard without apprehension, a demonstration which is practically in the direction of mob law..."[191] On the eve of the Demonstration, the *Digger's News* had warned the agitators: "Durban is not east of Suez, being situated on nearly the same great circle; but the Durbanites seem to enter into the category of those among whom 'there ain't no ten commandments,' to say nothing of the Imperial statute book. It is not a method of civilized men to bring about reform by shooting one another in the streets."[192] Though the Demons-tration had come to "an ignominious termination" and had ended in "a fiasco," responsible opinion in the Colony condemned the leaders since they "virtually and quite illegally superseded the Government."[193]

The Government of Natal came in for some strong criticism

---

[190] *Collected Works*, II, p. 225.
[191] *Ibid.*, II, p. 218.
[192] *Ibid.*, II, p. 220.
[193] *Ibid.*, II, p. 227.

for having allowed a dangerous situation to continue unchecked for a week. The Government had not been unware of the damage a white mob could do. A white gang had recently set fire to an Indian store in the village of Dundee; another gang had thrown fire crackers into Indian stores in a business section of Durban.[194] As *The Cape Argus* put it, " For a week the Natal Ministry permitted the situation to develop, without pretence at the feeblest intervention, their policy suggesting an unofficial sanction of the whole business."[195] Laughton had not been alone in his suspicion that there had been collusion between the Government and the leaders of the Demonstration. In the words of *The Natal Witness*,..."the fact remains that people will not believe that the whole business was not a plot between the Government and the leaders of the late remarkable movement...which claimed to represent the people... The concluding act of this pretty drama was played at the Point, when the Committee handed back their powers to Mr. Escombe, reinstated the Government, and everyone went home satisfied."[196]

Particular attention was focused on the dubious role played by Escombe, the Attorney General, in the whole affair. Apart from wishing to save Gandhi from a charge of cowardice, another reason which had prompted Laughton to ask Gandhi to accompany him openly into Durban had been his distrust of the motives of Escombe. *The Natal Advertiser* voiced this feeling that Escombe had been involved in backstairs intrigue with the leaders of the Demonstration. Analysing the events of the preceding week in its issue of January 14th, the *Advertiser* wrote, " A long series of negotiations ensues, during which the public is kept in a constant ferment of excitement, until at last the bugle sounds, and all Durban rushes to the Point,

---

[194] *Collected Works*, II, pp. 97-98.
[195] *Ibid.*, II, p. 228.
[196] *Ibid.*, II, p. 229.

prepared to do or die. Then, quite casually of course, at the psychological moment, the Attorney General ' bobs up serenely ', tells the people to be good boys, and he will do all that is necessary—' fix your eyes upon your Escombe and he will pull you through '—the Committee declare, they had the least idea of doing anything in opposition to Government, and are quite willing to leave it in the hands of Government— cheers for the Queen—blessings all round—everybody goes home happy—the demonstration melts away as quickly as it gathered—while the now forgotten Indians come quietly ashore, just as if there had never been any demonstration at all. Who can resist the suspicion that it was a pre-arranged and foregone conclusion ? "[197]

Escombe's shrewd handling of the assault on Gandhi is in keeping with the pattern of his previous behaviour—reflecting his unwillingness to take any action that would affect his personal popularity. Questions had been asked in the House of Commons about the incident, and Joseph Chamberlain, the Colonial Secretary, had cabled the Natal Government to prosecute Gandhi's assailants. Escombe sent for the young Indian lawyer. He was affable and solicitous. Gandhi was touched by his inquiries about his injuries and his repeated assurances that he had never intended that the Indian community should suffer in any way. When he emerged from Escombe's Chambers he had given the Attorney General a letter refusing to prosecute his attackers and admitting he had been wrong to leave the *Courland* without first informing the Water Police. Escombe had skilfully avoided further unpleasantness and enhanced his own prestige. Three months later, Escombe introduced three anti-Indian bills in the Natal Legislature; Gandhi realized then that he had been closeted with a man whose genial good nature served as the facade for an expedient politician.

---

[197] *Collected Works*, II, p. 227.

Escombe's ambiguous behaviour and the vacillations of the Natal Government with respect to the Demonstration are better understood in light of the fact that a general election was impending. *The Natal Witness* was blunt in its exposure of the motives behind the Government's attitude to the Demonstration: " Everyone is aware that we are rapidly nearing another general election, but no one could have possibly thought that any ministry would have played so low, to gain votes, as to give the population of a large town freedom to break the law."[198]   In 1895, Escombe had been described by the *Argus Annual* as " a magnificent man, big and impulsive " who " will fight hard to have his own way."[199] The Attorney General's subtle but risky handling of the Demonstration brought him the rewards of a bold gambler. Escombe emerged from the General Election of 1897 as the second premier of the Colony and represented Natal at the Colonial Prime Ministers' Conference held in London in connection with the Queen's second Jubilee. Some of the leaders of the Demonstration had their reward too. Harry Sparks was elected to the Legislature from Durban County and played an important role in pressing for anti-Indian legislation. He became the head of a butchers' ring which succeeded in raising the price of beef.[200] His business prospered without fear of Muslim Indian competition; the firms of Sparks and Young were the first to introduce cold storage into Natal.[201]   Dan Taylor, the most rabid of the leaders of the anti-Indian agitation, was elected to the Durban Town Council.[202]

---

[198] *Collected Works*, II, p. 229.

[199] *Ibid.*, p. 99.

[200] *Collected Works*, III, pp. 46-47.

[201] *Who's Who in Natal*, (Durban,   The Knox Printing and Publishing Co., 1933).

[202] *Collected Works*, III, p. 397; IV, p. 202.

Perhaps the wisest advice the white artisans received came from the *Diggers' Friend*. " The real grievance," declared this paper, " is an economical one based upon experience of which the theory is not generally understood. The soundest and most peaceable way is to form trade protection societies which shall insist upon a minimum price and a maximum wage..."[203] The same paper also pointed out that it was the white employers themselves who preferred cheap and easily controllable Indian labour to white workers. No legislation affecting indentured Indian labour could be introduced in the Natal Legislature in the face of the opposition of the white planters. In the end, the indentured system in Natal would be ended by the Indian Government, in 1917, because of the popular agitation against it in India.

It is idle to speculate as to what might have happened had white and Indian workers in Natal developed a common labour interest through trade unionism. The colour prejudice of the white artisans had already become deep and ineradicable. It also must be admitted that Indian labour at that time was too backward and ignorant to make such an alliance thinkable. Gandhi too had no such thoughts in his mind in the 1890's. He was much more involved in defending the interests of the Indian merchants than those of Indian labour. Just as Escombe was the leader of the white middle classes, Gandhi was the spokesman of Indian middle class interests. Even though he took up the cause of indentured labour during the last few years of his stay in South Africa, he did not conceive of the struggle in trade union terms. Thus the most tragic aspect of the battle of Durban Point would be the impassable gulf it opened up between white and black labour—a gulf which trade unionism has not been able to bridge to this day.

---

[203] *Collected Works,* II, p. 220.

The horrifying depth of the racial hatred which produced the Demonstration was seen most clearly in the attempt to turn the native Africans against the Indians. " A little explanation is still wanting," wrote *The Natal Witness*, " in regard to the presence of a force of several hundred kafirs in the Demonstration. Did it mean that the cause of the white man and the cause of the native are one and the same? Or, what else did it symbolise? "[204] A Durban attorney and prominent member of the Town Council, G. A. Labistour, wrote a letter asking for an investigation into the matter. His letter to the Town Council pointing out the evil results that would flow from this attempt to foster racial hatred received wide publicity.[205] Commenting on Labistour's letter, *The Natal Mercury* particularly condemned the white men who had escaped the fines inflicted on four native Africans they had brought to whoop and yell in front of Parsi Rustomji's house when Gandhi was besieged inside: " It was rather hard on the kafirs to make them scapegoats for really obeying the orders of men who ought to have known better. To call in the natives in a matter of the kind is to exhibit to them a weakness which, above all things, should be avoided, and we trust there will never be a repetition of so dangerous and disgraceful a practice as exciting the racial prejudice of so inflammatory an element as the natives."[206]

Gandhi had not completed his twenty-eighth birthday when he narrowly escaped being lynched in the streets of Durban. Still young and resilient, the Demonstration apparently left no serious scars on him. He would describe the period immediately following the incident as " the calm after the storm."[207] His refusal to prosecute his assailants

---

[204] *Collected Works*, II, p. 228.
[205] *Ibid.*, II, pp. 232-233.
[206] *Ibid.*, II, p. 234.
[207] *Autobiography*, p. 241.

created such an impression that it enhanced his prestige and made his work easier. There was also a considerable increase in his law practice. The attempted lynching made his name better known in South Africa and elsewhere.

If his name was now known, there was still a good deal of confusion as to his identity and motives. MacKenzie, a prominent leader of the Demonstration had referred to the Indians as " Gandhiites,"[208] thus acknowledging him as their leader. Frances Macnab, writing in 1897 about the problem of Indian immigration, said, " The matter assumed the form of a question when an Indian named Gandhi (*sic*), a barrister from Calcutta, arrived in Natal and took up the coolies. He first endeavoured to arouse in them the feeling that they were ill-used, and endeavoured to get them to agitate to procure the franchise. Something like a whirlwind of wrath was aroused in Natal by this proposition."[209] A few months after the Demonstration, Captain Francis Younghusband, then a special correspondent of *The Times* in South Africa, sought out Gandhi and wrote an interesting account of their meeting. Younghusband was under the impression that the lawyer was " the leading Indian merchant of Durban." " Mr. Gandhi, the spokesman of the Indian community and the butt of the agitators," he wrote, " is a particularly intelligent and well-educated man, who has studied for three years in England and lives in a well-furnished English villa at Durban."[210] Younghusband had the opportunity of meeting several Indian merchants at a dinner in Gandhi's home.

To all outward appearances Gandhi had recovered from the shock of his trying experiences. Yet the whole Demonstration had affected him deeply, leaving marks that were both physical and mental. More than forty years after the incident

---

[208] *Collected Works*, II, p. 268.
[209] *Op. cit.*, pp. 312-316.
[210] *Op. cit.*, p. 159.

in Durban, Gandhi would be mobbed by demonstrators opposed to him in Rajkot. Mahadev Desai, his secretary, in recording that event wrote, " All of a sudden he was seized by an attack of indescribable pain in the region of the waist and felt as if he would faint. This is an old symptom in his case that seizes him whenever he receives an acute mental shock."[211] Gandhi would be assaulted once more in South Africa, not by whites, but by an Indian, Mir Alam. The Mahatma's nervous system did not emerge unscathed from all the violence he had endured.

The Mahatma would remember how " the days dragged on their weary length "[212] when he was confined to the *Courland* for those three weeks. One of the reports about Gandhi which had circulated in Durban during the Demonstration was that " he was seen sitting on the deck of the *Courland* in a dejected mood." It may very well have been true, though indecent use had been made of the fact. Gandhi had spoken in India of conquering the hatred of the whites with love, of the need for the spirit of self-sacrifice. The long wait on the ship in Durban Bay tried both his patience and his stated ideals. As the reports reached him of the hostility of the whites (in particular the hatred towards him) he struggled not to dislike them in return. He tried, as he had done before, to find some explanation for their hatred and their prejudice.

This conflict of moods and feelings in Gandhi had found vocal expression on Christmas Day, 1896. Captain Milne and the ship's officers had invited the Gandhi family and the saloon passengers to a festive dinner. " I took part in the merriment, but my heart was in the combat that was going on in Durban. For I was the real target,"[213] the Mahatma

---

[211] *The Indian States' Problem*, p. 561.
[212] *Autobiography*, p. 235.
[213] *Autobiography*, pp. 233-234.

recalled. The convivial gathering called upon the Indian lawyer for an after-dinner speech. "I knew that this was not an occasion for a serious speech,"[214] Gandhi admitted, but he felt he had to unburden his mind of the thoughts that had plagued him during the preceding week. He treated his small but patient audience to a solemn discourse on the evil nature of " the civilization of which the Natal whites were the fruit, and which they represented and championed."[215] The only way to fight a civilization based on violence was by non-violence and love.

The *Courland's* officers had listened to him indulgently; they were well aware of the mental strain Gandhi was undergoing. That small group of people could not realize that he had stated deep convictions that would grow and mature until they found full expression in *Hind Swaraj*. This amplification of his Christmas Day speech would burst from him on another steamer, the *Kildonan Castle*, returning from London in 1909.

The postscript to the Demonstration of 1897 was written ten years later in the heart of Zululand. When the Zulu Rebellion broke out in 1906, Gandhi was found leading an Indian ambulance unit in that remote area. There he met again the men who had led the Demonstration against him. Colonel Harry Sparks and Colonel J. S. Wylie called on the man they had tried to prevent from landing in Durban to thank him warmly for his services; they also took him along to meet General MacKenzie.[216] South Africa then had not ceased entirely to be a land where a man's courage might be admired openly regardless of his colour. Gandhi now admired these men, who had once bitterly opposed him, for being volunteer soldiers. They also had learned by then to

---

[214] *Autobiography*, p. 233.
[215] *Ibid.*, p. 234.
[216] *Autobiography*, pp. 284-285.

admire the Indian lawyer of whom Laughton had written three days after Gandhi had escaped being lynched, "Throughout the trying procession, his manliness and pluck could not have been surpassed, and I can assure Natal that he is a man who must be treated as a man. Intimidation is out of the question because, if he knew the Town Hall were going to be thrown at him, I believe from what I saw, that he would not quail."[217]

Gandhi and Colour Prejudice

During his first period in Natal from 1894 to 1896, Gandhi's life was dominated by the struggle against the bill to disenfranchise the Indians on the dubious grounds that they had not enjoyed the right to vote in their own country. He also organized the opposition to the proposal to inflict a poll tax on labourers who did not reindenture or return to India. In 1895, however, an act was passed fixing the annual tax on Indian settlers at £ 3, and with the passing of Act 8 of 1896 the agitation to retain the Indian franchise also ended in failure.

The Colonial Office had shown reluctance to interfere in the affairs of an independent Colony. The angry Demonstration, which greeted Gandhi on his return to Durban at the beginning of 1897, was the prelude to further difficulties for the Indians. Though the methods employed by the leaders of the Demonstration were criticized, that agitation cemented the alliance between the merchants and the artisans—the two white groups most opposed to the Indians. Three bills were introduced in the Natal Legislature in March, 1897, seeking to tighten the Quarantine Laws, reduce and restrict licences given to Indian traders and hawkers and control the immigration of " free " Indians. The planting and farming

---

[217] *Collected Works*, II, p. 281.

interests were not opposed to the proposed measures since they did not affect the importing of indentured labour.

Gandhi was soon in the thick of the battle against this fresh spate of discriminatory legislation. A week after these bills were introduced, he wrote to Taleyarkhan, " The Indian question almost wholly occupies my attention."[218] The problems of the Indians kept Gandhi busy until he left for India in the middle of October, 1901, promising to return if necessary. By that time, Gandhi would have lived through all the excitement of the Boer War. Both the Anti-Indian legislation and the Boer War would have led him to ponder deeply the Imperial aspect of the treatment of Indians in South Africa. The details of his incessant warfare against the rising tide of racial discrimination through memorials to the Colonial Office, petitions to the Natal Legislature and test cases in the courts reveal his doggedness in an increasingly hopeless situation. It is more important, however, to trace the changes going on in Gandhi's mind. Outwardly, he appeared to be a loyal British citizen, joining enthusiastically in the general frenzy of patriotism exhibited both before and after the Boer War. Inwardly, he was steadily developing into a rebel against the British Empire. Beneath all his professions of loyalty there grew a mood of disillusionment as racism destroyed Gandhi's earlier faith in British goodness and justice.

When Gandhi first arrived in Durban in 1893, the generation of old colonists had been on the verge of acquiring political power under responsible government. He saw them enjoy a brief period of power which lasted until the turn of the century. Many of the leaders of that generation of colonists died soon after the Boer War ; Gandhi wrote appreciative obituaries of men like Escombe, Robinson, Binns and Saunders in *Indian Opinion*. The generation which succeeded

---

[218] *Collected Works*, II, p. 299.

them would suffer no twinges of liberal conscience, no feeling that mistakes could be made, as they steadily widened the area of racial segregation. They would not see the problem as a complex one facing " Anglo-Saxon law makers." Many principles of British democracy would be sacrificed as the legislature was converted into an instrument for maintaining a white minority in power.

Gandhi's rejection of parliamentary democracy was due partly to his observation of the South African Government's use of parliamentary institutions to implement policies of racial discrimination. In *Hind Swaraj*, written in the year of the Morley-Minto Reforms, this fear he had early developed of representative institutions influenced his opinion that parliamentary democracy was unsuited to India. Since Gandhi had seen how representative institutions could be abused by a minority, he foresaw clearly that the introduction of parliamentary democracy in India would aggravate the Hindu-Muslim problem. The Mahatma would fear the abuse of parliamentary institutions, not by minorities as in South Africa, but by Indian *majorities*.

The young Indian lawyer who settled in Natal in 1894, however, did not believe that racism was ineradicable. " The colour prejudice that I saw in South Africa was, I thought quite contrary to British traditions, and believed that it was only temporary and local, "[219] he recalled. Later he would realize that he had met a problem in South Africa affecting the status of Indians throughout the British Empire ; he interested himself in indentured labour in Mauritius, the West Indies, British Guiana, Ceylon, Burma, Malaya and Fiji. Yet, he spent a great deal of his time and energy in trying to educate the whites into a more liberal way of thinking. The various ways in which he tried to

---

[219] *Autobiography*, p. 212.

change the racial mentality of the whites form one of the most interesting aspects of Gandhi's career in South Africa. Gandhi was a patient man and his disillusionment about the possibility of effecting a change in the outlook of the whites was slow in coming. When the final disenchantment came, Gandhi had turned into one of the most determined opponents of British Imperialism.

Gandhi's earliest approach to the problem of racial prejudice in South Africa has an interesting connection with Cecil Rhodes. When Rhodes was Prime Minister of the Cape he had proposed that there should be a " Bill for Africa " giving the vote to every civilized man south of the Zambesi. This statement by Rhodes was one of the reasons for Gandhi's reading books on Indian civilization in Pretoria. He felt, at that time, that the whites could be educated to realize that India was a civilized country and Indians a civilized people. This assumption explains Gandhi's frequent references to Indian civilization in the *Open Letter* and the other appeals he wrote during his first period in Natal. In 1903, Gandhi referred to Rhodes while arguing in *Indian Opinion* that there may be some justification for a distinction between "civilized" and "uncivilized" provided that "uncivilized" is not made synonymous with " coloured."[220] As we have said before, Gandhi found it possible to admire Rhodes who derived some of his curious idealism from Ruskin.[221] Rhodes, who chose to be buried by the side of the African chief, Moselikatze, on the Matoppo Hills, had not been totally lacking in the ability to appreciate people of a different colour.

Lionel Trilling says of Kipling that his imperialism " is reprehensible not because it *is* imperialism but because it is a puny and mindless imperialism."[222] The colonial

---

[220] *Collected Works*, III, p. 334.
[221] See Sarah Gertrude Millin, *Rhodes*, (London, Chatto & Windus, 1952)
[222] *Op. cit.*, p. 121.

mind Gandhi encountered was conditioned largely by this type of imperialism. Gandhi asserted that "it is an unfortunate characteristic of the less cultured Englishman that, when he is brought into contact with what is strange and to which he is unaccustomed, he does not endeavour to investigate its nature, but spurns it contemptuously, as something foreign to his own outlook upon life, and he attributes to it every evil thing that can be imagined."[223] Gandhi discovered that no amount of rational argument could make any difference in the outlook of this class of whites to whom Kipling was superior. Trilling points out that Kipling was also "the first to suggest what may be called the anthropological view, the perception that another man's idea of virtue and honour may be different from one's own but quite to be respected."[224] Gandhi appreciated this redeeming quality in any Colonial leader who possessed it. During the Zulu Rebellion the tribesmen were classified as "friendlies" or "hostiles." A perusal of Gandhi's articles in *Indian Opinion* shows that Gandhi had unconsciously followed the same system of classification in dealing with the attitudes of the whites to the Indians. While outspoken in his exposure of ignorant and hostile attitudes, Gandhi cherished every crumb of comfort he could find in any statement friendly to the Indians.

An aspect of colour prejudice with which Gandhi became familiar was its effect on the minds of children. The pebbles thrown at him by the white boys who recognized him in the boat with Laughton at Cato's Creek were painful reminders of how racism could infect the attitudes of the young. The Mahatma would recall his surprise on discovering that the Zulu race "which is second to none in the point of physical

---

[223] *Collected Works,* IV, p. 334.
[224] *Op. Cit.,* p. 117.

strength, is so timid that a Negro is afraid at the sight even of a European child."[225] Ambrose Pratt, an American visitor to Durban, saw a little white boy of ten ordering about a huge Zulu ; and commented, " The white child is the king, the black is the white child's serf and vassal. Most white children born in South Africa acquire incurable habits of pride and insolence before they reach their teens. It is a common thing to see young boys and slips of girls treating the natives like dogs. By turns they are brutal and affectionate to their black attendants. Their manners are haughty and overbearing."[226]

" So deep-seated is the hatred," wrote Gandhi in 1896, " that children have begun instinctively to look down upon Indians."[227] When Gandhi was in India in 1902, he was saddened by the news that Indian school children in Natal would be debarred from receiving the Coronation comme-moration medals to be given to white pupils. Commenting on this, Gandhi wrote, "The exclusion is certainly not based on grounds of economy for the Indian children are, I think, about 3,000 against 20,000 European children. Evidently, the Coronation celebration day is to be marked out for the Indian children to realize as vividly as possible that the possession of a brown skin is a sure mark of humiliation and degradation in the estimation of the Government of the Colony."[228]

Gandhi sensed the need for some method of education to prevent white children from becoming contaminated by racial prejudice. Very early in his career in South Africa, Gandhi toyed with the idea that vegetarianism might

---

[225] *Satyagraha in South Africa*, p. 11.
[226] A.Pratt, *The Real South Africa*, (Indianapolis, The Bobbs-Merrill Co., 1914), p. 215.
[227] *Collected Works*, II, p. 87.
[228] *Ibid.*, III, p. 248.

provide the liberal element needed in the upbringing of the white child. Had he founded a youth movement, Gandhi would have insisted that the members practise vegetarianism. In a private letter to a friend (probably Oldfield) written in May, 1894, Gandhi described his efforts to convert white boys to vegetarianism.[229] Later he wrote, "Men cannot be really good or really civilized unless they can embrace in their goodness or their civilization all that lives."[230] Gandhi tried to convey to white children the gentler metaphysic which he believed was to be found in vegetarianism. The reverence for life implicit in vegetarianism would, he hoped, lead to compassion for both man and beast.

This trend in Gandhi's thought is made clear in an incident which he related about a white child. During his early years in Natal, Gandhi was a frequent visitor to an English home and had become very friendly with the little son of the family. He had succeeded in interesting the boy in vegetarianism. The parents were concerned lest Gandhi should create an aversion for meat in the child's mind and relations had become strained. A break in the friendship with this family occurred one Sunday when Gandhi, who had been re-reading Arnold's *Light of Asia*, compared Jesus unfavourably with Buddha. "Look at Gautama's compassion," said Gandhi. "It was not confined to mankind, it was extended to all living beings. Does not one's heart overflow with love to think of the lamb joyously perched on his shoulders? One fails to notice this love for all living beings in the life of Jesus."[231]

Gandhi was both tactless and inaccurate. The inaccuracy, however, was not the fault of the young lawyer but that of Edwin Arnold. Gandhi was referring to Book V which

[229] *Collected Works*, I, p. 89.
[230] *Ibid.*, p. 66.
[231] *Autobiography*, p. 199.

contains a description of Siddhartha bearing a sick lamb on his shoulder with a mother ewe walking beside him. Brooks Wright, in his careful and sympathetic analysis of *The Light of Asia*,[232] discusses the scene which had attracted Gandhi. Since no such scene is mentioned in the Buddhist scriptures, Wright concludes that "the incident seems deliberately designed to suggest an analogy with the Good Shepherd."[233] The important point, however, is not Gandhi's ignorance of higher criticism but his use of Arnold's Christianised portrait of Buddha to underline the connection between vegetarianism and reverence for life.

Vegetarianism naturally acquired a special significance for Gandhi in a land where hunting was common sport. Hunters had played a pioneer role in the opening up of Africa; some of them had become legendary figures. The image of the hunter had an understandable appeal for both young and old in South Africa. While there is need for caution in establishing a causal relationship between the hunting of animals and cruelty to men, there was undoubtedly a connection between the roles of hunter and warrior in Africa. That the two roles occasionally became interchangeable among white children is evidenced by Gandhi's reference to a picnic which turned into a manhunt. In 1896, he reported, "a picnic party of European children used Indian and Kaffir boys as targets and shot bullets into their faces, hurting several inoffensive children."[234] The air guns used by the white children had become symbols of cruelty. Had Gandhi read the account of Harry Sparks in *Who's Who in Natal*, which appeared in 1933, some facts about the man who had violently opposed him might have

---

[232] See *Interpreter of Buddhism to the West : Sir Edwin Arnold*, (New York, Bookman Associates, Inc., 1957), pp. 86-108.

[233] *Op. cit.*, p. 97.

[234] *Collected Works*, II, p. 87.

given the Mahatma food for thought—" At the age of 10, shot his first buck, and his first hippo, only four miles from Durban." It might have been difficult for the Mahatma to resist the temptation to conclude that Harry Sparks, ten years old in 1864, had put his early hunting abilities to good use in organizing the anti-Indian Demonstration of 1897.

His painful experiences of colour prejudice led Gandhi to compare racism to vivisection. He knew from his reading as a student in London that many prominent vegetarians were ardent anti-vivisectionists, participating in the activities of both the Vegetarian Society and the Humanitarian League. H. S. Salt, Anna Kingsford, Edward Maitland and Edward Carpenter were anti-vivisectionists with whose writings Gandhi was familiar.[235] Gandhi's first reference to vivisection occurred in his address to the public of Bombay in 1896, when he described the Indians as being " a proper subject for vivisection under the Natal Pasteur's deadly scalpel and knife."[236] Many things were to reinforce this feeling in Gandhi before he would compare the treatment of Indians to vivisection a second time. Both in Natal and the Transvaal, objections to the presence of Indians were raised on sanitary and medical grounds. The use of doctors and medical knowledge in the municipal campaigns to drive Indians out of the towns into " locations " appeared as a dreadful form of cruelty to Gandhi. This abuse of medical science made him say, in 1904, " It were a mercy to put the British Indians out of the country altogether rather than subject them to vivisection and kill them by inches."[237]

During his stay in Natal from 1893 to 1901, Gandhi

---

[235] See H. S. Salt, *Animals' Rights Considered in Relation to Social Progress*, (London, G. Bell & Sons, 1892); Edward Carpenter and E. Maitland, *Vivisection: An Address Given Before the Humanitarian League*, (London, The Humanitarian League, 1904).

[236] *Collected Works*, II, p. 78.

[237] *Ibid.*, IV, p. 134.

was involved in fighting stereotypes of coloured peoples as members of backward and uncivilized races. When he returned to South Africa in 1902, racial prejudice was so strengthened that Gandhi found coloured people regarded as members of a sub-human species. Gandhi felt angry and sad as he watched municipality after municipality enforce rules segregating Africans and Indians into "locations," driving them off pavements and footpaths and limiting their use of transport by labelling cabs and rickshaws "Europeans Only." "The true solution of the colour prejudice," Gandhi pleaded in 1903, "is not in treating every coloured man as a beast, an animal having no feelings...."[238]

When Gandhi settled in Natal in 1894, he had been sought out by Spencer Walton, the head of the South Africa General Mission, who had met the young Indian at the Wellington Convention. As in Pretoria, Gandhi made a number of Christian friends in Durban, such as Dr. Booth. He attended Sunday worship in the Wesleyan Church for a time. The indifference of the Church in Natal to colour prejudice, however, strengthened Gandhi's conviction that Christianity had nothing to offer which he could not find in his own religion. He judged the Christian professions of both the clergy and laity in terms of their attitudes to the racial problem.

In *The Indian Franchise*, which Gandhi subtitled "An Appeal to every Briton in South Africa," he made special reference to the role of the clergy. This pamphlet, printed and widely distributed in Natal just before Christmas in 1895, asked, "Why should the Clergy remain silent on this momentous question, momentous because it affects the future of South Africa?"[239] Racialism, Gandhi pointed out, was not a purely political question to be avoided in the

---

[238] *Collected Works*, III, p. 338.
[239] *Collected Works*, I, p. 283.

pulpit. Further, the clergy had not been averse to attending political meetings in connection with the disenfranchisement of Indians. " Will they see a race degraded and insulted," Gandhi concluded, " because of the ' unreasoning ' prejudice against it and sit still ? Is such indifference sanctioned by Christ's Christianity ? "[240]

Gandhi's attitude to prominent Christian laymen was clear in his references to Henry Bale. This leading lawyer and member of the Assembly succeeded Escombe as Attorney General ; he was knighted when he rose to the position of Chief Justice of Natal. In the *Green Pamphlet*, published in India in 1896, Gandhi deplored the fact that " matters have now reached such a stage that, for a good Christian gentleman, it is as natural to see nothing unjust in the persecution of the Asiatics, as it was in the olden days for the bonafide Christians to see nothing wrong or unchristian in slavery."[241] He then cited the example of the future Attorney General : " Mr. Henry Bale is a legislator in the Natal Assembly, a typical English gentleman, and is dubbed Bale the conscientious, because he is a converted Christian and takes a prominent part in religious movements and brings his conscience often into play on the floor of the Assembly House. Yet, this gentleman is one of the most powerful and uncompromising opponents of Indians . . . "[242] Gandhi succeeded in awakening the Christian conscience of a few individuals but could make no impression either on the churches or the people of South Africa for whom racialism had become part of their religion.

The most powerful argument Gandhi found against conversion to Christianity was the plight of the Indian Christians of South Africa. Their change of religion had

---

[240] *Ibid.*, I, p. 283.
[241] *Ibid.*, II, pp. 42-43.
[242] *Collected Works*, II, p. 43.

not won them acceptance or a better status. " They, of all others," wrote Gandhi, " know fully, and have been taught to understand, the advantages of Western culture. They are taught by their religious teachers the doctrine of equality. They are told, Sunday after Sunday, that their Great Master knew no distinction between a Jew and a Gentile, a European or an Asiatic."[243] The case of Roberts and Richards, two young Indian Christians, was a good illustration of the fact that a change of religion, name and dress could not save any dark-skinned person from colour prejudice. Roberts and Richards, dressed in suits, were returning from a park one night in March, 1896, when they were arrested under the Vagrant Law. Though they spoke English, both were refused bail and locked up for the night. The degree of westernization they had achieved only seemed to increase the contempt of the white constable dealing with them ; he laughed derisively when one of the young Indians gave his name as " Samuel Richards." They were called " upstarts " in court and fined. Richards was later refused a pass though Gandhi pleaded, " If he is not fit to be out after 9 p.m. he cannot be fit to be a Sunday School teacher."[244]

The constable's attitude on hearing the name of Samuel Richards was a familiar problem faced by many kinds of immigrants seeking recognition and acceptance. The prejudice in Durban against Indians with English names was similar to the prejudice against Jews who changed their names in Johannesburg. Samuel Richards (the son of an Indian indentured labourer) and his posterity had much less chance of acceptance in South Africa than the Jews. As late as 1933, only one Colonial-born Indian Christian, Bernard Gabriel, was to find a place among the personalities listed in *Who's Who in Natal*. " How can the children

---

[243] *Ibid.*, III, p. 85.
[244] *Collected Works*, I, p. 298.

of slaves escape the brand of slavery ? "[245] the Mahatma would ask. " The Europeans do not dispense the bounties and benefits of their culture with any less discrimination than the African shows in taking what is offered to him,"[246] wrote Malinowski. The same has been true of the relations between whites and Indians in South Africa.

During his residence in Natal, Gandhi shared the attitude of the Indian traders towards the Africans. The Indian trader in Africa had not shown much wisdom in his past relations with African peoples. The economic exploitation of the Africans by the whites had the advantage of remote controls. The Indian trader's business shrewdness was more visible to the Africans; his very closeness to them made him an easier object of their resentment. The need for some form of identification with the Africans was, therefore, greater for the Indian than for the whites. Yet, when Gandhi arrived in South Africa, one aspect of the struggle of the merchants had been an attempt to prevent any identification of the Indians with the Africans in the eyes of the whites or in their legislative enactments.

The Indians were right to oppose the attempt to apply to them " native policies "[247] such as the poll tax which came into effect in 1895. But in asking for facilities separate from those of the Africans, the Indians showed they shared some of the white attitudes to African peoples and set themselves apart by creating segregation within segregation. The young Gandhi reflected the attitude of the Indian traders when he complained in the *Green Pamphlet*, " We are

---

[245] *Satyagraha in South Africa*, p. 23.

[246] *Op. cit.*, p. 41.

[247] See E. H. Brookes, *The History of Native Policy in South Africa From* 1830 *to The Present Day*, (Cape Town, Nasionale Press, 1924); H. Rogers, *Native Administration in the Union of South Africa*, (Johannesburg, University of the Witwatersrand Press, 1933); I. L. Evans, *Native Policy in South Africa: An Outline*, (London, Cambridge University Press, 1934).

328

classed with the natives of South Africa—the Kaffir races."[248]
After showing how the registration and pass laws put
Indians on the same footing as the Africans, Gandhi further
illustrated " the proposition that the Indian is put on the
same level with the native in many other ways also."[249]
He described how lavatories not reserved for whites in the
railway stations had been marked " Natives and Asiatics "
like the separate entrances, similarly indicated in the Durban
post and telegraph offices. " We felt the indignity too much,"
Gandhi recalled, " and many respectable Indians were insulted
and called all sorts of names by the clerks at the counter. We
petitioned the authorities to do away with the invidious
distinction and they have now provided three separate
entrances for Natives, Asiatics and Europeans."[250] In scoring
a point, however, the Indians had unconsciously contributed
to the racialist theory of separate but equal facilities.

Gandhi's own attitude changed after he settled in Johannesburg in 1902. The multi-racial character of the Golden City
and the problems of mine labour taught him to look at the
treatment of the Indians with a larger perspective. He
worked closely with Leung Quinn, the leader of the Chinese
community in the Transvaal, for example, in opposing the
proposal to import indentured Chinese labour. The pages of
Indian Opinion show that he could be outspoken on behalf of the
Africans. Unlike the Indians and the Chinese, the Africans
were still inarticulate and unorganized so that it was not
possible to think in terms of a united front of coloured
peoples.[251] Throughout his career, Gandhi would remain an
Indian, rather than a South African, leader.

---

[248] *Collected Works*, II, p. 8.
[249] *Ibid.*, II, p. 13.
[250] *Ibid.*, II, p. 13.
[251] See E. H. Brookes, *The Colour Problems of South Africa,*(Lovedale, S. A., The
Lovedale Press, 1934); E. Hellmann and L. Abrahams, (ed.), *Handbook on
Race Relations in South Africa*, (London, Oxford University Press, 1949).

For more than a decade Gandhi believed, in the words of a familiar hymn, that racial animosity would be ended when Indian and white saw each other better after " the mists had rolled away."[252]   The little boy in Porbandar had seen mists rise from the sea and vanish time and again. Gandhi was not to see any lifting of the mists of racial prejudice in South Africa. It took him a long time to put to himself the question Malinowski would ask: " In reality, is not the European in Africa something profoundly different from the European at home? "[253]   Slow to realize that a community of white settlers are by no means " a direct replica of its mother community at home,"[254] Gandhi continued to appeal to them in the name of their European " hinterland " for many years. He wanted Indians in South Africa to be given opportunities " just as an Indian going to England would be able to avail himself of the institutions of England to as full an extent as any Englishman."[255]

Rejected by the whites in South Africa, Gandhi would end by rejecting the " hinterland " from which they derived their civilization as well.   Gandhi's visits to India are important in that they enabled him to maintain contact with his own religious and cultural " hinterland."   In *Hind Swaraj*, Gandhi would stage a return to his own " hinterland," his mother culture.   Racism was to teach the Mahatma to cut himself off from all forms of dependence on Western civilization and to look on it as childish and immature.   " The Englishman," Faucher wrote, " is disposed to believe that all the nations of mankind, with the single exception of the British, who in his opinion have reached maturity, are children."[256] The English-

252 *Collected Works*, IV, p. 95.

253 *Op. cit.*, p. 21.

254 *Ibid.*, pp. 17-18.

255 *Collected Works*, II, p. 78.

256 Léon Faucher, *Etudes sur l'Angleterre*, 1845, Vol. I, p. 8. (Quoted in *Victorian Years*, p. 410.)

man in South Africa, however, could justify his behaviour on the grounds of immaturity and youth. Referring to the Demonstration of 1897, the Johannesburg *Star* had said, " The whole country is still in its boyhood, and there is nothing a boy loves more than to refer his disputes to the gory arbitrament of physical force. Looked at in that way, this week's doings at Durban may be excused with an indulgent smile."[257] Gandhi accepted the South African whites at their own selfvaluation, but without an indulgent smile for what he called their " childish race sentimentalities."[258]

The Mahatma's career in India overshadowed his obscure and neglected South African period. He is better known to the world as a nationalist leader than as a fighter against racial prejudice. Great as the Mahatma was as a leader of his people, time may yet show that greater value and importance attach to his role in South Africa than to his part in winning independence for India. Gandhi's struggles against colour prejudice and his technique of Satyagraha, designed to help a racial minority in its fight for equality and justice, raise the Mahatma above the level of a nationalist leader and give him a universal significance and appeal.

The Imperial Angle*

" The Empire has been built up as it is on a foundation of justice and equity. It has earned a world-wide reputation for its anxiety and ability to protect the weak against the strong."[259] Those were the words of Gandhi writing in *Indian Opinion* in 1904. Sixteen years later, the Mahatma wrote " An Open Letter " to Lord Chelmsford, the Viceroy of

---

[257] *Collected Works*, II, p. 224.
[258] *Ibid.*, I, p. 276.
  * See C. W. de Kiewiet, *British Colonial Policy and the South African Republics*, (London, Longmans, Green & Co., 1929) and *The Imperial Factor in South Africa*, (London, Cambridge University Press, 1937).
[259] *Collected Works*, IV, p. 302.

India, in which he said of the British Empire, " I don't believe that it protects the weak. It gives free scope to the strong to maintain their strength and develop it. The weak under it go to the wall."[260] Written on the eve of the Khilafat Agitation, the letter was a ringing challenge from a man who had suffered in South Africa for three decades before he finally lost his faith in British Imperialism and all its works. He had struggled long and painfully to retain his belief in the essential goodness and integrity of the Empire; the weaknesses of the Imperial system had turned a staunch loyalist into a determined rebel.

Gandhi repeatedly argued that the Indians were not in South Africa on sufferance but as a matter of right. " Our existence in South Africa," he said, " is only in our capacity as British subjects."[261] Gandhi was aware that the problem of the Indians in South Africa did not affect that country alone. " What status will the Indians outside British India have? "[262] he asked. When interviewed aboard the *Courland* by a correspondent of *The Natal Advertiser*, Gandhi stressed that in the memorials sent by the Indians to the Colonial Office, " the Imperial view of the question has always been kept in the forefront."[263] On the eve of the Colonial Premiers' Conference in London in 1897, Gandhi repeated a question asked earlier by *The Times* in an article on Indian immigration: " May they or may they not go freely from one British possession to another, and claim the rights of British subjects in allied States? "[264] The fate of the British Empire in India was partly decided by the negative answer given to the Indians in South Africa.

---

[260] *Speeches*, p. 513.

[261] *Satyagraha in South Africa*, p. 72.

[262] *Collected Works*, II, p. 157.

[263] *Ibid.*, II, p. 158.

[264] *Ibid.*, II, p. 295.

Imperial problems in an area the size of the British Empire were bound to be complicated and difficult to solve. Gandhi was certainly not unaware of this. His struggle for objectivity was evident when he wrote in 1901 to the British Committee of the Indian National Congress, " I know that we who are on the spot suffer from nearness of vision and may consequently take merely a narrow and parochial view..."[265] Nearness of vision, however, had become an optical weakness throughout the British Empire ; both the Colonies and the Colonial Office were tending to look at Imperial issues from a narrow, parochial perspective. The sacrifice of wider Imperial ideals to narrower colonial interests was most clear in the racialist legislation, based on colour prejudice, enacted in many parts of the Empire. Yet neither Joseph Chamberlain, who tacitly agreed to these discriminatory forms of legislation, nor the Colonial premiers, who pressed for Imperial sanction for their racialist policies, were fully aware of the shortsightedness of their actions.

Gandhi fought for the old liberal ideals of Empire as opposed to the " New Imperialism " which had been gaining ground since the 1870's. This is illustrated in his appreciation for the Cape, which he considered the most liberal of the four Colonies. Table Mountain symbolised for Gandhi the old liberal traditions of South Africa. " Not being too high, it does not inspire awe. People are not compelled to worship it from afar, but build their houses upon it and live there. And as it is just on the seashore, the sea always washes its foot with its clear waters. Young and old, men and women, fearlessly move about the whole mountain, which resounds every day with the voices of thousands."[266] The Cape had been least affected by colour prejudice, and Gandhi regarded

---

[265] *Collected Works*, III, p. 195.
[266] *Satyagraha in South Africa*, p. 6.

it as " the chief centre of culture in South Africa."[267] The Mahatma later remembered with warmth the " sober, gentlemanly and large-hearted Europeans "[268] of the Cape such as Merriman, Molteno and Schreiner who had befriended him. Both the leaders and the newspapers of the Cape " were less hostile to Indians "[269] than their counterparts in the other Colonies.

Throughout his career in South Africa, Gandhi pleaded for a larger vision of the meaning and value of the Empire. " There can be no true imperialism," he said, " unless we have oneness, harmony and toleration among all classes of British subjects."[270] Gandhi could state his case in the language and spirit of Edmund Burke. In a letter written to *The Englishman* of Calcutta in 1902, he said, " Imperialism is on the lips of everybody, more especially in the Colonies. How to weld the different parts of the British Dominions into one beautiful unbreakable whole is a problem which the greatest British politicians of the day are endeavouring to solve, and yet, here is a Colony (Natal) which is making invidious distinctions between one class of British subjects and another in a most aggravating manner."[271] The student who studies the image of the British Empire Gandhi cherished until the aggravations in South Africa became unbearable, may conclude that a potential imperial statesman was lost in Gandhi. There was probably no non-European British subject anywhere in the Empire who strove harder than Gandhi to uphold what he described as " true imperialism."[272]

Gandhi's Kathiawadi background gave him an insight

---

[267] *Ibid.*, p. 36.
[268] *Ibid.*, p. 36.
[269] *Ibid.*, p. 37.
[270] *Collected Works*, III, p. 252.
[271] *Collected Works*, III, p. 251.
[272] *Ibid.*, III, p. 355.

into the attachment of the British for the system of monarchy. Coming from a family with traditional loyalties to the Ranas of Porbandar, he understood the fascination that royalty had for the British public. As a student in London he had been a regular reader of *Answers*, a magazine which showed him the place of the Crown in the interests of the average Englishman ; he had sensed the hold which the monarchy had on the minds of the working classes. Therefore, he was not surprised to find that the Crown and the Union Jack were powerful symbols in the colonial mind. As long as he continued to have faith in the Empire, Gandhi never hesitated to demonstrate publicly his loyalty to the British monarchy. He sang the National Anthem with fervour and saluted the Union Jack with pride.

Though his loyalty was sincere, Gandhi also used the Crown as a means of appealing to the sentiments of the whites in South Africa to regard Indians as their fellow British subjects. This use of the symbol of the Crown was seen most clearly in his actions at the time of the death of Queen Victoria. On February 1, 1901, Gandhi sent telegrams to leading Indians asking them to mourn the Queen's death by taking out processions with floral wreaths to be laid at the statues of the departed Empress.[273] On the same day a memorial souvenir was distributed by the Indian community in South Africa. This was obviously intended for wider consumption than the Indian school children to whom it was allegedly directed.

The memorial souvenir brought together all that Gandhi had been trying to make clear to Queen Victoria's white subjects in South Africa.[274] In the centre of the souvenir was a portrait of the Queen. In the left-hand corner above

---

[273] *Collected Works*, III, p. 174.
[274] See photographic reproduction of memorial souvenir, *Collected Works*, III, facing p. 184.

the portrait was an encircled map of India showing the extent of the British possessions in 1839. In the bottom right-hand corner was a similar map showing the whole of India painted red to indicate the extent of British rule in 1901. When Gandhi arrived in Pretoria in 1893, he had found that the Boers obstinately believed the Indian merchants were not British subjects but Turks. The souvenir was a continuing lesson in political geography which Gandhi had been teaching the whites.

Above the portrait of the Queen was an " Extract from The Gracious Proclamation of 1858, given to The People of India." The Queen's Proclamation of 1858 had been used frequently by Gandhi to prove to the people of Natal that the intention of the Imperial Government was to increase and not to limit the liberties of Her Majesty's Indian subjects. There is irony in the fact that the man who so strongly opposed British rule in India once stoutly defended the liberality of both the Imperial Government and the Government of India as contrasted with the oppressiveness of colonial rule. In South Africa, Gandhi strenuously defended his rights as a British citizen by pointing out that Queen Victoria was Empress of India, a fact printed below her portrait on the memorial souvenir. At the bottom of the souvenir was the story of how Victoria, informed at the age of twelve that some day she would be queen, had said, " I will be good." The memorial souvenir asked the whites of Natal to be good like Queen Victoria who had guaranteed the rights of the Indian people by her Proclamation of 1858.

On February 2, a great procession of the Indians of Durban wended its way to Queen Victoria's statue to pay tribute to the memory of the Empress. In the lead were Gandhi and Nazar carrying a huge floral wreath on their shoulders.[275]

---

[275] *Collected Works*, III, p. 174.

Gandhi's speech at the wreath-laying ceremony, as reported by *The Natal Advertiser*, again used the Queen for an object lesson to the whites. " Mr. M. K. Gandhi, " said the *Advertiser*, " dwelt on the noble virtues of the late Queen. He referred to the Indian Proclamation of 1858, and the Queen's deep interest in Indian affairs—how she commenced the study of Hindusthani language at a ripe age, and how, although she herself could not go to India to be in the midst of her beloved people, she sent her sons and grandsons to represent her."[276]

The boy who had grown up in the atmosphere of the princely states of Kathiawad knew the importance the British attached to royal visits. Gandhi was familiar with the way in which the visits of Victoria's sons and grandsons were commemorated. The old student of the Alfred High School was not surprised to find there was an Alfred County in Natal. When Gandhi wrote Prince Alfred's obituary in *Indian Opinion*, he drew attention to another imperial link between India and Natal. The visit of the Duke and Duchess of York to Durban in August, 1901, gave Gandhi an opportunity for drafting a Loyal Address full of sentiments intended to convey the importance of India as an imperial possession. Queen Victoria was referred to as " our late beloved Kaiser-i-Hind " and King Edward as " our Maharaja." The royal visit was credited with having " drawn tighter the silken cord that binds together the different parts of the British Raj."[277] Even the symbolism of the British flag was utilized. "We fully realize," the Address said, "the blessing of the munificent British rule. It is because we are in the folds of the all-embracing Union Jack that we have a footing outside India."[278] The visit of the King and Queen to Ireland in

---

[276] *Ibid.*, III, p. 175.
[277] *Collected Works*, III, p. 200.
[278] *Ibid.*, III, pp. 200-201.

1903 inspired Gandhi to write an article in *Indian Opinion* under a caption borrowed from the Irish-born dramatist, Oliver Goldsmith—" Stooping to Conquer." To claim that " the event has a special significance for India "[279] was rather far-fetched, but it did not stop Gandhi, as long as he could turn the activities of royalty in Dublin into a homily on " true imperialism."

The various ways in which Gandhi tried to raise the patriotism of the South African whites from a parochial to an imperial level by creating pride in " our Indian Empire " makes an interesting study. He tried to educate the whites to a realization that India was a partner and a full member of the imperial family. Gandhi turned *Indian Opinion* into a handbook on the Indian Empire, using the imperial motif to gain respect for Indians. Knowing the British penchant for royalty, Gandhi utilized all the glamour associated with the image of an Indian Maharajah. "The balls given by the Maharajah of Kuch Behar," he gravely reported, " attract the best European society."[280] Gandhi included Sir Pertab Singh, " the King-Emperor's personal friend and aide-de-camp,"[281] the Maharajah of Baroda, " one of the most cultured Princes of India,"[282] and Ranjitsinhji, the princely cricketer, to give colour to the drab image of India as a land of coolies in the minds of the whites. The same motive underlay Gandhi's sketches in *Indian Opinion* of a host of eminent Indians distinguished in various walks of life.

In order to counteract the impression that all Indians lived in insanitary conditions, Gandhi drew attention to " a very interesting description of the new palace which is being built

---

[279] *Ibid.*, III, p. 400.
[280] *Collected Works*, IV, p. 318.
[281] *Ibid.*, IV, p. 329.
[282] *Ibid.*, IV, p. 456.

at Mysore for the Maharajah "[283] in the weekly edition of *The Times of India* in September, 1903. Gandhi tried to offset the unfortunate stereotypes generated by the state of Eastern and Western Vlei (the colonies of the Indian employees of the Durban Town Council) and the Indian location in Johannesburg by treating the readers of *Indian Opinion* to an occasional lecture on Indian art and architecture. This, he hoped, would help the whites to realize " that India, as is often believed in South Africa, is not a place dotted merely with huts inhabited by savages."[284]   Even the loyal addresses to visiting royalty were utilized to proclaim the glories of India's past.   The Loyal Address to the Duke and Duchess of Cornwall and York was engraved on a silver shield along with pictures of the Taj Mahal, the Karla Caves of Bombay, the Bodh Gaya stupa, and indentured Indians working on Natal sugar estates.[285]   Gandhi's educational motive was also apparent in the Address presented by the Indian community to Lord Roberts in 1904.   The left side of the illuminated vellum Address was " taken up with a faithful representation of that most exquisite bird, the peacock of India."[286]   This " work of art," for which Gandhi had commissioned a Johannesburg artist, Ada M. Bissicks, was enclosed " in a solid silver casket, with lotus flowers engraved on it."[287]

The image of India as a land of famine and contagious diseases was wide-spread during the latter half of the nineteenth century.   Walt Whitman, for example, hailed the " plague-swarms of Madras "[288] in his *Salut au Monde*.   In South Africa, this fearful notion of India had been exploited to

---

[283] *Ibid.*, IV, p. 447.
[284] *Collected Works*, IV, p. 447.
[285] *Ibid.*, III, p. 200.
[286] *Ibid.*, IV, p. 294.
[287] *Ibid.*, IV, p. 294.
[288] *Op. cit.*, p. 123.

339

tighten the Quarantine Laws restricting immigration and to segregate Indians into "locations." Gandhi tried to convert this fear of contagion into sympathy and compassion for fellow-members of the British Empire. "It may be," Gandhi hoped, "that the threefold scourge in India—viz., famine, plague and cholera—black as it is, will be the means of forging another link in the chain that ties all together."[289] The Famine Funds launched by Gandhi had the same object of enlisting the concern of the Natal whites for the people of India in order to foster imperial ties.

When Gandhi told the Natal whites that the "British love of justice and fair play are the sheet-anchor of the Indian's hopes"[290] he showed that the sporting spirit inculcated in him as a boy by the public school tradition of the Alfred High School had stayed with him. Natal was such a British colony that the volunteers in the Zulu War of 1879 had taken their cricket gear with them; cricket bats, however, had been of no avail against the Zulu spears at Isandhlwana.[291] In Durban, where there was a cricket pitch in Albert Park, Gandhi became conscious of the value of the batting prowess of his friend, Ranjitsinhji. When, later on, Gandhi made a similar appeal to the "sportsmanlike instincts"[292] of Lord Harris (a former Governor of Bombay and Chairman of the Consolidated Gold Fields of South Africa), racialism had begun also to infect the arena of sports ; Gandhi noted that the Government in Pretoria had refused permission to an Indian football team from Pietermaritzburg "to pass the sacred precincts of the Transvaal."[293] In South Africa, the public school spirit the British had brought with them into

---

[289] *Collected Works*, III, p. 152.
[290] *Ibid.*, II, p. 365.
[291] Southey, *op. cit.*, p. 124.
[292] *Collected Works*, IV, p. 50.
[293] *Collected Works*, IV, p. 259.

Kathiawad, was proving compatible with segregated sports.
The young Kathiawadi had gained sufficient insight into
the military aspects of imperial pride to know the value of
public expressions of loyalty in times of crisis. The desire
to win acceptance by proving the loyalty of the Indian
community was particularly clear in Gandhi's activities in
connection with the Boer War. When the Durban Women's
Patriotic League complained that the Indian merchants
had not contributed liberally to their organization, Gandhi
promptly sent round a subscription list and appeased the
good ladies.[294] The Indian merchants also supplied free
gifts of cigarettes, cigars, pipes and tobacco for the troops,
and the Indian women sewed pillow-cases and handkerchiefs,
vying with the Durban Women's Patriotic League in looking
after the comfort of the men at the front.[295] Gandhi himself
was decorated for his services to the Empire in organizing an
Indian Ambulance Corps. Both Gandhi and the Indian
stretcher-bearers, who were in the firing lines during the
critical battle of Spion Kop, found a place in *The Times
History of The War in South Africa.*[296]

The same desire to show that Indians knew both their
rights and duties as British citizens prompted Gandhi to
lead a small Ambulance Unit during the Zulu Rebellion of
1906. Even after he had become known as an exponent
of non-violence, Gandhi continued to demonstrate his loyalty
to the Empire by recruiting men for the Imperial armies
during the First World War. Gandhi's services to the British
Empire in semi-military capacities made him a target of
Soviet criticism. *The Great Soviet Encyclopaedia* commented

---

[294] *Ibid.*, III, p. 120.
[295] *Ibid.*, III, p. 140.
[296] L. S. Amery, (ed.), *The Times History of The War in South Africa*, 1899-1902,
7 Vols., (London, Sampson, Low Marston & Co., 1909), III, p. 100; VI,
p. 134.

adversely on Gandhi, saying that " he actively helped British imperialism by organizing and leading an Indian sanitary unit which served the British army in its invasion in the land of the Zulus, destroying them with fire and sword."[297]   This view of Gandhi was not revised by the Russian *Encyclopaedia* until after 1956.

Gandhi not only actively served the Empire but also constantly stressed the part played by Indian troops in its expansion and protection.   In both cases, Gandhi had two objects in mind.   First, he argued the wrongness of excluding Indians, who had contributed to the growth of the Empire, from any part of it.   This view emerges clearly in his comments on the Tibetan Mission of 1904 in which Sikh troops had participated: " The Colonies would be prepared as part of the British Empire to appropriate the results of Sikh bravery, and if it were found that the great plateaus of Tibet were filled with gold, there would be a mad rush to the land. But it is a sad fact that they are not at all prepared to welcome the Sikh soldiers themselves or their compatriots as settlers in the Colonies.   It is to be wished that such an inconsistent attitude will strike the Colonial leaders as something to be rectified."[298]   In these remarks Gandhi obviously had in mind the Uitlanders whose possession of the gold of the Rand had been guaranteed by British troops sent from India and partly paid for by the Indian treasury.

Gandhi's second object was to gain respect for India's martial traditions in order to remove the South African impression that Indians were lacking in manliness.   Coming from a land of Rajput valour, Gandhi found this stereotype based on the docility of the humble, poverty-stricken indentured labourer obnoxious.   One aspect of his concern that Indians should take some active part in the Boer War was to prove

---

[297] Quoted in *The New York Times*, February 21, 1956, p. 5.
[298] *Collected Works*, IV, p. 165.

that even indentured labourers were not lacking in courage. The Indian Ambulance Corps proved that coolies were worth something on a battlefield. In an article entitled " Sepoy Bravery," Gandhi quoted Tennyson's " Charge of the Light Brigade " to describe the role of Indian troops on the battlefields of the Empire.[299]

Two other problems with an imperial relevance which Gandhi confronted relate to language and religion. Some of the Mahatma's objections to the use of English in India actually derived from his experience of the exploitation of that language to penalize Indians in South Africa, especially in Natal. An Indian might be refused admission to Natal for failing to satisfy the immigration authorities that he had a knowledge of English. Similarly an Indian trader might be refused a licence for an inability to maintain his accounts in English.[300] Gandhi agreed that English should be the common language of the Empire but objected to the aggressive uses to which it was put in South Africa.

As to the second problem, Gandhi appreciated Christianity as a religion, but he had little to say for its role within the imperial context. The exclusiveness of Christianity was not helpful in an Empire comprising peoples of different religions; this explains Gandhi's interest in the Esoteric Christian Union during his early years in Natal. The Esoteric Christianity of Anna Kingsford and Edward Maitland seemed to be a more inclusive form of belief than the religion of the churches in Natal. Gandhi thus became a representative of Edward Maitland's Esoteric Christian Union and sold Anna Kingsford's books with the zeal of a member of the Wellington Convention.

Hardly a year had elapsed since he had attended that gathering of Christians in Wellington when Gandhi wrote

---

[299] *Ibid.*, IV, pp. 215-216.
[300] *Collected Works*, II, p. 353.

to *The Natal Mercury* on November 26, 1894, commending Esoteric Christianity as " a system of religion which teaches universality, and is based on eternal verities and not on phenomena or historical facts merely. In that system there is no reviling Mahomed or Buddha in order to prove the superiority of Jesus. On the other hand, it reconciles the other religions with Christianity ... "[301] The superiority claimed for Jesus had become associated with the racial superiority asserted by the whites. Christianity could play the role of a civilizing but not a reconciling force within the British Empire ; where there was tolerance, it often rested on secular rather than religious assumptions. Ultimately, Gandhi would go back to concepts of tolerance evolved in the ancient empires of India. He would find in syncretism, a legacy from the imperial past deeply rooted in the Hindu mind, a useful method of reconciling racial and religious differences.

The Mahatma's opposition to the Empire in India was so determined precisely because his faith in the imperial system of the British had once been so great. A comparison of his appeals to the whites of Natal such as his *Open Letter* and *The Indian Franchise* with the stern denunciation of the British in the Mahatma's challenge entitled " To Every Englishman in India " reveals the depth of his disillusionment. The vision of the New Jerusalem he once saw in imperialism had turned into a picture of racist hell for the Mahatma when he declared, " A system that is responsible for such things is necessarily satanic."[302] Gandhi's struggles against racial prejudice in South Africa had made the British Empire diabolical in his eyes.

There were three significant elements in Gandhi's loss of

---

[301] *Collected Works*, I, p. 139.
[302] *Speeches*, p. 558. (Reproduced from *Young India*, October, 1920.)

faith in the British Empire—all based on his South African experience. First, he no longer believed the Empire could evolve into a better system of imperial government. This conviction stemmed from his reaction to the Imperial Government's surrender of its liberal principles to the racist interests of the white settlers in the Colonies. Gandhi regarded the Colonial Office as the arbiter between the various races in Africa. In 1899, he wrote, " In a continent like this, where there are diverse and conflicting interests belonging to the various races, the strong and powerful influence of the Home Government is ever necessary. Once give latitude to a particular section of the various peoples, and you never know when an ebullition will take place."[303] Gandhi, however, watched helplessly while Joseph Chamberlain and a Unionist Ministry abdicated their Imperial responsibilities in South Africa as far as the Indians were concerned. His spirits revived after the great Liberal victory of 1905. Gandhi visited London in 1906 and 1909 in order to present the Indian case to the Liberal Government. He returned empty-handed on both occasions because, with the Liberals striving to effect the union of South Africa, the Indians had become a forgotten factor. G. B. Pyrah's comment that " the Indians seem generally to have been forgotten in contemporary Liberal literature "[304] is indicative of the apathy which destroyed the last shreds of Gandhi's hope that the Colonial Office would safeguard the rights of the Indians. The Mahatma's apparent intransigence at the Round Table Conference in 1931 may be understood as the behaviour of a man who had ceased to trust the Imperial Government two decades before.

The second aspect of Gandhi's changed opinion of the Empire was his disillusionment with regard to the working

---

[303] *Collected Works*, III, p. 61.

[304] G. B. Pyrah, *Imperial Policy and South Africa*, 1902-1910, (Oxford, Clarendon Press, 1955), p. 33.

out in practice of responsible government in the colonies. In 1899, Gandhi wrote, " The poor Indians have known no rest since responsible government has been granted. One after another, the elementary rights of British citizenship have been snatched away from them ; and if Mr. Chamberlain and Lord Curzon are not wide awake, the British Indians in Natal will, one of these days, find themselves stripped of all that they have been taught to believe they possess as subjects of the Queen-Empress."[305] Gandhi was aware that what was happening in South Africa was not an isolated instance of colour prejudice in the British Empire ; he referred on more than one occasion to the racial policies of Australia. In a letter to Gokhale from Madras in October, 1896, Gandhi asked him to raise questions about the proposed racial legislation in Australia in the Imperial Council in Calcutta.[306] In 1903, Indian lascars on a ship wrecked off the Australian coast were refused permission to land in that country because they were coloured. Gandhi commended Chamberlain's attitude to the incident in *Indian Opinion* as an indication to the colonies that " coloured British subjects are entitled to be treated the same as other British subjects."[307] In the following year, Gandhi wrote an article entitled " British Indians in Australia, "[308] praising the good work being done by Mr. C. F. Sievwright and the British Empire League in fighting colour prejudice in that Dominion. Gandhi frequently argued with an almost prophetic foresight that the practice of racial discrimination in the colonies would result in the loss of India to the Empire.

A loss of confidence in British constitutional and legal procedures marks the third aspect of Gandhi's disillusionment

---

[305] *Collected Works*, III, p. 85.
[306] *Ibid.*, II, p. 90.
[307] *Ibid.*, III, p. 355.
[308] *Collected Works*, IV, p. 125.

with the Empire. As we have said before, the use made by the generation of Robinson and Escombe of the Natal Legislature to pass discriminatory laws partly accounts for Gandhi's distrust of representative institutions. He was particularly appalled by the manner in which the Natal Legislature managed to circumvent the Imperial Government's objections to discriminatory laws with what Gandhi, rightly or wrongly, considered the connivance of Chamberlain and the Colonial Office. Gandhi quoted Robinson's own words to show how the Natal premier had steered the discriminatory bills through the Assembly : " When a ship was heading against a wind, she had to tack, and bye and bye she accomplished her goal. When a man met difficulties, he fought against them, and if he could not knock them over, he went round them instead of breaking his head against a brick wall."[309]

Gandhi's suspicion of the South African legislatures deepened after the threatened mob violence of the anti-Indian Demonstration of 1897 was exploited to rush discriminatory laws through the Natal Assembly. An act of the Legislature, he concluded, was no longer backed by principles of British law and justice but by the threat of mob violence. The same doubts about legislative processes in South Africa assailed Gandhi after he settled in Johannesburg in 1903. The pages of *Indian Opinion* abound with Gandhi's often pungent comments on the racialist activities and terrorist threats of white Leagues and Vigilance Associations. In 1904, Gandhi wrote, " The history of British rule is the history of constitutional evolution. Under the British flag, respect for the law has become a part of the nature of the people."[310] It was an ironical statement addressed to the Vigilants of Potchefstroom who had launched a campaign of terror against

---

[309] *Ibid.*, II, p. 328.
[310] *Collected Works*, IV, p. 322.

the Indians by burning their shops, ostracising whites who bought goods from Indians and refusing permission for the building of a mosque. Gandhi did not demonstrate his loss of faith in constitutional methods by launching passive resistance until long after the whites had shown a disrespect for law and order by resorting to mob rule tactics to get their own way. The municipalities of South Africa had, like the legislatures, become local instruments for the maintenance of white power when Gandhi revealed a growing cynicism about the value of imperial ties. " Is it Imperial or Empirical ? "[311] he asked when the Transvaal Legislative Council was debating the Elective Municipalities Ordinance in 1903 which eventually debarred coloured voters from exercising their municipal franchise.

Gandhi's loss of faith in British Imperialism not only changed his images of the Empire but also his picture of India under British rule. The treatment of Indians in South Africa led Gandhi to describe India as " the Cinderella of the Empire."[312] The refusal of the South African whites to allow Indian merchants to make a living set Gandhi thinking about the economic exploitation of India by the British. After the anti-Indian Demonstration of 1897, a correspondent wrote to *The Natal Mercury* pointing out that " there are plenty of European stores in India, and well patronised and flourishing too."[313] Gandhi was quick to take the hint. Three months later, in April, 1897, Gandhi also wrote to *The Natal Mercury* enlarging upon the same theme : " India benefits hundreds of thousands of Europeans ; India makes the British Empire; India gives an unrivalled prestige to the British Empire ; India has often fought for England. Is it fair that European subjects of that Empire in this Colony, who themselves derive

---

[311] *Ibid.*, III, p. 339.
[312] *Collected Works*, III, p. 382.
[313] *Ibid.*, II, p. 239.

a considerable benefit from Indian labour, should object to the free Indians earning an honest livelihood in it?"[314]

These simple propositions in Gandhi's mind were further developed by reading the works of Dadhabhai Naoroji and R. C. Dutt ; he listed both authors in Appendix I of *Hind Swaraj*. The economic researches of Naoroji and Dutt shattered the rather unquestioning adulatory picture of British rule cherished by Indian liberals in the nineteenth century. This flattering image of the British was mirrored, for example, in Surendranath Bannerjee's speech in Finsbury on April 14, 1890. Praising Britain's role in India, the Bengali leader echoed Macaulay when he said, " To have found a great nation sunk in depths of superstition, to have raised them to a higher level of civilization, to have communicated to them the breadth of a new life—the pulsations of a new civilization—are titles to glory all her own."[315] The colour of truth in Bannerjee's encomium had faded by the end of the nineteenth century ; the dark shades of famine, plague and degrading poverty were more visible than the brighter sides of British rule.

The economic impoverishment of India by the British was a prominent and controversial theme from the 1890's to the 1920's until it was superseded by an interest in Indian constitutional problems. Naoroji's *Poverty and Un-British Rule in India*,[316] which appeared in 1901, was a collection of papers on the subject going back to 1876. Lajpat Rai's *Unhappy India* published in 1916 was followed a year later by *England's Debt to India*. Some of these writings on Indian economic problems were inspired by the spate of English books on the poverty of the London poor. The lines of argument for

---

[314] *Ibid.*, II, p. 309.
[315] *India*, April 25, 1890.
[316] Dadhabhai Naoroji, *Poverty and Un-British Rule in India*, (London, Swan Sonnenschien & Co., Ltd., 1901).

supporting the charge that the poverty of India was due mainly to British rule were developed by Naoroji in a paper read to the Bombay Branch of the East India Association of London. In this paper he put forward his " Drain Theory " which was inspired by reading J. W. Draper's *A History of the Intellectual Development of Europe*.[317] Draper described the " steady drain of money from every realm "[318] into the papal coffers during the time of Innocent III and Innocent IV. Naoroji drew an analogy between the picture drawn by Draper of the impoverishment of England as a result of the drain to Italy and the economic aspects of British rule in India.

These writings on Indian economics played an important part in fostering the violent nationalism of the first two decades of the twentieth century before the Mahatma channeled the angry emotions engendered into civil disobedience campaigns. The British were no longer seen as benefactors but as ruthless exploiters. The image of the British rule as a form of humanitarian benevolence was replaced by the picture of an oppressive imperialist power—a picture in which there was both truth and exaggeration. Interestingly enough, an American and a descendant of a prominent figure in the first colonial struggle against the British, made a contribution to the " Drain Theory " elaborated by Naoroji. Brooks Adams was in India studying conditions under British Imperialism when *The Law of Civilization and Decay* was published in London in 1895.[319] In his chapter entitled " Spain and India " Brooks Adams cast the British in the role of Spanish conquistadors.

Gandhi's reading of Naoroji and Dutt completed his image

---

317 J. W. Draper, *A History of the Intellectual Development of Europe*, (New York, Harper & Brothers, 1863).

318 Draper, *op. cit.*, p. 397. (Quoted in Naoroji, *op. cit.*, p. 52).

319 B. Adams, *The Law of Civilization and Decay*, (New York, Vintage Books, 1955).

of India as the Cinderella of the British Empire clad in the rags of a poverty " unparalleled in any civilized country,"[320] neglected and reduced to a drudge by her Imperial step-mother, despised and ill-treated by her unkind sister colonies. There was one analogy in Naoroji's book which would appeal greatly to Gandhi. Naoroji compared India's position to " that of a child to which a fond parent gives a sweet, but to which, in its exhausted condition, the very sweet acts like a poison, and, as a *foreign substance*, by irritating the weak stomach makes it throw out more, and causes greater exhaustion. In India's present condition the very sweets of every other nation appear to act on it as a poison."[321] Indians had been sent to Natal by the Imperial Government in the hope that they would share the sweets of sugar prosperity but were forced to take the bitter poison of racial prejudice. South Africa poisoned Gandhi's mind against the Empire to such an extent that even the good fruits of British rule in India lost their sweetness and became distasteful. The young Gandhi's child-like faith in the British was understandably replaced by the Mahatma's irremovable suspicion and distrust of Imperial designs.

Johannesburg

The thirty-three year old Gandhi who returned to South Africa in December 1902, after spending just over a year in India had acquired a better knowledge of his mother-country. His first leave in India had enabled him to meet the Anglicised political leaders of the major cities. He met them again at the Congress session of December, 1901 in Calcutta. Gandhi's experiences at the Calcutta Congress confirmed his impression that the westernized middle class

---

[320] R. C. Dutt, *India Under Early British Rule*, (London, Kegan Paul, Trench, Trubner & Co., 1908), p. vi.
[321] *Op. cit.*, p. 54.

leadership was out of touch with the Indian masses ; yet he had found in one of these national figures a man whom he could respect and admire. Gandhi had profited greatly by the interest Gokhale had taken in him. With the instinct of a professor, Gokhale saw in Gandhi the potential qualities of greatness that others such as Sir Pherozeshah Mehta, for all their kindness to him, had missed in the ordinary-looking young lawyer. The liberal statesman, Gokhale, deserves the credit for sowing the thought in Gandhi's mind that he was destined to play a role in the national movement in India.

This second holiday in India also gave Gandhi an opportunity to study the religious movements he had read about in South Africa. In Calcutta, he became acquainted with the Bengali Christian leader, Kalicharan Banerji, and Pratap Chandra Mazumdar, the biographer of Keshab Chandra Sen. He attended a Brahmo service in the home of Maharshi Devendranath Tagore and developed an appreciation for Bengali music. He walked to Belur Math in the hope of seeing Swami Vivekananda, but was disappointed ; he had, however, seen the Swami's English disciple, Sister Nivedita, queening it over her Chowringhee mansion, and was not much impressed. During his visit to Rangoon, the rats in the Shwe Dagon pagoda reminded him of Swami Dayanand Saraswati ; the founder of the Arya Samaj had become disillusioned with idol worship when, as a young boy, he had watched rats scampering over the image in the temple at Morvi. In Benares, Gandhi called on Annie Besant. He also learned much from Gokhale about Ranade, Telang, Mandlik and other leaders of the reform movement in Western India. During his second furlough the young man from the isolated peninsula of Kathiawad completed his discovery of India.

When Gandhi reached Pretoria on New Year's Day, 1903, he found a situation in the Transvaal which convinced him

that " peace was never to be my portion in this life." [322]   The
Provisional Government (set up after the Boer War by the
Vereeniging Peace treaty) [323] had acquired an Anglo-Indian
flavour owing to the presence of British military and civil
officials from India.   These former Indian officials had
brought the bureaucratic attitude with them turning the
administration into an efficient but impersonal machine.
Gandhi had his first brush with this new bureaucracy when
the Colonial Office refused to let him represent the Indians
as a member of the deputation to see Chamberlain, then on a
visit to South Africa.   Recalling the way he had been treated
as an agitator by the Anglo-Indian officialdom of the
Provisional Government, the Mahatma later wrote, " I saw
that I had to begin my work from the very beginning." [324]

The Indians in South Africa always faced the difficulty of
being represented by British officials with little sympathy or
understanding for their problems.   In Natal, for example,
the British Agent, Walter Peace, wrote a book entitled *Our
Colony of Natal* [325] in which he viewed the problem of Indian
labour as any colonial would.   The appointment of a Protector
of Indian Immigrants had not improved matters.   This
official, distant and aloof, spoke no Indian language.   He
was hardly the sort of person to whom a humble indentured
labourer could turn in his difficulties.   The Indians had
fared better under the old slow-moving and inefficient South
African Republic than they did in Natal.   The race prejudice
in the Transvaal had been tempered by the personal and
paternalistic methods of the Boers of Paul Kruger's generation.

After the Boer War, the British created the Department of

---

[322] *Satyagraha in South Africa*, p. 81.
[323] See G. W. Eybers, (ed.), *Select Constitutional Documents Illustrating South African History* 1795-1910, (London, George Routledge & Sons, Ltd., 1918),   p. 346.
[324] *Satyagraha in South Africa*, p. 83.
[325] Walter Peace, *Our Colony of Natal*, (London, Edward Stanford, 1883), pp. 130-131.

Asiatic Affairs to deal with the Indians and Chinese in the Transvaal. The bureaucratic traditions of this Department were inherited and maintained by the restored Government of the Transvaal after the elections of February, 1907. The attitude of the Asiatic Department was in striking contrast to that of the Imperial Government before the South African War when the Indian grievances had been listed among the *casus belli*. The stringent enforcement of the old Boer Republic's anti-Indian laws by the Provisional Government came as a shock to the Indians who had been led to believe that their grievances would be redressed after the British victory.[326] Gandhi's deep distrust of Imperial war-time promises may be traced back to the sympathy for the Indian cause shown before the Boer War and the harsh attitude of the Asiatic Department after the Vereeniging Peace Treaty of 1902. Gandhi's experience with the Asiatic Department and the continuation of its policies in 1907 by J. C. Smuts, the Colonial Secretary, induced him to launch Passive Resistance in the Transvaal.

Gandhi's conflicts with the Asiatic Department led him to reflect on the nature of government and the state. The boy who had grown up in an Indian native state now began to see virtues in a paternalistic form of government. The paternalism of the Boers seemed preferable to the ruthless efficiency of British bureaucracy. "The whole of the anti-Indian legislation in the Transvaal is being enforced with a vigour unknown before. The laxity of the late Government was totally in our favour,"[327] Gandhi had complained even earlier

---

[326] C. H. Thomas, *Origin of the Anglo-Boer War Revealed*, (London, Hodder & Stoughton, 1900), p. 38; "The Rights and Wrongs of the British Indian", in A. R. Colquhoun, *The Africander Land*, (London, John Murray, 1906); "The Treatment of the Asiatics," in Manfred Nathan, *The South African Commonwealth*, (Johannesburg, and Cape Town, The Speciality Press of South Africa, Ltd., 1919).

[327] *Collected Works*, III, p. 184.

in 1901. In 1903, Gandhi led a deputation of the British
Indian Association to interview Lord Milner. This interview
made it clear that the British High Commissioner himself was
the chief opponent of that Boer laxity which Gandhi admired.
When the Indian deputation pointed out that the South
African Republic had not strictly enforced Law No. 3 of 1885
according to which Indians had to register themselves and
pay a registration fee of £3, Lord Milner replied, " You
make a point of the fact that this law was not enforced by the
old Government. That is what I object to about the system
of the late Government of the Transvaal—it was so arbitrary.
The law was enforced and it was not enforced."[328]

In April, 1903, Gandhi was enrolled as a duly qualified
attorney of the Supreme Court and settled down in Johannesburg. His office was located in Rissik Street, (named after
Johannes Rissik, the Surveyor-General of the Transvaal).[329]
Gandhi was never to feel for Johannesburg the affection he
felt for London, yet the Golden City stimulated and challenged
him at a crucial time in the development of his personality.
The bracing climate of the Rand enabled him to work long
hours without tiring, and the din and bustle of the city
quickened his spirit. " It would be no exaggeration to say
that the citizens of Johannesburg do not walk but seem as if
they ran,"[330] the Mahatma remembered. The current of
Gandhi's life ran more swiftly in Johannesburg than it had
in Durban. Perched six thousand feet above sea level,
Johannesburg, the city which " gives men ardour in thought,
in act and competition and creates in them the vitality from
which spring the excitements of South Africa,"[331] was an

---

[328] *Ibid.*, III, p. 305.
[329] J. P. Fitzpatrick, *The Transvaal from Within*, (London, William Heinemann,
1899), p. 61.
[330] *Satyagraha in South Africa*, p. 4.
[331] Millin, *op. cit.*, p. 69.

appropriate place for the birth of Gandhi's Passive Resistance. His philosophy of Satyagraha was clarified through "the invigorating cut and thrust of conversation in a society where everyone must justify his existence by personal efforts."[332]

If Johannesburg stimulated Gandhi it also depressed him. Though the city had changed outwardly something of the evil reputation it had acquired in the 1890's still clung to its spirit. Only four years before Gandhi settled there, Johannesburg had been described as "Monte Carlo superimposed upon Sodom and Gomorrah" and "The central sin spot of civilization."[333] Gandhi's images of modern civilization were unfortunately based largely on his impressions of this incongruous city on the Rand. Indians listening to the Mahatma's strictures on modern civilization would naturally infer that he was critical of the civilization of Europe. Most of his later listeners were unaware of the fact that his dislike for European civilization stemmed from his experience of its distorted features seen at their worst in Johannesburg.

The greed for gold was written on the faces of the people and in the names of the streets of the city. "No one has the leisure to look at anyone else, and every one is apparently engrossed in thinking how to amass the maximum wealth in the minimum of time,"[334] the Mahatma wrote as he recollected the hurrying people in Gold Street, Quartz Street, Banker Street, Claim Street and Nugget Street. Gandhi lived with the sound of the roar of the Batteries on the Reef constantly in his ears, a daily reminder of the principal motive for the city's existence. Joseph Doke,[335] conscious perhaps of the impression the Batteries on the Reef had made on Gandhi, began his biography of his Indian friend by evoking the

---

[332] Hamilton Fyfe, *op. cit.*, p. 131.

[333] Hamilton Fyfe, *op. cit.*, p. 126.

[334] *Satyagraha in South Africa*, pp. 4-5.

[335] See W. E. Cursons, *Joseph Doke, The Missionary Hearted*, (Johannesburg, 1929).

constant roar from the mines which formed part of the background of Johannesburg. "That roar," said Doke, "never ceases. On calm, hot, sunny days it almost dies; it sinks away into a lazy hum like the drone of bees in the clover. But it is always there. The Batteries of the Reef are never still. Night and day, and every night and every day, without rest, the crushing of the great machinery goes on, and the rocks and stones and sand yield their golden treasure in response."[336] The incessant roar from the mines had much to do with Gandhi's dislike of machinery. In Johannesburg it was difficult to see the machine in any other light except as the servant of man's insatiable avarice. The gold mines on the Rand were largely responsible for the Mahatma's firm conviction that western civilization is essentially selfish and materialistic.

Gandhi's feeling that western civilization is pleasure-loving grew stronger in Johannesburg. In 1917, the Mahatma would say, " The divine word that India alone is the land of *Karma* (right action), the rest is the land of *Bhoga* (enjoyment) is imprinted on my mind."[337] Johannesburg was a city where fear walked in the streets. It was a fear engendered by a situation in which eighty-four thousand whites, unabashedly flaunted their wealth and sex in the faces of seventy-five thousand coloured people.[338] It had become a city of burglars and bulldogs; even Gandhi's friends, the Polaks, kept a watch-dog which Gandhi unsuccessfully tried to convert into a vegetarian.[339] Gandhi could almost feel an invisible wall of fear between the whites and the blacks as he moved around the city.

The Transvaal, which Gandhi called " the El Dorado of

---

[336] *Op. cit.*, p. 1.
[337] *Speeches*, p. 377.
[338] The figures given by Phillips for 1904, *Transvaal Problems*, p. 32.
[339] M. G. Polak, *op. cit.*, pp. 105-106.

the gold-hunters of the Western World,"[340] attracted a diversity of races which turned Johannesburg into a polyglot city. A considerable proportion of the population of the Rand consisted of Jews.[341]

Gandhi's relations with the Jews of Johannesburg is an absorbing subject for study. The manner in which different sections of the Jews reacted against the potential threat of anti-Semitism explains why Gandhi found both opponents and friends among them. Anti-Semitism in South Africa was to become marked after the rise of Hitlerism, but it was present in subtle forms when Gandhi lived in Johannesburg. The wealthier sections of the Jews shared the racist attitudes of the Rand aristocracy; it was a form of protective identification with the politically powerful Anglo-Saxon strata of British and Boer. If the wealthy Jews wanted to be identified with their economic class on the Rand, what the poor Jews feared most was to become identified with Asiatics or Africans. An example of the attitude of this section of the Jews was furnished by Langermann, a Polish refugee and a member of the Johannesburg Municipal Council in 1905. The Works Committee suggested that a by-law be passed whereby " every Native, holding a cycle permit and riding a cycle within the municipal area, should wear on his left arm, in a conspicuous position, a numbered badge which shall be issued to him, together with his permit."[342] Langermann not only strongly supported the proposal but also demanded that the badge should be worn in front. Langermann's explanation that this " was absolutely necessary to distinguish a native from the white man "[343] produced some amusement among the other members. These other members,

[340] *Collected Works*, II, p. 79.
[341] Marquard, *op. cit.*, pp. 218-219.
[342] *Collected Works*, IV, p. 345.
[343] *Collected Works*, IV, p. 345.

with names like Mackie, Niven, Rockey and Pim, could afford to laugh as they had no fear, as did some of the swarthy Jews, of being mistaken for a native. Gandhi was naturally shocked by Langermann's desire to pin the Star of David on the breasts of native cyclists. In his editorial on the subject in *Indian Opinion*, Gandhi went straight to *The Merchant of Venice* for his title—" Does a Kaffir feel? " In this editorial, Gandhi wrote, " Mr. Langermann is never slow in protesting against the persecution of his co-religionists in Russia. May not a Native ask the question— has he no feelings? "[344]

In between the wealthy and the poor Jews there was a middle section of professional men and women who were liberal and cultured in their outlook. These Jews played a prominent role in Johannesburg in encouraging art and education. Interested in a number of movements like Zionism, Theosophy and Vegetarianism, they were cosmopolitan and enlightened. It was from among this group that Gandhi found some of his closest friends and supporters outside the Indian community. It is interesting that each of the three major Jewish groups in Johannesburg supplied Gandhi with a close collaborator. Henry S. L. Polak was a British Jew whom Gandhi first met in a Vegetarian Restaurant. Polak became a law apprentice under Gandhi and lived as a member of his family. When Gandhi's family moved to the Phoenix Settlement, the Polaks provided him with a home and stimulating conversation. Hermann Kallenbach was a German Jew and a wealthy architect very close to Gandhi. The Tolstoy Farm was made possible by Kallenbach's generosity. Sonja Schlesin, a sixteen-year-old Russian Jewess, joined Gandhi as his personal secretary. Gandhi relied greatly on her youthful ability and entrusted her with the finances of the

---

[344] *Ibid.*, IV, p. 347; see also pp. 352-353.

Passive Resistance Movement. Both Polak and Kallenbach were arrested during the course of the last Passive Resistance struggle.

Quite early in his career, Gandhi had seen a similarity between the position of the Indians and the Jews, many of whom had come to South Africa as humble pedlars like Indian hawkers. He used many images in his writings and speeches linking the Indians and the Jews. In the *Green Pamphlet* he wrote, " Sufferance is, really and sincerely, the badge of the Indians in South Africa, especially in Natal."[345] Gandhi was glad when *The Times* compared the Indian " locations " to Jewish ghettos ;[346] he found the analogy useful in his arguments against this policy of segregation. In Johannesburg, he developed a considerable interest in the Jews and their problems. He came to know of Zionism and acquired an interest in Max Nordau's writings. The presence of Russian and Polish Jews gave him a knowledge of the problems of ethnic minorities in other countries. Gandhi quoted with approval Sir Lepel Griffin's comparison of the treatment of the Indians in South Africa with the hardships of the Jews in the Russian Empire.[347] In 1905, Gandhi wrote a comparative study of the Indian National Congress and Russian Zemstvos.[348] His interest in Russia derived from the Jews was further stimulated by the Russo-Japanese War.[349]

There are three particularly interesting examples of the close parallels that Gandhi quoted between the Indians and the Jews. In 1904, Gandhi discovered the almost identical manner in which Jews and Indians could be described in South Africa. He drew attention to the report of the Cape

---

[345] *Collected Works*, II, p. 8.
[346] *Ibid.*, III, p. 68.
[347] *Collected Works*, III, p. 375.
[348] *Ibid.*, IV, pp. 343-344.
[349] *Ibid.*, IV, pp. 466-467.

immigration authorities which described Russian Jews as
" unsatisfactory in most important respects, being ill-provided,
indifferently educated, unable to speak or understand any
language but Yiddish, of inferior physique, often dirty in
their habits, persons and clothing, and most unreliable in
their statements."[350] This report on Jewish immigrants
read exactly like a description of Indians in a petition of the
Pretoria Chamber of Commerce objecting to their presence
as merchants and hawkers in the Transvaal. Back in India
in the 1920's, the Mahatma drew a parallel between the use
of Yiddish by the Jews and the need to use the mother tongue
as the medium of instruction in India. Commending the
development of Yiddish, Gandhi wrote, " Even the Jews
could not satisfy the soul's yearning through the many foreign
tongues of which they are masters; nor did the learned
few among them wish to tax the masses of the Jewish
population with having to learn a foreign tongue before
they could realize their dignity."[351] The third interesting
parallel Gandhi drew was the nemesis he thought the Jews
and Indians had brought upon themselves by their exclusiveness. He attributed the sufferings of the Jews to their self-
regarding conception of themselves as a chosen people and
the treatment of Indians overseas to the caste system, based
on a distinction between Aryan and non-Aryan, of their
homeland.[352]

Three powerful businessmen who were strongly opposed
to the Indian merchants were H. R. Abercrombie,
E. F. Bourke and R. K. Loveday. Bourke and Loveday
were more open in their opposition. They organized the
Anti-Asiatic National Convention of 1904. Gandhi
commented at length in *Indian Opinion* on the proceedings

---

[350] *Ibid.*, IV, p. 180.
[351] *Speeches*, p. 307.
[352] *Autobiography*, p. 350.

of this racist convention, which met in the Opera House at Pretoria.[353]

The poor white in the Transvaal, like the white worker in Natal, was the victim of the white employer's preference for coloured labour. Yet it was easier for this frustrated section of the population to work off their anger against the Indians and Africans rather than the Rand lords. The deplorable conditions under which they lived in Johannesburg made them insecure and fearful of being submerged by the Africans. Many of these poverty-stricken people were Jews and Syrians who gave vigorous support to the White League of the Rand.[354] Gandhi betrayed a weariness with the constant threats of this White League when he wrote, " We would welcome a hanging or two in the East Rand, should an Indian open a store."[355]

Johannesburg was not only an appropriate setting for the launching of Passive Resistance but also provided a challenging atmosphere for Gandhi's spiritual development. He could only break completely or emerge victorious under the terrible sense of strain he experienced. The real drama of Passive Resistance is not in the events which led up to it but in the tremendous changes which took place in Gandhi himself. The very sordidness of the Golden City would impel Gandhi to demonstrate the need for " higher moral consciousness " that Violet Markham would later refer to. Like the Batteries on the Reef, Johannesburg pounded and crushed Gandhi till the true metal of his character emerged. Gandhi had become so transformed that when he entered the Johannesburg Jail in 1908 he was a truly free man.

In Johannesburg where the pursuit of wealth was almost a religious passion, Gandhi chose a life of poverty. In streets

---

[353] *Collected Works*, IV, pp. 300, 302.
[354] *Collected Works*, IV, p. 199.
[355] *Ibid.*, IV, p. 201.

where there was fear in men's eyes, he learned to look death in the face. In a place where the mining compounds were oppressive reminders of the power of Johannesburg to tear men from their homes and render them outcasts, Gandhi broke up his own family only to recreate it in a wider way in the Phoenix Settlement. In a city that denied the brotherhood of man, he learned how to affirm that all men are brothers.

CHAPTER SIX

The Manifesto of the Gandhian Revolution

The Writing of "Hind Swaraj"

A Mahatma often has early visions of his own greatness
before contemporaries probe through to his soul. By the
end of 1903 Gandhi had begun to emerge from the South
African crucible as a striking personality. The thirty-four-
year old barrister had arrived in Durban a decade earlier
as a timid young man. Since that time he had grown and
deepened through his many struggles on behalf of the Indians.
He had read, thought and written so much that he felt like
" a Triton among minnows."[1]

The Gandhi who sailed from Cape Town for London on
June 23, 1909, was even more experienced and mature than
he had been in 1903. The founding of *Indian Opinion* in 1903
was followed the next year by the Phoenix Settlement,
established in a burst of enthusiasm generated by his reading
of Ruskin's *Unto This Last.* 1904 was also the year when
Gandhi battled courageously with the bubonic plague which
broke out in the Indian Location of Johannesburg. He
witnessed another dance of death, in 1906, when he served

---

[1] *Autobiography*, p. 322.

364

as an ambulance worker in the Zulu Rebellion ; the battle-field strangely recalled to his mind both the peace and activity of the Trappist monastery in Natal. His Passive Resistance Movement in the Transvaal, inaugurated on September 11, 1906, was over two years old. He had served two terms in jail in 1908. Painful at first, these prison experiences proved valuable interruptions in a strenuous life enabling him to strengthen his convictions by his reading and meditation.

The Phoenix Settlement had been entrusted to the faithful Kallenbach ; Polak was to go to India to work with Gokhale to make the grievances of the Indians in South Africa better known; Doke was to edit *Indian Opinion*. Gandhi was grateful for the help of his European friends in his absence but, as he paced the deck of the *Kenilworth Castle* with his fellow-deputationist, Sheth Haji Habib, he was restless to return. He had been so immersed in the struggle of the Transvaal Indians that he had not been able to give undivided attention to the plans which had been taking shape for the creation of a Union of South Africa ;[2] but now the Indians were keen that their case should not be overlooked during the negotiations that were to take place in London under Asquith's Liberal Ministry. Gandhi had been in London in 1906 not long after Sir Henry Campbell-Bannerman had assumed office. He had met the Prime Minister, Lord Elgin, then Secretary of State for the Colonies, and Mr. Morley, Secretary of State for India. This visit, however, was even more important for it was essential to safeguard in advance the position of the Indians suffering under the Black Act if the Imperial Government was going to transfer power to South Africa.

J. X. Merriman, Prime Minister of the Cape and leader of the South African Party, was on board the same ship.

---

[2] See J. Van Heerden, *Closer Union Movement* 1902-1910: *A Bibliography*, (Cape Town, University of Cape Town, 1953).

General Botha and General Smuts were also on their way to London. Sheth Haji Habib, also a native of Porbandar, spoke very little English. Gandhi and the Meman merchant talked in Gujarathi, and all their thoughts were centered on the struggle in the Transvaal. Gandhi's mood is reflected in a letter he wrote : " Truth to tell, I rather prefer jail life than a first class cabin in this steamer... Alas! I cannot pray here with the same depth, earnestness and devotion."[3] He was so full of South Africa that little did he suspect that when he set foot in England his thoughts would be powerfully turned in the direction of Home Rule for India. Annie Besant, who would put forward the demand for Indian Home Rule, was in London that summer.

There could be no doubt that Gandhi was already an outstanding figure in 1909. Early that year the first of many biographies appeared in London, this one by his friend the Baptist minister, Joseph Doke. H. S. L. Polak, arriving in India in August, handed over his monograph on Gandhi to G. A. Natesan, the Madras publisher, one of the earliest to recognize Gandhi's services to the indentured labourers, the majority of whom were Tamil. Polak's brief biography which appeared in September made Gandhi better known to the Indian public.[4] The many ideas germinating in Gandhi's mind, however, had not yet fused into a logical whole. Christianity and Theosophy, the *Bhagavad Gita* and the Sermon on the Mount, the *Yoga Sutras* of Patanjali and the writings of Ruskin and Tolstoy, Vegetarianism and the Nature Cure Theories of Adolf Just and Louis Kuhne— a host of deep influences were among the elements contributing to the strong spiritual ferment within him. Only a spark was needed to touch off the blaze that would give

---

[3] D. G. Tendulkar, *Mahatma: Life of Mohandas Karamchand Gandhi,* (Bombay, V. K. Jhaveri and D. G. Tendulkar, 1951).

[4] H. S. L. Polak, *Mahatma Gandhi*, (Madras, G. A. Natesan, 1931).

coherence to his thinking. That vital spark was provided by his encounter with the Indian anarchists in London in the summer of 1909 ; a very different breed of men from the Bengali *bhadralog* and Parsi lawyers he had met at the Congress session in Calcutta in December 1901, these revolutionaries brought Gandhi up to date on the Indian situation and fired his imagination as it had never been fired before.

When Gandhi reached London on July 3rd, he found the atmosphere electric among the Indian residents. Only two days earlier the patriotic, but misguided, young revolutionary, Madanlal Dhingra, angered by the heavy sentence (transportation for life) inflicted on V. D. Savarkar's younger brother, Ganesh, for writing nationalist songs, had shot Sir Curzon-Wylie outside the Indian Institute. Dr. Lalkaka, a Parsi, met the same fate in trying to save the victim. A few hours later Gandhi began to drink in the new, turbulent spirit that was animating a younger generation of Indians on whose lips were the names of Tilak and Savarkar, Arabindo Ghosh and Bepin Chandra Pal, Har Dayal and Lajpat Rai.

Gandhi was both shocked and profoundly stirred as he met and talked with the Indians in London. In 1909, Gandhi was no weakling whose stomach was likely to turn at the thought of blood. There is a curious, but little noted episode which Gandhi recorded about his student days in London. When torn by doubts and anxieties about his legal career, he was advised to meet Mr. Frederick Pincott, a worthy Conservative with a genuine affection for Indian students. " I can never forget that interview," he wrote. Among the books Mr. Pincott asked him to read " to understand human nature " was Kaye and Malleson's *History of the Mutiny*. " I could not read Kaye and Malleson's volumes in England," Gandhi recalled, " but I did so in South Africa, as I had made a point of reading them at the first opportunity."[5]

---

[5] *Autobiography*, pp. 107-108.

We have no way of knowing what impression the younger Gandhi received from those scenes of cruelty and horror, with their lesson of what hatred and bitterness can do to both sides in a racial conflict. However, he was soon to see in real life what he had read on the printed page. During the Boer War, in the firing lines as a stretcher-bearer, he saw at first hand the havoc that modern warfare wreaks on the bodies of men. Polak even concludes that it was the South African War that completed Gandhi's maturity.[6] The Zulu rebellion from April to July of 1906, which saw him tending the lacerated bodies of the hapless Zulus, completed his education in the school of violence. Gandhi's pacifism was born, not simply of religious sentiment, whether Eastern or Western, but also of a compassion aroused by close and personal intimacy with the cruelty of war.

In the summer of 1909, Gandhi knew more about the realities of armed conflicts than any of the passionate revolutionaries who talked to him so earnestly. Yet he could not help being impressed by their manliness. The lesson was never lost on Gandhi. Earlier he had lovingly translated the last scenes in the life of Socrates from the *Phaedo* into Gujarathi. It was a composite image that was in his mind— that of the brave young man in the dock and the wise old Greek calmly drinking the cup of hemlock—when he wrote in *Hind Swaraj* : " Who is the true warrior—he who keeps death always as a bosom friend, or he who controls the death of others ? "[7] A satyagrahi would need all the courage of a Khudiram Bose or a Madanlal Dhingra, but not their lethal weapons.

Lord Acton used to say that the course of history in the nineteenth century was altered twenty-five times by assassination ; Gandhi changed the course of Indian history by

---

[6] Polak, Brailsford and Pethick-Lawrence, *op. cit.*, p. 35.
[7] *Op. cit.*, pp. 59-60.

rejecting the method of assassination. Gandhi returned to India early in 1915. His first public utterance, after the year's silence he had imposed on himself at the wish of the departed Gokhale, was his speech at the inauguration of the University of Benares in 1916. He began with an attack on the appeal for youth of anarchism. Unfortunately Annie Besant, misunderstanding the import of his words, confused the meeting and the country by staging a walk-out ; she was followed by indignant Indian Princes and British officials. Gandhi's message, however, was clear ; he had declared, " I honour the anarchist for his love of the country. I honour him for his bravery in being willing to die for his country ; but I ask him—'Is killing honourable ?' "[8]

Lord Bryce once wrote of the Boers, whom Gandhi admired in some ways, that " they have a slow tenacious intensity like that of a forest fire which smoulders long among the prostrate trunks before it bursts into flames."[9] Gandhi had been smouldering when he came to London that summer ; when he embarked on the *Kildonan Castle* on November 13th, winter had come, but the fire in him had been kept alive by his long discussions with the Indian anarchists. Gandhi had tried to put down the thoughts surging in him in a letter to Lord Ampthill, dated October 9th, from the Westminster Palace Hotel, where he was staying. The British aristocrat (who had written an introduction for Doke's biography the previous August) could not agree with Gandhi, but Ampthill's friendliness and courtesy lingered in his memory.

As Gandhi stood at the rails watching the shores of England recede, the exciting experiences of the crowded weeks in London flashed through his mind—Dhingra...Mrs. Pankhurst and Mrs. Despord, the leaders of the Suffragette Movement

---

[8] M. K. Gandhi, *To the Students*, (Ahmedabad, Navajivan Press, 1949), p. 20.
[9] *Op. cit.*, p. 482.

whose activities had interested him...the gay, lunch-time parties in his hotel room with the velvet cloth on his central table thrown aside to make room for newspapers, piles of oranges, apples, bananas, grapes and a big bag of unshelled peanuts...the picture of himself in his mirror, all dressed up in the Edwardian style with a starched shirt and collar, waistcoat and tailcoat, as he set off to interview some British political dignitary.[10]

And yet, what had it all amounted to? He had met Joseph Chamberlain in South Africa in 1902, and had learned not to expect too much from a Unionist Ministry. The great Liberal victory at the end of 1905 had filled him with hope even as it had encouraged Gokhale in India, but now his mood was more disillusioned. The Liberals, anxious for the goodwill of the Boers, were not prepared to press the Indian issue. His interviews with Lord Morley, Lord Crewe and several other British politicians and journalists had proved useless. " The more I see of them, the more I am tired of calling on all persons considered to be great. It is all a thankless, fruitless job...Far better to go to jail and suffer," he wrote.[11] Hardly anyone in London seemed concerned about the fate of the Indians in South Africa.

Gandhi's mission had been a failure but his mind refused to admit defeat. At this moment inspiration suddenly seized him. He hurried to the warm lounge, pulled out some of the ship's stationery and began to write like one possessed. " I wrote. .," he said, " only when I could hold myself no longer."[12] Ten days later he had covered 275 sheets with 30,000 Gujarathi words, using his left hand when his right became numb to write the last forty pages. Only three lines

---

[10] Tendulkar, *op. cit.*, I, p. 123.
[11] *Ibid.*, I, p. 123.
[12] P. Gandhi, *op. cit.*, p. 87.

were scratched out and a word changed here and there.[13] There had been a volcano inside him and his thoughts flowed onto the pages like molten lava, hot and vaporous, liquid and moving, but potentially as hard and adamantine as Porbandar stone.

Gandhi had celebrated his fortieth birthday that autumn. When he finished *Hind Swaraj* he had created a landscape which reflected those forty years—a volcanic landscape of jagged contours and harsh colours—softened only by the steady light of Truth as he had felt, experienced and practised it in an age of clashing civilizations. On that same voyage back to Cape Town he wrote an introduction to Tolstoy's *Letter to a Hindu* which he had previously translated into Gujarathi.[14] Tolstoy had been much in his mind that summer. He met Aylmer Maude who was popularising Tolstoy in England, and three days before he sailed, he wrote his first letter to Tolstoy. The philosophy of non-violence which was the bedrock of all his thinking in *Hind Swaraj* became a bond of sympathy between Gandhi and Tolstoy.

Despite the two biographies published in 1909, Gandhi would continue to be comparatively unknown outside South Africa and India. However, he was now sufficiently famous in India for his name to be proposed for President of the Congress in 1909 by the Bengal Provincial Committee. Gokhale's speeches in the closing months of 1909, undoubtedly stimulated by first-hand accounts of Polak who had arrived in India in August, are filled with an awareness of the fact that Gandhi was no ordinary man. However it was Tolstoy who had the most prophetic insight into Gandhi's future. A few weeks before his death, Tolstoy wrote Gandhi a long letter in which he said, "...your activity in the Transvaal, as

---

[13] *Ibid.*, p. 87.
[14] Polak, Brailsford and Pethick-Lawrence, *op. cit.*, p. 74.

it seems to us at this end of the world, is the most essential work, the most important of all the work being done in the world, wherein not only the nations of the Christians, but of all the world will unavoidably take part."[15] The letter went astray, and when it eventually reached Gandhi, he read it with sadness for Tolstoy was already dead. Lord Morley's *Recollections*, published in 1917, contain no references to the deputationist from South Africa ; he remembered Dhingra but had forgotten Gandhi.

Hind Swaraj attracted little attention when it appeared in serial form in *Indian Opinion* in 1910. The Gujarathi version was published in book form in India the same year. It was promptly proscribed by the Government of Bombay in March. Nine years later, Gandhi, back in India, launched his non-violent struggle, and *Hind Swaraj* was sold in the streets of Bombay in defiance of the ban. It had become the manifesto of the Gandhian Revolution.

Could the values of Indian civilization be combined with these Graeco-Roman, Western values of politics and patriotism? Dhingra had given his answer in a flaming Hindu nationalism ; a year later, Arabindo gave his by retiring from politics into the seclusion of his Ashram in Pondicherry. Gandhi stood midway between the two ; the smoking gun in Dhingra's hand seemed to him a betrayal of Indian spiritual values, but Sri Arabindo's retreat from the battlefield seemed an attempt to escape from inescapable problems.

Was it possible to live the full ascetic life of the *karmayogi* and still interpret his duties in terms of political conflict ? This was the daring idea that suggested itself to Gandhi as, indeed, it had also to Bal Gangadhar Tilak in his interpretation of the *Gita* as a gospel of " Energism." But it was in Gandhi,

---

[15] Tendulkar, *op. cit.*, I, p. 150.

rather than in Tilak, that the challenge of the West met one of its most tremendous responses as the *karmayogi* and the politician fused to produce a baffling but extraordinary man and leader. Swami Vivekananda had conceived the same idea in terms of the *karmayogi* and the social worker—a blend of the Franciscan and Dominican ideals. Gandhi outdared all his predecessors by taking the ideal in the direction of the Jesuits. Professor Catlin rightly compares *Hind Swaraj* to *The Spiritual Exercises of Ignatius Loyola*.[16]

Throughout *Hind Swaraj* one feels that politics plays a subsidiary role as it was to do throughout the rest of Gandhi's life, though he became one of the best known political figures of the twentieth century. This curious ambivalence produced by the blending of the saint and the politician struck the two Nehrus when they met Gandhi when he finally returned to India. Motilal preferred the manliness to the saintliness in Gandhi. In his introduction to *Current Thoughts*, a selection of Gandhi's writings, he said, " I have heard of saints and supermen, but have never had the pleasure of meeting them, and must confess to a feeling of scepticism about their real existence. I believe in men and things manly."[17] Jawaharlal, meeting him for the first time at the Congress Session of 1916, recorded his impression thus : " All of us admired him for his heroic fight in South Africa, but he seemed very distant and different and unpolitical to many of us young men."[18]

In his message to the special " *Hind Swaraj* Number " of *The Aryan Path* published in September, 1938, Gandhi, after reaffirming his faith in the views he expressed in 1909, referred

---

[16] George Catlin, *In the Path of Mahatma Gandhi*, (Chicago, Henry Regenery Co., 1959), p. 150.

[17] Quoted by Frank Moraes in *Jawaharlal Nehru: A Biography*, (New York, Macmillan, 1956) , p. 6.

[18] *Ibid.*, p. 4.

to " the opinion of a dear friend, who alas! is no more, that it was the production of a fool." Mahadev Desai informs us that the friend was Gokhale to whom Gandhi had shown *Hind Swaraj* when he visited South Africa in 1912. Gokhale " thought it so crude and hastily conceived that he prophesied that Gandhiji himself would destroy it after spending a year in India."[19] Gokhale was such a careful and thoughtful writer that his reaction to the many crudities with which *Hind Swaraj* was littered is understandable enough. When Gandhi twitted Gokhale once about the length of time he took over the writing of a simple letter the reply he got was : " I will think about it and consider the central idea. I will next deliberate as to the language suited to the subject and then set to write. If everyone did as I do, what a huge saving of time there would be. And the nation would be saved from the avalanche of half-baked ideas which now threatens to overwhelm her."[20]

Gandhi's reactions to the political events of the first decade of this century in India are concentrated in the first four chapters of *Hind Swaraj*, and were the obvious results of his conversations with the Indian anarchists in London. Though Gandhi himself nowhere mentions any of these anarchists by name, Asaf Ali, who later became the first Indian ambassador to the United States (1947—1948), provided some useful clues to their identity in his account of his meeting with Gandhi in September, 1909 : " In a quiet corner of Bayswater, London, one Nazimuddin maintained a restaurant of Indian cuisine which catered for Indian students and non-Indian visitors. It was there that a publicly subscribed Dussehra dinner was held to honour and hear Mr. Gandhi. I, like most of the other freshers, was just a callow youth who had barely been able to pick up his bearings. Among the

---

[19] *Hind Swaraj*, p. 12.
[20] *Satyagraha in South Africa*, pp. 249-250.

Indian student community there were many budding speakers and would-be leaders of today, by far the most arresting personality of whom was Vinayak Damodar Savarkar. Around him had been built a flaming ring of violent revolutionarism, and he presided over a galaxy of young revolutionaries of the India House of the late Shyamji Krishnavarma. As far as I can recollect, it was Savarkar's group who had organized the Dussehra dinner, with Mr. B. C. Pal in the chair and Mr. M. K. Gandhi as the chief guest of honour."[21]

Asaf Ali then described how Gandhi, like the one hundred and fifty dinner guests, was dressed in the conventional evening dress of the period consisting of " a well-cut swallow-tail coat and a white waistcoat and bow in the Bond Street style of the day."[22] When Gandhi rose to speak after he had been introduced by B. C. Pal with his stentorian voice, the guests could hardly hear him. " To the best of my recollection," said Asaf Ali, " Gandhiji's voice and speech were no different then from what they were afterwards—calm, unemotional, simple, and devoid of rhetoric."[23] The young revolutionaries at the dinner were unimpressed though they greeted the end of Gandhi's speech with polite applause.

Gandhi knew of Shyamji Krishnavarma's activities in England even prior to 1905, as he had been receiving copies of *The Indian Sociologist*.[24] The object of this journal edited by Krishnavarma was to spread the teachings of Herbert Spencer. In 1909 Savarkar published his book on the Mutiny entitled *The Indian War of Independence of* 1857; he was arrested in 1910 and sent to the Andamans. When he returned to India, Savarkar became the founder of the

---

[21] *Reminiscences of Gandhiji*, p. 17.
[22] *Ibid.*, p. 17.
[23] *Reminiscences of Gandhiji*, p. 17.
[24] *Collected Works*, IV, p. 458.

Hindu Mahasabha. It is interesting that the advocate of violence and the prophet of non-violence should have met and argued with each other in London that summer. One wonders whether Gandhi met Har Dayal ; that brilliant but erratic man would also have struck fire in him. Lajpat Rai had been in London in 1905 and again in 1908 ; his influence on the young revolutionaries there was considerable. Many of the views Gandhi encountered among the anarchists found expression in Lajpat Rai's *Young India* published in America in 1916.

It was fortunate that Gandhi met the Indian anarchists in London in 1909, because it put him in touch with the " New Nationalism "—so different from the earlier Anglicised, middle class outlook of the Indian National Congress—which was born during the first decade of the twentieth century. Gandhi, who was to give to the last phase of the Indian national struggle the colour of his own character and outlook, was stimulated by his meeting with the Indian revolutionaries to formulate his ideas and organize them into a coherent work in *Hind Swaraj*.

The Contents of "Hind Swaraj"

Hind Swaraj consists of twenty brief chapters which can be divided, for the purpose of study, into five sections. Chapters I to III form the first section, which is a discussion of the political situation in India in 1909 ; they indicate the position Gandhi took in his arguments with the Indian anarchists in London in the summer of that year. He pleaded for a patient understanding of Gokhale and the Moderates in this year of the Morley-Minto Reforms (which he indirectly referred to later only in connection with the Muslims); he urged that " to treat the Congress as an institution inimical to our growth as a nation would disable us from using that body."[25] He

---

[25] *Hind Swaraj*, p. 17.

then went on to show, however, in his discussion of the Partition of Bengal, that he had certain sympathies for the Extremists. It can be demonstrated that what the Paris Commune was for Marx, the Partition of Bengal was for Gandhi; he combined the tactics employed by the Bengalis in the Anti-Partition campaign with the techniques of Satyagraha he had evolved and tested in South Africa. This section ends with an appraisal of the meaning of " Discontent and Unrest,"—words very much in vogue in describing the Indian situation at that time. It is here the reader begins to feel that Gandhi's approach became strangely unpolitical. The language he employed is that of *ascesis*—the ancient Indian doctrine of the Awakening, associated with Buddhism.[26] Like the Buddha's sermon in the Deer Park at Sarnath after he achieved enlightenment, *Hind Swaraj* was the significant declaration of a man who had found his mission in life. An important part of Gandhi's mission was to teach that political freedom without the moral awakening of each individual member of the nation would be of no avail.

This theme is developed further in the second section comprising chapters IV to XIII, in which Gandhi explained what he understood by *Swaraj*. The term " Hindvi Swarajya" had been used by Shivaji in his correspondence[27] and was popularized by Tilak, who declared in 1905, " *Swaraj* is my birthright and I will have it." In 1906, when excitement was running high over the Partition of Bengal, Dadhabai Naoroji, the President of the Congress session that year, declared that *Swaraj* was to be the political goal of India, and in 1909 B. C. Pal was editing a journal in London called *Swaraj*. No one, however, was very clear as to the exact

---

[26] See J. Evola, *The Doctrine of The Awakening* (trans.), H. E. Musson, (London, Luzac & Co., 1951).

[27] Surendra Nath Sen, *Military System of The Marathas*, (Calcutta, The Book Company Ltd., 1928), p. 24, fn. 50.

meaning of *Swaraj*. The Moderates interpreted it in constitutional terms while the Extremists used the language of Hindu revivalism ; neither side imagined its meaning absolute independence from Britain. The Moderates thought in terms of responsible government on the Canadian or South African model ; the Extremists, inspired by the Irish agitation, spoke of Home Rule. In 1916, Tilak, the leader of the Extremists, gave his support to Annie Besant's Home Rule League.

In *Hind Swaraj* Gandhi set out to show both Moderates and Extremists that " what you call *Swaraj* is not truly *Swaraj*."[28] Yet his own interpretation of *Swaraj* was closer to the Hindu revivalism of the Extremists and repudiated the constitutionalism of the Moderates. It is interesting to compare Gandhi's feeling that parliamentary democracy was not suited to India with the views of Lord Morley (whose speeches were widely read by Indians) on the same subject. Their views are almost identical and in certain respects both were aware of dangerous implications for the future of Hindu-Muslim relations. Morley and Gandhi agreed that the parliamentary system did not suit the genius of Indian civilization with its stabilized pluralism. Gandhi, however, parted company with Morley when, as a philosophical anarchist, he rejected both democracy and the state.

In chapter VII Gandhi asked " Why was India lost ? " and gave an answer that closely follows the line taken by Sir John Seeley's *Expansion of England* which he had read.[29] Gandhi accepted Seeley's contention that British rule was made possible by Indian support, " The sword is entirely useless for holding India. We alone keep them (the British)." Gandhi agreed with Seeley only in order to apply the lesson

---

[28] *Hind Swaraj*, p. 17.
[29] *Collected Works*, III, p. 383.

learned from Thoreau, William Lloyd Garrison and Tolstoy. That lesson was that the withdrawal of Indian support for the British would bring on the collapse of their rule. It is here that Gandhi made his sweeping condemnation of "modern civilization," attacking railways, lawyers and doctors. Gandhi's rejection of middle class leadership affords an interesting parallel with Lord Dufferin's notion that the British should not entrust power to such a "microscopic minority."

In many ways these are the most absorbing chapters in the booklet. Gandhi's Hindu revivalism had blended with an anarchism derived from Western sources as a result of his experience in South Africa. The insight of the historian here must be reinforced by the sympathetic understanding of the cultural anthropologist and sociologist in order to interpret adequately the whole of this section, which ends with the affirmation that "it behoves every lover of India to cling to the old Indian civilization even as a child clings to the mother's breast."[30]

In the third section comprising chapters XIV to XVII, Gandhi discussed the ways in which India could become free, and developed his concept of passive resistance or Satyagraha. In the chapter entitled "Italy and India" we have an example of how Gandhi constantly used the bifocal lenses of Hinduism and anarchism to interpret ideas and experiences in *Hind Swaraj.*

The same type of reasoning he used in Chapter VII leads Gandhi to criticize Cavour, Garibaldi and Victor Emmanuel, while espousing the cause of Mazzini. The existence of certain affinities between India and Italy had long been recognized when Gandhi took up the question in *Hind Swaraj.* The influence of the *Risorgimento* in general and of Mazzini

---

[30] *Hind Swaraj*, p. 46.

in particular on the development of Indian nationalism is a study in itself. In 1875, Surendranath Bannerjee and Ananda Mohan Bose organized a Students' Association in Calcutta; one of Surendranath's favourite lectures to the members was " The Life of Mazzini."[31] Mazzini, with his passionate devotion to the ideal of a united Italy, had inspired the minds of English-educated Bengalis. Mazzini's works and studies of his life were also available in many Indian languages.

Gandhi's approach to the *Risorgimento* had little of the romanticism which coloured Nehru's account of the unification of Italy in his *Glimpses of World History*.[32] While a schoolboy at Harrow, Nehru filled himself " with the joy and anguish of the struggle " by reading the story " in three books by Trevelyan—*Garibaldi and the Fight for the Roman Republic, Garibaldi and the Thousand*, and *Garibaldi and the Making of Italy*."[33] Nehru's graphic sketch of this period in Italian history also acknowledges the glow of inspiration he received in reading the poetry of Byron, Swinburne, Meredith, and Elizabeth Barrett Browning extolling Italy.

What appealed to Gandhi in Mazzini's *Duties of Man* was his teaching that " every man must learn how to rule himself."[34] *Swaraj* means " self-rule "; the term, however, had been used by Shivaji to denote Hindu as opposed to Muslim rule. Gandhi read Mazzini's " self-rule " into *Swaraj* which he interpreted in terms of Hindu ethics. Gandhi would have agreed with Morley's verdict on Mazzini that " his was the moral genius that spiritualized politics, and gave a new soul to public duty in citizens and nations."[35] But

---

[31] P. Griffiths, *op. cit.*, p. 262.

[32] J. Nehru, *Glimpses of World History*, (London, Lindsay Drummond Ltd., 1942) pp. 507-510.

[33] *Glimpses of World History*, p. 510.

[34] *Hind Swaraj*, p. 48.

[35] Morley, *Recollections*, I, p. 75.

Gandhi's anarchist predilections were also at work in his estimate of Mazzini. He admired those visionary qualities in Mazzini which Carlyle feared most in the man he was proud to claim as a friend.[36] In this respect, Gandhi's attitude was similar to that of most of Mazzini's Indian admirers—an attitude which stemmed from the fact that there is a basic problem common to the history of both India and Italy. This problem was canvassed by Professor d'Entreves, in his inaugural lecture in Oxford in 1947, entitled *Reflections on the History of Italy*.[37] He pointed out that the major problem of Italian history is that it " sorely lacks a central motive around which the infinite variety of its details can be brought into order and unity..."[38] Professor d'Entreves then discussed Croce's contention that " it must be admitted as evident that the unified history of Italy can begin only with 1860." There were strong reactions to Croce's statement because " for one thing, the assertion that Italy could not claim a distinctive history until the establishment of an Italian State embracing and uniting all Italians, had an unpleasantly Hegelian flavour, which seemed to endorse the Fascist doctrine that only in the State and through the State could a people assert its personality." Yet the fact that the Italian people had " managed to survive through so many centuries " clearly indicated that " the unity of Italian history could be provided by the continuity of their national consciousness." Therefore, Italians have had a natural tendency to fall back on the idea of a nation as " a spiritual unit " transcending political and racial differences.[39]

Indians, confronted by the lack of a central motive which

---

[36] Julian Symons, *Thomas Carlyle*, (London, Gollancz, 1952), pp. 170-173.
[37] A. P. d'Entreves, *Reflections on the History of Italy*, (Oxford, The Clarendon Press, 1947).
[38] *Reflections on the History of Italy*, p. 6.
[39] *Ibid.*, pp. 7-8.

would contribute to order and unity, reacted precisely as many Italians did. An Indian claiming that the unity of India really begins with the imposition of British rule over the whole country would be accused, even as Croce was, of being unpatriotic. Further, to associate the emergence of India with the state raised the problem of how that political institution could express the personality of a people so divided by culture and religion. Therefore, as in Italy, the myth of an ancient unity rooted in an enduring national consciousness based on Hindu culture became a necessary element in modern Indian nationalism. This partly explains why Gandhi rejected the state in *Hind Swaraj*, preferring the concept of a nation as " a spiritual unit " capable of transcending religious and cultural differences. It is the permeation of the present " secular " state by this still surviving " spiritual " outlook that makes for a certain political ineptness—in dealing with the problem of minorities, for example.

Gandhi expressed an antipathy for Cavour, but his own career showed him to be capable of emulating that statesman. In supporting the British in the Boer War and World War I, Gandhi followed a line of expedient reasoning not very different from that of Cavour in his justification of Italy's participation in the Crimean War. Thus, the statesman and the anarchist frequently conflicted in Gandhi's political outlook.

One other interesting coincidence should be mentioned in connection with Gandhi and Mazzini. In chapter I, Gandhi mentioned the expression " Young India," which was popular in India at that time and owed its origin to the " Young Italy " movement of Mazzini. *Young India*, a phrase in vogue among the Extremists, was the title of Lajpat Rai's book published in America in 1916. When Gandhi became the Editor of *Young India*, its title would have more significance for him than for most of his readers not so aware of the attraction Mazzini had both for nineteenth century India and for the Extremists in the decades before the Great War.

The discussion of Italian history is the prelude to Gandhi's exposition of Satyagraha in chapters XVI and XVII. He had launched his Satyagraha movement in the Transvaal in 1906, and these chapters reflect the concrete, personal decisions involved in his leadership of that struggle—such as his vows of poverty and chastity.

The fourth section consists of two chapters, XVIII and XIX, and contains Gandhi's application of the principle of *Swadeshi* to education and industry. The examples of his father and the Indian merchants in South Africa, men of common sense and ability in spite of their little schooling, inclined Gandhi towards an Aristotelian preference for experience and habit rather than academic learning. He deplored the teaching of English to Indians, suggested that Hindi should be the national language, and touched briefly on the problem of religious education. The middle-classes had been enslaved by English learning and culture; " through our slavery the nation has been enslaved, and it will be free with our freedom," Gandhi argued. " Only the fringe of the ocean," he said, " has been polluted and it is those within the fringe who alone need cleansing."[40] The youth of nineteen, who had risked pollution by crossing the ocean, seemed to repent his action at forty: " In order to restore India to its pristine condition, we have to return to it." Gandhi was returning—returning to the influences of childhood and boyhood, returning to the illusion of a lost innocence. To recover these things only one effort was required, " and that is to drive out Western civilization. All else will follow."[41]

Chapter XIX, entitled " Machinery," contains the germ of the Gandhian theory of economics. Gandhi was not unique in his reaction to industrialism. There are echoes going back to the Luddites and the embattled American

---

[40] *Hind Swaraj*, p. 67.
[41] *Hind Swaraj*, p. 67.

farmers in the nineteenth century in his assertion that " machinery is the chief symbol of modern civilization; it represents a great sin."[42] Now added to these echoes is Gandhi's experience of industrialism in Kathiawad and South Africa. The chapter contains a significant reference to " the ancient and sacred handlooms."[43] When Gandhi wrote *Hind Swaraj* he had not even seen an Indian *charka*, but he was already feeling his way towards the question:

> When Adam delved and Eve span
> Who was then the gentleman?

The spinning wheel was more to Gandhi than a means of regenerating cottage industries or emphasizing the dignity of manual labour. " But in the case of the spinning wheel something else was added, something beyond economics, sociology or politics, a kind of mystical concentration upon service as a form (and to him the pervading form) of religion,"[44] claimed Vincent Sheean, with insight into Gandhi's spirit.

The last chapter of *Hind Swaraj* forms a fifth and concluding section in which Gandhi addressed himself to the Extremists and the Moderates, the British and the Nation. He asked the Extremists to eschew violence and the Moderates to cease petitioning the British because he felt such action to be derogatory and a confession of inferiority. He appealed to both to accept his concept of *Swaraj* and to submerge their differences. Gandhi always distinguished between petitioning one's opponent as an inferior and appealing to him as an equal. His appeal to the British, however, is an interesting example of the lack of communication which may exist between the value systems of two cultures, particularly when one is

---

[42] *Ibid.*, p. 68.
[43] *Ibid.*, p. 69.
[44] *Op. cit.*, p. 159.

dominant. " We hold the civilization that you support to be
the reverse of civilization. We consider our civilization to be
far superior to yours,"[45] Gandhi asserted and asked the
British to give up eating beef for the sake of the Hindus and
bacon and ham for the sake of the Muslims. In spite of its
sometimes ludicrous tone, Gandhi's appeal is filled with those
generous impulses which he never ceased to feel for the British.
The appeal to the Nation, consisting of nineteen points, sets
forth many of the ideals which Gandhi made part of the
discipline of the satyagrahi in his Civil Disobedience campaigns
in India. He concluded, " I have endeavoured to explain it
(Swaraj) as I understand it, and my conscience testifies that
my life henceforth is dedicated to its attainment."[46]

The Significance of " Hind Swaraj "

Gandhi's flair for journalism went back to his student days
in London when he had written articles for *The Vegetarian* in
1891.[47] Soon after he established himself in Pretoria in 1893,
he began wielding his pen on behalf of the Indian community
in a series of letters to editors of numerous English newspapers
in all the four Colonies of South Africa. In addition to
numerous petitions, he wrote three pamphlets setting forth
the grievances of the Indians: *The Indian Franchise — An Open
Letter* in 1894, *An Appeal to Every Briton in South Africa* in 1895
and, in 1897, *The Green Pamphlet*, which was widely distributed
in India.[48] In 1904, he founded and edited *Indian Opinion*,
which became the propaganda organ of Indians in South

---

[45] *Hind Swaraj*, p. 72.
[46] *Ibid.*, p. 76.
[47] *Collected Works*, I, pp. 24-52.
[48] *Collected Works*, I, pp. 142-163, 256-286. *The Green Pamphlet* w   ·:tled
The Grievances of the British Indians in South Africa. It derived its
its green cover. *Collected Works*, II, pp. 1-52. (The frontispiece
photostat copy of the green cover.)

Africa in their struggle for civil rights.[49] But *Indian Home Rule* (or *Hind Swaraj* as it came to be known later), written in November 1909, was the first real blast from the Triton's horn announcing the emergence of a man of strange genius from the sea of history.

Since Gandhi was assassinated in 1948, we are still too near him in time for an adequate perspective—or a fresh interpretation of the kind of man he was and the role he played in Indian history. Yet any new attempt at reinterpretation must at least take into account *Hind Swaraj*; for it is one of the most important landmarks to guide the historian in his exploration of the life and thought of Gandhi. Written only a few weeks after his fortieth birthday, *Hind Swaraj* shows all the influence of the formative years in Gandhi's career. So many of Gandhi's experiences are reflected in the pages of *Hind Swaraj* and it is so rich in allusions to contemporary events, that the reader is reminded of G. M. Young's comment on Tennyson: " Only an Historical Index of his works could make clear at how many points he touched the passing interests of his day."[50] A detailed analysis of the formative influences which led to *Hind Swaraj* provides a corrective to the ethnocentric apotheosis which began to obscure the historical Gandhi even in his life-time. Any student of Gandhi should be aware of Vincent Sheean's pithy comment that " in a country which, like India, has been all too inclined to excessive deification, the aseptic value of Gandhi's sanity could not be more clearly shown."[51] The influences injected by three countries—India, England, South Africa—and the impulses radiated by three continents—Asia, Europe, Africa—clash and fuse in the pages of *Hind Swaraj*. Gandhi's image of himself as a Triton has an uncanny accuracy; his genius rests

---

[49] *Satyagraha in South Africa,* pp. 141-144.
[50] *Op. cit.,* p. 243.
[51] *Op. cit.,* p. 301.

on his attempt to surmount the tidal waves raised by the swift-flowing currents of history in a period of conflicting civilizations and cultures.

Hind Swaraj, born of his vast and varied experience, shows that Gandhi was not simply a great Indian, but also one of the great men of a new era of internationalism. As George Catlin puts it, " He is the nationalist and also the internationalist, the leader of the Indian masses who yet never for one moment ceased to be the citizen of the world."[52] Gandhi's universal appeal lay not only in his ability to represent the moral elements of Indian culture, but also in his capacity to speak to the heart of a torn and divided world. Roy Walker points out that Gandhi "is not so much an Eastern as a universal figure, his philosophy and example are essentially valid for all humanity or none because they work at a level deeper than that at which cultural, social and technological variations are of conclusive importance."[53] George C. Marshall once said that " Mahatma Gandhi was the spokesman for the conscience of mankind."[54] There are three lines from Walt Whitman's *Salut Au Monde*! which could have come from Gandhi:

> My Spirit has pass'd in compassion and
> determination around the whole earth;
> I have look'd for equals and lovers, and
> found them ready for me in all lands;
> I think some divine rapport has
> equalized me with them.[55]

---

[52] *Op. cit.*, p. 150.

[53] "Gandhi's Message to the World," *Viswa Bharati Quarterly*, Gandhi Memorial Peace Number, (ed. Khitis Roy), 1949, p. 54.

[54] Quoted by Louis Fischer in *Gandhi: His Life and Message for the World*, (New York, The New American Library, 1954), p. 8.

[55] Walt Whitman, *Leaves of Grass*, 8th ed., (New York, Rhinehart & Co.,1959), p. 121. For a comparison between Gandhi and Whitman see Bijoylal Chatterjee, " Gandhi and the New World," in *The Modern Review*, January 1957.

Hind Swaraj shows that as early as 1909 Gandhi was ready for the moment when the finger of destiny would beckon him to assume the leadership of the Indian national movement. South Africa had prepared and matured him, and out of his experiences there he had developed the diverse roles he would play in India: nationalist critic of Western civilization, reformer and consolidator of Hindu society, champion of Hindu-Muslim unity, friend of Christians and opponent of Christian missions, amateur physician, dietician, educator and economist. When on July 18, 1914, Gandhi left South Africa, never to return, he spoke of the great wrench he felt in leaving the land " where I had passed twenty-one years of my life sharing to the full in the sweets and bitters of human experience, and where I had realized my vocation in life." [56]

Hind Swaraj looks toward India, but it was written by a man who had hardly lived there since he left as a young student in 1888. Since Gandhi was the first Indian barrister to arrive in South Africa, the small uprooted Indian community welcomed him gladly. The task of uniting Indians on this foreign soil, away from their own country and in the midst of a hostile white population, was comparatively easy; the different roles Gandhi played did not conflict with one another. His greatness is that he succeeded so largely in transferring his South African experience to the vast and infinitely more complicated setting of India. But his failures must also be attributed in part to the sheer impossibility of repeating, on the enormous Indian scale, either his success in uniting Hindu and Muslim in South Africa or the peaceful nature of the Satyagraha campaign in the Transvaal. Nor could Gandhi succeed in being all things to all men amid the deep-seated prejudices and tensions of India's various communities. His

---

[56] *Satyagraha in South Africa*, p. 338.

diverse roles in India conflicted dangerously and caused great bewilderment among his people; the greatest Hindu of this age was killed by a fanatic convinced that the Mahatma was betraying Hinduism by his defence of the Muslims.

The most positive evidence of the importance of *Hind Swaraj* for an understanding of Gandhi comes from Gandhi himself. He had an almost touching attachment to this early expression of his ideas and ideals; he even asserted rather naively, " It is a book which can be put into the hands of a child."[57] Writing in *Young India* in January, 1921, under the caption " A Word of Explanation," he reaffirmed his faith in *Hind Swaraj*, while regretfully admitting that " the only part of the programme which is now being carried out is that of non-violence."[58] In his message for the special number devoted to *Hind Swaraj* by the *Aryan Path* in September, 1938, he said, " I might change the language here and there, if I had to rewrite the booklet. But after the stormy thirty years through which I have since passed, I have nothing to make me alter the views expounded in it."[59] *Hind Swaraj* was written on a steamer, and Gandhi rather wistfully regarded his booklet as a boat carrying the precious cargo of his early ideals. He had been steadfast in his determination to keep them bright and steady despite the waves that constantly buffeted them in " the stormy sea of Indian political life."[60] One of the books recommended by Gandhi for further study of his ideas in *Hind Swaraj* is *The Defence and Death of Socrates from Plato*. The reference is to a Gujarathi booklet written by Gandhi himself and containing a translation of the last scenes in the life of Socrates from the *Phaedo*. It may be said that what *The Republic* was for Plato, *Hind Swaraj* was destined to

---

[57] *Hind Swaraj*, p. 11.
[58] *Ibid.*, p. 12.
[59] *Ibid.*, p. 12.
[60] *Autobiography*, p. 471.

become for Gandhi. The aging Gandhi echoed the melancholy of the aging Plato when he sadly admitted that the ideals of *Hind Swaraj* remained unattainable because " it requires a higher simplicity and renunciation than the people are today prepared for."[61] Gandhi, like Plato, never fully resigned himself to the fact that human institutions, at best, can only imperfectly partake of the ideal.

Hind Swaraj was written on board the *Kildonan Castle* which brought him back from his futile mission to London in November, 1909; it appeared in serialized form in the Gujarathi editions of *Indian Opinion* from the end of that same year. Copies of the Gujarathi version of *Hind Swaraj* found their way to India at this time when the British Government was tightening its regulations relating to the publication of books suspected of being seditious. In a statement on January 25, 1910, the Viceroy, Lord Minto, announced that " the preaching of a revolutionary press " would no longer be tolerated, and that the Government had decided " to bridle literary licence."[62] *Hind Swaraj* attracted the attention of the Criminal Investigation Department and was proscribed in March of the same year by the Government of Bombay using the fresh powers it had acquired through the Indian Press Act of 1910. Interestingly enough, V. D. Savarkar's *The Indian War of Independence of 1857*[63] and Har Dayal's *Social Conquest of the Hindu Race* were proscribed at the same time.

Gandhi returned to India early in 1915. Four years later *Hind Swaraj* sprang into prominence in a dramatic fashion. In 1919, an English edition of *Hind Swaraj*, which Gandhi had translated himself, was selling in the streets of Bombay in defiance of the ban. Actually, he had made this translation

---

[61] *Autobiography*, p. 471.

[62] M.V. Krishna Rao, *The Growth of Indian Liberalism in the Nineteenth Century*, (Mysore, H. Venkataramiah & Sons, 1951), p. 114.

[63] (London, 1909). Published anonymously " by an Indian Nationalist."

for the benefit of his friend, Hermann Kallenbach, the Johannesburg architect. The idea of selling *Hind Swaraj* as a revolutionary pamphlet, however, emanated from two students of Wilson College in Bombay, Sankarlal Banker and Omar Sobhani. They had come under Gandhi's influence when the Satyagraha Sabha was formed during the agitation against the Rowlatt Act of 1919. In narrating the episode to Gandhi's associate, Kaka Kalelkar, Banker said, " Gandhiji's book had already been banned by the Government—while he was still in South Africa...So I got thousands of copies printed, and started selling them openly in the streets of Bombay. They sold like hot cakes and at fancy prices." [64]

In the 1920's, *Hind Swaraj* became a textbook for students seeking to understand the ideas and techniques of Gandhi's Civil Disobedience campaigns. Romain Rolland, while recognising that it went counter to Western ideals, called it " the gospel of heroic love." [65] John Haynes Holmes felt that *Hind Swaraj* had " unique value as the only book written as such by the Mahatma." [66] Lord Lothian advocated the booklet as the best means of understanding the " germinal ideas " of Gandhi. [67] Mahadev Desai called on all Indians to study this " seminal book " before deciding whether Gandhi's principles should be accepted or rejected. [68] However, a provocative booklet like *Hind Swaraj* was bound to have critics as well as admirers. It was also during this decade that Gandhi's views in *Hind Swaraj* were most strongly attacked. The Allahabad *Leader* ridiculed his criticism of lawyers, and Lord Ronaldshay, then Governor of Bengal,

---

[64] Kaka Kalelkar, *Stray Glimpses of Bapu*, (Ahmedabad, Navajivan Publishing House, 1950), p. 30.

[65] *Op. cit.*, p. 19.

[66] In his Introduction to Haridas T. Mazumdar (ed.), *Sermon on the Sea*, (Chicago, Universal Publishing Co., 1924), p. 10.

[67] *Hind Swaraj*, p. 9.

[68] *Ibid.*, p. 10.

criticized his conception of Swaraj in the booklet. Gandhi defended himself in *Young India*[69] and reaffirmed his faith in *Hind Swaraj*. Sir Sankaran Nair rejected certain aspects of the booklet in his *Gandhi and Anarchy*.[70] Katherine Mayo made use of *Hind Swaraj* to attack Gandhi in her *Mother India*, a book that gained much notoriety and did a certain amount of harm to Indo-American relations.[71]

The interest in *Hind Swaraj* had largely waned by the 1930's. His ideas had become more familiar and attention was focussed on Gandhi himself and the statements that issued almost daily from his mouth and pen. There was a brief revival of interest in the booklet when Madame Sophia Wadia, editor at the time of the *Aryan Path*, brought out a special number of that journal devoted to *Hind Swaraj*. Appearing as it did in the same month as the September Crisis of 1938, the special number gathered the views on *Hind Swaraj* of a group of distinguished British thinkers. The purpose of this examination was to see if it had any relevance for a world on the verge of another great war. Articles were contributed by Professor Soddy, G. D. H. Cole, C. Delisle Burns, J. Middleton Murry, J. D. Beresford, Hugh Fausset, Claude Houghton, Gerald

---

[69] " Courts and Schools," August, 1920; " On the Wrong Track," December 8, 1920.

[70] (Madras, Tagore & Co., 1922).

[71] Katherine Mayo, *Mother India*, (New York, Harcourt, Brace & Co., 1927). The book ran into four editions in 1927. The furore it caused and the rejoinders it elicited in the form of articles and books form a study in itself. The following are some of the replies it evoked: Lajpatrai, *Unhappy India*, (Calcutta, 1928); Natarajan K., *Miss Mayo's Mother India: A Rejoinder*, (Madras, Natesan, 1930); Dhan Gopal Mukerji, *A Son of Mother India Answers*, (Dutton, 1928); Ranga Iyer, *Father India: A Reply to Mother India*, (New York, Louis Carrier & Co., 1928); Syam Sundar Chakravarty, *My Mother's Picture*, (Calcutta, Sanjiboni Book Depot, n.d.); Harry H. Field, *After Mother India*, (New York, Harcourt, Brace & Co., 1929); Ernest Wood, *An Englishman Defends Mother India*, (Madras, Ganesh & Co., 1929).

G. A. Natesan with Gandhiji, Kasturba and Muhammed Yakub Hasan,

Heard and Irene Rathbone. Though the special number of the *Aryan Path* did not attract much attention at the time, it makes poignant reading, more as an expression of what some sensitive men and women felt on the eve of an impending tragedy, rather than for any new light it throws on *Hind Swaraj*.[72]

The booklet continued to find an occasional student. In 1947, George Catlin, who carried *Hind Swaraj* around with him during his travels in India, felt that " it resembled more the Spiritual Exercises of St. Ignatius Loyola than a party pamphlet of National Independence."[73] Its importance has been taken for granted and statements like Roy Walker's that there has been nothing essentially new in Gandhi's thoughts after he wrote *Hind Swaraj* have never been seriously examined.[74] So far as it can be ascertained, no student has yet subjected this little volume to a thorough and careful scrutiny.

There is nothing surprising in the fact that the earliest publishers of *Hind Swaraj*—G. A. Natesan and Co., S. Ganesan and Co., Ganesh and Co.,—were all from Madras. Gandhi's name became dear to South Indians first, since they were naturally interested in the fate of indentured labourers in South Africa. *Hind Swaraj* crossed the Atlantic when an American edition, prepared by H. D. Mazumdar and entitled *Sermon on the Sea*, was published in Chicago in 1924.[75] Later the publication of *Hind Swaraj* was taken over by the Navajivan Publishing House, which has printed several editions, the latest dated 1958. Fortunately, and thanks to the foresight of Chhaganlal Gandhi, the manuscript copy of the booklet is preserved by the Navajivan Publishing House. During the

---

[72] Mahadev Desai reviewed the Special " Hind Swaraj Number " of the *Aryan Path* in the *Harijan* of December 11, 1938.

[73] Catlin, *op. cit.*, p. 215.

[74] *Mahatma Gandhi: Essays and Reflections*, (ed.), S. Radhakrishnan, (Bombay, Jaico Books, 1956), p. 356.

[75] See footnote 22, *supra*.

agitation against the Rowlatt Act, Chhaganlal had the manuscript sent to him in India from the Phoenix Settlement.[76]

Hind Swaraj, despite its many readers, has not achieved anything like the popularity of Gandhi's *Autobiography*, perhaps because the booklet needs a good deal of annotation before it can be properly understood. " As a matter of fact," Gandhi once asserted, " my writings should be cremated with my body. What I have done will endure, not what I have said and written."[77] It would have been a pity if his wishes had been carried out, especially in regard to *Hind Swaraj*, for this prophetic pamphlet contains the seeds of both the greatness and the weakness, the reason and the irrationality, of the last phase of the Indian national struggle. Gandhi's thoughts in *Hind Swaraj* mirror both the triumph and the tragedy of the remarkable man who dominated the political scene in India for nearly thirty turbulent years. The 30,000 words of *Hind Swaraj* give us some indication of the wide sweep of Gandhi's various interests; they contain nearly all his ideas which took root in the political soil of India and branched out into every aspect of Indian life.

The Style of "Hind Swaraj"

A generation accustomed to the image of Gandhi in the 1930's and 1940's as " Bapu," the kindly father-figure, will read *Hind Swaraj* with a slight sense of shock. It was written in Gujarathi for a comparatively uneducated Indian community in South Africa half a century ago. Even the reader who realizes this cannot help feeling rather appalled, at first, by many examples of what seems like Gandhi's ability to

---

[76] P. Gandhi, *op. cit.*, p. 87.

[77] Quoted by Rajendra Prasad in his Introduction to Pyarelal's *Mahatma Gandhi, The Last Phase*, 2 Vols., (Ahmedabad, Navajivan Publishing House, 1956), I, p. 8.

" thrust into a bare primitive "—to use a phrase once employed by C. F. Andrews about him in another connection.[78] At first sight the booklet appears to be littered with simple or crude analogies—" parliament is simply a costly toy of the nation "—or vast, oversimplified generalizations—" the tendency of the Indian civilization is to elevate the moral being, that of the Western civilization is to propagate immorality "; one even finds examples of unthinking naivete—" Hospitals are institutions for propagating sin "—and an occasional lapse from good taste such as the reference to the Mother of Parliaments as a " prostitute," the one word Gandhi was willing to withdraw " in deference to a lady friend," Mrs. Annie Besant.[79]

" Language at best is but a poor vehicle for expressing one's thoughts in full," said Gandhi.[80] We must remember that his English style in *Hind Swaraj* was largely derived from his reading in a particular genre of nineteenth century literature expressive of moral indignation. *Hind Swaraj* contains many echoes of Carlyle, Ruskin, Tolstoy and the other writers Gandhi lists in the first appendix. A familiarity with these recommended books is essential for understanding both the style and content of the booklet. *Hind Swaraj* can be compared to Tolstoy's *The Kreutzer Sonata*, of which Janko Lavrin wrote, " Deliberately bald and rugged, it keeps only to the essentials, and so outspokenly too, as to stun the reader."[81] If Gandhi's language is sometimes harsh and painful in its moral indignation, it is also taut and earnest in its high purpose. His

---

[78] The phrase was employed about Gandhi, but in another connection, by C. F. Andrews in a letter to Tagore, dated January 26, 1931. Quoted by Banarsidas Chaturvedi and Marjorie Sykes in *Charles Freer Andrews*, (London, Allen & Unwin, 1949), p. 176.

[79] *Hind Swaraj*, pp. 11, 23, 42, 46.

[80] *Selected Writings of Mahatma Gandhi*, (ed.), Ronald Duncan, (London, Faber & Faber Ltd., 1951), p. 63.

[81] Janko Lavrin, *Tolstoy: An Approach*, (New York, Macmillan, 1946), p. 125.

style often has a simplicity and directness which is refreshing when contrasted, for example, with the rather florid, rhetorical exuberances of nineteenth century Congress politicians like Surendranath Bannerjee. Perhaps he also owes some of his bluntness and directness to Gokhale, his first political tutor, whose forthright Maratha speech Gandhi has preserved for us in his memoirs.[82] Gandhi had a gift for recording conversations in a vivid and dramatic manner. He had a fondness for simple illustrations, of which there are some examples in *Hind Swaraj*. Chapter XVI, entitled " Brute Force," contains a long and involved illustration based on the analogy of a householder and an armed robber.

A good example of the imagery in *Hind Swaraj* is the following: " A man with a stick suddenly came face to face with a lion and instinctively raised his weapon in self-defence. The man saw that he had only prated about fearlessness when there was none in him. That moment he dropped the stick and found himself free from all fear."[83] While it is true that lions abound in South Africa, and a few survive in the Gir Forest in India, it was not " the Untia Bagh—the lion of the Gir—fiercest and strongest of its race "[84] that leaps to the reader's mind, but another lion, the British lion.

Gandhi could also turn a phrase that would haunt the mind of any sensitive reader. It was Catlin who noted one of the most expressive sentences in the whole of *Hind Swaraj*: " That nation is great which rests its head upon death as its pillow."[85] H. S. L. Polak drew attention to another haunting phrase in the booklet: " Who is the true warrior—he who keeps death

---

[82] *Satyagraha in South Africa*, pp. 259-270; *Autobiography*, pp. 285-291, 435-437 457-459. See also M. K. Gandhi, *Gokhale, My Political Guru*, (Ahmedabad, Navajivan Publishing House, 1955).

[83] *Hind Swaraj*, p. 63.

[84] James Douglas, *Bombay and Western India*, (London, Simpson Low & Co., 1893), p. 294.

[85] *Op. cit.*, p. 229.

always as a bosom friend?"[86] Gandhi was thinking of Swami Nagappan, a Satyagrahi who had died in July, 1909, of whom he later wrote that he had " embraced death for his country's sake as he would embrace a friend."[87]

Gandhi's Gujarathi excerpts from the *Phaedo* entitled *The Defence and Death of Socrates* (also proscribed by the Bombay Government in 1910) influenced not only the contents of *Hind Swaraj*, but also its form. The form of *Hind Swaraj* was inspired by Madame Blavatsky's *Key to Theosophy*, which he read as a student in London, and the Platonic dialogues. Gandhi had experimented with the conversational form in *Indian Opinion*, probably because he found the method of the Platonic dialogues useful in dealing with readers who were not highly educated. When Gandhi made a " gentleman's agreement " with General Smuts in 1905, he wrote many articles for *Indian Opinion* explaining the terms of the settlement including an imaginary dialogue. " I believe that this dialogue produced a good effect," he said, throwing further light on why he chose the dialogue form when he wrote *Hind Swaraj*.[88] *Hind Swaraj* is in the form of a dialogue between " editor " and " reader; " the former plays a Socratic role while the latter voices all the views and opinions that Gandhi was intent on demolishing. The procedure is reminiscent of Mrs. B. and poor Caroline in Jane Marcet's *Conversations on Political Economy*.[89] It is fascinating to watch Gandhi at work through the dialectic processes of *Hind Swaraj* where " he really opens his mind and allows the interviewer to see how the machine inside works."[90]

---

[86] *Mahatma Gandhi: Essays and Reflections*, p. 180.

[87] *Satyagraha in South Africa*, p. 224.

[88] *Satyagraha in South Africa*, p. 186.

[89] The book was translated by Viswanath Narayan Mandlik into Marathi in the 1850's.

[90] Louis Fischer, *A Week with Gandhi*, (New York, Duell, Sloan & Pearce, 1942), p. 116.

The voice of the editor in *Hind Swaraj* was the voice that the young Nehru heard for the first time in February, 1919. " But this voice was somehow different from the others," wrote Nehru, recalling the impression it made on him, " it was quiet and low, and yet it could be heard above the shouting of the multitude; it was soft and gentle, and yet there was something grim and frightening in it; every word used was full of meaning and seemed to carry a deadly earnestness. Behind the language of peace and friendship there was power and the quivering shadow of action and determination not to submit to a wrong."[91]

To read *Hind Swaraj* for the first time is to hear the voice that Nehru describes, and like him we will " not know quite what to make of it " even if we are " thrilled."[92] Gandhi confessed that Gokhale used to laugh at some of his ideas in *Hind Swaraj* and say: " After you have stayed a year in India, your views will correct themselves."[93] It is easy to laugh at some of Gandhi's statements in *Hind Swaraj* because, in the words of Louis Fischer, " His brain has no blue pencil; he doesn't censor himself."[94] What Gandhi said about the *Gita* can be aptly applied to *Hind Swaraj*: " Because a poet puts a particular truth before the world, it does not necessarily follow that he had known or worked out all its great consequences, or that having done so, he is able to express them fully."[95]

The Cultural Conflict in "Hind Swaraj"

Matthew Arnold died in April, 1888, the year that Gandhi arrived in London. It may be said that the forty years of

[91] Jawaharlal Nehru, *Glimpses of World History*, (New York, John Day, 1944), p. 713.

[92] Jawaharlal Nehru, p. 713.

[93] *Autobiography*, p. 467.

[94] *A Week with Gandhi*, p. 118.

[95] Duncan, *Selected Writings of Mahatma Gandhi*, p. 40.

Gandhi's life from 1869 to 1909 were concerned with the two problems dealt with by Arnold in his essay on *Culture and Anarchy*.[96] The thought of *Hind Swaraj* is structured around two poles—the positive pole of Gandhi's affirmation of the superiority of Indian culture and the development of his concept of Satyagraha, and the negative pole of his rejection of Western industrial civilization reinforced by his anarchism. These two poles, like an anode and a cathode, served to electrify the political life of India after 1920. However, the problem remained of how to provide new sources of energy when the Gandhian battery ran dry. The polarisation in Gandhi's thought made it difficult to create a stable synthesis from Eastern and Western culture from which an adequate conception of freedom and unity could emerge.

As we have seen, Gandhi's life until the writing of *Hind Swaraj* is a study in acculturation,[97] the unfolding story of his response and reaction to Western culture and civilization. In her study of St. Augustine, Rebecca West says, " The child must be naughty and run away, get dirty and hungry and tired, and know the terror of loneliness and a pricking conscience; and then be suddenly picked up and carried home again to be washed and fed and rocked to rest, to be loved and

---

[96] His brother, William Delafield Arnold (1828-1859), was Director of Public Instruction in the Punjab.

[97] *The American Anthropologist* contains a very helpful article entitled " Acculturation: An Exploratory Formulation," LVI, (December, 1954), p. 473-500. For the problems of acculturation see also the following books and articles: H. G. Barrett, *Innovation: The Basis of Cultural Change*, (New York, McGraw Hill, 1953); R. L. Beals, "Urbanism, Urbanization and Acculturation," *The American Anthropologist*, LIII, (January-March, 1951), 1-10; E. M. Bruner, " Cultural Transmission and Cultural Change," *The South West Journal of Anthropology*, XII, (Summer, 1956), 191-199; L. W. Doob, " An Introduction to the Psychology of Acculturation," *Journal of Social Psychology*, XLV, (May 1957), 143-160; J. Gillin, " Acquired Drives in Culture Contact," *The American Anthropologist*, XLIV, (October-December, 1942), 545-554; and A. I. Hallowell, *Culture and Experience*, (Philadelphia, University of Pennsylvania Press, 1955).

forgiven. So the mystic sees himself as the child of God,. playing truant in time and the finite, being brought home to the eternal and the infinite."[98] Gandhi was happily free from the ritualism and irrational mysticism associated with some Indian cults. For example, he was rather appalled by the animal sacrifice he witnessed at Kalighat in 1901.[99] His robust common sense saved him from religious excesses;. he had a practical mysticism akin to that of the Quakers. The reader of *Hind Swaraj* will be struck by how well the symbolism and imagery employed by Rebecca West illuminate Gandhi's relation to Indian civilization as his mother-culture. To return to the " unpolluted," " uncontaminated," " uncorrupted " Indian matrix, to float on the timeless " ocean " in its " pristine purity," " to cling to the old Indian civilization even as a child clings to the mother's breast "—these are the meaningful symbols in Gandhi's experience.[100]

As a critic of Western culture, Gandhi's desire to " return to India " confirmed in him the feeling that he had played the truant, that he had dirtied and soiled himself. This idea was almost an obsession with him and explained " the pricking conscience " involved in his exposure to the " disease " of modern civilization. For instance, Gandhi, who often needed dental attention in his early manhood, had what looked like " gold coverings shining on two of his lower teeth "[101] in South Africa. Though the coverings were actually made of platinum, Gandhi's later refusal to wear false teeth seems like a form of atonement. The very thought of gold had become anathema to the Mahatma who had seen the seamy side of Johannesburg, a city built on reefs rich with the yellow metal.

Gandhi's anarchism was rooted in his cultural revulsion

---

[98] *Saint Augustine*, (London, Thomas Nelson & Sons Ltd., 1938), p. 111.
[99] *Autobiography*, p. 289.
[100] *Hind Swaraj*, p. 46.
[101] P. Gandhi, *op. cit.*, p. 44.

400

against modern civilization. Reacting strongly against the type of anarchy he saw as a boy in Kathiawad, as a student in London and as a lawyer in South Africa, he idealized forms of benevolent, anarchistic government which he believed had existed in India in the past. His anarchist ideal was *Ramrajya,* a form of polity derived from the *Mahabharata.* No man can divest himself of his present; Gandhi's "return to India" could never be complete or innocent of modern influences. His Hinduism could never be the mere repetition of his childhood. The Indian peasant was for Gandhi what the Scholar Gypsy had been for Matthew Arnold. Yet, despite his idealization of the past, Gandhi, like Arnold, could criticize contemporary Indian national culture with a view to improving it both socially and morally.

Any sensitive individual caught in an acculturative situation always finds within himself elements of both response and reaction; in different periods of his life, however, one or the other may prevail, depending on the circumstances of his existence. Gandhi himself wrote, "I have gone through deep self-introspection, searched myself through and through, and examined and analysed every psychological situation.... But at every step I have carried out the process of acceptance or rejection and acted accordingly."[102]

We have viewed this process of acculturation at work in Gandhi in two periods of response followed by two periods of reaction until he discovered himself in *Hind Swaraj.* The first period of response in Gandhi's life was from his birth (in 1869) to 1888 in India; the second was from 1888 to 1896 in England and South Africa. Gandhi told Louis Fischer, "I was a loyalist in respect to the British and then I became a rebel. I was a loyalist until 1896."[103] His shattering

---

[102] *Autobiography,* p. 5.
[103] *A Week with Gandhi,* p. 97.

experiences in South Africa destroyed the mood of response. His new outlook developed in a period of gradual, imperceptible reaction starting vaguely in 1893 and continuing to 1901, and a period of self-conscious reaction dating from his return to South Africa, after a brief interlude in India in 1902. This phase came to a head in 1909 and resulted in the writing of *Hind Swaraj*.

Gandhi's *Autobiography*, which Glorney Bolton felt to be " as remarkable as the *Confessions* of Rousseau,"[104] is invaluable for deciphering his psychological development;[105] it may, however, be both a help and a hindrance. Many biographers use this book to focus attention on the inner turmoil and ferment of his life in such a way that Gandhi emerges as a powerful force moulding history. The same attention is not always paid to the economic, social and historical forces that moulded Gandhi. As Ben Halpern puts it, " It is the task of the historian...on the basis of his theory of the underlying nature of history, to interpret both events and the rationalizations of the actors in them in the light of the deeper dynamics of history."[106] To depend on his autobiographical writings without attempting to examine the totality of the situations through which he lived is an inadequate approach which lacks objectivity. Gandhi himself showed an awareness of this fact when he wrote, " I understand more clearly today what I read long ago about the inadequacy of all auto-biography as history."[107]

The attempt to reconstruct the different kinds of *milieus* in which he was immersed as a youth in Kathiawad, as a student

---

[104] *The Tragedy of Gandhi*, (London, George Allen & Unwin Ltd., 1934), p. 2.

[105] See James S. Plant, *Personality and the Cultural Pattern*, (New York, The Commonwealth Fund, 1948).

[106] Ben Halpern, " History, Sociology, and Contemporary Area Studies, " *The American Journal of Sociology*, LXIII, (July, 1957), 1-10.

[107] *Autobiography*, p. 342.

in London, and as a public figure in South Africa, was vital for a more perceptive understanding of Gandhi's views in *Hind Swaraj*. The study in depth of the period of Gandhi's life from 1869 to 1909 has enabled us, in the conceptual language of David Riesman, to trace how the " outer-directed " youth, steeped in the regional culture of Kathiawad, emerged in *Hind Swaraj* as a powerful " inner-directed " person with drives rooted in—but transcending—the traditional patterns of his inheritance.[108]

Sylvia Thrupp suggests that " the kinds of hypotheses that historians are best fitted to contribute..are those that probe intercultural contacts and historical continuities in search of common origins for recurrent attempted solutions of human quandaries."[109] In this book I have attempted to probe Gandhi's life and thought for "intercultural contacts and historical continuities " during his first forty years in order to uncover the " common origins for recurrent attempted solutions of human quandaries " in the story of his struggles. Gandhi's genius lay in his ability to reinterpret and transform old solutions and methods drawn from the past, as the Indian people, assailed by the human quandaries and perplexities of the twentieth century, sought to preserve their cultural identity and their sense of continuing history.

---

[108] *The Lonely Crowd* and *Faces in the Crowd*, (New Haven, Yale University Press, 1953).
[109] " History and Sociology: New Opportunities for Co-operation," The *American Journal of Sociology* LXIII, (July, 1957), p. 11-16.

BIBLIOGRAPHY

I. Reference Works

Argus Annual and South African Gazetteer, 1895, Johannesburg, Cape Town and Pretoria.

The British Crown and The Indian States. An outline sketch drawn up on behalf of the Standing Committee of the Chamber of Princes. London, 1929.

Brown's " South Africa ": A practical and complete guide for the use of Tourists, Sportsmen, Invalids, and Settlers, Cape Town and Johannesburg, 1893.

Buckland, Charles E., *Dictionary of Indian Biography*, London, 1906.

Capuchin Mission Unit, *India & Its Missions*, London, 1923.

Cross, K. E., *Pretoria: A Bibliography*, Cape Town, 1948.

Descriptive Catalogue of the Secret and Political Department Series 1755–1820, compiled by V. G. Dighe, Bombay, 1954.

Deshpande, P. G., *Gandhiana: A Bibliography of Gandhian Literature,* Ahmedabad, 1948.

Hellman, Ellen and L. Abrahams, eds., *Handbook on Race Relations in South Africa*, London, 1949.

Hunter, W. W., *The Imperial Gazetteer of India*, 9 Vols., London, 1881.

Imperial Gazetteer of India, rev. ed., 26 Vols., Oxford, 1907–1909.

Index to South African Periodicals, issued by The South African Library Association, First Annual Cumulative Volume, 1940, Pretoria, 1941.

Johannesburg's 40th Birthday, Official Souvenir, Johannesburg, 1926.

MacKenzie, W. D., *The Library of South Africa*, Chicago, 1899.

Pictorial Atlas of The History of The Union of South Africa, Pretoria, 1949.

Theal, George M., *Catalogue of Books and Pamphlets, Relating to Africa South of the Zambesi, in the English, Dutch, French and Portuguese Languages*, Cape Town, 1912.

Thornton, Edward, *A Gazetteer of the Territories Under the East India Co.*, London, 1858.

Van Heerden, J., *Closer Union Movement, 1902–1910: A Bibliography*, Cape Town, 1953.

Watson, J. W., ed., *Gazetteer of the Bombay Presidency*, Bombay, 1884.

Who's Who in Natal, Durban, 1933.

II. Primary Sources

Aga Khan, *Memoirs of the Aga Khan*, New York, 1954.

Aitchinson, C. U., *A Collection of Treaties, Engagements and Sunnuds*, 7 Vols., Calcutta, 1896.

Amery, L. S., ed., *The Times History of the War in South Africa 1899–1902*, 7 Vols., London, 1909.

Anderson, Phillip, *The English in Western India*, London, 1856.

Arnold, E., *India Revisited*, London, 1886.

Bayley, Edward Clive, *The Local Muhammadan Dynasties: Gujarat*, in *The History of India as Told by Its Own Historians*, London, 1886.

Beal, Samuel, *Hiuen Tsiang and Valabhi : Buddhist Records of the Western World*, 2 Vols., London, 1906.

Besant, Annie, *The Changing World*, Chicago, 1909.

Bigelow, Poultney, *White Man's Africa*, New York, 1898.

Blavatsky, H. P., *The Key to Theosophy*, London, 1889.

Blunt, Wilfred, *India Under Ripon: A Private Diary*, London, 1909.

Booth, Robert B., *Life and Work in India*, London, 1912.

Brown, John Cave, *Indian Infanticide*, London, 1857.

Bryce, James, *Impressions of South Africa*, 3rd. ed., London, 1899.

Buckland, Charles T., *Sketches of Social Life in India*, London, 1884.

Buist, George, "Kathiawar," *Bombay Quarterly Review*, VII (Jan. 1855).

Carpenter, Edward and E. Maitland, *Vivisection: An Address Given Before the Humanitarian League*, London, 1904.

Chailley, Joseph, *Problems of British India*, London, 1910.

Chapman, Mrs. E. F., *Some Distinguished Indian Women*, London, 1891.

Collier, Price, *The West in The East*, London, 1911.

Colquhoun, A. R., *The Africander Land*, London, 1906.

Conway, Moncure, *My Pilgrimage to the Wisemen of the East*, Boston, 1906.

Cotton, H. J. S., *New India*, London, 1885.

Cumberland, Stuart, *What I Think of South Africa: Its People and Its Politics*, London, 1896.

Dajie, Bhawoo, *An Essay on Female Infanticide*, Bombay, 1847.

Doke, Joseph J., *M. K. Gandhi: An Indian Patriot in South Africa*, London, 1909.

Dosabhai, Edalji, *A History of Gujarat from the Earliest Period to the Present Time*, Ahmedabad, 1894.

Douglas, James, *Bombay and Western India*, London, 1893.

Dufferin and Ava, Marchioness of, *Our Viceregal life in India*, 2 Vols., London, 1890.

Dufferin & Ava, Marquis of, *Speeches Delivered in India*, London, 1890.

Duncan, Ronald, ed., *Selected Writings of Mahatma Gandhi*, London, 1951.

Eybers, G. W., *Select Constitutional Documents Illustrating South African History*, 1795–1910, London, 1918.

Field, Harry A., *After Mother India*, New York, 1929.

The First Hindoo Convert: A memoir of Krishna Pal, a preacher of the Gospel to his countrymen more than 20 years, Philadelphia, 1852.

Fitzpatrick, Sir James P., *The Transvaal From Within*, London, 1899.

Forbes, A. K., *Ras Mala*, 2 Vols., London, 1924.

Forbes, James, *Oriental Memoirs: A Narrative of Seventeen Years Residence in India*, 2 Vols., London, 1854.

Fyfe, H. Hamilton, *South Africa Today*, London, 1911.

Gandhi, M. K., *Bapu's Letters to Mira*, Ahmedabad, 1928.

Gandhi, M. K., *Christian Missions: Their Place in India*, Ahmedabad, 1941.

Gandhi, M. K., *Collected Works of Mahatma Gandhi*, 4 Vols., New Delhi, 1958.

Gandhi, M. K., *Correspondence with the British Government 1942–1944*, Ahmedabad, 1945.

Gandhi, M. K., *From Yerravada Mandir*, Tr. by Valji G. Desai, Ahmedabad, 1933.

Gandhi, M. K., *Gokhale, My Political Guru*, Ahmedabad, 1955.

Gandhi, M. K., *Hind Swaraj or Indian Home Rule*, Ahmedabad, 1946.

Gandhi, M. K., *The Indian States Problem*, Ahmedabad, 1941.

Gandhi, M. K., *Satyagraha in South Africa*, Ahmedabad, 1928.

Gandhi, M. K., *Songs from Prison*, New York, 1934.

Gandhi, M. K., *Speeches and Writings of Mahatma Gandhi*, Madras, 1922.

Gandhi, M. K., *The Story of My Experiments with Truth, Gandhi's Autobiography*, Washington, D. C., 1954.

Gandhi, M. K., *To the Students*, Ahmedabad, 1949.

Gidumal, Dayaram, *Behramji M. Malabari: A Biographical Sketch with an Introduction by Florence Nightingale*, London, 1892.

Gladwin, Francis, Tr., *Ayeen Akbery or The Institute of the Emperor Akbar*, Tr. from the Persian, 3 Vols., Calcutta, 1834.

Great Indian Questions of the Day Series, London and Madras, 1903.

Griffith, M., *India's Princes: Short Life Sketches of the Native Rulers of India*, London, 1894.

Guthrie, Mrs., *Life in Western India*, 2 Vols., London, 1881.

Haggard, H. Rider, *The Days of My Life: An Autobiography*, 2 Vols., London, 1926.

Haggard, H. Rider, *A History of the Transvaal*, London, 1899.

Hart-Synnot, Arthur F., *Letters of Major-General FitzRoy Hart-Synnot*, B. M. Hart-Synnot, ed., London, 1912.

Heber, Reginald, *Narrative of a Journey through the Upper Province of India from Calcutta to Bombay*, 2 Vols., London, 1834.

Holden, William C., *History of the Colony of Natal*, London, 1855.

How to be Happy Though Married, New York, 1886.

Bibliography

Ingram, J. Forsyth, *The Colony of Natal: An Official Illustrated Handbook and Railway Guide*, London, 1895.

Jeffry, R., *The Indian Mission of the Irish Presbyterian Church*, London, 1890.

Jubilee Commemoration at Bombay of the British & Foreign Bible Society, Bombay, 1854.

Kavakaria, R. P., *India: Forty Years of Progress and Reform*, London, 1896.

Keane, A. H., *The Boer States*, London, 1900.

Kingsford, Anna, *Her Health, Beauty and the Toilet*, London, 1886.

Kingsford, Anna, *The Perfect Way in Diet*, London, 1881.

Labour and Other Questions in South Africa: Being Mainly Considerations on the National and Profitable Treatment of the Coloured Races Living There, London, 1903.

Lalchandra, V. D., *Jubilee Paramodika*, Ajmere, 1889.

Latimer, E. W., *Europe in Africa in The Nineteenth Century*, Chicago, 1895.

Lee-Warner, William, *The Native States of India*, London, 1910.

Letters from South Africa: by the Times Special Correspondent, London, 1893.

Lipsett, H. Caldwell, *Lord Curzon in India, 1895–1903*, London, 1903.

Macfayden, W. A., Tr., *The Political Laws of the South African Republic*, London, 1896.

Macnab, F., *On Veldt and Farm*, London, 1897.

Maitland, Edward, *Anna Kingsford: Her Life, Letters, Diary and Work*, 2 Vols., London, 1896.

Malabari, Behramji Merwanji, *Gujarat and the Gujaratis: Pictures of Men and Manners Taken from Life*, Bombay, 1889.

Mann, R. J., *The Colony of Natal*, London, 1859.

Markham, V. R., *The South African Scene*, London, 1913.

Mitchell, J. M., *In Western India*, Edinburgh, 1899.

Moor, Edward, *Hindu Infanticide*, London, 1811.

Morley, James, *Recollections*, 2 Vols., New York, 1917.

Morley, James, *Speeches on Indian Affairs*, Madras, 1917.

Mozoomdar, Pratap Chandra, *The Oriental Christ*, Boston, 1910.

Muller, Max, *India—What can it teach us—A Course of Lectures Delivered Before the University of Cambridge*, London, 1883.

Naoroji, Dadhabhai, *Poverty and Un-British Rule in India*, London, 1901.

Nathan, Manfred, *The South African Commonwealth*, Johannesburg and Cape Town, 1919.

Nazim, Muhammad, *The Life and Times of Sultan Mahmud of Ghazni*, Cambridge, 1931.

Nehru, J., *Nehru on Gandhi, a selection arranged in the order of events, from the writings and speeches of J. Nehru*, New York, 1948.

Noble, M. E., *The Web of Indian Life*, London, 1904.

Nordau, Max, *Degeneration*, Tr. from the 2nd ed. of the German work, 5th ed., New York, 1895.

Olcott, H. S., *Old Diary Leaves: The True Story of The Theosophical Society*, New York and London, 1895.

Parker, Joseph, *The People's Bible: Discourses Upon Holy Scripture*, London, 1889.

Peace, Walter, *Our Colony of Natal*, London, 1883.

Pearson, J. R., *Remarkable Providence and Proofs of Divine Revelation*, London, 1876.

Phillips, Lionel, *Some Recollections*, London, 1925.

Phillips, Lionel, *Transvaal Problems: Some Notes on Current Politics*, London, 1905.

Phillips, Mrs. Lionel, *Some South African Recollections*, London, 1899.

Pillai, G. Parameswaran, *Representative Indians*, London, 1897.

Pratt, A., *The Real South Africa*, Indianapolis, 1914.

Radhakrishnan, S., ed., *Mahatma Gandhi: Essays and Reflections*, Bombay, 1956.

Rajagopalachari, C. and J. C. Kumarappa, eds., *The Nation's Voice*, Ahmedabad, 1947.

Robinson, John, *A Life Time in South Africa*, London, 1900.

Bibliography

Ross, E. Denison, ed., *An Arabic History of Gujarat...by...al-Asafi*, London, 1910.

Ross, E. Denison, ed., *The Travels of Marco Polo*, Tr. by Aldo Ricci, London, 1931.

Salt, H. S., *Animals' Rights Considered in Relation to Social Progress*, London, 1892.

Salt, H. S., *A Plea for Vegetarianism and other Essays*, Manchester, 1886.

Sanderson, Edgar, *Africa in the Nineteenth Century*, London, 1898.

Scidmore, E. R., *Winter India*, New York, 1903.

Shore, Frederick John, *Notes on Indian Affairs*, 2 Vols., London, 1838.

Southey, Rosamund, *Storm and Sunshine in South Africa*, London, 1910.

Tangye, H. Lincoln, *In New South Africa*, London, 1896.

Temple, Richard, *India in 1880*, London, 1881.

Temple, Richard, *Men and Events of My Time in India*, London, 1882.

Theal, George M., *Progress of India in the 19th Century*, London, 1902

Theosophical Movement: A History and a Survey 1875–1925, New York, 1925.

Tod, James, *The Annals and Antiquities of Rajasthan*, 2 Vols., Calcutta, 1894.

Tod, James, *Travels In Western India*, London, 1839.

Wallace, Robert, *The Guicowar and His Relations with the British Government*, Bombay, 1863.

Wells, James, *Across India*, Glasgow, 1901.

Williams, Howard, *The Ethics of Diet: A Catena of Authorities, Deprecatory of the Practice of Flesh-eating*, Manchester, 1883.

Williams, G. F., *The Diamond Mines of South Africa*, New York, 1905.

Wilson, John, *History of the Suppression of Infanticide in Western India*, Bombay, 1855.

Wilson, Sarah, *South African Memoirs*, London, 1909.

Younghusband, F. E., *South Africa of Today*, London, 1898.

III. Secondary Sources

Abercrombie, H. R., *The Secret History of South Africa*, Johannesburg, 1951.

Adams, Brooks, *The Law of Civilization and Decay*, New York, 1955.

Agar-Hamilton, J. A. I., *South Africa*, London, 1934.

Akhilananda, Swami, *The Hindu View of Christ*, New York, 1949.

Alteker, Anant Sadasiv, *A History of Important Ancient Towns and Cities in Gujarat and Kathiawad (From the Earliest Times Down to the Moslem Conquest)*, London, 1922.

Andrews, C. F., *Mahatma Gandhi's Ideas*, New York, 1930.

Appasamy, J. B. *Indians in South Africa*, Bombay, 1943

Application of Psychiatric Insights to Cross-Cultural Communication, Symposium No. 7, New York, 1961.

Bannerjee, A. C., "Lord Minto and the Rajput States," *Journal of Indian History*, XXII (April 1943).

Bannerjee, A. C., *Rajput Studies*, Calcutta, 1944.

Bannerjee, Surendranath, *A Nation in the Making*, London, 1925.

Barnett, H. G., *et al.*, " Acculturation: An Exploratory Formulation; Results of the SSRC Seminar on Acculturation," *American Anthropologist*, LVI (Dec. 1954), 973-1002.

Barnewell, P. J. and A. Toussant, *A Short History of Mauritius*, London, 1949.

Barrett, H. G., *Innovation: A Basis of Cultural Change*, New York, 1953.

Beals, R. L., " Urbanism, Urbanization and Acculturation," *The American Anthropologist*, LIII (January-March 1951), 1-10.

Beauchamp, Joan, *British Imperialism in India*, London, 1934.

Bharsinji, H. H., *Forty Years of the Rajkumar College*, 1870–1910 London, 1911.

Birla, G. D., *In the Shadow of the Mahatma*, Calcutta, 1953.

Bloomfield, Maurice, *The Life and Stories of the Jaina Savior Parcvanatha*, Baltimore, 1919.

Bolitho, Hector, *Jinnah: Creator of Pakistan*, New York, 1955.

Bolton, Glorney, *The Tragedy of Gandhi*, London, 1934.

Bowle, John, *Politics and Opinion in The Nineteenth Century*, New York, 1954.

Bibliography

Boyd, R. H., *Couriers of the Dawn*, Belfast, 1940.

Boyd, R. H., *The Prevailing Word*, Belfast, 1951.

Boyd, R. H., *Trophies for the King*, Belfast, 1950.

Brailsford, H. N., H. Pethick-Lawrence, and H. L. Polak, *Mahatma Gandhi*, London, 1909.

Brinton, Crane, *English Political Thought in The Nineteenth Century*, London, 1954.

Brooks, E. H., *The Color Problems of South Africa*, Lovedale, S. A.,1934.

Brooks, E. H., *The History of Native Policy in South Africa from 1830 to the Present Day*, Cape Town, 1924.

Bruner, E. M., " Cultural Transmissions and Cultural Change," *The Southwest Journal of Anthropology*, XII (Summer 1956), 191-199.

Bullhatchet, Kenneth, *Social Policy and Social Change in Western India*, 1817–1830, London, 1957.

Bulpin, T. V., *The Golden Republic: The Story of the South African Republic from Its Foundation until* 1883, Cape Town, 1957.

Bulpin, T. V., *Storm Over The Transvaal*, Cape Town, 1955.

Burgess, James, and Henry, Cousens, *The Architectural Antiquities of Northern Gujarat*, London and Calcutta, 1903.

Burgess, James, *Report on the Antiquities of Kathiawad and Kachh*, London, 1876.

De Burgh-Edwardes, S. B., *History of Mauritius* (1507–1914), London, 1921.

Burtis, M. E., *Moncure Conway*, New Brunswick, New Jersey, 1952.

Bush, Douglas, ed., *The Selected Poetry of Tennyson*, New York, 1951.

Butler, Clementine, *Pandita Ramabai Saraswati*, New York, 1922.

Butler, Joseph, *The Analogy of Religion*; *Natural and Revealed, to the Constitution and Course of Nature*, London, 1736.

Carrington, C. E., *The British Overseas*, London, 1950.

Catlin, George, *In the Path of Mahatma Gandhi*, Chicago, 1950.

Chakravarty, S. S., *My Mother's Picture*, Calcutta, n.d.

Chatterjee, Bijoylal, " Gandhi and the New World," *The Modern Review*, CI (Jan. 1957), 43-44.

Chaturvedi, B. and M. Sykes, *Charles Freer Andrews*, London, 1949.

Churchill, Winston S., *A History of the English Speaking Peoples*, IV, *The Great Democracies*, New York, 1958.

Commissariat, Manekshah S., *A History of Gujarat*, II, *The Mughal Period*, Bombay, 1957.

Coomaraswamy, Ananda K., and I. B. Horner, ed., *The Living Thoughts of Gotama, The Bhuddha*, Bombay, 1955.

Cousens, Henry, *Somnath and Other Medieval Temples in Kathiawad*, Archaeological Survey of India Imperial Series, XLV, Calcutta, 1931.

Cursons, William E., *Joseph Doke, The Missionary-Hearted*, Johannesburg, 1929.

Davids, T. W. Rhys, ed. and Tr., *The Questions of King Milinda*, Oxford, 1890–1894.

Davie, Maurice R., *World Immigration*, New York, 1936.

Desai, A. R., *Social Background of Indian Nationalism*, Bombay, 1948.

Dikshit, K. N., *Prehistoric Civilization of the Indus Valley*, Madras, 1939.

Dikshitar, R., *Mauryan Policy*, Madras, 1932.

Doob, L. W., " An Introduction to the Psychology of Acculturation," *Journal of Social Psychology*, XLV (May 1957), 143-160.

Draper, J. W., *A History of the Intellectual Development of Europe*, New York, 1863.

Dubois, Cora, *Foreign Students and Higher Education in the United States*, Washington, D. C., 1956.

Duff, Grant J. C., *History of the Marathas*, London, 1921.

Dutt, K. Iswara, " Political Oratory in India," *The March of India*, VIII (April 1956), 7-9; (May 1956), 18-21.

Eaton, Jeanette, *Gandhi: Fighter Without a Sword*, New York, 1950.

Elliot, Him, *The Arabs of Sind*, Vol. 3 of *The History of India as Told By Its Own Historians*, 8 Vols., Cape Town, 1853.

d'Entreves, A. P., *Reflections on the History of Italy*, Oxford, 1947.

Erikson, Erik H., *Young Man Luther: A Study in Psychoanalysis and History*, New York, 1958.

Evans, I. L., *Native Policy on South Africa: An Outline*, London, 1934.

Evola, J., *The Doctrine of the Awakening*, Tr. from the Italian by H. E. Musson, London, 1951.

Ferguson-Davie, C. J., *The Early History of Indians in Natal*, Johannesburg, 1953.

Bibliography

Fischer, Louis, *A Week With Gandhi*, New York, 1942.

Fischer, Louis, *Gandhi: His Life and Message for the World*, New York, 1954.

Fisher, Frederick B., *That Strange Little Brown Man Gandhi*, New York, 1932.

Gandhi, Manubehn, *Bapu My Mother*, Ahmedabad, 1949.

Gandhi, Prabhudas, *My Childhood With Gandhiji*, Ahmedabad, 1957.

George, S. K., *Gandhi's Challenge to Christianity*, Ahmedabad, 1947.

Ghurye, G. S., *Caste and Race in India*, New York, 1932.

Gillin, T., "Acquired Drives in Culture Contact," *The American Anthropologist*, XLIV (October-December 1942), 545-554.

Gooch, G. P., *History of Modern Europe*, 1878–1919, London, 1923.

Griffiths, Sir Perceval Joseph, *The British Impact on India*, London, 1952.

Habib, Mohammed, *Sultan Mahmud of Ghazni*, Bombay, 1927.

Halevy, Elie., *Victorian Years*, Vol. 4 of *A History of the English People in the Nineteenth Century*, "Essay and Chronological Table 1852–95" by R. B. McCallum, London, 1951.

Halifax, Edward F. L. W., "Working with Churchill, Talks with Gandhi and Lady Astor's Parties" *Ladies Home Journal*, LXXIV (January 1957), 154 ff.

Hallowell, A. I., *Culture and Experience*, Philadelphia, 1955.

Halpern, Ben, "History, Sociology and Contemporary Area Studies," *The American Journal of Sociology*, LXIII (July 1957), 1-10.

Handlin, Oscar, ed., *Immigration as a Factor in American History*, Englewood, New Jersey, 1959.

Hardy, P., *Historians of Medieval India*, London, 1960.

Hattersley, Alan F., *Later Annals of Natal*, London, 1938.

Heilbroner, Robert L., The Worldly Philosophers, New York, 1953.

Heras, S. J., Rev. H., *The Conversion Policy of the Jesuits in India, Studies in Indian History of the Indian Historical Research Institute*, No. 8, Bombay, 1933.

Hurwitz, N., *Agriculture in Natal*, 1800–1950, London, 1957.

415

Hutchison, Keith, *The Decline and Fall of British Capitalism*, London, 1951.

Hyatt, S. P., *The Old Transport Road*, London, 1914.

Iyer, Ranga, *Father India: A Reply to Mother India*, New York, 1928.

James, Robert Rhodes, " Charles Stewart Parnell," *History Today*, VII (January 1957), 11-17.

James, William, *The Varieties of Religious Experience*, New York, 1936.

Jhaveri, Mansaplal, " Gujarati Literature," *Contemporary Indian Literature: A Symposium*, Delhi, 1959.

John, Joseph, ed., *Gandhi As Others See Him*, Colombo, 1933.

Kalelkar, Kaka, *Stray Glimpses of Bapu*, Ahmedabad, 1950.

Kalelkar, Kaka, *To A Gandhian Capitalist*, Bombay, 1951.

Khan, Ali Mohammed, *The Political and Statistical History of Gujarat*, Tr. from the Persian by James Bird, London, 1835.

Kincaid, C. A., *Forty-Four Years A Public Servant*, Edinburgh and London, 1934.

Kincaid, C. A., and A. B. Parasnis, *A History of the Maratha People*, 3 Vols., London, 1918.

Kincaid, C. A., *Lakshmibai, Rani of Jhansi*, Bombay, n.d.

Kincaid, C. A., *The Land of ' Ranji ' and ' Duleep '*, Edinburgh and London, 1931.

Kincaid, C. A., *The Outlaws of Kathiawar*, Bombay, n.d.

Kincaid, Dennis, *British Social Life in India*, 1608–1937, London, 1938.

Kipling, Rudyard, *Verse*, New York, 1938.

de Kiewiet, C. W., *British Colonial Policy and the South African Republics*, London, 1929.

de Kiewiet, C. W., *The Imperial Factor in South Africa: A Study in Politics and Economics*, London, 1937.

Konclap, C., *Indians Overseas*, London, 1951.

Krishna Rao, M. V., *The Growth of Indian Liberalism in the Nineteenth Century*, Mysore, 1951.

416

Bibliography

Lajpat Rai, Lala, *Unhappy India*, Calcutta, 1928.

Lambert, Richard D., and M. Bessler, *Indian Students on an American Campus*, Minneapolis, 1956.

Lavater, John Caspar, *Essays on Physiognomy Calculated to Extend the Love of Mankind*, 3 Vols., Tr. by C. Moore, London, 1797.

Lavrin, Janko, *Tolstoy: An Approach*, New York, 1946.

Logan, Frenise A., " The American Civil War: A Major Factor in the Improvement of the Transportation System of Western India " *Journal of Indian History*, XXIII (April 1955), 91-102.

Lovett, H. Verney, *A History of the Indian Nationalist Movement*, London, 1920.

Low, Sidney, *The Indian States and Ruling Princes*, London, 1929.

McCrindle, J. W., ed., *Ancient India as Described by Ptolemy*, Calcutta, 1885.

Macphail, J. M., *Asoka* in *The Heritage of India Series*, Calcutta, 1908.

Majumdar, Asoke Kumar, *Chalukyas of Gujarat*, Bombay, 1956.

Malgonkar, M., *Kanhoji Angrey: Maratha Admiral*, Bombay, 1959.

Malinowski, Bronislaw, *The Dynamics of Culture Change: An Inquiry into Race Relations in Africa*, New Haven, Conn., 1961.

Mandy, C. R., " New Cathay," *The Illustrated Weekly of India*, (August 20, 1960).

Manshardt, Clifford, ed., *The Mahatma and the Missionary*, Chicago, 1949.

Marquard, Leo, *The Peoples and Policies of South Africa*, Cape Town, 1960.

Masani, R. P., *Dadhabhai Naoroji, The Grand Old Man of India*, London, 1939.

Mashruwala, K. G., *Sahajanand Swami*, Ahmedabad, 1923.

Mathews, J. K., *The Techniques of M. K. Gandhi as Religious*, unpublished Ph. D. thesis, Columbia University, 1957.

Mayhew, Arthur, *Christianity and the Government of India... 1600–1920*, London, 1929.

Mayo, Katherine, *Mother India*, New York, 1927.

Mazumdar, Haridas T., ed., *Sermon on the Sea*, Chicago, 1924.

Millin, Sarah G., *The People of South Africa*, London, 1951.

27   **417**

Millin, Sarah G., *Rhodes*, London, 1952.

Moraes, Frank, *Jawaharlal Nehru: A Biography*, New York, 1950.

Morton, Eleanor, *The Women in Gandhi's Life*, New York, 1953.

Mukerji, Dhan Gopal, *A Son of Mother India Answers*, New York, 1928.

Mulji, Karsandas, *History of the Sect of Maharajas, or Vallabhacharyas in Western India*, London, 1865.

Munshi, K. M., *The Early Aryans in Gujarata*, Bombay, 1941.

Munshi, K. M., *The Glory That Was Gujaradesa*, Bombay, 1943.

Munshi, K. M., *Gujarata and Its Literature, A Survey from the Earliest Times*, Foreword by Mahatma Gandhi, London, 1935.

Munshi, K. M., *Somnath: The Shrine Eternal*, Bombay, 1950.

Nair, Pyarelal, *Mahatma Gandhi: The Last Phase*, 2 Vols., Introduction by Rajendra Prasad, Ahmedabad, 1956–1958.

Nanda, B. R., *Mahatma Gandhi*, London, 1958.

Narain, A. K., *The Indo-Greeks*, London, 1957.

Natarajan, K., *Miss Mayo's Mother India: A Rejoinder*, Madras, 1928.

Nehru, Jawaharlal, *Glimpses of World History*, New York, 1944.

Oaten, Edward Farley, *A Sketch of Anglo-Indian Literature*, London, 1908.

O'Brien, R. Barray, *The Life of Charles Stewart Parnell*, 2 Vols., New York, 1898.

Oldfield, Josiah, " Vegetarianism," *Encyclopedia Britannica*, 11th ed., Vol., 27, pp. 967-968, Cambridge, 1911.

Orwell, George, *A Collection of Essays*, Garden City, New York, 1954.

Oxford Book of Modern Verse, W. B. Yeats, ed., New York, 1936.

Oza, Kevalram C., *Reconstruction of Life and Polity in Kathiawar States*, Rajkot, 1946.

Palmer, Mabel, *The History of the Indians in Natal*, London, 1954.

Panikkar, K. M., *Asia and Western Dominance 1498–1945*, New York, 1954.

Panikkar, K. M., *Geographical Factors in Indian History*, Bombay, 1951.

Bibliography

Panikkar, K. M., *Indian States and the Government of India*, London 1932.

Parekh, M. C., *Sri Vallabhacharya*, Rajkot, 1943.

Penrose, Boies, *Sea Fights in the East Indies in the Years* 1602–1639, Cambridge, Mass., 1931.

Pithawala, M. B., "The Gujarat Region and the Parsees: A Historic-geographical Survey," reprinted from *The Journal of the Gujarat Research Society*, VII (April and July 1945), 88-111.

Plant, James, S., *Personality and the Cultural Pattern*, New York, 1948.

Plot, J., *Reconstruction of Life and Polity in Kathiawar States*, Rajkot, 1946.

Polak, H. S. L., *Mahatma Gandhi*, 9th ed., Madras, 1931.

Polak, M. G., *Mr. Gandhi: The Man*, London, 1931.

Polanyi, Karl, *The Great Transformation*, Boston, 1957.

Prabhu, R. K., *This Was Bapu*, Ahmedabad, 1945.

Pyrah, Geoffrey B., *Imperial Policy and South Africa*, 1902–1910, Oxford, 1955.

Prasad, J., "A Comparative Study of Rumours and Reports in Earthquakes," *British Journal of Psychology*, XLI (December 1950), 129-144.

Prasad, Rajendra, *At the Feet of Mahatma Gandhi*, Bombay, 1955.

Radhakrishnan, S., *Dhamma Padha*, London, 1950.

Ranchodji, Amarji, *Tarikh-i-Sorath*; *A History of the Provinces of Sorath and Halar in Kathiawad*, Tr. from the Persian by J. Burgess, Bombay, 1882.

Ranade, M. G., *Rise of the Maratha Power*, Bombay, 1900.

Rapson, E. J., *Ancient India*, Cambridge, 1912.

Rawlinson, H. G., *Bactria: The History of a Forgotten Empire*, London, 1912.

Ray, H. C., *Dynastic History of Northern India*, Calcutta, 1931.

Redfield, Robert and M. B. Singer, "The Cultural Role of Cities," Economic Development and Cultural Change, III (October 1954), 53-73.

Riencourt, Amaury de., *The Soul of India*, New York, 1960.

Riesman, David, *Faces in the Crowd*, New Haven, Conn., 1950.

Riesman, David, *et al.*, *The Lonely Crowd*, New Haven, Conn., 1950.

Rogers, H., *Native Administration in the Union of South Africa,* Johannesburg, 1933.

Rolland, Romain, *Mahatma Gandhi,* New York, 1924.

Rolland, Romain, *Prophets of New India,* New York, 1930.

de Rougement, Denis, *Love in the Western World,* Garden City, New York, 1957.

de Ruggiero, Guido, *The History of European Liberalism,* Tr. by R. G. Collingwood, Boston, 1959.

Ryan, C. J., *H. P. Blavatsky and the Theosophical Movement,* Point Loma, Calif., 1937.

Saletore, B. A., *Medieval Jainism, with Special Reference to the Vijaya-nagara Empire,* Bombay, 1939.

Sankalia, D., *The Archaeology of Gujarat,* Bombay, 1941.

Sarda, Har Bilas, *Life of Dayanand Saraswati,* Ajmer, 1946.

Sardesi, G. S., *New History of the Marathas,* 3 Vols., Bombay, 1948.

Sarma, D. S., *Studies in the Renaissance of Hinduism in the Nineteenth and Twentieth Centuries,* Benares, 1944.

Sastri, K. A. Nilakanta, ed., *Age of Nandas and Mauryas,* Bombay 1952.

Sastry, K. R. R., *Indian States and Responsible Government,* Allahabad, 1941.

Savarkar, V. D., *The Indian War of Independence of* 1857, London, 1909.

Seesodia, I. S. J., *The Rajputs: A Fighting Race,* London, 1915.

Semenoff, Marc, ed., *Gandhi et Tolstoi,* Paris, 1958.

Sen, Surendranath, *Military System of the Marathas,* Calcutta 1925.

Shahani, R., *Mr. Gandhi,* New York, 1961.

Sharma, J., *Mahatma Gandhi, A Descriptive Biography,* Delhi, 1955.

Sharma, S. R., *Maratha History Re-examined,* Bombay, 1944.

Sharpe, Elizabeth, *Thakore Sahib Sir Jaswant Singh of Limbdi,* London, 1931.

Sheean, Vincent, *Lead Kindly Light,* New York, 1949.

Shejwalker, T. S., *Panipat: 1761,* Poona, 1946.

Sherrins, M. A., *History of Protestant Missions in India,* 1700–1882, London, 1884.

Sheth, C. A., *Jainism in Gujarat,* Bombay, 1953.

Bibliography

Shukla, C., ed., *Reminiscences of Gandhiji*, Bombay, 1951.

Singh, Sirdar Jogendra, *B. M. Malabari*: *Rambles with the Pilgrim Reformer*, London, 1914.

Sinha, D., " Behaviour in a Catastrophic Situation: A Psychological Study of Reports and Rumours," *British Journal of Psychology*, XLIII (August 1953), 200-209.

Slade, Madeleine, *The Spirit's Pilgrimage*, London, 1960.

Smith, George, *The Life of John Wilson*, London, 1878.

Smith, V. A., *Asoka, The Buddhist Emperor of India*, 2nd ed., Oxford, 1909.

Somervell, D. C., *English Thought in the Nineteenth Century*, London, 1957.

Somervell, D. C., ed., *A Study of History* by A. J. Toynbee, London, 1956.

Stevenson, Mrs. Sinclair, *The Heart of Jainism*, London, 1915.

Stokes, E., *The English Utilitarians and India*, Oxford, 1959.

Strachey, Lytton, *Queen Victoria*, New York, 1931.

Summerson, John Newenham, *The Microcosm of London, by T. Rowlandson and A. C. Pugin*, London and New York, 1943.

Symons, Julian, *Thomas Carlyle*, London, 1952.

Tarn, W. W., *The Greeks in Bactria and India*, 2nd ed., Cambridge, 1951.

Tarn, W. W., " Notes on Hellenism in Bactria and India," *Journal of Hellenic Studies*, XXII (1902), 268-293.

Tendulkar, D. G., *Mahatma*: *Life of Mohandas Karamchand Gandhi*, Bombay, 1951.

Thomas, C. H., *Origin of the Anglo-Boer War Revealed*, London, 1900.

Thomas, P., *Christians and Christianity in India and Pakistan*, London, 1959.

Thompson, Edward and G. T. Garrat, *Rise and Fulfilment of British Rule in India*, London, 1934.

Thoothi, N., *The Vaishnavas of Gujarat, Being a Study in Methods of Investigation of Social Phenomena*, Bombay, 1935.

Thrupp, Sylvia, " History and Sociology: New Opportunities for Co-operation," *The American Journal of Sociology*, LXIII (July 1957), 11-16.

Tillich, Paul, *The Protestant Era*, Tr. by James Luther Adams, Chicago, 1948.

Tolstoy, Leo N., *The Kingdom of God is Within You, Christianity and Patriotism, Miscellanies*, Tr. by Leo Wiener, London, 1905.

Toynbee, A. J., *Civilization on Trial*, London, 1948.

Trevelyan, G. M., *British History in the Nineteenth Century and After*, London, 1957.

Useem, John and Ruth Useem, *The Western Educated Man in India*, New York, 1955.

Uys, C. J., *In the Era of Shipstone, Being a Study of British Expansion in South Africa*, Lovedale, S.A., 1933.

Viriji, K. T., *Ancient History of Saurashtra*, Bombay, 1955.

Vyas, K. C., *The Social Renaissance in India*, Bombay, 1957.

Walker, Eric A., *A History of South Africa*, London, New York and Toronto, 1957.

Walker, Roy, " Gandhi's Message to the World," *Viswa Bharati Quarterly*, Gandhi Memorial Peace Number, ed. by Khitis Roy, 1949.

Wedderburn, William, *Allan Octavian Hume: Father of the Indian National Congress*, London, 1913.

West, Rebecca, *St. Augustine*, London, 1938.

Whitman, Walt, *Leaves of Grass*, 8th ed., New York, 1959.

Wilberforce-Bell, Harold, *The History of Kathiawad from the Earliest Times*, London, 1916.

Wild, Roland, *Ranjit Sinhji*, London, 1934.

Winsten, Stephen, *Salt and His Circle*, with Preface by Bernard Shaw, London, 1950.

Wint, Guy, *The British in Asia*, New York, 1954.

Wood, Ernest, *An Englishman Defends Mother India*, Madras, 1929.

Working Abroad: A Discussion of Psychological Attitudes and Adaptations on New Situations, New York, 1958.

Wright, Brooks, *Interpreter of Buddhism to the West: Sir Edwin Arnold*, New York, 1957.

Young, G. M., *Victorian England: Portrait of an Age*, London, 1953.

INDEX

423

Index

Index

427

Index